# Southern Manhood

# Southern Manhood

## Perspectives on Masculinity in the Old South

EDITED BY *Craig Thompson Friend & Lorri Glover*

The University of Georgia Press *Athens and London*

© 2004 by the University of Georgia Press
Athens, Georgia 30602
All rights reserved
Set in Ehrhardt by G&S Typesetters, Inc.

Most University of Georgia Press titles are
available from popular e-book vendors.

Printed digitally

Library of Congress Cataloging-in-Publication Data

Southern manhood : perspectives on masculinity in the
Old South / edited by Craig Thompson Friend and
Lorri Glover.
xvii, 234 p. ; 24 c.
Includes bibliographical references (p. ).
ISBN 0-8203-2423-X (hardcover : alk. paper) —
ISBN 0-8203-2616-X (pbk. : alk. paper)
1. Men—Southern States—History—19th century.
2. Masculinity—Southern States—History—19th century.
3. Southern States—History—1775–1865.   I. Friend,
Craig Thompson.   II. Glover, Lorri, 1967–
HQ1090.5.S68P47    2004
305.31′0975—dc22
2003021627

Paperback ISBN-13: 978-0-8203-2616-0

British Library Cataloging-in-Publication Data available

# CONTENTS

# Rethinking Southern Masculinity: An Introduction

## Craig Thompson Friend and Lorri Glover

In 1862, James B. Griffin wrote to his wife in Edgefield, South Carolina, from the Virginia front: "We cannot see, My Darling, into the future," he penned, "but I trust & have confidence in our people to believe, that if the unprincipled North shall persist in her policy of subjugating the South, that we, who are able to resist them, will continue to do so, until we grow old and worn out in the service, and that then, our Sons will take the arms from our hands, and spend their lives, if necessary, in battling for Liberty and independence." If the war lingered that long, he anticipated that his own son would proudly "take his Father's place in the field, and fight until he dies, rather than, be a Slave." Griffin consoled his wife with assurances that Confederates would always "meet the issue like *men*." [1] Many white southerners similarly interpreted the war as a maturation process, one that transformed boys into men by compelling them to fulfill roles as citizens and soldiers. Southerners held that if boys like the younger James Griffin hoped to be known as men one day, they needed to replicate their fathers' quest for liberty, independence, and the right to exclusively govern one's self and family. [2]

Eighty-six years earlier, another southern man enunciated similar themes as he assigned purpose to another war. "We hold these truths to be self-evident," began Thomas Jefferson's immortal words, "that all men are created equal, that they are endowed by their Creator with certain unalienable Rights, that among these are Life, Liberty, and the pursuit of Happiness." Independence and self-determination reverberated throughout revolutionary political tracts, justifying rebellion and inspiring civilian soldiers to find gendered meaning in war. The Declaration of Independence was, in its own fashion, a call to manly service, endowing masculinity with civic purpose through duty (to avoid "enslavement"), fortitude (in opposing the King's "tyranny"), and commitment (of "our Lives, our Fortunes, and our sacred Honor").

As manifested through honor, civic identity shaped southern masculinity between the American Revolution and the Civil War. In the late nineteenth century, as white southerners became nostalgic over the Old South and the "Lost Cause," memory of that honor—equal parts reality and fantasy—became central to conceptualizations of southern history and southern men. At monument unveilings, orators linked the Confederate cause to the American Revolution, reaffirming the centrality of honor to war and to southern male culture. Sons and daughters of the Confederacy remembered with pride the gallantry and discipline that their fathers manifested during wartime. Revising collective memory, late-nineteenth-century southerners celebrated those characteristics by venerating the most honorable of all men: Confederate officers who valiantly defended the South.[3]

Although described and analyzed by several generations of historians, the power of that hegemonic version of southern manhood has persisted in the historiography. W. J. Cash described the quintessential southern man as intensely individualistic, independent, and resentful of authority. Most important, he "did not (typically speaking) think; he felt; and discharging his feelings immediately, he developed no need or desire for intellectual culture in its own right."[4] Ironically, Cash's southern man was not the aristocrat with whom we typically associate the external presentations of southern manhood: chivalry, autonomy, and aggression. Instead, he was a middling white yeoman farmer who, in Cash's rendering, lusted after the lifestyles of colonial southern elites. Aristocratic culture, which had found its fullest expression in colonial tidewater Virginia and the South Carolina lowcountry, persisted in the Old South where men still pursued honor even though they lacked the gentility of their forefathers.

In one of the most important contributions to understanding southern manhood, Bertram Wyatt-Brown's *Southern Honor* unraveled the mysteries of the code of honor that Cash's yeomen sought. Unlike Cash, Wyatt-Brown put elite men at the center of the antebellum South. His subjects' wealth and lineage allowed them to perpetuate a code of honor increasingly outdated in early national America, clashing with the rationalism, restraint, and respectability sought by northern middle-class men. Honor as a relic of medieval European culture reinforced how truly and distinctively traditional the South remained in the young modernizing nation. Like Cash, however, Wyatt-Brown found that emotion rather than intellect drove southern masculinity. His southerners immortalized valor through vengeance, exalted individual will, and defended masculinity through duels, vigilantism, and lynching.[5]

Since the publication of Wyatt-Brown's pathbreaking work, honor—which encapsulated the values lauded by nostalgic Confederates and lamented by W. J. Cash—has dominated historical understanding of southern masculinity. Historians use honor to explain the relationships of husbands to wives and children, sons to parents, men to men, and citizens to society; they employ it to reason the Missouri Crisis, the Nullification Controversy, Indian removal, the Mexican War, Bleeding Kansas, and the Civil War; they blame it for the subordination of women, the oppression of blacks, and the extension of slavery.

A related but less transcendent analytical framework for understanding masculinity in the Old South centers on mastery. According to this line of argument, men internalized a sense of manliness through relationships to wives, children, and slaves by subverting challenges to white male authority leveled by these dependents and by heading autonomous, self-sufficient households. Masculine mastery, sometimes labeled patriarchy or paternalism, was primarily internally realized. Historians have long parsed the chronology and nature of the division between patriarchy and paternalism. Patriarchy is generally linked with the monarchical colonial era and is depicted as more pervasive (encompassing law, religion, and politics) than paternalism. Paternalism is associated with feigned benevolence in the nineteenth century and is often considered both a kinder and more insidious form of power. Kathleen Brown has persuasively argued that these concepts were two sides of the same coin.[6] Whether distinct forms of mastery or intimately related, both patriarchy and paternalism depended more on personal conduct than on public acknowledgment. Although social values informed male behavior, each patriarch or paternalist mastered his household as he saw fit and derived his identity as a man from the successful realization of that power.[7]

Family and the household were the crucibles in which mastery was forged. Manhood therefore required an independent household and landownership, a submissive wife and children, and, ideally, slaves. Vigilant household authority over those subordinates mixed with self-restraint thus made a man in his own mind and in his home.[8] Stephanie McCurry described this type of manhood, one built on controlling others, in *Masters of Small Worlds*. She returned to the yeoman farmers at the heart of Cash's interpretation of the South and found that in their quests to construct identities as free men these southern whites sought mastery over women, children, slaves, and land.[9] In that regard, mastery and manhood were made possible through the agrarian vision espoused by Thomas Jefferson and embraced by Southern yeoman farmers.

Slavery was the South's peculiar contribution to Jefferson's ideal of land acquisition and household autonomy. The mastering of slaves propelled white culture and male identity in the early South by exaggerating the power of the planter class and by promoting a sense of racial solidarity among white southern men.[10] The connection between manhood and the mastery of slaves was peculiarly southern as well. Visitors from the North and from Europe criticized the idleness and entitlement of southern slaveholders, lamenting how dominance of slaves heightened the violence and dissipation of southern whites and sapped commercial development and personal initiative. Mastering slaves, then, contributed to an increasingly self-conscious regionalism among white men, fueling sectionalism in the late antebellum era and that folly of war in 1861.

Although mastery and honor often appear interconnected in the historiography of the Old South, an important distinction should be drawn between the two as we seek to reveal how southern men defined themselves. Honor was a set of expectations determined and perpetuated by the community, which differentiated men in the eyes of others through public rituals. Achieved by controlling households and commanding slaves, mastery was less scripted and more of consequence to a man's self-identity. To be certain, mastery had a profound secondary public dimension that permeated southern society. Men's refusal to be mastered by others and their insistence on mastering slaves, after all, lay at the heart of antebellum southern political culture.[11] Conversely, honor was bound up in individual identity. But at their core, these two sets of values differed. Honor was externally presented for public consumption; mastery was internally realized for personal fulfillment.[12]

Clearly, the historiographical emphasis on honor and mastery is worthwhile; for these interrelated masculine values shaped the families, communities, economies, and political lives of the white male leadership of the Old South. Yet scholars' reliance on this framework has reinforced the planter-cavalier model that, idealized by nineteenth-century southern gentlemen, marginalized men outside gentry ranks. As important as honor and mastery are to Old South historiography, they cannot fully reveal the diversity of southern masculinities.

This collection of essays contextualizes and complicates the honor-mastery paradigm. Collectively these original works of scholarship demonstrate that race, class, age, and locale allowed and sometimes forced communities and individuals to alter their perceptions of and requirements for manhood. Honor and mastery were the dominant idealized masculine traits among southern whites, but as the works of our contributors demonstrate, these values were co-opted, transformed, and even rejected on occasion by the diverse men who populated the South between the Revolution and the Civil War.[13]

A complexity of factors influenced southern men's identification with and realization of these dominant masculine values. Since mastery and honor were deeply rooted in the perceived independence endowed by the ownership of land and slaves, only those owning land or slaves could act upon those ideals. Yet such ownership among southern white men was never consistent between the Revolutionary and Civil wars. Figures vary by region and time, but often less than half, and seldom more than two-thirds, of white men owned land in the Old South.[14] And while slave ownership may have been slightly more attainable, there was no meeting of the minds between large slaveholders and the more numerous small slaveholders. The two dominant historiographical themes of southern masculinity lay beyond the claims of many, and in some locales most, white men. What becomes apparent in considering the inconsistency of land and slave ownership is that as the South and the nation came into being and then came apart, definitions of what it meant to "be a man" were unsettled as well. Urban dwellers, men of color, and those who owned no land or slaves collectively composed the majority of men living in the early South. Thus it is essential to explore the ways in which those who fell outside the hegemonic ideals thought about masculinity and marked themselves as men. The current historiography offers no place for them except at the margins, in conflict with southern society's dominant values—a deduction that should not ring true.

Of course, these so-called marginalized men lived within a society dominated physically, politically, and culturally by slave-holding patriarchs. Not surprisingly, their notions of manhood bore the imprint of elite values. The most obvious instances involved enslaved black men. Domination of blacks bought manhood for whites. White male mastery and the code of honor provided a variety of practices designed to subordinate and brutalize black men, including political exclusion, cultural abuse, legal violence, and economic exploitation. In the eyes of whites, black men were the antithesis of honor and mastery—dependent, acquiescent, externally controlled. From the point of view of whites, enslavement equaled emasculation.

African American men resented and sometimes violently resisted such denials of manhood. As the contributions by Diane Barnes, Edward Baptist, and Heather Williams evidence, slaves as well as free blacks struggled to exert their own definitions of masculinity and to perform their duties as men. A host of factors impeded their efforts, including southern laws, owner violence, family retribution (the rape, beating, or sale of loved ones), and the indifference of most white Americans. As Edward Baptist argues, the forced migration of slaves compromised black definitions of manhood. Westward expansion of plantation agriculture severed slaves' conjugal ties and undermined the ability of slave men to fulfill key functions within their communities. But, as Heather Williams demonstrates, whites did not hold all the cards. Black men sought to empower themselves through education, financial autonomy, and physical escape from slavery. Although they enjoyed far more opportunities and rights than bondsmen, free African Americans also saw their lives circumscribed by the peculiar institution;

white mastery necessarily informed their definitions of masculinity. Diane Barnes illuminates the intersections of race and class in her analysis of artisans, and she concludes that as they resisted the efforts of white society to subvert their autonomy free African American men self-consciously differentiated themselves from bondsmen.

Although far less intensely, white men lacking the requisite age, wealth, or family ties also struggled to claim manhood within the framework of mastery and honor. As Harry Laver and Jennifer Green reveal, middling young men turned to education and public displays of martial prowess to counterbalance their lineage and lack of gentility. Freed from subordination by virtue of their race, they participated in oppressing women and black men to gain political, economic, or cultural advantage. Their actions both challenged and reinforced hegemonic masculine culture. In Lorri Glover's essay, we see the limitations of honor and mastery within the ranks of southern gentry boys, as stage of life undermined the discipline required of honorable patriarchs. And Craig Friend's case study illustrates the desperation of one middling young man to use courtship to emulate the behaviors and merit the attention of his "betters." In these four pieces, class, family ties, and stage of life represent obstacles—but not insuperable impediments—to the claiming of southern manhood. Collectively they reveal both the hold that honor and mastery exerted over the lives of southern white men and the ways in which men defined themselves when those manly attributes were not fully attained.

The rise of consumerism, which transformed not only the American economy but also the nature of families and society, further complicated masculine values in the late eighteenth and early nineteenth centuries. In the North, economic changes led to industrial growth, wage labor, and an erosion of localistic perspectives.[15] In the South, the new economy changed life by expanding agricultural markets, increasing demands for farmlands in the Old Southwest, incorporating white men into broader economic networks, and validating slavery as a lucrative and appropriate form of labor. Some southern men, black and white, immersed themselves in the emerging liberal market economy. As Diane Barnes demonstrates, those men often resented the South's conservative social and political structures; they consequently created alternative ideals of manhood that rejected the conventional values of the plantation gentry. And as John Mayfield relates, conservative southerners felt at odds with the new values of masculinity among an emerging middle class. Southern literature often took on a distinctly antimarket tone, largely because of concerns about maintaining traditional notions of manhood, particularly honor and mastery.

The evolving market economy also influenced definitions of masculinity among Choctaw Indians, who found themselves torn between tradition and innovation in the early national South. As Greg O'Brien argues, southeastern Indians' sense of masculinity both reflected and contrasted with white ideals of honor and mastery. The expansion of slavery onto Indian lands inspired the redefinition of manhood in native communities and reconfigured racial and gender assumptions among Indians. For many Choctaw, the collision between traditional and Americanized culture manifested in new, contentious ideas about what it meant to be a Choctaw and a man.

Significantly, although richly diverse in sources and interpretation, the following essays share many common themes. Each suggests that manhood did not exist except in contrast to womanhood. Unlike their white contemporaries, Indian and black men seldom denigrated women and women's work, but throughout the triracial South, femininity was the antithesis of, and the greatest threat to, manliness. Before contact with whites, southeastern Indian nations sharply divided male and female duties. The divergence in functions ran so deep that many Indians inhabited gender-segregated communities. After a century of contact with whites—and their concerted efforts to "civilize" Indians—and with the intrusions of the market economy, native peoples faced difficult choices about maintaining their gender divisions without appropriating white assumptions about sexual inequality. Within African American communities as well, gender patterns came under attack. Because slave women labored beside slave men in the fields and in the house, bondsmen struggled to preserve distinctive male roles. They carved out niches of masculinity in plantation artisan shops, as disciplinarians to their children, and through adept hunting and fishing. Likewise free black men publicly affirmed their differences from women, pursuing trades and skills closed to most females. Gender distinctions and the subordination of women to men were most pronounced in patriarchal white households. And in the white South, duties of men and women were not simply different, they were oppositional. If men performed women's work, expressed feminine sentiments, failed to marry and master households, or pursued too eagerly the frills of the emerging consumer culture, they imperiled their claims on manhood.

Moreover, as described in each of these essays, conflicts over manhood necessarily took place before the community. Conservative white southern writers publicly mocked newer forms of masculinity inspired by market forces and an emerging middle class. Planters' college-aged sons rebelled against their fathers' private directives and instead wanted peer validation. Other young men turned to courtship and refinement to prove their worth. Such non-elites as artisans and militia members sought community affirmation by parading and by exhibiting their prowess. Such public expressions of manhood often emphasized physical power and violence. Musters and military education offered preparation for anticipated exhibits of masculine aggression. Duels and street brawls displayed personal justice. The whipping of enslaved blacks and the policing of free blacks, often violent in their consequences, were overt methods of racial oppression. Indian rituals of maturation, particularly those related to hunting and warring, were publicly performed. Striking an owner was the manliest and, consequentially, the deadliest thing a bondsman could do, for it constituted the ultimate abrogation of white masculine power and the assertion of black manhood. And warring—for former slaves, rebellious Confederates, Native Americans, and men as prominent as Thomas Jefferson and as anonymous as James Griffin—was the ultimate expression of manly character.

Finally, these essays also bring the new tools of masculine studies to the Old South, enriching both masculinity studies and southern history by pushing them beyond a white male paradigm of honor and mastery. Throughout the 1990s, masculinity studies have concentrated on the nineteenth-century North.[16] The few southernists who broached the topic overemphasized honor and mastery.[17] The essays compiled here collectively demonstrate that nineteenth-century masculinity was far more varied than men's historians or southernists have previously understood. We trust that the authors' research and interpretations will inspire further inquiry into the fertile field of southern masculinities.

### NOTES

The editors are particularly grateful to Charles E. Crosby and Ashley E. Moreshead, who assisted with typing and proofreading this collection.

1. James B. Griffin to Leila Griffin, 29 February 1862, Papers of James B. Griffin, Center of American History, University of Texas at Austin, reprinted in *"A Gentleman and an Officer": A Social and Military History of James B. Griffin's Civil War*, ed. Orville Vernon Burton and Judith N. McArthur (New York: Oxford University Press, 1996), 163.

2. Reid Mitchell, "Soldiering, Manhood, and Coming of Age: A Northern Volunteer," in *Divided Houses: Gender and the Civil War*, ed. Catherine Clinton and Nina Silber (New York: Oxford University Press, 1992), 44.

3. Catherine W. Bashir, "Landmarks of Power: Building a Southern Past, 1885–1915," *Southern Cultures*, inaugural issue (1993): 5–46; Gaines M. Foster, *Ghosts of the Confederacy: Defeat, the Lost Cause, and the Emergence of the New South, 1865 to 1913* (New York: Oxford University Press, 1987).

4. W. J. Cash, *The Mind of the South* (1941; reprint, New York: Vintage, 1991), 30–35, 56–58, 99. Other historians similarly have portrayed the yeoman farmer as the essence of "southerness": see Grady McWhiney, *Cracker Culture: Celtic Ways in the Old South* (Tuscaloosa: University of Alabama Press, 1988); Frank L. Owsley and Harriet C. Owsley, "The Economic Basis of Society in the Late Ante-Bellum

South," *Journal of Southern History* 6 (1940): 24–45; Frank L. Owsley, *Plain Folk of the Old South* (Baton Rouge: Louisiana State University Press, 1949).

5. Bertram Wyatt-Brown, *Southern Honor: Ethics and Behavior in the Old South* (New York: Oxford University Press, 1982), 20, 34; Elliott J. Gorn, "'Gouge and Bite, Pull Hair and Scratch': The Social Significance of Fighting in the Southern Backcountry," *American Historical Review* 90 (1985): 18–43; Kenneth S. Greenberg, *Masters and Statesmen: The Political Culture of American Slavery* (Baltimore: Johns Hopkins University Press, 1985); Steven M. Stowe, *Intimacy and Power in the Old South* (Baltimore: Johns Hopkins University Press, 1987), chap. 1; Kenneth S. Greenberg, *Honor and Slavery: Lies, Duels, Noses, Masks, Dressing as a Woman, Gifts, Strangers, Humanitarianism, Death, Slave Rebellions, the Proslavery Argument, Baseball, Hunting, and Gambling in the Old South* (Princeton: Princeton University Press, 1996); Edward L. Ayers, *Vengeance and Justice: Crime and Punishment in the Nineteenth-Century South* (New York: Oxford University Press, 1984); Gail Bederman, "Manly Civilizations/Primitive Masculinity: Race, Gender, and Evolutions of Middle-Class American Manhood" (Ph.D. diss., Brown University, 1992); Joanne B. Freeman, *Affairs of Honor: National Politics in the New Republic* (New Haven: Yale University Press, 2001).

6. Kathleen M. Brown, *Good Wives, Nasty Wenches, and Anxious Patriarchs: Gender, Race, and Power in Colonial Virginia* (Chapel Hill: University of North Carolina Press, 1996).

7. On paternalism, see Ulrich B. Phillips, *American Negro Slavery: A Survey of the Supply, Employment, and Control of Negro Labor as Determined by the Plantation Regime* (1918; reprint, Baton Rouge: Louisiana State University, 1966); Robert W. Fogel and Stanley L. Engerman, *Time on the Cross: The Economics of American Negro Slavery* (Boston: Little, Brown, 1974); Eugene Genovese, *The World the Slaveholders Made: Two Essays in Interpretation* (1969; reprint, Middletown: Wesleyan University Press, 1988); Joan Cashin, *A Family Venture: Men and Women on the Southern Frontier* (New York: Oxford University Press, 1991). On patriarchy, see Daniel Blake Smith, *Inside the Great House: Planter Family Life in Eighteenth-Century Chesapeake Society* (Ithaca: Cornell University Press, 1990), 284–87; Jane Turner Censer, *North Carolina Planters and Their Children, 1800–1860* (Baton Rouge: Louisiana State University Press, 1984); Carol Bleser, ed., *Secret and Sacred: The Diaries of James Henry Hammond, a Southern Slaveholder* (New York: Oxford University Press, 1988).

8. Eugene D. Genovese, *Roll, Jordan, Roll: The World the Slaves Made* (New York: Vintage, 1974), 73–75, 93–96; Catherine Clinton, *The Plantation Mistress: Woman's World in the Old South* (New York: Pantheon, 1982), 36–37.

9. Stephanie McCurry, *Masters of Small Worlds: Yeoman Households, Gender Relations, and the Political Culture of the Antebellum South Carolina Low Country* (New York: Oxford University Press, 1995), 81, 83–85; Orville Vernon Burton, *In My Father's House Are Many Mansions: Family and Community in Edgefield, South Carolina* (Chapel Hill: University of North Carolina Press, 1985), 99–103.

10. Edmund S. Morgan, *American Slavery, American Freedom: The Ordeal of Colonial*

*Virginia* (New York: Norton, 1975); Brown, *Good Wives;* and McCurry, *Masters of Small Worlds.* As James Oakes phrased it, "For the paternalistic master, slaveholding was not simply a duty, it was a destiny" (*The Ruling Race: A History of American Slaveholders* [New York: Knopf, 1982], 203).

11. Masters so typically believed in the validity of their power that they were nonplussed and then offended when slaves ran away, children rebelled, or wives grew distant—such behaviors abrogated the patriarch's power and compromised his manhood; Clinton, *The Plantation Mistress*, 204–5; Jon L. Wakelyn, "Antebellum College Life and the Relations between Fathers and Sons," in *The Web of Southern Social Relations: Women, Family, and Education,* ed. Walter J. Fraser Jr., R. Frank Saunders Jr., and Jon L. Wakelyn (Athens: University of Georgia Press, 1985), 107–26; Elizabeth Fox-Genovese, *Within the Plantation Household: Black and White Women of the Old South* (Chapel Hill: University of North Carolina Press, 1988), 203; Oakes, *The Ruling Race,* 218–19.

12. Bertram Wyatt-Brown, *The Shaping of Southern Culture: Honor, Grace, and War, 1760s–1880s* (Chapel Hill: University of North Carolina Press, 2001), xii.

13. Our discussion of dominant masculinities and alternative masculinities is shaped in part by R. W. Connell's typologies in *Masculinities* (Berkeley: University of California Press, 1995), 76–81.

14. For examples of varying land ownership in different southern locations at different times, see Stephen Aron, *How the West Was Lost: The Transformation of Kentucky from Daniel Boone to Henry Clay* (Baltimore: Johns Hopkins University Press, 1996), 203 (table A.5), 205 (table A.8); McCurry, *Masters of Small Worlds,* 53 (table 2.4); Lee Soltow, "Land Inequality on the Frontier: The Distribution of Land in East Tennessee at the Beginning of the Nineteenth Century," *Social Science History* 5 (1981): 277. For various slaveholding figures, see Daniel S. Dupre, *Transforming the Cotton Frontier: Madison County, Alabama, 1800–1840* (Baton Rouge: Louisiana State University Press, 1997), 36 (table 2); Lisa C. Tolbert, *Constructing Townscapes: Space and Society in Antebellum Tennessee* (Chapel Hill: University of North Carolina Press, 1999), 202.

15. The shift to a market economy is seen as the defining milestone in altered masculine behaviors and ideals in the urbanizing North. See E. Anthony Rotundo, *American Manhood: Transformations in Masculinity from the Revolution to the Modern Era* (New York: Basic Books, 1993); Shawn Johansen, *Family Men: Middle-Class Fatherhood in Early Industrializing America* (New York: Routledge, 2001); Mark E. Kann, *A Republic of Men: The American Founders, Gendered Language, and Patriarchal Politics* (New York: New York University Press, 1998); Nancy Cott, *The Bonds of Womanhood: "Women's Sphere" in New England, 1780–1835* (New Haven: Yale University Press, 1977).

16. Johansen, *Family Men;* Rotundo, *American Manhood;* Mark C. Carnes and Clyde Griffin, eds., *Meanings for Manhood: Constructions of Masculinity in Victorian America* (Chicago: University of Chicago Press, 1990); David G. Pugh, *Sons of Liberty: The Masculine Mind in Nineteenth-Century America* (Westport, Conn.: Greenwood

Press, 1983); Lisa Wilson, *Ye Heart of a Man: The Domestic Lives of Men in Colonial New England* (New Haven, Conn.: Yale University Press, 1999); Stephen M. Frank, *Life with Father: Parenthood and Masculinity in the Nineteenth-Century American North* (Baltimore: Johns Hopkins University Press, 1998); Robert L. Griswold, *Fatherhood in America: A History* (New York: Basic Books, 1993).

17. Only recently have historians challenged the dominance of honor and mastery in understanding southern masculinity: see John Mayfield, "'The Soul of a Man!': William Gilmore Simms and the Myths of Southern Manhood," *Journal of the Early Republic* 15 (1995): 477–500; Janet Moore Lindman, "Acting the Manly Christian: White Evangelical Masculinity in Revolutionary Virginia," *William and Mary Quarterly* 57 (2000): 393–416; Anya Jabour, "Male Friendship and Masculinity in the Early National South: William Wirt and His Friends," *Journal of the Early Republic* 20 (2000): 83–111; Daniel Kilbride, "Southern Medical Students in Philadelphia, 1800–1861: Science and Sociability in the 'Republic of Medicine,'" *Journal of Southern History* 65 (1999): 697–732; Jim Cullen, "'I's a Man Now': Gender and African American Men," in Clinton and Silber, *Divided Houses*, 76–96.

# Southern Manhood

# Refuge of Manhood: Masculinity and the Militia Experience in Kentucky

*Harry S. Laver*

The men who came of age after the American Revolution could have easily identified with Thomas Paine's 1776 pronouncement that the times tried men's souls. Although ratification of the Constitution settled the issue of an American system of government, the country struggled to preserve its independence, adjust to the volatile market economy, and shape a national identity. Social and political disorder threatened to overwhelm the nation as the post-Revolutionary generation appropriated the sacred ideal of liberty and seemingly perverted it to justify luxury, vice, and even corruption. The nation's growing pains also created a crisis of confidence among white males, as Americans' definition of masculinity began to change. The eighteenth-century model of manhood, identified by historians as "republican" or "communal," set forth that a male, as head of household, place the good of the community above individual desires, that he subordinate self-interest to the commonweal. In the early nineteenth century, this accepted gender construct came under assault from the market economy's protagonist, the "liberal" or "self-made man," who unapologetically pursued wealth, power, and self-advancement. The republican emphasized consistent self-sacrifice for the community as a whole as the preeminent quality of a man. Conversely, the liberal promoted self-enrichment without the sense of responsibility to neighbor or nation.[1]

These irreconcilable meanings of manhood fostered confusion and anxiety among American males; what defined a man was no longer clear. Sons and grandsons of the founding generation struggled to make sense of conflicting expectations that pitted their forebears' community-oriented manhood against modern society's seductive call to self-aggrandizement. These contested notions of manhood struck particularly deep in the minds of southern white males. Their position at the pinnacle of the South's hierarchical order rested upon the dual foundations of race and gender. Claims to social, economic, and political authority emanated from a fusion of whiteness and maleness. Skin color visibly, and in most cases instantly, established an individual's racial identity. Claims of whiteness were rarely challenged. The legitimacy of one's manhood, however, was not so readily apparent. As the contest between the communal man and the self-made man suggests, the definition of masculinity was open to debate, and in the South such ambiguity could threaten the white patriarchal order.

With their self-confidence and social standing made insecure by the evolving nature of manhood, men sought to demonstrate their masculinity in ways that had remained unaffected by competing concepts of masculinity. They found such a refuge in the militia experience. A bastion of masculine culture, the militia provided the means to authenticate manhood through actions and images that dated from ancient Greece and Rome and continued to resonate among nineteenth-century southerners. Western cultures had equated martial behavior with masculinity for centuries, and southerners continued that association through the militia. In the centuries-old martial role of citizen-soldier, men saw the opportunity to confirm their masculinity, irrespective of communal or self-made ideas of manhood.[2]

An examination of the Kentucky militia in the early republic reveals the intimate relationship southerners saw between citizen-soldiers and manhood. Kentucky's progression from frontier settlements to mature communities provides an opportunity to identify the militia's significance to maintaining masculinity as social and economic progress brought some elements of manhood into question. Beginning in the 1790s and continuing for the next fifty years, wilderness outposts such as Fort Boonesborough gave way to thriving cities, including Lexington and Louisville, and itinerant peddlers surrendered to the market economy's shopkeeper and his market house. Amid these changes, white males, regardless of their attitudes toward—or even their awareness of— competing gender definitions, found in the militia a safe harbor of masculinity, a place of uncontested manhood.[3]

In multiple ways, militia participation reinforced a masculine self-identity. First, the militia helped create and sustain a unified white male community. The militia experience was a racially proscribed experience, a gathering of white men that bridged class differences without threatening the hierarchical order among those same men. Second, the exclusion of "others," namely women and racial minorities, from direct participation buttressed white males' power and reinforced their collective identity. Third, citizen-soldiers embraced weapons and uniforms, symbols of the militia's martial, masculine, and exclusionary qualities.

Finally, through the militia, men could experience battle and thus claim their forebears' manly legacy of self-sacrifice and bravery. The Revolutionaries of 1776 and the patriots of 1812 demonstrated their manhood in the crucible of war. And as militiamen, succeeding generations hoped to prove themselves both soldiers and men.[4]

In the South, the most apparent way the militia experience supported traditional male gender norms was through the reinforcement of a shared white male identity. A rigid social structure based upon race, class, and gender characterized southern society from its early-seventeenth-century origins. Southern elites hoped to recreate an aristocratic social order similar to that maintained in Old England. In the 1670s, wealthy planters and poor whites set aside their economic and social differences to unite in the face of an increasingly black, and potentially dangerous, labor force. By the late eighteenth and early nineteenth centuries, rich and poor had bridged their differences to create a unified community of white men, their shared belief in black inferiority producing a democracy of whiteness. Widespread militia participation sustained this alliance of race, since every white male enjoyed the opportunity, and in some instances was expected, to join the local company of citizen-soldiers.[5]

Events such as Independence Day and Washington's Birthday celebrated freedom and liberty, but this patriotism also spurred the militia, thus uniting the white male population. When the militia mustered, fathers, brothers, sons, and neighbors gathered to break bread and parade as a company of citizen-soldiers. Marching ranks of militiamen presented onlookers with a model of order and deference, as regimented columns responded to their officers' commands. The many became one.[6] Furthermore, the company's homogeneity reinforced the citizen-soldiers' collective self-identity and solidarity. Companies mixed men from different walks of life whose disparate economic and social positions normally defined separate worlds. Historian Dana Nelson's observation that nineteenth-century organizations like the Masons created an environment conducive to the formation of masculine bonds applies to militia units that welcomed, and in some cases required, participation of all white males. Their coming together as militiamen bridged their differences, creating a single shared world, if only for a few hours. In 1834 Shelbyville captain James Allen organized a company of relatively poor men and covered the cost of their uniforms himself, going two hundred dollars in debt to purchase caps, feathers, and other paraphernalia. Allen's willingness to underwrite the expense suggests more than a desire to command a militia company. His actions affirmed his elevated social position, supported the participants' commitment to each other, diminished potential interclass resentment, and constrained overt expressions of disaffection. A *Kentucky Gazette* writer, struck by the harmony and nostalgia at an 1835

Fourth of July gathering, commented on the day's power to unite militiamen as well as observers: "Harmonious and good feelings . . . appeared upon every countenance. The invited guests, according to modern parlance, would be deemed heterogeneous, but they with the whole assemblage seemed to fall in side by side, with a full determination, that however we might have slight family jars, in the cause of the country, and a determination to support the government, no one would yield to his neighbor." For the family and friends who gathered that summer day, the militia represented their unity as Americans; for the citizen-soldiers who marched in the parades, their companies exemplified the exclusive fraternity of white males.[7]

The veneer of harmony, however, masked the militia's internal divisions. Militia organization based on rank preserved the community's social order without threatening unity among white men. Poor white males marched in parades with their social and economic betters, who generally served as officers, thus maintaining society's organic nature. At the dinners that followed the parades, militia officers and town elders proposed the toasts and made the speeches. Access to the stage equaled power, and only the elite found the podium open. Especially in the South, gifted orators and military men commanded respect and admiration. In his history of Independence Day celebrations, Len Travers demonstrated how those in power maintained tight control over celebrations and rituals and how the speeches, songs, food, and drink of these events strengthened their grip on social and political power. The common sort who filled the ranks as privates listened silently, notwithstanding the occasional cheer for the United States, General Washington, or the "American fair" (a reference to women). Not surprisingly, the poor never found themselves initiating these holiday rituals; only the better sort enjoyed this honor. Yet despite these socioeconomic divisions, differences among militiamen remained subordinate to the fraternalism of the white male community. For most southern males, maintaining the social and economic pecking order within their militia companies seemed a small price to pay for an equality of whiteness and the confirmation of their manhood as citizen-soldiers.[8]

The second way militia service supported traditional manhood was by excluding all but white males. As holiday dinners concluded and celebrants turned to toasting such ideals as Jefferson's declaration of life, liberty, and equality, white men of every class closed the doors to women and blacks. Sociologists and gender historians have demonstrated that individuals create an identity in opposition to an "other." The identification of those who are different defines the traits and mannerisms, innate or otherwise, that one is *not*. In the nineteenth century, being a man meant in part not being a woman or a child; in other words, not being effeminate or immature. In the slave South, most damning was the unmanly fault of dependency. Dependents lacked the ability to care for themselves, and nineteenth-century southern society branded women and African Americans as thus deficient, relegating them to the margins of the public sphere.[9]

Women rarely found themselves directly involved in militia events. At best they participated as spectators, attending the parades and listening to the orations. The practice of toast-making, however, was strictly a male domain. Women excused themselves before the rounds began, where the universal acknowledgment of the American fair and the occasional observation of their need for protection emphasized women's dependent, subordinate status. Women's attendance at parades, musters, and barbecues enlivened the social intercourse and contributed to the perception of social harmony, but more subtly, their presence gave tacit approval to the day's gendered subtext: white male hegemony. The willingness of women to participate in the day's events and their acquiescence to all-male rituals confirmed these practices. Women were women, militiamen were men—an arrangement reiterated by the sights, sounds, and participants of every militia gathering.[10]

African Americans were even further removed from celebration rituals. Their status as slaves relegated them to absolute dependence and social irrelevance, and thus their direct participation in militia activities was out of the question. This exclusion applied both to slaves and to free blacks. In social matters, legal differences between slave and free mattered little; skin color was the determining factor. The inclusion of African Americans as passive observers during militia events is difficult to document, but in the South the demands of life and business produced an integrated public sphere. African Americans constituted a significant portion of the population in southern society, reaching majority in a few communities. On any given day, they purchased and transported goods from town to plantation and back. They shared life's daily journeys with the master and his family. They were the silent and all but invisible participants in southern life. One can hardly imagine the Fourth of July or Washington's Birthday without the faces of black men, women, and children peering out of the crowd. But the presence of African Americans, like that of women, made even more explicit the exclusive nature of the militia and the organic structure of society. In the South, race contributed an essential element to the social hierarchy by defining blacks as inferior and reinforcing white superiority and unity. Slaves' participation at musters and parades was limited to nothing more than their position as back-row spectators. It was always clear who occupied the bottom rungs of the social ladder and who maintained control at the top.[11]

The third element of the militia experience that confirmed manhood, and perhaps the most popular with southerners of the era, was the military ornaments of weapons and uniforms. Swords, pistols, muskets, and an occasional cannon enhanced the sights and sounds of militia celebrations. More important, weapons symbolically affirmed the militia's responsibilities as the nation's first defenders and dramatized the relationship between guns and manliness. Fear of foreign invaders, civil insurrections, and, especially in the South, slave revolts demanded that men achieve and retain a degree of proficiency with powder and ball. Historian John Hope Franklin noted that in the South handling a gun was part and parcel of growing up and becoming a man, confirming Daniel R. Hundley's 1860 description of the southerner as a "yeoman, . . . always possess[ing] a manly independence of character. . . . He marches right on to where duty and honor call, and with unblanched cheek meets death face to face," carrying only "the deadly rifle . . . and this he handles with such skill as few possess." Such observations confirm the popular perception that southerners were all Daniel Boones, men who learned to handle a gun in the cradle and who could peg a squirrel's eye at a hundred paces.[12]

As a consequence of the Revolution and the War of 1812, faith in America's citizen-soldiers to handle guns became part of the national mythology. During the Revolution, Americans credited the militia with going toe-to-toe with British regulars and, even with more losses than victories, holding their own. By war's end, despite their essential contribution to victory, General Washington's Continental Army received little credit, the populace preferring to praise the supposed innate martial skills of family and friends who fought in the militia. The performance of citizen-soldiers in the War of 1812 was not unlike that in the Revolution; despite rare but well-publicized victories at Baltimore and New Orleans, the militia exhibited little ability against British regulars. Even the famed Hunters of Kentucky, glorified in story and song with securing the final American victory at New Orleans, in truth fired only a few shots from behind barricades while artillery decimated the poorly led British troops. The legend of the Hunters, noted historian John William Ward, arose from the wishful mythmaking of Americans. Fact or fiction, the accepted memory of the militia at New Orleans reinforced the South's popular image of its citizen-soldiers: southern men ready to defend loved ones and liberty with a stout heart, a steady rifle, and manly courage.[13]

In the 1830s and 1840s, Texas independence and the Mexican War presented a chance for another generation to join the militia, shoulder arms, and demonstrate their manliness. Reacting to Texas fever, young men throughout Kentucky and across the nation formed independent, volunteer militia units whose existence depended on procuring arms from the government. In 1832, hoping to secure weapons for a Louisville regiment, George W. Chambers wrote to the quartermaster general that the men "seem to display considerable Military spirit and . . . no doubt will take special care of the arms." Five years later, Captain

John Brown sought similar support: "We are anxious to obtain [arms] before the river closes. Should we fail in getting them I am fearful the company will fail." James Allen, who had incurred a substantial debt to help uniform his company, feared for his financial future if weapons failed to arrive soon. "There is considerable dissatisfaction," he wrote in 1834, "on account of not receiving the arms and if we do not receive the arms by the fall muster I am afraid the company will break up and leave me in the lurch." Although few if any of the men in these units owned weapons, firearms were the essential ingredient that legitimated their existence as a military organization and their masculine image.[14]

Ostensibly, a desire for sufficient firepower motivated the demands for weapons, but closer examination shows that concern for public appearances outweighed military preparedness. In his *History and Present State of Virginia* (1705), Robert Beverley revealed that in the early eighteenth century the militia used weapons for ceremonial purposes, "to fire upon some Joyful Occasions," a tradition continued into the nineteenth century. In 1840 a Louisville commander recorded that his men had suffered for months without arms and would be "sadly disappointed if again deferred" in their request for rifles: "We have a *parade* in a few days and shall need arms." Colonel E. G. House, also of Louisville, informed Kentucky's adjutant general that his company was "rapidly progressing in the uniforming which is after the style of the United States officers," but that guns were necessary to allow them to "parade as a company."[15]

Weapons not only added to the pageantry of a parade but also improved members' morale, promoting "a proper military spirit (a thing much to be desired)," according to a group of Lexington volunteers in 1841. In a request for arms in 1852, men from Russellville, Kentucky, confessed, "We have again the Military fever. We have formed an Infantry Company which we are vain enough to hope will do credit to our town and country." Weapons improved morale, but their loss proved to be the quickest cure for "military fever." Captain William Bradford discovered as much in 1842, when the adjutant general threatened to recall his company's muskets: "if our arms were reduced there would be a corresponding reduction in the Military pride of our company, which perhaps might tend to its demolition." Bradford articulated the feelings of citizen-soldiers across the South: guns were his company's lifeblood. Removing their weapons eliminated the symbol of their existence as a military and masculine organization.[16]

Kentucky's military fever was epidemic in the 1840s, as war with Mexico approached, and militia companies overwhelmed state officials with requests for government-issue weapons. Responding to the demand, the state began to recall arms from units that appeared inactive, initiating competition and resentment among companies. In 1840 Jesse Stevens of Princeton responded to a request for the return of state weapons by arguing that "the citizens would be very unwilling to give [up their guns] as they have a large company and made extensive arrangements for equipping them." A rumor in 1845 that the quartermaster general intended to recall his artillery company's cannon mortified Captain S. D. McCullough of Lexington. Hoping to head off such a calamity, McCullough warned that "if the gun should now be taken from us, or even a *fear* that such will be the case, it will have the effect to dishearten the men and may soon to disband the company." Two weeks later, Quartermaster Ambrose Dudley acceded to the captain's request to keep the cannon, but with a caveat: "you can retain it until it is required for another portion of the state and *no longer*." Captain Marshall of the Louisville Guards took great offense when the state recalled a portion of his company's muskets: "Your requisition for the return of [the muskets] will break up the handsomest company in Kentucky. . . . I do not know why or how the Dutch Company of this place holds seventy muskets when the Guards are required to be limited to forty! . . . I cannot fancy why the arms should be returned to rust in an arsenal when in the armory of the Guards they are preserved in first rate order, kept bright and clean and always inspected once a week." As the emotions of McCullough and Marshall suggest, once companies secured weapons, they were not inclined to surrender them without protest.[17]

Weapons took on such significance that the battles between militia companies to obtain and keep them turned malicious and personal. False rumors of his company's imminent dissolution prompted William Bradford to defend his artillery unit in a letter to Quartermaster Dudley. "I deemed it my duty to correct any erroneous impressions," Bradford wrote in 1845, "knowing that [accusations] have been made by those who desire the overthrow of the Volunteer company, which has at all times been without a successful competition in acquiring a knowledge of Military tactics." He assured Dudley that his unit had no intention of disbanding, blaming a "Counter Encampment" for rumors to the contrary: "We care not for the machinations of those who are disposed to crush us, but we do object to have false impressions made upon your mind, by our enemies." Bradford remained confident that the general would not withdraw the "pride of our Corps," a trust that appears well laced, as he received no demand to surrender the cannon.[18]

General Dudley normally operated as the moderator for these disputes over muskets and cannon, but in 1851 he found himself in the middle of a tug-of-war between a Lexington artillery company and Captain Thomas Coons's Jessamine County militiamen. Coons's unit apparently expected to take charge of a cannon held by the Lexington company, and so he paid a visit to a Mr. Winchester, "one of the men who [had] the gun in his possession." Winchester admitted that his company had disbanded, but he remained unwilling to part with the artillery piece. According to Coons, Winchester then told him that he and others there "would see you and our company at the *devil* before we should have it, and that you was a d——d old fool and had no right to demand it." Unfortunately, Dudley's response went unrecorded. Nevertheless, the fighting and fretting of militiamen over acquisition and control of weapons demonstrate that military preparedness remained secondary to public perception.[19]

These disputes over weapons expose their significance to the life of militia companies and to the public image southern militiamen hoped to create. In the most practical sense, guns were necessary to the militia's traditional responsibility as the community's defenders; citizen-soldiers without weapons were hardly soldiers. Weapons, however, had a purpose beyond the obvious, as the comments of company commanders attest—they were an essential part of the pageantry the militia created in their parades and ceremonies. Gunfire and thunderous cannonades drowned out the tedium of daily life; drilling with brooms and cornstalks did little to raise recruits, crowds, or confidence. Lexington militiamen revealed as much in an 1841 request for weapons. They assured the quartermaster general of their willingness, "if there should not be pistols sufficient in the arsenal, as they are not absolutely necessary for common parade, . . . to take swords & holsters." Guns were preferred, swords would do, but *some* kind of weapon was necessary.[20]

The preoccupation with uniforms in southern militia circles reveals the same subordination of martial fitness to public appearance. At military schools in the South, concern over uniforms often superseded attention to academics. To viewers of holiday parades, the sight of uniforms set citizen-soldiers apart from the rest of society, further underscoring their martial and masculine qualities. In 1835 Captain Tarlton of Louisville proudly announced that "the company I have raised have uniformed themselves splendidly which cost them at least $100 each." Richmond captain John Miller informed the quartermaster that "the young men of our town have arranged a very handsome company and gone to considerable expense in uniforming, etc." Captain Bradford of the Lexington Artillery Company was pleased with the efforts of his troops, "all of whom are gradually equipping with an entire full and dress uniform, as this is somewhat expensive, we are compelled to progress by degrees—but a better spirit I never saw manifested." Uniforms did not, however, always produce "a better spirit." One company in eastern Estill County became so divided over changing their uniforms that the captain thought "it very probable that the old company will be dissolved."[21] Mary Ann Clawson, in her sociological study of nineteenth-century fraternal organizations, found a similar obsession with military uniforms, where members turned out for public events adorned in all manner of colors, ribbons, feathers, and ornaments. This visual festival induced admiration if not envy among other males, who could not fail to notice the attention paid well-dressed citizen-soldiers. Edmund Cooper, for example, who in 1836 joined the White Oak Sprouts, a politically oriented youth militia company in Columbia, Tennessee, found the unit's extravagant uniforms far more appealing than political campaigns or debates.[22]

Beyond the showmanship, military trappings were also great discriminators. Consumer goods, including uniforms and weapons, conveyed messages of exclusivity, power, and hierarchy. At militia events where the restriction of direct participation to white males underscored their privileged position, the vivid display of colorful uniforms further marked the otherness of those who could only watch. Expensive uniforms and weapons emphasized the economic disparities within the white male fraternity. Few could afford such opulence, and those who could not were relegated to the company's lesser ranks or the role of spectator, joining the anonymous crowds of women, children, and slaves. Uniforms and weapons thus enhanced citizen-soldiers' manly image with visual evidence that confirmed both their elevated status and their ostensible willingness to risk life and limb in the community's defense. Should the British feel the inclination to try their luck yet again, the parading militia at least *appeared* well prepared. And an impressive appearance mattered most.[23]

Seeking arms from Governor Letcher in 1844, B. H. Reeves confessed that he and his company did "not profess to be military men nor to know what are the requirements of the law in relation to the public arms. . . . [Nevertheless,] the young men of our town and vicinity would be gratified in obtaining [guns] at as early a period as practicable." For this company, *looking* like soldiers was more important than *being* soldiers. In 1841 Brigadier General W. S. Pilcher heaped praise upon his men for "the splendid and ample preparations they have made, their full band of Martial Music, their equipage, their Military air"; nothing, however, concerning their proficiency with weapons or their military preparedness. Governor Gabriel Slaughter, in his annual message to the Kentucky legislature in 1816, summed up the nexus of arms, martial spirit, and manliness: "Arms produce discipline, inspire a spirit of manly independence, give the people confidence in their strength, and prepare them for resistance to oppression." Whether the governor's observation identified the reality of the militia's confidence and skill or was simply a political platitude, his words reveal the powerful symbolic role that weapons and uniforms played in defining a masculine image. A military appearance indeed created a manly aura.[24]

The final element of the militia experience, one that produced the most convincing evidence of manhood, was participation in battle. In the South, no other act more conclusively demonstrated an individual's masculinity than his prowess on the battlefield. Southerners looked upon military men with deep respect, and the militia offered men an opportunity to be soldiers without the long-term commitment of a military career. Many became officers in their local companies, earning places of prominence and coveted military titles. It is not surprising that travelers through the South often commented on the preponderance of captains, majors, and colonels. Although a military title brought respect, that respect never equaled the honors accorded those who faced the challenges of battle. The white southern male understood that duty and obligation called him to the battlefield, where manly courage and honor conquered effeminate luxury and sloth.[25]

For these aspiring soldiers, it was the men who won the Revolutionary War and those who ensured victory in the War of 1812 who set the standard for virtue, heroism, and manhood. Historian George B. Forgie noted that for males who came of age after the Revolution, nearly all social, political, personal, and moral questions were resolved after pausing to consider the standards set by the founding generation. Especially in the South, veneration of the dead played an important part in male culture, furnishing role models and inspiring younger generations. The previous generations' legendary accomplishments, however, engendered not only respect but anxiety as well. Faced with the Revolutionary era's legacy of republican sacrifice, southerners questioned their ability to maintain their forefathers' storied integrity, honor, and courage.[26]

The boastful toasts Kentuckians offered to the militia at Fourth of July celebrations hinted at the younger generation's yearning to prove their courage and manhood: "The militia of the United States—May their military ardor prove to tyrants that citizens are the proper guardians of national honour," and "The Militia of Kentucky—With fixed bayonets always ready to avenge the blood of their countrymen." Fine speeches and toasts of bravado satisfied holiday crowds but did little to assuage the anxieties that plagued the deeper recesses of young men's minds. Only battle struck deep enough to drive out doubt and apprehension.[27]

The War of 1812 offered an opportunity for young men to prove themselves equal to the men of the founding generation. By risking their lives for liberty and justice, men of the nineteenth century could assert themselves as legitimate heirs of the Revolutionaries.[28] Kentucky's most prominent native son, Henry Clay, argued on the floor of the United States Congress in 1812 that war with England would not only notify the world of the nation's determination but also redeem national honor damaged in recent disputes with Great Britain over unfair trade policies and the impressment of American sailors. A confrontation with the British, Clay advised, would end with an American victory after an "open and manly war." According to the Clay, "a certain portion of military ardor . . . is essential to the protection of the country." Moreover, an additional benefit of war would be "the reproduction and cherishing of a martial spirit amongst us." Men were fighting not simply to protect liberty from a tyrannical monarch but to regain the courage, discipline, and honor of the Revolutionaries, to prove themselves worthy heirs to the "spirit of '76."[29]

Such recollections fortified the country's second generation of warriors as the nation again prepared to battle the British. At the same time, however, their memories raised doubts about their ability to sustain their fathers' manly virtues. During the congressional debate over the Non-Intercourse Act in 1810, Clay warned his fellow representatives not to expect leadership and protection from "the illustrious founders of our freedom," for time had "withered arm and wrinkled brow." With the founders' "deeds of glory and renown" passed to memory, the representatives "shall want the presence and living example of a new race of heroes to supply their place, and to animate us to preserve unviolated what they atchieved." South Carolinian John C. Calhoun, as chairman of the Committee on Foreign Relations, expressed similar sentiments in a report on the war with England presented to Congress in June 1812. He recommended resistance, by armed force if necessary, to maintain the nation's honor and independence. "Americans of the present day," he declared with confidence, "will prove to the enemy and to the world, that we have not only inherited that liberty which our fathers gave us, but also the will and power to maintain it."[30]

Six months before Calhoun's report, Kentucky governor Charles Scott summoned the spirit of America's Revolutionaries in a message to the legislature. Writing with the authority of experience, the old Indian-fighter-turned-politician reminded the state's political leaders of where and how men were made: "It is in the rough school of adversity, that the nobel [sic] virtues of valor, patriotism and fortitude shine forth with distinguished lustre. The spirit of '76 has too long slumbered. Let it again breathe in our councils and animate the children of worthy sires." The Kentucky House of Representatives responded by proclaiming their support for war with Great Britain: "The time has perhaps arrived when some of the people of Kentucky will have to exchange the *plowshare* for the *musket*." Acknowledging the military sacrifices and accomplishments of Scott and other Revolutionary heroes, House members said, "We should do injustice to the veterans who have toiled before us, by a comparison of their sufferings with the sufferings of those who may be now called to war." Their own place in the memories of future generations left no alternative course of action. Great Britain, they said, "has driven us to the last alternative—*unqualified, base submission,* or *war.* The American people cannot hesitate which of the two to choose. The curses of posterity would be upon us by *submission.*" The legislators' message was clear: the weak cowered in surrender; men proved their courage in war. Three months later, when Scott called for fifty-five hundred militia volunteers, he again summoned the nation's forefathers: "Remember '76. I will continue to indulge the hope that the same spirit still animates the children that did their fathers."[31]

Sharing the same sentiments as the state's political leaders, military commanders and ordinary citizens promoted their ancestors as exemplars of manhood. Preparing for battle in October 1813, General Robert Butler reminded his men of their obligation to fight for "the rights of *their* insulted country," and told them that they must not falter as "the sons of sires whose fame is immortal." The same message reached citizen-soldiers and civilians at Fourth of July celebrations and political rallies, where speakers preached of the preceding generations' model virtues. At a barbecue in Lexington to celebrate the declaration of war in June 1812, one resident lifted his cup to the mustering militia and declared, "May the volunteers of this regiment never disgrace their predecessors." Kentuckians also held up the frontiersmen who first explored and settled the wilderness as examples of courage and masculinity. A *Kentucky Gazette* writer, comparing a company of 1812 volunteers to the first tramontane explorers, boasted that "men more hardy and determined, or more capable of braving the fatigues of an active campaign, we have never seen. They are the sons and *true representatives of those old warriors, who first conquered and defended, and then settled Kentucky. They will support the reputation which Kentucky has acquired for valour and patriotism.*" Apparently, as reported by the *Kentucky Gazette*, Captain George Trotter's militiamen did not disappoint: "From all the information we can collect, both officers and men, did their duty and maintained the credit which our first settlers acquired for Kentucky."[32]

Some writers voiced concern that the second generation of Americans might fail to maintain the virtue of their Revolutionary fathers, raising further doubt about their contemporaries' manhood. In 1801 Stanley Griswold preached a sermon of doubt and despair, asking, "Where are our fathers? . . . Where are our former men of dignity . . . who in their day appeared like men?" He feared that American males had become "more disposed to act like children than men." Kentucky poets reiterated Griswold's theme, suggesting that their fellow citizens lacked the military ardor and patriotism of the heroes of 1776. The 1811 poem "New Yankee Doodle" questioned American resolve in meeting British atrocities:

> I guess if father was not dead
> He'd think us very blandly
> And ask where all the fire had fled
> Of yankee doodle dandy.

Similar sentiments appeared in the 1814 poem "Martial Hymn":

> Vile party spirit, hence!
> Like brothers all unite;
> Nature's first law is self defense
> And Liberty her right
> For this our patriots fought,
> for this our fathers bled;
> And shall they bleed and die for nought?
> O, never be it said![33]

Despite the doggerel's pessimism regarding American manhood and the dismal record of U.S. troops in the war, the country survived as a sovereign nation, prompting "A Virginian, Retired in Kentucky," to praise the "Citizens of Kentucky, brave sons of the West" and to declare them a credit to the men of 1776. "You have done your duty," he wrote with reverence, "and future generations will say, *you were worthy of your sires, and the sacred legacy which they bequeathed.*"[34] In battle, the citizen-soldiers of 1812 convinced some that they were indeed the sons of their fathers and men in their own right.

The generation that followed the "brave sons of the West" and participated in the Mexican War suffered the same doubts and anxieties as their fathers, exacerbated by the additional accomplishments of the men who fought in the War of 1812. By the 1840s, Americans enjoyed an abundance of heroes, from Washington to Jackson, each contributing to a mythological national manhood. In 1846, when H. Groesbeck of Covington volunteered his artillery unit for service, he assured the governor that "the blood of Kentuckians courses in their veins, and they desire to emulate the deeds of their fathers." The volunteer cavalry of Henry County informed Governor Owsley of their lineage and eagerness to carry on. First Lieutenant Charles Marshall insisted that he had "a company of *Kentuckians born free,* . . . panting to sustain the reputation given to them by their ancestors." Joseph Powell of the Covington Guards, fearing the governor might reject his company of infantry, averred that he and his men were "anxious to sustain . . . the glory and chivalry of our fathers." They wanted a chance to prove they "had lost none of that noble impulse that animated the spirit of [their] fathers." C. C. Kelly, recommending a fellow resident of Louisville for a command, thought it worth mentioning the officer's legendary ancestor: "As a descendant of the hardy and chivalrous Daniel Boone, his name alone would give éclat to his regiments, and afford a prestige of success in his enterprise." Whether descendants of a famous frontiersman or the sons of anonymous farmers, southerners wanted to show that they, like their fathers and grandfathers, commanded the courage and fortitude of soldiers and men. Battle could authenticate the civic virtue of those who embraced the competition and selfishness of the market economy. In combat militiamen subordinated self-preservation to attain an absolute and eternal masculinity. War might take a man's life, but in return, it redeemed his manhood.[35]

War has always carried with it the risk of death, but the soldier who falls in battle assures himself a place among his nation's heroes as the embodiment of bravery and manhood. In a 1783 sermon, George Duffield made this point when he eulogized the patriots of the Revolution: "Number them not of the dead. They are enrolled in the list of glory and fame, and shall live immortal, beyond the death of the grave." In 1813 Elizabeth Love of Frankfort heartened her son James with the same lesson. "Should you fall in battle," she wrote from Frankfort, "the praise of your good deeds will shine through." The words of Duffield and Love demonstrate the relationship southerners saw between manhood, battle, and death. Man's anxiety over his eventual death and disappearance from the community's memory pushed him to find a means to secure his immortality, figuratively if not literally. For many, the answer lay on the battlefield. Death in combat assured an eternal life on earth. A man's death and subsequent rebirth in the masculine community of fellow fallen soldiers manifested itself in the community's collective memory, where he achieved immortal manhood.[36] An 1811 verse commemorating Kentuckian Joseph H. Daviess illustrates this relationship between death in battle and eternal life in memory:

> Who to their country's welfare freely give
> The sacrifice of life, forever live
> As bright examples to the unborn brave,
> To shew how virtue rescues from the grave.

"Virtue rescues from the grave"—death in battle secured citizen-soldiers a place of honor in their communities, proved them equal to their forefathers' virtue, and authenticated their courage and masculinity.[37]

In 1861 presidents from two American nations asked that volunteers from North and South accept the challenges and dangers of a civil war. Newspapers from Baton Rouge to Boston trumpeted the call for men to defend their country, their families, and their manhood. Many of those who answered the call believed themselves fortunate, a generation blessed with the opportunity to win manly glory. For their fathers and grandfathers, however, demonstrating one's courage and manhood was not so simple. Fate produced no grand war. Moreover, the eighteenth-century masculine ideals of self-sacrifice and civic virtue were being swept aside by self-interest and individualism. Indeed, just who was the true man? The father who sacrificed time and sweat for the betterment of family and community, or the entrepreneur who toiled long hours for greater personal profit? In the militia, both found a martial experience that demonstrated beyond doubt their manhood. The exclusion of all but white males, the accouterments of weapons and uniforms, and the discerning process of the occasional battle established militiamen as men, a process essential to maintaining the South's hierarchy of race and gender. For nineteenth-century southern males, the militia was indeed a refuge of masculinity.

### NOTES

1. Daniel T. Rodgers, "Republicanism: The Career of a Concept," *Journal of American History* 79 (1992): 11–38; E. Anthony Rotundo, *American Manhood: Transformations in Masculinity from the Revolution to the Modern Era* (New York: Basic Books, 1993), 10–25; Mark E. Kann, *A Republic of Men: The American Founders, Gendered Language, and Patriarchal Politics* (New York: New York University Press, 1998), 1–51, 109; Michael Kimmel, *Manhood in America: A Cultural History* (New York: Free Press, 1996), 18; Charles Sellers, *The Market Revolution: Jacksonian America, 1815–1846* (New York: Oxford University Press, 1991), 246.

2. Kimmel, *Manhood in America,* 59, also 43–45, 78; Peter N. Stearns, *Be A Man! Males in Modern Society* (New York: Holmes and Meier, 1979), 7, 23–25; Kann, *A Republic of Men,* 2, 22; David G. Pugh, *Sons of Liberty: The Masculine Mind in Nineteenth-Century America* (Westport, Conn.: Greenwood Press, 1983), 6.

3. Lowell H. Harrison and James C. Klotter, *A New History of Kentucky* (Lexington: University Press of Kentucky, 1997); Lowell H. Harrison, *Kentucky's Road to Statehood* (Lexington: University Press of Kentucky, 1992). For a review of community study methodology, see Colin Bell and Howard Newby, *Community Studies: An Introduction to the Sociology of the Local Community* (New York: Praeger 1971), 29–30, 39.

4. For a history of the English militia, see John R. Western, *The English Militia in the Eighteenth Century: The Story of Political Issue, 1660–1802* (London: Routledge and Kegan Paul, 1965). Lawrence Delbert Cress explores the early American militia in *Citizens in Arms: The Army and Militia in American Society to the War of 1812* (Chapel Hill: University of North Carolina Press, 1982).

5. Edmund S. Morgan, *American Slavery, American Freedom: The Ordeal of Colonial Virginia* (New York: Norton, 1975); James Oakes, *The Ruling Race: A History of American Slaveholders* (New York: Knopf, 1982), 41, 83–86, 138–42; Bertram Wyatt-Brown, *Southern Honor: Ethics and Behavior in the Old South* (New York: Oxford University Press, 1982), 39, 63–69, 157; John Hope Franklin, *The Militant South, 1800–1861* (Cambridge: Beacon Press, 1956), 63–66; Len Travers, *Celebrating the Fourth: Independence Day and the Rites of Nationalism in the Early Republic* (Amherst: University of Massachusetts Press, 1997), 86–87, 153; Lisa C. Tolbert, *Constructing Townscapes: Space and Society in Antebellum Tennessee* (Chapel Hill: University of North Carolina Press, 1999), 75, 80–81; Dana D. Nelson, *National*

*Manhood: Capitalist Citizenship and the Imagined Fraternity of White Men* (Durham: Duke University Press, 1998).

6. Malcolm J. Rohrbough, *The Trans-Appalachian Frontier: People, Societies, and Institutions, 1775–1850* (New York: Oxford University Press, 1978), 7, 116–17; Elizabeth A. Perkins, *Border Life: Experience and Memory in the Revolutionary Ohio Valley* (Chapel Hill: University of North Carolina Press, 1998), 132, 138, 142; David Waldstreicher, *In the Midst of Perpetual Fetes: The Making of American Nationalism, 1776–1820* (Chapel Hill: University of North Carolina Press, 1997), 68. Waldstreicher also pointed out that by the 1780s, unruly celebrations had given way to more structured and ordered popular displays as Americans learned "how orderly nationalist rejoicing could express their political differences" (107).

7. Nelson, *National Manhood*, 184–88. Also see R. Claire Snyder, *Citizen-Soldiers and Manly Warriors: Military Service and Gender in the Civic Republican Tradition* (Lanham, Md.: Rowman and Littlefield, 1999), 35; and Kann, *A Republic of Men*, 28, 155, 160. James W. Allen to Quartermaster General John Woods, 20 August 1834, Militia Records, Kentucky Military Records and Research Branch, Frankfort (hereafter KMRRB); *Kentucky Gazette* (Lexington), 11 July 1835. Wyatt-Brown and Franklin both noted the importance of militia events to engendering white male identity across class lines, as well as to creating community unity: see Wyatt-Brown, *Southern Honor*, 340–41, and Franklin, *The Militant South*, 173–85. For national accounts of the relationship between public events, white male unity, and community identity, see Waldstreicher, *Perpetual Fetes*, 105, 242–43; Simon P. Newman, *Parades and the Politics of the Street: Festive Culture in the Early American Republic* (Philadelphia: University of Pennsylvania Press, 1997), 103; Travers, *Celebrating the Fourth*, 184–85; Tolbert, *Constructing Townscapes*, 80–81; Don Harrison Doyle, *The Social Order of a Frontier Community: Jacksonville, Illinois, 1825–70* (Urbana: University of Illinois Press, 1978); and Hugh Dalziel Duncan, *Communication and Social Order* (New York: Bedminster Press, 1962), 275. By tradition and statute, company officers were elected by the rank and file; "An Act to regulate and discipline the Militia of this Commonwealth, and for other purposes," 1792, Second Session, chap. 5, sec. 3, in *Laws of Kentucky: comprehending those of a general nature now in force, and which have been acted on by the legislature thereof. Together with a copious index and a list of local or private acts, with the dates of the sessions at which they were passed. To which is prefixed the Constitution of the United States, with the amendments, the Act of Separation from the state of Virginia, and the Constitution of Kentucky* (Lexington: John Bradford, 1799–1807), 6.

8. Wyatt-Brown, *Southern Honor*, 69; Travers, *Celebrating the Fourth*, 153; John F. Kutolowski and Kathleen Smith Kutolowski, "Commissions and Canvasses: The Militia and Politics in Western New York, 1800–1845," *New York History* 63 (1982): 5–38; Rohrbough, *The Trans-Appalachian Frontier*, 7, 116–17. For the relationship between the control of public ceremonies and speeches and the concomitant access to power, see Wyatt-Brown, *Southern Honor*, 47, 330; Franklin, *The Militant South*, 189–92; Waldstreicher, *In the Midst of Perpetual Fetes*, 225; Susan G. Davis, *Parades*

and *Power: Street Theatre in Nineteenth-Century Philadelphia* (Philadelphia: Temple University Press, 1986), 70–71; and Duncan, *Communication and Social Order,* 264. Cynthia A. Kierner demonstrates how restrictions on speakers reinforced southern social order in "Genteel Balls and Republican Parades: Gender and Early Southern Civic Rituals, 1677–1826," *Virginia Magazine of History and Biography* 104 (1996): 198. For a discussion of the role of audiences in rituals and community events, see Waldstreicher, *Perpetual Fetes,* 71–72; and Duncan, *Communication and Social Order,* 262.

9. Wyatt-Brown, *Southern Honor,* 138–40, 170–71, 251; Nelson, *National Manhood,* ix–x; Kann, *A Republic of Men,* 17, 26, 153–54.

10. Kierner, "Genteel Balls," 195–204. Also see Wyatt-Brown, *Southern Honor,* 43, 51–52, 234, 347–48. For a discussion of women and the concept of dependency in the Revolutionary era, see Joan R. Gundersen, "Independence, Citizenship, and the American Revolution," *Signs: Journal of Women in Culture and Society* 13 (autumn 1987): 59–77. For additional interpretations of women's participation, exclusion, and significance to public events, see Newman, *Parades and the Politics,* 66–67, 85–86; Waldstreicher, *Perpetual Fetes,* 82, 168–71, 233–35; and Travers, *Celebrating the Fourth,* 139–41.

11. Travers, *Celebrating the Fourth,* 145–52; Newman, *Parades and the Politics,* 81, 103; Tolbert, *Constructing Townscapes,* 72. On the participation of free blacks in celebrations, see Waldstreicher, *Perpetual Fetes,* 243–45, and Newman, *Parades and the Politics,* 103. Also see Morgan's overall argument in *American Slavery.*

12. Franklin, *The Militant South,* 14–62. Wyatt-Brown verified the promotion of gun use among young boys in the South in *Southern Honor,* 156. Daniel R. Hundley, *Social Relations in Our Southern States* (1860), 199. Also see Morgan, *American Slavery,* 239–40, and Stephen Aron, *How the West Was Lost: The Transformation of Kentucky from Daniel Boone to Henry Clay* (Baltimore: Johns Hopkins University Press, 1996), 103, 113.

13. Charles Royster, *A Revolutionary People at War: The Continental Army and American Character, 1775–1783* (Chapel Hill: University of North Carolina Press, 1979). See Donald Hickey, *The War of 1812: A Forgotten Conflict* (Urbana: University of Illinois Press, 1989), for an account of the defense of Baltimore, 202–4. See also, Robert V. Remini, *The Battle of New Orleans* (New York: Viking, 1999), and John William Ward, *Andrew Jackson: Symbol for an Age* (New York: Oxford University Press, 1962), 16, 29. For a discussion of the Kentucky frontiersmen and their legendary reputations, see Arthur K. Moore, *The Frontier Mind: A Cultural Analysis of the Kentucky Frontier* (Lexington: University Press of Kentucky, 1957), 77–106.

14. George W. Chambers to Quartermaster General John Wood, 2 May 1832; Captain John Brown to Colonel P. Dudley, 14 October 1837; James W. Allen to Quartermaster General John W. Wood, 20 August 1834; William Myers to Quartermaster General John Woods, 15 May 1836; and Captain John D. Crafton to Quartermaster Pettit, 1 June 1840, all in KMRRB.

15. Robert Beverley, *History and Present State of Virginia,* ed. Louis B. Wright (Chapel Hill: University of North Carolina Press, 1947), 269, 271; J. B. Marshall to Adjutant General Ambrose Dudley, 6 May 1840 (emphasis added); Colonel E. G. House to Quartermaster General Ambrose Dudley, 22 April 1843, both in KMRRB.

16. H. K. Berry et al. to Quartermaster General Ambrose Dudley, 7 July 1841; Payton, Bibb, Harrison, and Caldwell to J. B. Temple, 11 August 1852; William R. Bradford to General A. Dudley, 16 January 1842, all in KMRRB.

17. Jesse Stevens to General Hughs, 29 May 1840; Capt. S. D. McCullough to Quartermaster General Dudley; 15 July 1845; General Dudley to Capt. McCullough, 22 July 1845; Captain H. Marshall to Quartermaster General A. W. Dudley, 4 June 1842, all in KMRRB. Despite the intense competition to obtain weapons, some companies were willing to share their muskets if they had a surplus, as did Captain W. R. Bradford's company, which offered "to send over . . . 50 stand arms" to another company; see Captain Bradford to Colonel P. Dudley, 22 March 1841; for another example, see James Kelly to Quartermaster General John Woods, 9 May 1836, both in KMRRB. For additional examples of arms requests, see J. D. Hill to Governor R. P. Letcher, 10 October 1843; Bob McKee to Governor Letcher, 22 May 1844; Colonel R. T. P. Allen to Quartermaster General Ambrose Dudley, 22 April 1845; N. W. Maddux to Governor William Owsley, 3 May 1847; and A. M. Brown to Governor William Owsley, 10 May 1847, all in KMRRB.

18. Captain William R. Bradford to Quartermaster General Ambrose Dudley, 21 July 1845, KMRRB.

19. Captain Thomas M. Coons to Quartermaster General A. W. Dudley, 23 July 1851, KMRRB.

20. H. K. Berry et al. to Quartermaster General Ambrose Dudley, 7 July 1841; for an additional example, see Ratliff Baines to Adjutant General Dudley, 22 July 1848, both in KMRRB.

21. Franklin, *The Militant South,* 167. Rod Andrew Jr. explored the South's martial culture in a study of military academies: see *Long Gray Lines: The Southern Military School Tradition, 1839–1915* (Chapel Hill: University of North Carolina Press, 2001). A. Tarlton to unknown recipient, 11 March 1835; John Miller to Quartermaster General A. W. Dudley, 29 May 1841; Captain William R. Bradford to Quartermaster General A. W. Dudley, 21 July 1845; William P. Chiles to Quartermaster General A. W. Dudley, 8 June 1847, all in KMRRB. For additional examples, see Captain J. F. Busby to Governor William Owsley, 5 March 1841; C. A. Preston to James Harland, 21 August 1843, both in KMRRB.

22. Mary Ann Clawson, *Constructing Brotherhood: Class, Gender, and Fraternalism* (Princeton: Princeton University Press, 1989), 234–36. The story of Edmund Cooper is found in Tolbert, *Constructing Townscapes,* 158. Sociologist David Gilmore argued that societies around the world expect men to "take an active part in the ritualized dramas of community life." Such public demonstrations represent "a moral commitment to defend the society and its core values against all odds": see David

Gilmore, *Manhood in the Making: Cultural Concepts of Masculinity* (New Haven: Yale University Press, 1990), 91–93, 224. Also see Franklin, *The Militant South*, 176; and Davis, *Parades and Power*, 61–64.

23. Elizabeth A. Perkins, "The Consumer Frontier: Household Consumption in Early Kentucky," *Journal of American History* 78 (1991): 509; Davis, *Parades and Power*, 55; Clawson, *Constructing Brotherhood*, 236.

24. B. H. Reeves and F. M. Burton to Governor Letcher, 18 June 1844; Brigadier General W. S. Pilcher to Adjutant General Dudley, 9 June 1841, both in KMRRB; Annual Message of Governor Gabriel Slaughter printed in the *Kentucky Gazette*, 9 December 1816. Also see, Snyder, *Citizen-Soldiers*, 87. Richard L. Bushman discussed the increasing significance of dress and appearance in *The Refinement of America: Persons, Houses, Cities* (New York: Knopf, 1992), 69–74.

25. Wyatt-Brown, *Southern Honor*, 34–40, 191–92; Franklin, *The Militant South*, 146–92; Stearns, *Be A Man!* 23–25. The majority of studies on the relationship between manhood and battle focus on the Civil War and Victorian eras, but the findings are similar. For the Civil War, see Reid Mitchell, "Soldiering, Manhood, and Coming of Age: A Northern Volunteer," in *Divided Houses: Gender and the Civil War*, ed. Catherine Clinton and Nina Silber (New York: Oxford University Press, 1992), 43–51. For the Victorian period, see Rotundo, *American Manhood*, 222–46, and Donald Mrozak, "The Habit of Victory: The American Military and the Cult of Manliness," in *Manliness and Morality: Middle-Class Masculinity in Britain and America, 1800–1940*, ed. J. A. Mangan and James Walvin (New York: St. Martin's, 1987), 220–39.

26. George B. Forgie, *Patricide in the House Divided: A Psychological Interpretation of Lincoln and His Age* (New York: Norton, 1979), 7–8; Wyatt-Brown, *Southern Honor*, 31, 39, 44–45, 118–22; James Oakes, *The Ruling Race*, 202–203. In her study of the post-Revolution United States, Joyce Appleby argued that the influence of the founding generation rapidly diminished. She did not, however, address the role of the Revolutionaries' military legacy: see *Inheriting the Revolution: The First Generation of Americans* (Cambridge: Harvard University Press, 2000).

27. *Kentucky Gazette*, 9 July 1796, 21 July 1826. For examples of similar toasts, see *Kentucky Gazette*, 9 July 1791, 12 July 1803, 13 July 1820, 7 August 1823, and 12 July 1838; Wyatt-Brown, *Southern Honor*, 118; Travers, *Celebrating the Fourth*, 216. See also Stearns, *Be A Man!* 19, in which the author asserts that society's expectations required "the son . . . to approximate the same attributes of the father." As Mark Kann wrote in *A Republic of Men*, "Each male generation must measure up to prior generations," 162, also 33, 79, 139–40.

28. Steven Watts, *The Republic Reborn: War and the Making of Liberal America, 1790–1820* (Baltimore: Johns Hopkins University Press, 1987), 74, 102, 271–74; Wyatt-Brown, *Southern Honor*, 40. For similar ideas, see Mark E. Kann, *On the Man Question: Gender and Civic Virtue in America* (Philadelphia: Temple University Press, 1991), 17, 293; and Travers, *Celebrating the Fourth*, 206.

29. Henry Clay, "Address to Congress," 14 April 1812, in *The Papers of Henry Clay*, ed. James F. Hopkins (Lexington: University Press of Kentucky, 1959), 1:645; Henry Clay, "Speech on Proposed Repeal of Non-Intercourse Act," 22 February 1810, in Hopkins, *Papers of Henry Clay*, 1:450; Watts, *The Republic Reborn*, 88.

30. Henry Clay, "Speech on Proposed Repeal of the Non-Intercourse Act," 22 February 1810, in Hopkins, *Papers of Henry Clay*, 1:450; John C. Calhoun, "Report on the Causes and Reasons for War," 25 June 1812, *Annals of the Congress of the United States* (Washington, D.C., 1853), 24:1546–54.

31. *The Palladium* (Frankfort, Kentucky), 4 December 1811, 6 May 1812; *Kentucky Gazette*, 11 February 1812.

32. *Kentucky Gazette*, 12 October 1813, 30 June 1812, 8 September 1812, 29 December 1812. For other examples, see Kann, *A Republic of Men*, 34.

33. Stanley Griswold, "Overcoming Evil" (1801), in *Political Sermons of the American Founding Era, 1730–1805*, ed. Ellis Sandoz (Indianapolis: Liberty Fund, 1991), 1551–52; *Kentucky Gazette*, 3 September 1811, 5 December 1814. Also see Kann, *A Republic of Men*, 95, for further discussion of the older generation's doubts.

34. *Kentucky Gazette*, 13 March 1815.

35. H. Groesbeck to Governor William Owsley, 23 May 1846; Charles E. Marshall to Governor William Owsley, May 1846; Joseph W. Powell to Governor William Owsley, 22 May 1846; C. C. Kelly to Governor William Owsley, 26 May 1846, all in Governor William Owsley's Executive Papers, Kentucky Historical Society, Frankfort; Damon Eubank, "A Time for Heroes, A Time for Honor: Kentucky Soldiers in the Mexican War," *Filson Club Historical Quarterly* 72 (1998): 176.

36. George Duffield, "Sermon" (1783), in Sandoz, *Political Sermons*, 785; for an additional example, see Daniel Shute, "Election Sermon" (1768), in *American Political Writing during the Founding Era, 1760–1805*, ed. Charles S. Hyneman and Donald S. Lutz, 2 vols. (Indianapolis: Liberty Fund, 1983), 1:131; Elizabeth Love to James Love, 7 June 1813, James Young Love Papers, Filson Club Historical Society, Louisville, Kentucky; Nancy C. M. Hartsock, "Masculinity, Heroism, and the Making of War," in *Rocking the Ship of State: Toward a Feminist Peace Politics*, ed. Adrienne Harris and Ynestra King (Boulder: Westview Press, 1989), 135–45. Also see George L. Mosse, *The Image of Man: The Creation of Modern Masculinity* (New York: Oxford University Press, 1996), 50–51; Philipe Aries, *Western Attitudes toward Death: From the Middle Ages to the Present*, trans. Patricia Ranum (Baltimore: Johns Hopkins University Press, 1974), 72–79; Kann, *A Republic of Men*, 163–67; Moore, *The Frontier Mind*, 81–82; and Wyatt-Brown, *Southern Honor*, 45.

37. *Kentucky Gazette*, 18 February 1812. Len Travers wrote that during the War of 1812 "new heroes, worthy inheritors of the Revolutionary tradition, took their places with George Washington and Thomas Jefferson in the pantheon of American patriots": see *Celebrating the Fourth*, 207.

# "Let Us Manufacture Men": Educating Elite Boys in the Early National South

*Lorri Glover*

For elite boys from southern states who came of age between the 1780s and the 1820s, higher education was the centerpiece of their transformation into "southern men." As adults, this first generation of self-conscious southerners guided their region through sectional crises and into Civil War.[1] Like young men throughout the nation, southern students saw their college years as a time to secure reputations and to acquire knowledge. But universities also taught profound sectional lessons. When changes in the American economy and political culture challenged the southern gentry's historical reliance on lineage and slave-holding, the job of defending these traditions and securing the future of their families and their region fell to these southern sons. Thus, in addition to fostering success and respectability, university education laid the foundation for southern nationalism. Historians typically locate the emergence of sectionalism either in the political crisis regarding Missouri statehood in 1819–20 or in the heightened tensions over slavery in 1831 following the founding of William Lloyd Garrison's *Liberator* (a radical abolitionist newspaper) and the Nat Turner slave rebellion in Virginia. These episodes certainly signified the strident political sectionalism that divided antebellum America. But the origins of sectional identity and defensiveness appeared a generation earlier, among college students in the early Republic.

Beginning in the 1780s, the university experience represented the first milestone in maturation for southern gentry boys and shaped their emergent sectional identity. Completion of formal education preceded other manifestations of manhood: courtship and marriage, career proficiency, mastery over estates and slaves. Southern students shared much in common with young men in other parts of the early United States. But family correspondence, which offers the clearest and most comprehensive description of southern masculine values available to scholars, demonstrates the dawning of a self-conscious southern identity at the turn of the nineteenth century. Although influenced by the emergent national culture, sectional demands, particularly the interwoven defense of slavery and family, eventually played the dominant role in these students' lives. Between the 1780s and 1820s, elite boys from southern states moved gradually but unmistakably toward thinking about themselves as southern men.

Three factors drove this shift in southern manhood: the institutions southern students attended, the parental directives they received, and the peer culture they created. The South's peculiar institution informed each. Slavery bought the accoutrements of southern elites' exaggerated refinement and allowed them and their sons to lead leisured, genteel lifestyles. Because slavery increasingly earned the rebuke of northern intellectuals in the early Republic, family slaveholding made southern boys stand out at northern universities; as outsiders, they congregated together and reified their regional distinctiveness. Moreover, slavery underlay parents' fears about educating their sons in the North and contributed to their determination to build southern state universities. Finally, slavery exaggerated southern elite boys' sense of independence as well as their proclivity for violence—values that lay at the core of southern youth culture.

Changes in American educational expectations in the early Republic gradually pushed southern parents and their sons toward regional pride and defensiveness.[2] In the decades after American independence, transformations in economy and political culture increased the importance of attending a university. In addition to ensuring independence, the American Revolution advanced an ideology of individual rights and self-determination that challenged lineage and class entitlement. Furthermore, the expansion of a market economy encouraged competitiveness and individualism in the broader culture.[3] In the colonial period, a man's family name and his inherited wealth determined his political power and status in society. While formal education enhanced a man's worldliness, it was not essential for social recognition. But in the early Republic, family and class no longer ensured a man's position. Instead, men needed to prove individual merit and to compete with others for power and wealth. A university education increasingly provided the means by which a boy could become his own man.

In the wake of the American break from the British Empire, education also became more politicized. Parents increasingly associated Europe with decadence, which they juxtaposed with American virtue. Thus, they determined a more appropriate education could be found at home, in the United States. Since Americans believed that the success of their republican experiment required an educated, virtuous citizenry, universities also represented important centers for the adoption of national values. As one southern educator explained, America triumphed against Britain because of "principles and accomplishments established in the minds of her sons, rather than in her property and external resources." American society could persist only by instilling those same qualities in each succeeding generation through education. Inculcation of those national values began in youth, according to Abraham Baldwin, since "there is no place in which the forming hand of Society may be more conspicuous than upon their youth, and more thoroughly pervade and insinuate into every part."[4]

Southern aristocrats initially embraced the idea of nationalist education. Parents encouraged teenage boys to see college as an opportunity to groom themselves for service to their states and the new nation. When, for example, wealthy South Carolinian John Ball Jr. headed off to Harvard in 1798, his parents urged him to conduct himself so that the Ball family would be honored and so that his country would be "ornamented by" him. Fellow Carolinian Ralph Izard concurred. Writing during the debates over ratification of the Constitution, he insisted, "There are two objects very near my Heart, which if I live to see accomplished, will be an ample compensation for every thing that I have suffered. I wish to see a good solid federal Government established, & my Sons so educated as to afford me a prospect of their being Men of abilities, & honour, & their becoming useful, valuable Citizens of their Country." In a typical letter of encouragement, Virginian Daniel Guerrant urged his younger brother to excel in his studies: "We hail the day when you will return to your native soil, aquiting yourself with honor at School and qualified to render Services to your Country." Between the 1780s and the 1800s scores of students from the southern states heard and internalized similar messages about national service and pride. Imbued with patriotism, Henry Rutledge said of the time he spent studying in Europe in the 1790s, "[It] has been enough to sicken and disgust [me]. . . . [I] thank my fate which had made me an American."[5]

Parents in the North and in the South sent boys to college to become good Americans: men of refinement, self-determination, and virtue fully prepared to lead their families and their nation. Elite southerners shared with prominent northerners other assumptions about masculine values as well. In both regions, whiteness formed a critical part of masculine civic identity.[6] Throughout most of the nation, only white men enjoyed the full benefits of citizenship. Moreover, advice literature encouraging meticulous attention to public perceptions of character and privileging refinement above all other qualities influenced American men of the upper and middle classes.[7] The first generation of southerners identified with the emergent national ethos, but the pull of sectional loyalties soon compromised their national allegiance.

Southern parents wanted to buy the best for their boys, so they sent sons to the nation's most prestigious universities, located predominantly in New England. But at schools such as Harvard, Yale, and Princeton, southern and northern boys saw how different they were from one another. Many southerners openly criticized their hosts. South Carolinian William Martin found New Englanders "industrious & parsimoning in the extreme . . . [and] almost invariably homely." Others found qualities worth praising. Virginian Edmund Ruffin Jr. lauded New Englanders as "enlightened and polished . . . all very industrious and hard working, a sober and religious people." Fearful that his father might think he had "been praising Conneticutt too much," he added, "Yankees sometimes cheat if they can, and they will try to get as much out of you as they can." John C. Calhoun, a Yale student in 1803, offered a mixed assessment. Northerners appeared "certainly more penurious, more contracted in their sentiments, and less social, than the Carolinians. But as to morality," Calhoun conceded, "we must yield."[8] By and large, southerners prided themselves on their superior wealth, attractiveness, and gentility but admitted that northerners, while often frugal, evidenced greater respect for religion and education. Whether they praised or condemned their northern counterparts, southern students clearly acknowledged regional distinctiveness.

Northerners who traveled south or who encountered southern students at universities similarly pointed out sectional differences, in particular they criticized southern inattention to education and religion. Edward Hooker, a native of Connecticut, arrived in South Carolina in 1807 to tutor at South Carolina College. In a letter home he said to a friend, "we used when together, frequently to talk of the Southern States. I believe you thought I entertained in some particulars undue prejudice respecting them." While Hooker admitted that class lines seemed more fluid than he imagined, southerners confirmed his suspicions about illiteracy, indolence, and impiety. He expressed particular concern about the dearth of churches in Columbia, home of South Carolina College: "Eighty rising youths of just the proper age to be forming their moral and religious principles which are to govern them in life and stay them in death—and no stated preaching in town."[9] Richard Furman, a Baptist minister, concurred. In 1799 Furman published a sermon on "the languishing state of religion in the southern parts of these United States." The "luke-warmness and backsliding" of the South he juxtaposed with the piety of the North: "a pleasing contrast . . . exciting our emulation and encouraging our hope."[10] Northerners and southerners recognized a host of differences from the mundane to the profound. Massachusetts native William Blanding found the early June heat in South Carolina nearly unbearable. Amazed, he wrote in his diary that "the people say this is nothing— if this is nothing what will something be?" Even eating patterns varied by region.

While boarding at a Connecticut school, Edmund Ruffin Jr. noted that every northern student ate hominy with molasses and that every southerner did not.[11]

The most striking difference between North and South in the early Republic centered on slave-holding. Like many northerners, Massachusetts native Davis Thacher marveled at the inhumanity of southern slaveholders who tracked runaways "with dogs & guns like deer . . . hunting the human species like wild beasts."[12] Other northerners, indifferent to the plight of slaves, commented on the dissipation that pervaded the southern slave-holding class. Timothy Ford, traveling to Charleston in 1785, complained that the gentry ignored their businesses: "Pleasure becomes in great measure their study." This he attributed to slavery: "Accustomed to have every thing done for them they cannot or will not do anything for themselves."[13]

Such differences, thrown into bold relief when large numbers of boys from the two regions lived together, increasingly encouraged students from the southern states to think of themselves as "southerners." As early as the turn of the nineteenth century, southern students evidenced a subtle regional identification, measuring themselves against their southern classmates. When sixteen-year-old Harry Manigault entered the freshman class at Princeton in 1804, his uncle George Izard accompanied him. George Izard decided to hand over to Harry all the money his parents had designated for Harry's expenses. As George explained to Harry's father, Gabriel Manigault, "much of the youth from the Southward of the same age were entrusted by their Friends with the Money deemed necessary for all their expenses. Your son was desirous to have the same confidence placed in Him, & I judged it was proper to gratify him."[14] Students from southern states also roomed and socialized with boys from their own state or region.

By the 1810s southern students gave voice not only to regional identification but also to regional tensions that played out in college conflicts. The South Carolina Ball brothers complained that northern boys abused them at their Vermont school. Hoping for money to fund a vacation, Hugh insisted, "we don't wish to stay here with a parcel of Yankees for they have stolen enough from us already, they have stolen two beautiful watches from some of the Southerners, and they have the impudence to come in our rooms at night and steal." Attending a Connecticut school in the 1820s, Virginian Edmund Ruffin Jr. recounted the teasing one southern boy endured from his northern classmates and the solidarity of southern students. After "the Yankees" laughed at the schoolboy's speech patterns, southern boys rose to his defense and "a great dispute between the Southerners and the Northerners" ensued.[15]

Southern gentry encouraged this growing regionalism among boys, for they feared that young men might form allegiances with northerners or adopt northern values. Their fears were not always baseless. In the first few months of his residence in Cambridge, John E. Colhoun Jr. complained about homesickness and the local girls. After two years at Harvard, he changed his mind: "I have but lately found out that the Yankee girls are very fine and upon due consideration, think they would make much better wives . . . than the southern." Although he missed his family while studying in Philadelphia, Marylander Richard Hopkins dreaded returning to his rural home: "I feal much anxiety of mind when I contemplate spending my life confined to the narrow limits of a Neighbourhood to be rusticated among unlettered and unpolished rustics." [16]

Although parents worried that their sons might remain in northern cities or fall in love with northern women, their most profound fears arose over northern skepticism of southern slave-holding. Beginning in the 1770s and inspired by the values of the American Revolution, northern states adopted programs of gradual emancipation and abolition. During this same era, the South intensified its reliance on slave labor (especially after the development of the cotton gin in 1794) and commitment to the westward expansion of slavery. The first national crisis did not arise until 1819, with the struggle over Missouri statehood. But as early as the 1790s, southerners expressed fears of northern animosity toward slavery. For example, as John Ball Jr. studied at Harvard in 1799, his father, one of South Carolina's wealthiest slaveholders, directed the younger Ball to avoid "imbibing principles . . . against the interest of the southern states." "Carry in mind," he warned, "that whenever a general emancipation takes place in So[uth] Carolina & Georgia you are a ruined man and all your family connexions made beggars." [17]

Elite parents, the vast majority of whom owned slaves, believed that the future of their families depended on their sons and that the future of their region depended on slavery. In 1805 South Carolinian Henry DeSaussure lamented the passing of the revolutionary generation but took solace in the youth of his state and the potential offered by education: "we have lost a few of our venerable men, the remains of the revolution—By degrees they are removed, and a new generation occupy the stage of life—. . . [but] the diffusion of education gives the hope that we shall have able & worthy men for every department of government." [18] The precise nature of the education southern sons received at northern schools scared some parents. Imagine, for example, the reaction of Edmund Ruffin Sr. upon reading his fourteen-year-old son's praise of his Connecticut headmaster for taking students to hear a recently liberated "African Prince" recount his harrowing experience of bondage in America. Little wonder that the following year Edmund Ruffin Jr. transferred to the University of Virginia. [19]

Thus the first hints of sectional identity and protectionism came as adults considered the future of the most malleable and most important members of the society: the next generation of leaders. Consequently, between the 1790s and the

1820s, parental fixation on prestigious northern schools gave way to anxieties over their sons' adopting the wrong values. Fears about southern boys' identifying with northern classmates, particularly regarding the increasingly divisive issue of slavery, coupled with local pride encouraged southerners to open the doors of their own state universities: the University of North Carolina in 1795, South Carolina College in 1805, the University of Virginia in 1819, and the University of Georgia in 1823.[20] Abraham Baldwin, a Yale graduate and founder of the University of Georgia, argued that the school would protect Georgia's sons as well as the state's reputation within the nation: "To send them [southern students] abroad to foreign countries for their education will always be the cause of so great foreign attachment that could our national pride brook such a dependence, upon principles of good policy it would be insufferable. To send them to other States . . . is too humiliating an acknowledgment of the ignorance and inferiority of our own."[21]

In the 1810s and 1820s, universities became powerful symbols of state pride. Henry Clay promoted the establishment of Transylvania University in his hometown of Lexington, Kentucky, convinced that it would "shed particular lustre upon that State." Local leaders seeking to establish a medical school in Kentucky in the 1800s argued that the school would "tend to show an air of polish, and refinement over the minds, and the manners of the Citizens, and thereby exalt [Kentucky] in the estimation of [its] sister States." Edmund Hubard insisted that the University of Virginia, which he attended in 1825, promised to reverse the decline in reputation that Virginia suffered after its heyday in the colonial and revolutionary eras. Every Virginian, he proclaimed, could take pride in the prominence of the university.[22] The significance of universities to their states proved so great that some men feared voicing criticism of these institutions. After David Swain questioned the morality of the students at Chapel Hill and the educational benefits of attending the university, his father urged him to be "silent as possible on the subject of Chapel Hill. . . . every North Carolinian feels interested in its welfare and so strong is the partiality . . . that the least imprudent expression may raise you a host of adversaries and injure your popularity during life." Similarly after condemning the waywardness of his Chapel Hill classmates, John Pettigrew asked his father to keep their discussions private, insisting, "I should be sorry to be the means of spreading a report which might injure the University."[23]

Southern state universities recruited few students from outside the region; instead, they became havens for state pride and sectional defensiveness. By the 1820s, the northern colleges once praised by southerners as centers of republican virtue became the objects of contempt. "My God can't we be educated at the South" demanded a North Carolina student in 1828. "It is all a mere cheat. . . .

We have worshipped their literary deities, Princeton, Yale & Cambridge long enough. . . . Let the Yankees manufacture woolen clothing, let us manufacture men."[24]

As the locus of education shifted to accommodate regional interests, the lessons southern adults taught also grew more sectionalized. Deeply influenced by advice literature, particularly that of the English writer Lord Chesterfield, whose *Letters to His Son* swept America in the late eighteenth and early nineteenth centuries, southerners stressed social refinement and reputation over book learning.[25] Chesterfield and his compatriots advised readers to rigorously groom the self for presentation in society. Only through careful and constant control could men act out proper behaviors, suppress inappropriate actions, and thereby acquire a reputation of refined manhood. A boy seeking such a reputation needed to vigilantly attend to his dress, speech, and physical comportment as well as to the elements of his conversation, his leisure pursuits, and his social network. Chesterfield bragged that forty years had passed since he had said or done anything without considering the impact on his reputation.[26] Southern parents mimicked the advice of Chesterfield, coaching their sons to smile, dress, speak, and socialize gracefully.

Neither southern parents nor their sons would have equated this self-mastery with present-day notions of self-control or moderation. Rather the self-mastery they sought focused on a limited range of activities and related exclusively to behavior in genteel society. Drinking, gambling, sexual experimentation, and dueling and other forms of orchestrated violence were accepted and even encouraged in southern male culture. These behaviors, which today connote an absence of self-control, did not, in the early Republic South, compromise a refined man's reputation. Southern elites instead viewed these actions as another manifestation of self-mastery: a man was not controlled by anyone but himself. This self-mastery distinguished elite men from other members of society and laid the foundations for their dominance over wives, children, and, particularly, slaves. Aggression and independence thus dovetailed with social niceties in the minds of southern elites.

Universities provided the proving grounds on which young southern men could adopt these behaviors and thereby move from boyhood to refined manhood. Southern adults clearly cared more about these matters than the intellectual preparation offered at these institutions. Indeed one of the biggest surprises in reading advice to college students is the infrequency with which relatives discussed classes, books, or ideas. Most correspondence concentrated on the young men's social contacts and their comportment in society. While Marylander Richard Hopkins studied medicine in the 1780s, his cousin warned that "Books dont do alone" and reminded him that "a little Chesterfieldian politeness is essentially necessary." South Carolinian Ralph Izard expressed a similar sentiment when he sought a tutor for his friend Edward Rutledge's son, informing the prospective teacher that "an attention to the morals, conduct, & behaviour were points as important . . . as those parts of education which were to be acquired from Books."[27] Parents wanted their sons to balance social activity with study and self-improvement. As Kentuckian William Barry explained to his son, "To pass life in an agreeable manner, a man should not devote himself so entirely to pleasure as to neglect or postpone necessary business, nor should he be so much a man of business as to dislike elegant amusements: a proper mixture of both should be observed." Sterling Ruffin concurred and advised his son Thomas, "be not only attentive to your books, but particularly so to your manners. A man may be better read than his neighbor, & yet not acquire half the respect if the other should be more accommodating."[28]

Of course, teenage boys could take this emphasis on socializing to extremes. While attending school in Paris, young Harry Manigault looked forward to studying under a renowned mathematician because, as he explained, it offered "the pleasure of being some part of my time with a portion of the fairer sex, for he has a tolerable good looking better part, and two handsome daughters to boot." As James Strobhart reflected on his South Carolina College days, he bragged, "I spent the months in Columbia as pleasantly as I ever spent any in my life. I . . . visited the ladies regularly, and went to all the balls and parties. You may judge by this that I did not injure any matter by hard study."[29]

Northerners similarly concerned themselves with refinement and sociability, but residents of both regions agreed that they cared far more about formal education than did southerners. In an oft-repeated criticism, Timothy Ford lamented, "there is but little of the spirit of Education" present in South Carolina. Southerners traveling to the North expressed the opposite reactions. South Carolinian William Martin praised the people of Connecticut for their attention to education: "Its importance & necessity are held in the highest estimation." Some southerners, including Martin, envied northern educational standards and urged emulation: "it is uncommon to find a man [in Connecticut] who does not write an intelligible hand: and one who does not read is never heard of. In Carolina, one third at least, can not read at all, & another third I am convinced, cannot write legibly. . . . I feel for my country and blush at the comparison."[30]

Southern elite boys could more easily sidestep the educational demands placed on northern students, for their future wealth rested on inheriting slaves and land, and their social standing hung on connections and reputation. So as northerners prepared for careers, southerners crafted reputations. Repeatedly, southern boys heard that securing a proper reputation represented their first duty at college, since public perceptions would dictate their future status in the

South. One father explained, "Public Opinion has great influence on the conduct of men & he who is regardless of it, will sooner or later sink into disgrace and contempt or into vice & immorality—It is the standard by which men are generally measured & . . . [must] be sought for & desired."[31] Thomas Armstrong echoed this sentiment when his son Martin left home to study at the University of North Carolina in 1815. In an extensive advisory letter, Thomas wrote: "You are now arriving at that age when it is necessary for a young man to assume to himself a character. And above all other times you ought to be most circumspect in your conduct . . . it is an easy matter for a man to stray from the paths of rectitude; but it is not so easy to regain his course. . . . One devious step will require many to make it good." In a subsequent letter, Thomas continued his discussion of the importance of acquiring a proper reputation: "Your future success and respect will depend greatly upon your demeanor during the next year. If you come out of college with unsullied character and maintain deportment suited a young man of education, it will command respect and afford an opportunity to begin in the world under favorable circumstances. First impressions of a man's character are apt to be lasting."[32] Southern boys recognized the power of reputation and worked to adopt a persona that would merit the esteem of their peers and secure their position in society.

The development of the right social circle promoted a refined reputation and provided future political and economic contacts. Young men and their parents selected schools with an eye toward the connections that boys might secure. Preparing to attend William and Mary in 1803, William Barry confided to his brother: "I anticipate many advantages . . . amongst others, that of making new acquaintances. I expect to become acquainted with some of the first characters of Virginia, and possibly by a lucky throw of fortune recommend myself to their favour, which at some future day may be advantageous to me . . . my success will depend very much on the influence of friends and acquaintances."[33] Even when universities suffered from poor academic ranking, men attended for social reasons. George Swain and his son, David, agreed that attending the University of North Carolina did not necessarily promise a quality education. But, as the elder Swain explained, studying at Chapel Hill "would be the most ready way to popularity however inferior the Institution."[34]

Throughout the young nation, men understood that appearance shaped reputation, but wealthy slave-holding southerners took this national interest to extremes. Northerners often found them "showy, their clothes ostentatious."[35] Dress, an immediately discernible symbol of status and therefore a critical basis of judgment, garnered outsized attention from both southern students and their benefactors. John Ball Sr. ascertained that his son dressed in a fashion to "keep way with the finest circles at Cambridge." The proper clothing mattered so much to Virginian Severn Eyre that he complained upon arriving in London of being "confined to the house 'till thursday for want of fashionable cloaths."[36] Students regularly reported home on the style and expense of their classmates' wardrobes. Even when cash poor, many parents allowed the purchase of new suits and shoes.

Speech similarly symbolized a man's worth in gentry society. Henry DeSaussure informed his charge, John Colhoun, that "the right knowledge of your own tongue is essential; & no man can be expected to succeed without [it]." In his instruction to his son, Joel Lyle agreed about the importance of language: "Have your speeches well digested . . . [and] to give you confidence in yourself . . . let your fellow students hear you . . . before you make your grand Debute." Distressed at his son's inability to speak confidently, one father directed his son to practice speaking nightly before a mirror.[37] Letters about excessive mirth and anger, stilted gestures, and weight followed these directives about dress and speech and demanded near obsessive detail to controlling the self for the express purpose of earning a proper reputation.

Letter writing, like stylish dress and artful conversation, gave genteel Americans an opportunity to publicly display their refined status. Letter recipients used content and penmanship to evaluate writers. Furthermore, letters typically provided the sole means of communication with sons who had left home to attend universities. Therefore, in addition to allowing parents to advise and evaluate their offspring's progress, letters perpetuated emotional bonds between parents and sons.[38] Not surprisingly, parents expected, and even demanded, frequent, lengthy letters from college boys. One father insisted, "I wish you to write once a week by Post untill I countermand the order." Another, also requiring weekly letters, set up a schedule for correspondence with his son.[39] But adults were often frustrated by youthful responses to such directives.

Unlike dress and speech, correspondence with family seldom mattered among the peer groups formed by southern students. Getting sons to write home was often as difficult as it was important. If college boys failed to write home, relatives complained bitterly. After not hearing from his younger brother Charles, a student at West Point in the 1810s, John Guerrant expressed his "mortification" at not having received a letter for two months: "I am sorry to find you so negligent, in a matter which whilst it would consume so little of your time would add to the comfort & satisfaction of your friends & would contribute to your own edification & improvement." When John Jones's brother Thomas went to Chapel Hill in 1809, John claimed that Thomas wrote so seldom that he had "almost forgotten" his brother's name.[40]

When students did write home, their families scrutinized the style of their letters. Although happy with the frequency with which her son Charles wrote home from school in Philadelphia, Margaret Izard complained that he wrote sloppy, brief letters. In one letter she found nine misspelled words on a single page and charged, "If you knew how disgraceful such faults are, you would spare no pains to correct them." Edmund Hubard, a student at Hampden-Sydney in the 1820s, corresponded with his brother Robert Thruston Hubard, who offered repeated and varied advice about writing. First, he instructed Edmund to "fill up the sheet with something and dont scribble off a few lines and say you are in a hurry." Then Robert criticized Edmund's handwriting: "it is miserable. . . . a bad hand & a bad composition are intolerable." Nathaniel Middleton's mother proved equally frank in her criticism of one of his letters, which was riddled with errors. Alicia Middleton declared, "I am ashamed to shew it to any body."[41] In a fascinating revelation of values, Severn Eyre begged his brother Littleton never to share his writings (a diary kept in the form of letters to Littleton). One might initially suspect this was owing to Severn's repeated liaisons with London prostitutes. Not only did Severn Eyre discuss the frequency and price of his dalliances, he claimed a medicinal benefit from them: "speaking physically [I] think nature has clearly pointed out their advantages in clearing the head & stomach . . . for I declare positively that Dr. Saunder's lecture is more easily comprehended after such an indiscression." Indeed, the style, not the content, of Severn's writings caused his embarrassment: "they are wrote in a cursory manner just as thoughts present themselves, without any attention to diction or the usual forms of letter writing."[42] Eyre, like most southern men, knew that prose, vocabulary, length of letter, penmanship, and even the size and quality of paper selected would be used to gauge his refinement and social worth.

Southern parents encouraged boys to give the same scrutiny to their emotions as they did their writings; they were far less successful on this front than on any other. According to parents, a dutiful son carefully monitored and molded his feelings to earn a reputation of refined manhood. Offering typical parental advice, Joel Lyle wrote to his son that mastering one's emotions mattered more than "all your acquirements" at college. Adults frequently counseled sons to repress anger, mirth, and sadness. Roger Pinckney's benefactor, for example, warned his fourteen-year-old charge to avoid "immoderate laughing."[43] Hoping to encourage emotional restraint, parents praised young men who controlled their feelings. The physical act of leaving their families to attend college afforded boys a first chance to master their emotions. When sixteen-year-old John Grimball left South Carolina for Princeton in 1816, he feared he might never see home again. His grief grew strong: "I could hardly support it, however I restrained my feelings as much as I could." Although John Legaré assured his family that he felt "contented and happy" studying in Connecticut, his uncle James Legaré doubted the assurances: "I apprehend [that] is not the case, but [John] has very properly suppressed his feeling." Arthur Morson's guardian proudly reported Arthur's successful suppression of grief upon leaving home: "[in hopes of] making himself a comfort and ornament to his Parents . . . from the time we arrived in Washington till we parted at New Haven [Arthur] controlled his feelings remarkably well, and in his whole conduct gave me entire confidence of his future success."[44] Such emotional restraint was, however, the exception, not the rule, among southern college students. Unlike dress (which won the esteem of peers) or even letters (which earned parental approval and ensured the flow of money), college boys saw few advantages to exerting this sort of emotional self-control. More typically they seemed out of control: fighting, drinking, carousing, and squandering money.

This generational struggle over comportment reflected a disagreement between southern adults and boys about the nature of self-mastery. Parents stressed restraint of emotions and behaviors—sons should master themselves. Young men, however, emphasized self-determination and independence—they refused to be mastered by anyone. Both versions of self-mastery were linked to the practiced domination required of slaveholders. Planters had to exercise absolute authority over their chattel and simultaneously be restrained in the public expression of that power. A slaveholder who perpetually whipped his slaves could lose respect among his peers—not because of the violence inflicted (slavery required cruelty in order to work, and whites felt little remorse at brutalizing their slaves), but rather because his actions bespoke a lack of control over himself and his chattel. Parents actively encouraged and from a young age sons accepted this pronounced male commitment to autonomy and superiority. Adolescence thus proved to be the wrong time to begin teaching restraint.

Unwilling and unable to compel compliance, most southern parents viewed college as a testing ground of their sons' personal choices and their future promise as men. Parents routinely reminded sons of the transcendent significance of the years spent in college. North Carolinian Charles Pettigrew insisted that, "the time of life is but short, & *youth* is the season for improvement, improve therefore every moment." Ralph Izard concurred: "This is the time of Life, in which by proper, or improper management, the foundation will be laid for his becoming either a very useful, & valuable Member of Society, or the contrary."[45] The future lay in each boy's hands. Familial wealth could buy the finest education, and familial status opened doors. What young men made of the opportunities offered by family membership, however, rested squarely on their own shoulders. Boys received frequent reminders of the responsibility they held for themselves and the effort future prominence required. Cary Whitaker advised and funded his cousin Matthew Whitaker while he studied medicine in Baltimore. But, insisted Cary, Matthew needed to be self-reliant: "the main thing on which your future eminence and usefulness will depend, rests within yourself." [46]

As in their obsession with refinement, southerners' focus on masculine autonomy differed from that of northerners. Hoping to foster independence and to test judgment, parents allowed boys to make many of their own decisions about living arrangements, academic paths, friends, careers, and lifestyles. Even the length of study could be left to teenage boys. In a letter from his mother, eighteen-year-old Princeton student and South Carolinian John Gibbes was encouraged to determine the course of his study: "Mr. Hutson seems anxious for you to stay long enough to take your degree, he says it will be of infinite service to you: however we put so full a confidence that you will most certainly act for the most advantage for Yourself; that we leave it to y'r opinion." [47] Certainly parents advised on these matters, but by and large they encouraged self-reliance. Virginian Thomas Armstrong explained to his son his desire to inspire rather than control: "I don't wish to be understood as forbidding those innocent amusements, which are perhaps necessary for the health of the body, and the recreation of the mind. But I wish to inculcate that you avoid such practices that you would in your own sober judgment condemn in others." [48]

Even when adults anticipated boys' making bad choices, they often opted to let matters run their course. For example, Gabriel Manigault lamented the friendship his son shared with Pinckney Horry, a notoriously dissipated South Carolinian, but he also viewed the relationship as an important test: "We cannot expect that my Son is to escape bad examples. He must be exposed to them, as he must be to various kinds of temptation. If he has good sense he will escape them. They may even be a service. . . . I will caution him about this young man, & that being all that can be done, we must hope for the best." [49] To circulate among bad company, believed John Ramsey, was an important test of maturation: "the great mass of mankind though wicked, ignorant, and ignoble affords lessons which fill the youthful bosom with sound and extensive learning." South Carolinian Richard Beresford put things more bluntly: "Much of the success attendant upon Education depends upon the Knowledge of the Student's Character; even his vices may be productive of valuable Ends, corrupted Substances may form a rich Manure." [50]

Not surprisingly, parental desires to promote self-determination exacerbated willfulness among sons. Gabriel Manigault had a particularly difficult time reining in his son's independent streak. "I was sorry to hear," wrote Gabriel to the boy's European benefactor, "that my Son had become disgusted with the Lycee. But I must confess that considering the spirit of independence which he imbibed in America . . . and which he carried with him to France, I am not surprised at the circumstances." Family members even joked about willful children. When John Ball Jr. complained about his two-year-old son, John's brother William expressed surprise: "You say your Son is much spoiled, or self willed . . . but I suppose You would not count him a true *Ball* if he was not a little headstrong."[51]

Exaggerating familial encouragement of reputation-building and independence, southern students embraced peer-group values that set them apart from their parents' generation and their northern contemporaries. Conflict between parents and sons over issues of money and family duty evidence the obstinacy of adolescent boys and the power of their youth culture. Southern students similarly challenged the authority of university administrators and used group violence to express their will. With their classmates, young men began to learn to use power publicly and successfully—essential knowledge for southern patriarchs.

Friendships formed the foundation of college youth culture in both the North and the South. Away from all things familiar and surrounded by young men of similar age and circumstance, university students formed close friendships with their classmates. College friendships helped assuage John Grimball's homesickness; he reported having a "number of very agreeable companions," which made "the time more pleasant." Kentuckian Alfred Beckley formed typically close attachments with his schoolmates, writing to one friend, "I often think of you and my other school mates with affection & regret that I am absent from them. I trust we will meet some future day, when we are men to renew our acquaintance and friendship."[52]

Friends marked a man's refinement and provided vital political and economic contacts, so southern parents, like their northern contemporaries, cautioned sons to select friends wisely. "Great care," advised one father "ought therefore to be exercised by a young man in first setting out, in his choice of company; for by it he must and will be judged." As Anne Hart's son left Charleston for Philadelphia in 1806, she explained the importance of selecting friends wisely: "You will be at liberty to Choose your Company—O, make a wise choice . . . you enter on New Scenes—A stranger in a strange Land—yet many will know from whom you derived birth—Many eyes will be on you—then be circumspect in all your Actions—all your dealings—be sober, wise, and temperate—Civil to all—but choose select friends."[53] Family members routinely stressed "the necessity and absolute propriety of being particularly cautious who you admit as your intimate and busom friends."[54]

Although northern and southern college boys had parents concerned about their reliance on school friendships, they created different student cultures. Choosing to be in concert at northern schools and having few northern classmates at southern institutions, southern boys congregated to produce a powerful and regionally distinct peer group. The upbringing of southern gentry boys, the wealth of their families, the intentions of their education, and the legacy of slave-holding combined to produce far more truculence and violence among southern college boys than among their northern counterparts.

University administrators freely acknowledged the difficulty of governing large groups of adolescent boys—particularly southerners—and they structured school regulations to militate against youthful disorder. Most colleges enacted elaborate codes of conduct, but few could consistently enforce their rules.[55] Educators tended to blame campus disorder on youthful character, and they labeled southerners as particularly egregious violators of school rules.

Even students recognized the negative implications of this southern distinctiveness. John Pettigrew, for example, criticized the younger students at the University of North Carolina, "half of whom do little or nothing with regard to improvement." In 1825 Robert Hubard conveyed his concern that his younger brother Edmund, while studying at Hampden-Sydney, was "surrounded by a number of wild young fellows, who delighted in dissipation."[56] Moving to the University of Virginia, Edmund reported that some of his classmates there seemed "to have forgotten what was their intention. . . . Instead of attending to their Books, they are sauntering about from one days end to another in all kind of rascality, and mischief." When Kentuckian William Barry moved to Virginia to attend William and Mary, he wrote to his brother, describing his disappointment in the school and in the character of students. He attributed low enrollments at the college to "the dissipation of the place. People are afraid to send their children here, least their morals should be perverted." In another letter, he complained about the "dissipated habits of the students, which for some years past has been carried to an extreme," and warned that unless a young man practice constant vigilance, "he is apt to be drawn into the licentious vortex."[57]

With little control over peer culture, parents concentrated on another troubling aspect of student behavior: excessive spending. The wealth of southern gentry families, their zeal for refinement, and their encouragement of male self-determination exacerbated extravagance in adolescent boys. Parents, however, wanted to instill in their sons a sense of fiscal responsibility. To southern parents, money mattered far beyond the bottom line. Spending patterns afforded men the opportunity to display their refinement and self-mastery. If boys were to acquire a genteel reputation, they had to handle money in a fashion that would merit the esteem of their peers. On a more practical level, southern sons needed to learn to manage finances to protect the fiscal future of their families. To spend money wisely and independently was an important part of maturation from boyhood to manhood. For these reasons, and owing to the great expense of college and the potential for financial ruin from overspending, money was an oft-discussed and contentious topic in student correspondence.

According to southern parents, refined men earned their reputations in part by controlling their use of money. Boys therefore needed to walk the fine line between excessive frugality (a frequent criticism of northerners) and decadence (associated with Europeans). Parents and sons often wrote about the importance of spending money genteelly. Arthur Morson explained, "I have endeavored to keep from all extravagance, but at the same time to avoid appearing too close to be respectable." Charles Carter Lee seconded the connection between spending money and genteel status: "If the company of which I happen to be a member wish for a bottle of wine or any other trifle, it would be very ungentlemanly for me or any other individual to object to its being bought. . . . For if you alledge you are unable to contribute your share to bye it, you must at the same time say you are unable to keep genteel company, & accordingly sneak off." [58] Parents and guardians advised their sons to spend money to "keep way" with peers, but warned against excessive spending that would empty family coffers and compromise reputations.

Headstrong students, typically in charge of their own finances and immersed in a raucous peer culture, seldom heeded parental advice about spending. Letters between southern students and their families showcased the conflict between parental values and student behavior. Honoring their commitment to their sons' self-determination and seeking to encourage rather than compel their sons, guardians handled minor money problems in a subtle manner. This approach gave young men the opportunity to independently correct the problem, avoided conflict, and built confidence. Robert Hubard, for example, tried to flatter his younger brother into more responsible spending: "I was a little surprised on the receipt of your letter, to find that you are in want of money, though I do not attribute it to your want of economy, but to the unavoidable expenses, which you have to incur—I am very glad of one thing that you are not disposed to imitate your companions." George Swain blended guilt with flattery in coaching his son's spending: "You know that it will give me a considerable scuffle to support you through the term, but I have the pleasure of knowing or believing that you will use my hard earnings with all the economy consistent with propriety." [59] More excessive or repeated overspending could result in recriminations. After John Pettigrew sent an accounting of his expenditures at the University of North Carolina, his father objected to John's patronizing taverns: "I think it by no means reputable, for Students to be found in public houses. . . . And I hope you do not go for the sake of *company*, particularly the company of such as your fellow students." [60] In particularly egregious cases, parents took more dramatic steps. Roger Pinckney's relatives in South Carolina and his benefactor in Europe cut off his money supply until the fifteen-year-old corrected his errant ways. His mother complained: all of Roger's thoughts "runs on spending what I send you." In 1801, exasperated with his son Warner's ceaseless spending, Ralph Wormeley threatened to disinherit the wayward boy, to "leave my estate to my daughters, and only so much to you, as may keep you from indigence and want."[61]

Given the independence, youth, and wealth of southern students, early Republic colleges and universities were, not surprisingly, often chaotic places. Boys in their teen years, separated for the first time from families and communities, living together with minimal supervision, encouraged by their culture to be independent and self-possessed, and in control of their own finances were a recipe for disaster. College offered myriad opportunities for students to act mischievously. Distressed by his waning control at South Carolina College in the 1820s, President Thomas Cooper reported that a group of boys "stole [his] horse out of the stable shaved its tail & mane, and rode it about in the night till it was nearly exhausted." While attending Hampden-Sydney in 1824, Edmund Hubard reported that "some of the Students drove a gang of Turkies in the dn [dining] Hall last week. . . . They were sometimes in the coffee, sometimes in the butter, and very often on the Students."[62] This kind of mischievous behavior could produce serious consequences from school administrators. John Jones was suspended from the University of North Carolina in 1814, when he and some friends, contemptuous of the school's president, "formed an association to harass him as much as they could by committing depredations on his property. According to this resolution of theirs, they on different nights shaved the hairs on his horse's tail . . . upset a house on his lot at two different times, carried away a cart and hid it in the woods; and loosed his gate from its hinges and concealed it in some secret place. The repetition of these acts indicated a malicious design against Mr. Chapman in order to render his life as miserable as possible."[63] Families, however, took this sort of behavior as a benign if unfortunate phase through which boys would eventually pass. When Margaret and Gabriel Manigault struggled to right their willful son Harry, Margaret's mother urged patience: "He is so amiable in his manners, & appearance that he must turn out well. Great excuses are to be made for youthful follies." Alice Izard reminded them that "some of the first characters of the World commenced by being wild youths."[64]

Southern students not only engaged in such "youthful follies" but also committed acts of debauchery and violence. According to Leander Hughes, his classmates Augustus Alston and Leonidas King were expelled from the University of North Carolina in October 1824 after they "committed violence upon the persons of some of the faculty viz Mr. Betner, Mr. Sanders." Hughes further reported that in the previous year one student had been dismissed from the school "for having a pistol for the purpose of exploding gunpowder," and two others were involved in a stabbing. In 1806 South Carolina College student Samuel DuBose informed his brother William that "twice since the New Year have these blades of metal thought proper to behave themselves in a seditious and turbulent manner unbecoming lads receiving their education." Less than three months after arriving in Charlottesville, Edmund Hubard wrote to his brother that six students had been expelled from the University of Virginia, including William Eyre, who "stayed 4 or 5 days, and then was expelled without ever going even to a lecture."[65]

Left to their own devices, young gentry men could behave in perfectly contemptible ways. Despite being a model student in his own youth, John Ball Jr. of South Carolina struggled mightily against his three wayward half-brothers. In 1823 he sent the boys (Alwyn, age 16; Hugh, age 15; and Elias, age 14) to a military academy in Vermont. The problems they caused at the school included gross overspending, drunkenness, fighting, and a suspension for disrupting church services. Within six months of arriving in Vermont, Alwyn and Elias ran away from the school. The headmaster met privately with the two after they returned to the academy, and upon explaining to them the gravity of their misbehavior and the long-term effects of such actions on their reputations, reported that the boys "appeared to be affected by what [he had] said and promised to do better in future." Within a week the two ran away again.[66] Georgian Milledge Galphin behaved even worse than the Ball brothers. In 1812 Moses Waddel dismissed Galphin from his school for card playing, running away, and general "shameful behavior." Waddel wrote to Galphin's uncle and benefactor, John Milledge, regarding the incident. But the letter never arrived, and Waddel charged Galphin with stealing it. As evidence, he offered a series of anonymous letters, "the contents of which for prophanity obscenity & personal abuse far exceed any language I have ever seen or heard used."[67] In 1822 the entire senior class of the South Carolina College fell into such insolence. Thomas Cooper, professor and president of South Carolina College, detailed the disorder at the school: "The Senior Class have adopted as their guiding system of morality, that they are under no obligation to obey the Laws of the College, but merely to abide by the punishment inflicted on disobedience *if they should* be discovered." Moreover, "Every Student in College, holds himself bound to conceal any offence against the Laws of the Land as well as the Laws of the College." Cooper insisted that the students "were guilty . . . of every outrage that they had the power to commit. The Professors were threatened, pistols were snapt at them, guns fired near them, . . . the windows of my bed room have been repeatedly shattered at various hours of the night, & guns fired under my window." At a number of southern schools, students likewise organized to thwart school rules, challenge professors, and defend classmates.[68]

Administrators and students reported a host of less dangerous but disturbing misdeeds committed by southern boys: they fought, cursed, drank, gambled, ran away, and engaged in sexual misconduct. John Pettigrew and his younger brother Ebenezer enrolled in the first class at the University of North Carolina. The brothers did not stay long at the school, however, for they informed their father, an Episcopal priest, that "cursing & swearing [was] carried on [there] to the greatest perfection; even from the smallest to the largest." Despite Chapel Hill's prohibition against drinking alcohol, one observer complained that "you will find some trifling, dissipated giddy youths slyly smuggling the forbidden object. . . . What a pity that those who might otherwise be the ornament of the Nation should blindly rush headlong to their own destruction."[69] Severn Eyre was one of the few southern boys willing to discuss his sexual indiscretions. When he first arrived in London in 1785 to study medicine, he showed far more interest in the city's prostitutes than in academics: "Saturday evening took a walk merely to view the fine girls of the town, as [they] are commonly called. . . . I forbade ever temptation 'till induced (more from curiosity than any other motive) by a little creature between ten & twelve years of age to take her in a coach & here I'll end my letter."[70]

Although violence, sexual misconduct, and excessive spending occurred at northern universities, contemporary observers agreed that southern students and southern schools far exceeded the disorder of northerners.[71] Edward Hooker, a Connecticut native who taught at South Carolina College in 1807, insisted, "That Southern students require a different management from those in the northern colleges is, I believe, undoubtedly true. I do not suppose the same rigid discipline of the North can easily be introduced here." Thomas Cooper of South Carolina College concurred: "In my own opinion the parental indulgence to the South, renders young men less fit for collegiate government than the habits of northern people." Davis Thacher moved from Massachusetts to South Carolina in 1816 to work as a private tutor on a lowcountry plantation. He lasted just over a year in the job, leaving, as he explained, because the mother of his pupils "thwarts my attempts in governing the children—she seldom if ever cross'd their inclination by denying improper requests—in this she seem'd to over look their best good, & have regard only to their present gratification."[72]

Contemporaries located the roots of this exaggerated dissipation and intransigence in the wealth of southern planters and in their domination over slaves. One student, describing the University of North Carolina, said, "The students are generally the sons of wealthy men, & are in search of pleasure & any thing else but mental improvement. Dissipation and badness & profanity too generally prevail, & I am quite certain that few good scholars are made." Others linked collegiate disorder directly to slave-holding. Responding to his son's complaints about the University of North Carolina, George Swain explained, "The dissipation you speak of pervades all the States where Slavery abounds. Were you conversant with the habits of So. Carolina or Georgia University you would find darker traces there than at Chapel Hill."[73]

The practiced domination that slave-holding required, the tremendous wealth it created, and the sense of self-importance it encouraged among the slave-holding class underlay the unique sectional identity that southern students adopted in the early Republic. Abetted by parental directives, peer culture, and the emphasis on sectional loyalty that occurred at their state universities, these boys from southern states grew into "southern men." It should come as no surprise that these boys, schooled in self-reliance backed up by violence, believing themselves the guardians of family as well as of regional wealth and power, and nearly obsessed with self-mastery and social reputation would, given the events that unfolded in the antebellum era, become the architects of southern nationalism and the instigators of civil war.

## NOTES

1. Bertram Wyatt-Brown argued that "honor" was the central feature of nineteenth-century southern gentry culture. While parents and, to a lesser degree, students evoked this term in correspondence, honor does not appear to have exercised such pervasive influence over student life as Wyatt-Brown finds among southern adults. Perhaps this is partially owing to the inability of college students to fully experience independence and physical mastery, which, according to Wyatt-Brown, were essential for honor; *Southern Honor: Ethics and Behavior in the Old South* (New York: Oxford University Press, 1982); idem, *The Shaping of Southern Culture: Honor, Grace, and War, 1760s–1880s* (Chapel Hill: University of North Carolina Press, 2001). For a perceptive analysis of education and gentry family culture a generation later in the antebellum South, see Steven M. Stowe, *Intimacy and Power in the Old South: Ritual in the Lives of the Planters* (Baltimore: Johns Hopkins University Press, 1987). Joyce Appleby investigated the national significance of this generation in *Inheriting the Revolution: The First Generation of Americans* (Cambridge: Harvard University Press, 2000).

2. For additional general information on university life and youth culture in this period, see Joseph F. Kett, *Rites of Passage: Adolescence in America, 1790 to the Present* (New York: Basic Books, 1977); E. Anthony Rotundo, *American Manhood: Transformations in Masculinity from the Revolution to the Modern Era* (New York: Basic Books, 1993); and Lawrence A. Cremin, *American Education: The National Experience, 1783–1876* (New York: Harper and Row, 1980). Jon L. Wakelyn investigated the relationships between southern fathers and their sons attending colleges in the antebellum era

in "Antebellum College Life and the Relations between Fathers and Sons," in *The Web of Southern Social Relations: Women, Family, and Education*, ed. Walter J. Fraser, R. Frank Saunders Jr., and Jon L. Wakelyn (Athens: University of Georgia Press, 1985), 107–26. Jane Turner Censer studied educational patterns among North Carolina gentry families in *North Carolina Planters and Their Children, 1800–1860* (Baton Rouge: Louisiana State University Press, 1984), chap. 3. See also Robert F. Pace and Christopher A. Bjornsen, "Adolescent Honor and College Student Behavior in the Old South," *Southern Cultures* 6 (2000): 9–28.

3. For a thorough analysis of the social implications of the American Revolution, see Gordon Wood, *The Radicalism of the American Revolution* (New York: Knopf, 1992). The fullest discussion of the social transformations caused by the market revolution is Charles Sellers, *The Market Revolution: Jacksonian America, 1815–1846* (New York: Oxford University Press, 1991).

4. "Abraham Baldwin's Speech to the University of Georgia Trustees," *Georgia Historical Quarterly* 10 (1926): 326–34.

5. John Ball Sr. to John Ball Jr., 12 August 1798, Ball Family Papers, South Carolina Historical Society (hereafter SCHS); Ralph Izard to Dr. Johnson, 20 December 1787, Ralph Izard Papers, South Caroliniana Library (hereafter SCL); Daniel Guerrant to Charles Guerrant, 4 May 1816, Guerrant Family Papers, Virginia Historical Society (hereafter VHS); Henry Middleton Rutledge to Edward Rutledge, 1 November 1797, reprinted in *South Carolina Historical Magazine* 83 (1982): 235–40.

6. Scholars recently exploring the cultural power of whiteness include Dana D. Nelson, *National Manhood: Capitalist Citizenship and the Imagined Fraternity of White Men* (Durham: Duke University Press, 1998); Lacy K. Ford Jr., "Making the 'White Man's Country' White: Race, Slavery, and State-Building in the Jacksonian South," *Journal of the Early Republic* 19 (1999), 713–37; and David Roediger, "The Pursuit of Whiteness: Property, Terror, and Expansion, 1790–1860," *Journal of the Early Republic* 19 (1999), 579–600.

7. For a fuller discussion of refinement, see Richard L. Bushman, *The Refinement of America: Persons, Houses, Cities* (New York: Knopf, 1992).

8. William Dickinson Martin Diary, 1809, SCL; Edmund Ruffin Jr. to Edmund Ruffin Sr., 28 March 1829, in "School-Boy Letters of Edmund Ruffin, Jr., 1828–1829," ed. Mrs. Kirkland Ruffin, *North Carolina Historical Review* 10 (1933): 318; John C. Calhoun to Andrew Pickens Jr., 23 May 1803, *The Papers of John C. Calhoun*, 26 vols. (Columbia: University of South Carolina Press, 1959–1999) 1:9–10.

9. Edward Hooker to Samuel Whitman, 5 May 1807; Edward Hooker to David Lilly, 8 May 1807, both in Edward Hooker Letters, SCL.

10. Richard Furman Sermon, 1799, reprinted in "The Baptist Courier," 3 May 1934, Richard Furman Papers, SCL.

11. William Blanding Journal, 7 June 1807, William Blanding Papers, SCL; Edmund Ruffin Jr. to Edmund Ruffin Sr., 6 November 1828, in Ruffin, "School-Boy Letters," 301–2.

12. Davis Thacher Diary, 16 March 1817, SCL.

13. Joseph Barnwell, ed., "Diary of Timothy Ford, 1785–86," *South Carolina Historical and Genealogical Magazine* 13 (1912): 203, 143.

14. George Izard to Gabriel Manigault, 29 May 1804, Ralph Izard Papers, SCL.

15. Hugh Ball to John Ball Jr., 20 November 1823, John Ball Sr. and John Ball Jr. Papers, Duke University Library (hereafter DUL); Edmund Ruffin Jr. to Edmund Ruffin Sr., 6 November 1828, in Ruffin, "School-Boy Letters," 302.

16. John E. Colhoun Jr. to William Moultrie Reid, 10 December 1818, John Ewing Colhoun Papers, SCHS; Richard Hopkins to Elizabeth Thomas Hopkins, 7 January 1784, in "A Maryland Medical Student and His Friends," *Maryland Historical Magazine* 23 (1928): 286.

17. John Ball Sr. to John Ball Jr., 29 September 1799, Ball Family Papers, SCHS.

18. Henry DeSaussure to Ezekiel Pickens, 27 October 1805, Henry William DeSaussure Papers, SCL.

19. Edmund Ruffin Jr. to Edmund Ruffin Sr., 8 October 1828, in Ruffin, "School-Boy Letters," 294–95.

20. These dates represent the first classes at the respective schools. In many cases charters were granted by state or colonial legislatures before the dates provided.

21. "Abraham Baldwin's Speech to the University of Georgia Trustees," *Georgia Historical Quarterly* 10 (1926): 329.

22. Henry Clay to [probably Horace Holley], 24 December 1819, *The Papers of Henry Clay*, 11 vols. (Lexington: University Press of Kentucky, 1959–92) 2:735; Charles Henry Warfield to William Bullitt, 14 December 1808, Bullitt Family Papers, Filson Historical Society (hereafter FHS); Edmund Wilcox Hubard to B. Walker, 26 July 1825, Hubard Family Papers, Southern Historical Collection, University of North Carolina at Chapel Hill (hereafter SHC).

23. George Swain to David Swain, ca. June 1822, David Swain Papers, North Caroliniana Collection, University of North Carolina at Chapel Hill (hereafter NCC); John Pettigrew to Charles Pettigrew, 27 June 1797, Pettigrew Family Papers, SHC.

24. M. F. Bryan to William Ruffin, 19 June 1828, Thomas Ruffin Papers, SHC.

25. The often printed letters of Philip Dormer Stanhope, fourth Earl of Chesterfield, to his son and namesake were widely read by Americans and Britons. Numerous reprints include R. K. Root, ed., *Lord Chesterfield's Letters to His Son* (London: J. M. Dent, 1929). For more on advice literature, see Sarah Newton, *Learning to Behave: A Guide to American Conduct Books before 1900* (Westport, Conn.: Greenwood Press, 1994); C. Dallett Hemphill, "Class, Gender, and the Regulation of Emotional Expression in Revolutionary Era Conduct Literature," in *An Emotional History of the United States*, ed. Jan Lewis and Peter Stearns (New York: New York University Press, 1998), 33–51; C. Dallett Hemphill, *Bowing to Necessities: A History of Manners in America, 1620–1860* (New York: Oxford University Press, 1999); Bushman, *The Refinement of America*, chap. 2; and Arthur Schlesinger, *Learning How to Behave: A Historical Study of American Etiquette Books* (New York: Macmillan, 1946).

   Chesterfield was not without critics. His advice regarding dalliances with French women, for example, sparked controversy. Many parents simply counseled their sons to ignore the indelicate aspects of his writing and to concentrate on his suggestions regarding sociability. John Ball Sr. directed his son to "regard with abhorrence the part of duplicity & seduction which his letters contain," but he owned several copies of the letterbook, often paraphrased Chesterfield in advisory letters to John Jr., and pressed the boy to read Chesterfield's guidance on sociability and style; John Ball Sr. to John Ball Jr., 14 April 1799, Ball Family Papers, SCHS. John Ramsey, a fellow Carolinian, agreed: "Women and even men may say as much as they please against the letters of Chesterfield & many subjects are indeed blameable, but there are so many polite reflections and useful lessons that no man can be well accomplished either in mind or body with but their perusal"; John Ramsey to Thomas Jones, 26 May 1810, Thomas Williamson Jones Papers, SHC. See also, Edmund Hayes, "Mercy Otis Warren versus Lord Chesterfield, 1779," *William and Mary Quarterly* 40 (1983): 616–21.

26. Philip Stanhope to Philip Stanhope, 9 December 1749, in Root, *Lord Chesterfield's Letters,* 138–39.

27. Unknown to Richard Hopkins, 27 May 1783, "A Maryland Medical Student and His Friends," *Maryland Historical Magazine* 23 (1928): 282; Ralph Izard to Edward Rutledge, 24 April 1789, Ralph Izard Papers, SCL.

28. William Barry to John Barry, 23 September 1801, William Taylor Barry Papers, FHS; Sterling Ruffin to Thomas Ruffin, 5 May 1803, Thomas Ruffin Papers, SHC.

29. C. H. Manigault to Gabriel Manigault, 27 April 1800, Manigault Family Papers, SCL; James Strobhart to John Kirk, 22 June [1833], Kirk Family Papers, SCHS.

30. Barnwell, "Diary of Timothy Ford, 1785–1786," *South Carolina Historical and Genealogical Magazine* 13 (1912): 192; William Dickinson Martin Diary, 1809, SCL.

31. Thomas Todd to Charles Todd, 5 February 1812, Charles Stewart Todd Papers, FHS.

32. Thomas Armstrong to Martin Armstrong, 6 December 1815; Thomas Armstrong to Martin Armstrong, 30 April 1817, both in Martin W. B. Armstrong Papers, SHC.

33. William Barry to John Barry, 23 September 1803, William Taylor Barry Papers, FHS.

34. George Swain to David Swain, ca. June 1822, David Swain Papers, NCC.

35. Joanne B. Freeman, *Affairs of Honor: National Politics in the New Republic* (New Haven: Yale University Press, 2001), 6.

36. John Ball Sr. to John Ball Jr., 17 June 1799, Ball Family Papers, SCHS; Severn Eyre Diary, 14 August 1785, VHS.

37. Henry DeSaussure to John E. Colhoun, 20 January 1808, Henry William DeSaussure Papers, SCL; Joel Lyle to William Lyle, 14 February 1828, Lyle Family Papers, University of Kentucky Special Collections (hereafter UKSC); John Ball Sr. to John Ball Jr., 21 October 1798, Ball Family Papers, SCHS.

38. In *The Refinement of America,* Richard Bushman persuasively argued that participating in literate culture symbolized a person's refinement in early America. A thorough analysis of letter writing among antebellum elite southern families can be found in Steven M. Stowe, "The Rhetoric of Authority: The Making of Social Values in Planter Family Correspondence," *Journal of American History* 73 (1987): 913–33; and Stowe, *Intimacy and Power.* In his extensive investigation of letter writing among

antebellum southerners, Stowe concluded that letters were "the best, and often the only, evidence that sons and daughters were growing up to be worthy persons"; *Intimacy and Power*, 142. Tamara Plakins Thornton offers a detailed and fascinating investigation into the meaning and styles of handwriting in *Handwriting in America: A Cultural History* (New Haven: Yale University Press, 1996).

39. John Ball Sr. to John Ball Jr., 15 September 1798, Ball Family Papers, SCHS; George Swain to David Swain, miscellaneous correspondence, David Swain Papers, NCC.

40. John Guerrant to Charles Guerrant, 10 January 1817, Guerrant Family Papers, VHS; John Jones to Thomas Jones, 4 September 1809, Thomas Williamson Jones Papers, SHC.

41. Margaret Izard Manigault to Charles Izard Manigault, 2 February 1812, Manigault Family Papers, SCL; Robert Thruston Hubard to Edmund Wilcox Hubard, 19 November 1824; Robert Thruston Hubard to Edmund Wilcox Hubard, 13 December 1824, both in Hubard Family Papers, SHC; Alicia Hopton Middleton to Nathaniel Russell Middleton, 28 July 1817, Middleton Family Papers, SCL.

42. Severn Eyre Diary, 5 September 1785, VHS.

43. Joel Lyle to William Lyle, 24 December 1828, Lyle Family Papers, UKSC; J. Wilson to Roger Pinckney, 16 May 1784, Roger Pinckney Correspondence, SCHS.

44. John Grimball to William Reid, 13 October 1816, John Berkley Grimball Papers, SCL; James Legaré to Jedidiah Morse, 11 November 1811, Thomas Legaré Papers, DUL; William Cleaveland to Alexander Morson, 20 July 1819, Arthur Alexander Morson Papers, SHC.

45. Charles Pettigrew to John Pettigrew, 8 October 1797, Pettigrew Family Papers, SHC; Ralph Izard to Mr. Bird, 25 June 1794, Ralph Izard Papers, SCL.

46. Cary Whitaker to Matthew Whitaker, 31 January 1824, Matthew Cary Whitaker Papers, SHC.

47. Sarah Gibbes to John Gibbes, 11 August 1783, Gibbes Family Papers, SCHS.

48. Thomas Armstrong to Martin Armstrong, 6 December 1815, Martin W. B. Armstrong Papers, SHC. See also, Kett, *Rites of Passage.*

49. Gabriel Manigault to Mr. DuPont, 13 April 1807, Manigault Family Papers, SCL.

50. John Ramsey to Thomas Jones, 26 May 1810, Thomas Williamson Jones Papers, SHC; Richard Beresford to unknown, 21 April 1785, Richard Beresford Papers, SCL.

51. Gabriel Manigault to Mr. DuPont, 13 April 1807, Manigault Family Papers, SCL; William Ball to John Ball Jr., 17 April 1807, William James Ball Family Correspondence, SCHS.

52. John Grimball to William Reid, 13 October 1816, John Berkley Grimball Papers, SCL; Alfred Beckley to George Washington Love, 10 October 1819, James Young Love and Thomas Love Papers, FHS. While some scholars argue that friendships between students could become homoerotic and even homosexual, no evidence of this exists among the southern boys in this study. Regarding homosociability and homosexuality, see Caroll Smith-Rosenberg, "The Female World of Love and Ritual: Relations between Women in Nineteenth-Century America," *Signs: Journal of Women in Cul-*

*ture and Society* 1 (1975): 1–29; Karen Hansen, "'Our Eyes Beheld Each Other': Masculinity and Intimate Friendship in Antebellum New England," in *Men's Friendships*, ed. Peter M. Nardi (London: Sage, 1992), 35–58; and Donald Yacovone, "'Surpassing the Love of Women': Victorian Manhood and the Language of Fraternal Love," in *A Shared Experience: Men, Women, and the History of Gender*, ed. Laura McCall and Donald Yacovone (New York: New York University Press, 1998), 195–221.

53. Thomas Armstrong to Martin Armstrong, 6 December 1815, Martin W. B. Armstrong Papers, SHC; Anne Hart to William Hart, 7 November 1806, Oliver Hart Papers, SCL.

54. Daniel Guerrant to Charles Guerrant, 4 May 1816, Guerrant Family Papers, VHS.

55. For an extensive discussion of the difficulty of controlling students at early national universities, see Kett, *Rites of Passage,* 51–61.

56. John Pettigrew to Charles Pettigrew, 27 June 1797, Pettigrew Family Papers, SHC; Robert Thruston Hubard to Edmund Wilcox Hubard, March 1825, Hubard Family Papers, SHC.

57. Edmund Wilcox Hubard to Robert Thruston Hubard, 8 November 1825, Hubard Family Papers, SHC; William Barry to John Barry, 20 January 1804; William Barry to John Barry, 6 February 1804, both in William Taylor Barry Papers, FHS.

58. Arthur Morson to Alexander Morson, 9 October 1819, Arthur Alexander Morson Papers, SHC; Charles Carter Lee [to mother], 20 June 1819, Lee and Marshall Family Papers, SHC.

59. Robert Thruston Hubard to Edmund Wilcox Hubard, 22 March 1825, Hubard Family Papers, SHC; George Swain to David Swain, 7 June 1822, David Swain Papers, NCC.

60. Charles Pettigrew to John Pettigrew, 8 October 1797, Pettigrew Family Papers, SHC.

61. Francis Pinckney to Roger Pinckney, 14 July 1785, Roger Pinckney Correspondence, SCHS; Ralph Wormeley to Warner Wormeley, 29 June 1801, Wormeley Family Papers, VHS.

62. Thomas Cooper, 14 February 1822, Thomas Cooper Papers, SCL; Edmund Wilcox Hubard to Robert Thruston Hubard, 15 December 1824, Hubard Family Papers, SHC.

63. Abner Stith to Thomas Williamson Jones, 31 March 1814, Thomas Williamson Jones Papers, SHC.

64. Alice Izard to Margaret Izard Manigault, 2 March 1805, Manigault Family Papers, SCL.

65. Leander Hughes to John Hughes, 2 October 1824; Leander Hughes to John Hughes, 23 August 1823, both in Leander Hughes Papers, SHC; Samuel DuBose to William DuBose, April 1806, Samuel DuBose Papers, SHC; Edmund Wilcox Hubard to Robert Thruston Hubard, 17 October 1825, Hubard Family Papers, SHC.

66. Miscellaneous correspondence, John Ball Sr. and John Ball Jr. Papers, DUL; quotation from Alden Partridge to John Ball Jr., 8 January 1824, John Ball Sr. and John Ball Jr. Papers, DUL.

67. Moses Waddel to John Milledge, 7 April 1812, Milledge Family Papers, DUL.

68. Thomas Cooper, 14 February 1822, Thomas Cooper Papers, SCL. In some cases, student rebellions appear justified. At the University of South Carolina and at the University of North Carolina, students rebelled because of the food provided by stewards. According to Chapel Hill student John Pettigrew, "The steward provides very sorrily. There is not one in Colledge that does not complain . . . it is impossible to describe the badness of the tea and coffee, & the meat generally stinks, & has maggots in it"; John Pettigrew to Charles Pettigrew, 3 October 1795, Pettigrew Family Papers, SHC.

69. John Pettigrew to Charles Pettigrew, 12 April 1796, Pettigrew Family Papers, SHC; George Swain to David Swain, 26 April 1822, David Swain Papers, NCC.

70. Severn Eyre Diary, 22 August 1785, VHS.

71. For a general discussion of student disorder, see Steven Novak, *The Rights of Youth: American Colleges and Student Revolt, 1798–1815* (Cambridge: Harvard University Press, 1977).

72. Edward Hooker to Addin Lewis, 4 June 1807, Edward Hooker Letters, SCL; Thomas Cooper, 14 February 1822, Thomas Cooper Papers, SCL; Davis Thacher Diary, November 1817, SCL.

73. David Swain to George Swain, 2 May 1822; George Swain to David Swain, ca. June 1822, both in David Swain Papers, NCC.

# Trying to Look Like Men: Changing Notions of Masculinity among Choctaw Elites in the Early Republic

*Greg O'Brien*

Southeastern Indians such as the Choctaws held notions about gender roles that were different from the ideas of their eighteenth-century European neighbors, although both groups drew sharp distinctions between the ideal attributes of men and women. In Choctaw society, women created life and accordingly assumed responsible for planting, tending, and harvesting crops. Men hunted large animals, waged war, and dominated diplomacy with foreigners. As with all social ideals, exceptions occurred to these rules. For instance, men, especially old men, assisted in the labor-intensive clearing of new agricultural fields and the harvesting of crops; women sometimes went to war.[1]

Nevertheless, success as a hunter and warrior was the minimal requirement for a Choctaw boy to become a man and served as a principal marker of gender identity. Choctaw notions of masculinity accordingly emphasized martial and hunting prowess for all eighteenth-century, and most early nineteenth-century, men. During the late 1700s, however, masculinity began to change, especially among elite Choctaw men and their families. They expanded the sources of their own power and selectively adopted Anglo-American notions of economy, politics, and gender. Masculinity was one of the fundamental cultural customs that required modification in this period of change, and elite Choctaws blazed the path to a new understanding of what it meant to be a man.

Recent research reveals the importance of studying American Indian societies with regard to gender. Focusing on gender and gender roles provides new insight into the cultural imperatives at work within Native communities, illuminating the sometimes widely divergent ways men and women viewed the world and the manner in which cultural change occurred. In fact, shifting ideas about gender

49

often heralded fundamental cultural transformation. Thus far, scholars of the Native Southeast employing an explicit gender analysis have focused primarily on the world of women or on the gender metaphors employed by Indian and European males engaged in diplomacy. These scholars have opened new ways of understanding southeastern Indians and have suggested that using gender as a category of analysis will reveal still further insight into American Indian cultures.[2]

Although many of the ideas about masculinity expressed by Choctaws mirrored the gender notions of other Indian groups, the Choctaws employed a particular vocabulary and specific cultural manifestations to express gender ideals. In addition, they lived through a unique history that promoted change in gender ideas. In their familial and societal responsibilities, and in the deerskin trade with Europeans, eighteenth-century Choctaw men expressed gender norms through oral traditions, warfare, hunting, and clothing. Symbols and signifiers of elite Choctaw masculinity included adult names, gendered terminology, social privileges, and physical accoutrements. Gradually, European contact altered these venues for displaying masculinity. Notions of proper male behavior remained more or less constant in the first half of the eighteenth century, but the rate of alteration quickened in the last half and continued to change rapidly in the early nineteenth century. Elite Choctaw men adapted most readily to new notions of masculinity and tried out new economic, political, and spiritual ideas selectively adopted from their Euro-American neighbors. In the process, they forever altered what it meant to be an elite Choctaw man.

In the eighteenth century and before, Choctaws intimately associated masculinity with spiritual power. Accomplishment as a warrior provided the basic requirement for a Choctaw male to become manly. War and hunting were decidedly spiritual activities that required careful ritual preparation and adherence to cultural rules about the spilling and handling of blood. This need to publicly demonstrate manipulation of spiritual forces pervaded every eighteenth-century Choctaw man's existence. Women, as creators of life, inherently held spiritual power, but men had to prove that they could tap into and manipulate similar powers. Those Choctaw men who repeatedly demonstrated spiritual abilities, especially if they descended from leading families or enjoyed connections with high-ranking individuals, became elites in their own right. Other Choctaws trusted them to protect and strengthen society by interacting with foreigners, traveling beyond the bounds of Choctaw territory, leading war parties, and gaining rare foreign goods for communal use through diplomacy and trade. These elite responsibilities existed in precontact Mississippian times (ca. 1000 to ca. 1600) and continued throughout the eighteenth and early nineteenth centuries. Contact with French, British, Spanish, and American cultures altered these notions concerning elite male attributes and responsibilities, forcing elite men to modify their notions of power and masculinity to maintain their positions in society. Paying close attention to masculinity among the Choctaws and other large southeastern Indian groups, therefore, sheds new light on the process of cultural change among Indians in the late colonial and early national South.[3]

In diplomatic documents, oral traditions, songs, and other eighteenth-century sources, elite Choctaw men frequently employed gendered language that exposed both traditional notions of gender ideals and alterations in those ideas over time. Such sources allow us to observe elite Choctaw men and determine the symbols of masculinity within Choctaw society. Although three principal political, ethnic, and geographic divisions (the Western, Eastern, and Six Towns Divisions) composed the Choctaw confederacy, definitions of masculinity adhered to long-established beliefs common to all Choctaws. Not until the late eighteenth century did new concepts of masculinity enter the cultural belief system of certain Choctaw men.

Names were the fundamental signifiers of masculinity, and they meant everything to a Choctaw male. By participating in a successful war party that killed an enemy or by demonstrating exceptional hunting skills, a boy received an adult title bestowed by elite men. These titles usually contained some version of the root words *abi* (anglicized to "tubby" in the nineteenth century) meaning "to kill" or "killer," *humma*, indicating red, the color of war, or *tashka*, signifying a lower-ranked warrior. The root word *hacho* similarly indicated warrior status. Related to the Creek word *hadjo* ("mad" or "crazy"), *hacho*, among the Choctaws, was "part of the war names of men" and had "an honorable meaning."[4] Describing the naming process for southeastern Indian men, eighteenth-century British trader James Adair wrote, "When the Indians distinguish themselves in war, their names are always compounded, drawn from certain roots suitable to their intention and expressive of the characters of the persons, so that their names joined together, often convey a clear and distinct idea of several circumstances—as of the time and place, where the battle was fought, of the number and rank of their captives, and the slain."[5] As men garnered additional war honors and further proved their ability to manipulate spiritual power, they earned new titles such as *Hopaii Minko* denoting a "war chief" or "prophet chief," and a "far-off or distant chieftain," a person who possessed power to control the destiny of a battle from afar.[6] Adair, who lived much of his adult life among the Chickasaw Indians, neighbors and close cultural relatives of the Choctaws, explained further the relationship between manhood and warring among southern Indians. Adair contended that "their titles of war invariably bespeak the man, as they always make them the true attendants of merit, never conferring the least degree of honour on the worthless."[7] Until the late eighteenth and early nineteenth centuries, to fail as a warrior rendered a Choctaw male "worthless" and stripped him of his manhood.

War titles separated men from women in Choctaw society and were essential to adult male identity. Because mothers gave boys their childhood names in the matrilineal society of the Choctaws, boys were very conscious of their need to accomplish feats that merited a war title. Consequently, young men who thought "to gain Reputation and Name of Warrior" eagerly pursued any opportunity to go to war and kill an enemy.[8] Choctaw men often drew distinctions between their sphere of influence and that of women, sometimes by singing a song about women that reflected gender expectations and described activities, such as farming and sewing, in which men refused to engage:

> Go and grind some corn, we will go camping,
> Go and sew, we will go camping,
> I passed on [died] and you were sitting there crying,
> You were lazy and your hoe is rusty.[9]

General Choctaw terms for men and women further exposed gender roles and the ideal attributes of men and women. *Nakni,* a Choctaw term that designated "the male sex of all creatures," intimately connected martial virtues with manhood. *Nakni* also meant "brave" and "masculine" and served as a synonym for warrior, thus connecting manhood with warrior status.[10] Conversely, a common term used to designate woman in Choctaw, *ohoyo,* meant to be a "harvester, a gather of fruits, a searcher for harvest grounds," and "a person who makes demands," thus linking women to agriculture and domesticity.[11]

The ultimate insult for an accomplished warrior was to be called "a woman." Chiefs rebuked men who failed to exhibit martial prowess and publicly derided them as effeminate.[12] Europeans also used the term "woman" to insult men or to persuade them to act a certain way; thus we find in documents the curious phenomenon of both Europeans and Indians calling one another "woman." For example, in 1729, French commandant Bernard Diron d'Artaquette of Mobile called the "Great Chief," or *Chikacha Oulacta,* of the Choctaw village of Couëchitto "a woman" for seeking a trade relationship with the English. The Great Chief reacted to the insult by temporarily renouncing his alliance with France, believing that Diron had forsaken him and "did not wish to see [him] anymore."[13]

As this instance demonstrates, the label "woman" sometimes designated dishonorable or unfaithful behavior. In Choctaw society, women not only controlled the households and domestic economy, they also retained a high degree of independence from their husbands and divorced their mates at any time by simply leaving them.[14] Both Diron and the Great Chief seemed to have had this definition of "woman" (someone who has abandoned a reciprocal relationship) in mind as they responded to the words and actions of each other. A real man adhered to kinship and diplomatic commitments and did not quit his family or allies, whether European or Choctaw. In 1732 this same Great Chief further exposed loyalty as essential to masculinity when he described French interpreter Marc Antoine Huché as having "three good qualities: he is brave, firm and faithful." Demonstration of loyalty provided a crucial notion of masculinity that persisted as American agents and businessmen pressured Choctaw chiefs to live up to new financial and social obligations.[15]

As the Great Chief suggested, a real man remained "firm and faithful," but he also demonstrated bravery. This emphasis on bravery typified Choctaw beliefs about how a man should act. The famous Choctaw war leader Red Shoes, also known as Shouloustamastabe, responded to French accusations that he was "a woman" (for also seeking trade with the English in the late 1720s) by insisting that he proved he "was a true man in the Chickasaw war by the large number of scalps and of skulls that [he] brought back."[16] For Red Shoes and other Choctaw warriors, the opposite of a "woman" was a successful warrior who killed enemies and mastered the spiritual power necessary to spill blood and return to Choctaw society unharmed. As late as 1786 this martial model of masculinity remained pervasive, as when a young Choctaw man named Tinctimingo, speaking to the governor of South Carolina, said, "[A]t present I am a youth, but I hope to live and become a man and a warrior."[17] It is this definition of manhood as warrior that Choctaw men and women most often promoted and expected.

Successful participation in war parties also made men contenders for elite status. Once men convinced others that they could manipulate spiritual power, other Choctaws looked to them to assume additional duties on behalf of the people, such as leading war parties, negotiating with Europeans and other outsiders, preserving social cohesion, and acquiring foreign items for the use of the community, especially European manufactured trade goods. Throughout most of the eighteenth century, skill in warfare laid the foundation for elite male power and masculinity. The nineteenth-century chronicler of the Choctaws, Horatio Cushman, only slightly overstated the case when he wrote that "the dignity of chieftainship was bestowed upon him who had proved himself worthy by his skill and daring deeds in war."[18] Similarly, a late-eighteenth-century French observer of Creek Indian society, Luis LeClerc de Milford, contended that "eligibility for any kind of office was contingent upon having scalped at least seven enemies."[19] Although Choctaws did not insist on a specific number of killed enemies for higher office as the Creeks did, one Choctaw man, "distinguished by his birth," lost authority among his fellow villagers in the 1730s "because he had never liked war, which had caused his village to choose another than him to take the place of his brother who was chief." This prospective leader failed to meet the basic requirement of participating in and succeeding in war, thus leading others to question his masculinity and his ability to serve in the gender-defined role of chief.[20]

Additional problems arose for apathetic males unwilling to participate fully in war. According to one early-eighteenth-century trader, Chickasaw men who faltered on the path to becoming warriors risked lifetime bachelorhood. "The Beautys are so engrossed, by the men of Action, by great Warriors and expert hunters," Thomas Nairne suggested in 1708, "that ordinary Fellows who are sloathfull [sic] and unfortunate, are obliged to take up with very mean stuff."[21] Nairne's description paralleled Milford's depiction of the Creeks: "A young Creek who had been to war and not brought back at least one scalp always bore his mother's name and was unable to find a wife."[22] The centrality of warfare in a boy's journey to manhood and respectability linked all southeastern Indians, including the Choctaws. Once they had become great warriors, or "men of note," as Nairne called them, men often supported multiple wives. Women, who possessed inherent spiritual power as child bearers, gravitated toward men who demonstrated their mastery of spiritual forces through martial prowess.[23]

Among Choctaw warriors, bravery became even more pronounced if they suffered the misfortune of falling into the hands of an enemy. Warriors tried to avoid capture at all costs, but if seized, they insulted and taunted their tormentors by singing about war exploits and by refusing to express pain. Captors expected such behavior, and they were genuinely disappointed if a victim broke down because of the pain of torture. Choctaws trained boys from an early age to be physically fit and to withstand pain without complaint.[24] Sometimes, a tortured prisoner so bravely confronted enemies that he achieved martyrdom among his countrymen. In 1767 Choctaw warrior Red Captain led a war party into a Creek ambush. Outnumbered at least three to one, the Choctaws fought hard. Red Captain reportedly killed thirteen Creeks by himself, but the group suffered defeat in the end. Twenty-four Choctaws died, and the Creeks captured Red Captain alive. Though wounded, he "bravely told who he was." The Creeks then skinned him alive and "tortured him most inhumanely." All the while, Red Captain refused to cry out in pain. His bravery and stoicism so impressed other Choctaws that the incident remained "fresh in everyone's memory" six years later. Although he led a war party into an ambush, Red Captain redeemed his reputation by withstanding even the worst tortures of his enemy.[25]

Choctaw men like Red Captain demonstrated bravery and trustworthiness to prove their masculinity, but that did not necessarily prevent other men from questioning their manhood in other, more inflammatory ways. Indians and Europeans in the Southeast also used "woman" and similar designations to emasculate one another by questioning whether or not a man could sexually perform. Choctaw men took extreme offense at any suggestion that they lacked virility, equating such insults with the questioning of other manly duties, including warfare, hunting, and providing for one's family. At the first large-scale meeting between the Choctaws and British, held in 1765 after the Seven Years' War and French rule, a chief named Tomatly Mingo complained about the abusive conduct of British traders "who often Treat our Warriors [sic] with Indecent Language they often call them Eunuchs *(Ubacktubac)* which is the most opprobrious Term that can be used in our Language, Such treatment will enrage our people and we cannot answer for the Consequences."[26] *"Ubacktubac,"* or *hobak toba,* which early-nineteenth-century missionary Cyrus Byington described as "a word of particular reproach and offense," meant "to be castrated" and also designated someone as a coward of the first order.[27] Trader James Adair claimed that the Choctaws and other Indians viewed *hobak toba* and similar emasculating terms as "the sharpest and most lasting affront, the most opprobrious, indelible epithet, with which one Indian [or European] can possibly brand another."[28]

Similarly, when a man propositioned a Choctaw's wife, he challenged the husband's masculinity at another basic level. At the 1765 conference, Chief Alibamon Mingo complained that British traders "put their hand upon the Breast of [our] Wives which was not to be admitted, for the first maxim in our Language is that Death is preferable to disgrace."[29] Later in the eighteenth century, an overeager Choctaw boy took this notion of male protection of female chastity to a rare extreme. After his father died, his mother slept with another man. The son murdered his mother, blaming her for disgracing his honor. Not yet a warrior or a man, the boy perceived himself as protector of his mother, much as Alibamon Mingo insisted that a husband guarded his wife. This boy immediately fled the Choctaw nation to lands west of the Mississippi River, where, for several years, he killed enemy warriors. Despite those accomplishments, his defense of masculine reputation by killing his mother went beyond acceptable behavior. When grown, the boy returned home to seek recognition of his war deeds but instead was killed by the community. This warrior's actions broke Choctaw cultural norms, revealing a hyperdeveloped sense of masculinity among late-eighteenth-century Choctaw youth.[30]

Obviously, Choctaw men did not take insults to masculinity or to reputations lightly and threatened violence if humiliation continued. This common feature of southern Indian masculinity—to react with intimidation or violence to any insult to one's sexual prowess, female companion, or masculinity—seems eerily reminiscent of antebellum southern white concepts of masculinity. Dickson Bruce argued in his seminal work on antebellum southern white violence that men's feelings of vulnerability encouraged them to react with violence in order to restore their reputations, especially if other men threatened to intrude upon their family life or questioned their abilities to act in masculine ways. Such threats challenged ideas of male independence. Trader Nathaniel Folsom, writing at the end of the eighteenth century after decades spent living among the Choctaws, asserted that young Choctaw men reacted bitterly toward others when they did not kill enough wild game to feed themselves and had to rely upon the food reserves of women and old men.[31] Ideas about masculinity that emphasize independence and violence were not confined to the antebellum South, but writers throughout American history have insisted upon the antebellum South's conformity to this masculine ideal. Cultural connections and interactions between southern Indians and Euro-Americans in the eighteenth- and early-nineteenth-century South suggest that such shared beliefs derived from this ongoing cultural contact.[32]

Elite Choctaw men learned to employ the imagery of dependence and effeminacy to their advantage in meetings with Europeans. Choctaw chiefs drew upon the common Indian and European association of masculinity with warfare to insist upon adequate supplies of guns and ammunition. Choctaw men prized the large quantities of European weaponry that colonial traders and officials provided to them, because these goods enabled them to fulfill the traditional masculine duties of hunting, warfare, and defense of their villages. For example, in the midst of a war against the Creeks that lasted from 1765 to 1777, Shouloustamastabe urged the British to give him ammunition, saying, "[V]ery soon I hope you will hear that all the Chactaws are not old Women."[33] Shouloustamastabe employed a gendered symbol understood equally well in both societies. He exploited "old women" imagery to cajole the British into supplying his warriors, knowing that the British did not consider women as soldiers. In Choctaw society, a healthy adult woman sometimes participated in war, but old women never engaged in battle. Historian Nancy Shoemaker has recently exposed the frequent juxtaposition of old women and young warriors within eastern Indian rhetoric. An old woman was expected neither to go to war nor to be sexually active, whereas younger women fought in wars and chose warriors as mates. Thus, from a male point of view, an old woman was the antithesis of a warrior, and the designation acted as a useful reference point understood by southeastern Indian men and European men alike.[34]

Southeastern Indians like the Choctaws also understood that gendered imagery could be used to their advantage. They criticized the unmanly appearance of Englishmen in Charles Town and in other settlements, calling them "young, lazy, deformed white men, with big bellies, who seemed to require as much help to move them along as over-grown old women." Upon discovering that some of these corpulent individuals served as British military officers, Indians called them "effeminate" men who bought status with "yellow stone." Military titles, these Indians insisted, "should only be conferred on those who excel in martial virtue." The English men in Charles Town, they maintained, "were not fit even for the service of an old woman."[35] Indian criticism of portly British officers fit general Choctaw understandings of manhood linked to physically demanding warfare, and it supplied Indians a way to deride the masculinity of European men.

Choctaws and other southeastern Indians doubted the manliness of British officers, but their desires for such British material items as guns and ammunition remained constant. The need to obtain manufactured items contributed directly to shifts in the concept of Choctaw masculinity, as the methods for procuring such goods changed in the late eighteenth century. After the arrival of French officials on the Gulf Coast in 1699, Choctaws relied upon European guns, ammunition, blankets and other manufactured cloth, clothing, metal products, and sundry utilitarian commodities. Continued acquisition of ammunition and other European-made trade goods placed Choctaws on a slippery slope of dependence. European and then American presence in the Gulf South resulted in changed trade expectations. From 1699 to 1763, the French supplied Choctaws from bases in Mobile, New Orleans, and Natchez. The British offered supplies from their posts on the Atlantic coast. From 1763 to 1781, Britain, then in possession of the entire North American southeast, and Spain, through its presence in New Orleans, competed for Choctaw trade allegiances. After the American Revolution, Spain dominated the trade. From 1781 to 1795, the United States intruded into the area, eventually securing a dominant position in the lower Mississippi Valley upon the Treaty of San Lorenzo between Spain and the United States in 1795. In time, Choctaw dependence on European and American trade threatened their traditional notions of masculinity—which rested upon avoiding dependence on others for basic necessities—and forced changes in what it meant to be a man, particularly an elite man.

Appearance also shaped the idea of masculinity among southeastern Indians and Europeans. After decades of trade relations with Europeans, Choctaws came to depend upon European-made objects to physically define status and masculinity. European clothing became highly sought markers of elite masculinity. Choctaw chief Appapaye (*Hopaii*—"war prophet") appealed at a conference with the British in 1771 to "make us look like men by Cloathing us[,] a poor Chactaw miserably wrapped up in a Bear Skin for Cloathes, is despicable[,] but Cloath us and Let the great King be told that his Children the Chactaws look like men."[36] To Appapaye, looking manly and elite were one and the same, made possible by European clothing and merchandise.

Archeological evidence indicates that to confirm status, long before contact with Europeans, elites within southeastern Indian societies monopolized access to foreign prestige items. To enhance standing, elites redistributed many goods throughout the community, but they reserved certain items as symbols of their abilities and rank. In the eighteenth century, Europe became the primary source of many of these prestige articles.[37]

The importance of European clothing as a marker of both prestige and elite masculinity cannot be overestimated. Manufactured fabrics, blankets, shirts, and military-style overcoats designated a Choctaw's importance. Because red was the color of war, the red coats supplied by the British to elite Choctaw men during British rule in the Gulf South reinforced their positions as great warriors and war leaders. Any manufactured clothing provided a marker of prestige. Three Choctaw prisoners among the Chickasaws in 1758 described this phenomenon when they told British traders "that their Nation was reduced to the lowest degree of poverty, that they had no other Cloathing than skins."[38] Trader Nathaniel Folsom reported that when a Choctaw died, if his personal resources permitted it, he was buried in European-made clothing and blankets. But poor Choctaws wore "sum [sic] other old worn out [animal] skin" upon burial.[39] By wearing European manufactured clothing, elite Choctaw men co-opted European symbols of dress and respectable appearance and made them their own.

Besides military overcoats given them by Europeans, another item worn by elite Choctaw men—medals stamped with the image of the monarch of the European country—explicitly designated high status and an intimate connection with European goods and power. "[All] the chiefs wore a silver medallion with the bust of the King [of Britain] on their chest, others had mirrors hanging [around their necks], which is much in style with them," described Hessian chaplain Philipp Waldeck during a meeting with Choctaw warriors while stationed in Pensacola in 1780.[40] The medallion placed around the neck of an elite Choctaw man, like the small and large medals bestowed on chiefs by various European powers in the Gulf South over the course of the eighteenth century, entitled him to extra gifts while visiting European posts and provided a visible marker of his elite masculine status. Choctaws placed tremendous significance on the medals that European governments bestowed, calling them *tali hullo*, or "sacred piece of stone."[41]

The late-eighteenth-century connection between European garb, high status, and masculinity was further revealed in the case of a war leader named Chocoulacta, who, though the recipient of a small medal from Britain, lost status when he and his warriors accidentally killed a British traveler in 1767. Olacta Houma, "landlord" of Chocoulacta's village, denied the privilege of war titles and honors to the young warriors and apparently considered executing Chocoulacta. Certainly, the killing of an Englishman threatened trade relations at a time when Britain remained the only reliable source of manufactured goods, but Chocoulacta's actions in attacking a lone innocent traveler also appeared unmasculine; the victim was not an enemy warrior prepared to battle the Choctaws. Olacta Houma and other high-ranking Choctaw men decided that Chocoulacta should live, but they took his British medal and threatened to remove his European clothing and to force him to wear animal skins instead. Since the 1760s, European clothing provided a principal marker of masculine elite status enabling other Choctaws to immediately recognize an elite man when they saw him. Chocoulacta's loss of the medal and European clothing served as visible reminders to other Choctaws of his diminished rank and authority. Not until the 1771 Choctaw conference with Britain did Chocoulacta regain his medal and status after performing a public ceremony demonstrating repentance and peaceful intentions.[42]

European goods as markers of masculinity and status grew in importance in the late eighteenth century. As more merchandise poured into Choctaw villages owing to unregulated British trade after 1763, however, elite Choctaws necessarily redefined what possession of such items meant, as they had done with other prestigious items since precontact times. As manufactured merchandise became available to larger numbers of Choctaws regardless of status, elites sought to preserve certain rarer items as emblems of prestige. Otherwise, they risked losing the physical manifestations of their masculinity and status. By the early nineteenth century, when nearly all Choctaws enjoyed access to blankets, strouds (blue and red wool fabric), and broadcloth, American businessman George Strother Gaines reported that the "more wealthy [Choctaw] Indians . . . of that [elite] class wore in lieu of strouds fine scarlet cloth with highly ornamented mockascins and head dressed."[43] To reinforce their high status, elite Choctaws, like those Gaines witnessed, persistently redefined the meaning of European manufactured goods. For elite men, such quality items also demonstrated their masculinity, just as certain prestige articles had historically indicated a Choctaw man's ability to manipulate spiritual power as a warrior, hunter, or diplomat. By the late 1700s, these men needed to retain access to such merchandise to preserve the physical manifestations of their elite masculine identities.

The maintenance of a certain physical image in order to display masculine character entangled elite Choctaws in a Euro-American market economy and contributed to their adoption of Euro-American notions of manhood. However, obtaining trade goods grew increasingly problematic, and in the last two decades of the eighteenth century, elite Choctaws had to actively pursue new ways of procuring wares.

For most of the century, two principal methods of acquiring manufactured commodities existed; both reinforced chiefly and masculine authority. From the early days of the century, Choctaws traded deerskins with Europeans. Until the mid-1760s, Choctaw hunters turned deerskins over to village chiefs, who then exchanged them with traders for manufactured commodities. This manner of handling trade supported chiefly power and elite masculinity by enabling the chiefs to directly control the disbursement of merchandise, thus securing reciprocal obligations among warriors and their families. Conferences with European governments provided the other major source of European goods. At these conferences all Choctaws received gifts of food, clothing, weapons, ammunition, and sundry other items; chiefs and noted warriors received the largest allotments. Until the Seven Years' War (1756–63), France held such conferences with the Choctaws on an annual basis. Here, too, chiefs controlled the flow of trade items. After the end of the Seven Years' War, both systems disintegrated when British traders began exchanging rum and other goods with any Choctaw who possessed deerskins, and the British government refused to hold gift-giving conferences.[44]

If, theoretically, any Choctaw man or woman could obtain status-laden manufactured goods, and if chiefs no longer received gifts, then an elite chief and his family needed to find other methods of acquiring prestige items. Since elite Choctaw men no longer played the dominant role of economic mediator between the Choctaws and Europeans after 1763, the very basis of their masculinity became threatened. Chiefs attempted to solve this social crisis by pushing their society to adopt more Euro-American notions of economics and gender roles. To stem the social disruptions caused by British trade and increasing tensions between chiefs and young warriors, Choctaw elites planned strategy according to traditional masculine duties of warfare. From 1765 to 1777, the Choctaws and Creeks (neighbors to the east in present-day Alabama) fought a war ostensibly over control of hunting territory located between the two peoples. Chiefs in both societies, however, promoted war and their own masculinity by leading young warriors in battle. In addition, war required the British guns and ammunition that chiefs redistributed among their warriors, thus reinforcing chiefly rank.[45] This temporary solution failed, however, to ensure the long-term procurement of European-made merchandise.

Choctaw elites then asked European traders to live in their villages on a semi-permanent basis. Consequently, the elites were able to control trade while simultaneously maintaining their chiefly role as redistributors of prestige items. By having traders reside in their villages, chiefs connected themselves to a source of high-status merchandise. This strategy seemed to solve several social concerns. To make the goods the chiefs received more valuable than those obtainable by most other Choctaws, chiefs fastened reputations and careers, both their own and those of their families, to certain traders, gaining access to a full range of merchandise in return. Furthermore, a new generation of men emerged from intercultural unions and used their Choctaw mothers' kinship connections and their European fathers' business skills to push elite Choctaw culture in new directions. On one level, chiefs who initiated cross-cultural relationships still exerted traditional chiefly responsibilities to manage the flow of externally derived items and to oversee labor resources and production. But resident traders replaced the hunters and warriors who had once handed over animal skins to chiefs.[46]

The stable economic relationship that resident traders provided, however, did not solve the problems that trade and new social strains presented. Competition erupted between trading companies and independent traders during Spanish rule in the Gulf South (1781–95).[47] Deer became increasingly scarce east of the Mississippi River, requiring more time and effort by Choctaw hunters to enable them to profit from the deerskin trade.[48] Choctaw chiefs began to realize, as did Franchimastabé, the principal Western Division chief of the late 1700s, that "the time of hunting and living by the Gun was . . . near its end," and that soon his "people would have to live by labor like the White Men."[49] This shift from hunting deer to laboring like white men required a fundamental reformulation of Choctaw masculinity, one that necessarily relied more on American market-oriented ideas about elite manliness.

Franchimastabé and other Choctaw chiefs knew that Euro-Americans supported their economy in a way different from the way of the Choctaws: "the whites by recourse to money always find the means to carry on trade," Franchimastabé observed in 1787, "but the poor red men have no other recourse than peltries."[50] When deerskins and resident traders no longer sustained elite authority, Choctaw chiefs sought access to the money that underlay Euro-American elite status. Amassing goods by building personal relationships with traders, by becoming traders themselves, or by producing goods for the open market were the primary options open to chiefs and their families who wanted to increase or protect status and power according to the new market definitions. Such economic activities enabled elite Choctaw men to continue looking like men.

Business-oriented pressures on the Choctaws forced elites to conform to a new set of economic rules that further transformed masculinity in the early nineteenth century. American officials coerced Choctaw chiefs in the early national era by appealing to their sense of honor and ethics in a new business environment. In 1805 Western Division chief Apuckshunubee confronted the result of decades of deerskin trading as the primary method for Choctaws to gain Euro-American goods. The Choctaws had amassed a large debt to fur trading companies because their warriors failed to harvest enough deer to pay the obligation. The United States insisted that to pay these debts the Choctaws cede land, but Apuckshunubee's warriors told him that "he must pay the debt with a small spot of ground." He replied: "I have tried that already, was made ashamed, and it will not do, we must give up enough to satisfy the claim."[51] Apuckshunubee "was made ashamed" by Euro-American officials and businessmen who defined masculinity by contractual obligations and honor gained through trustworthiness. Warriors, in contrast, opposed land cessions because the loss of hunting territory threatened the basis of their traditional notions of masculinity and economic independence. Choctaw chiefs had confronted this resistance to change by warriors as early as the 1790s, when Franchimastabé tried to persuade his warriors to agree to a small land cession to the Spanish at Nogales (then called the Walnut Hills by the Americans, today the site of Vicksburg). Insisting that he "wished to be in good standing" with the whites, Franchimastabé nevertheless stalled the land transfer, in part because he worried about his warriors: that "the red men laugh at me saying that I am a King who sells the land of my Women and children for goods to clothe them."[52]

It is not hard to imagine warriors laughing at their chief for acting in a way they deemed unmasculine: to trade land for manufactured cloth revealed a dependence on Europeans that warriors and chiefs disdained. After two years of negotiation, the land sale to Spain transpired, but not before Franchimastabé learned that the tightrope between traditional Choctaw masculinity and emerging gender constructions was a slippery one.[53] Until Choctaw elites found other ways to pay debts and other means to obtain money, the sale of land furnished the only alternative. While paying debts and living up to business contracts offered opportunity in the form of more credit extensions, they also pressured Choctaws to adapt to a new set of rules. Apuckshunubee and other chiefs met the challenge, demonstrating a new standard of manhood by proving themselves trustworthy to their American creditors. American ideas about male responsibility appealed to elite Choctaw men, who found that they could exploit ties with American officials to enhance their own economic prosperity.

After employing various strategies to preserve control over trading goods in the late eighteenth century, Choctaw elites of the early nineteenth century found that the emerging American market system provided some answers to their problems. Because of economic changes, hunting and warfare had become less important to defining elite manhood. Increasingly, like their American counterparts, elite families engaged in cash-crop agriculture, traded horses and African American slaves, raised livestock, adopted notions of individual land ownership, and promoted inheritance through the male line (a change from the Choctaw traditional of matrilineal succession).[54]

At the Fort Adams Treaty negotiations with the United States in 1801, Mingo Homastubbee, a dominant Eastern Division chief, expressed a Choctaw readiness to embrace more of the American economy, even as he recognized the changes in gender norms that such economic activities required. He requested that American women be sent "to learn our women to spin and weave. These women may first go amongst our half breeds and learn them, and the thing will then extend itself; one will learn another, and the white women may return to their own people again." Most Choctaws adhered to a traditional division of labor in which women farmed, but interest in the new material culture signaled a profound realignment of femininity and masculinity. Recognizing the technological revolution already under way within elite Choctaw families, Mingo Homastubbee asked for help, "as we have half breeds, and others accustomed to work, that ploughs may be sent us, weeding hoes, grubbing hoes, axes, handsaws, augers, iron wedges, and a man to make wheels, and a small set of blacksmith's tools for a red man." [55]

Although certain chiefs like Mingo Homastubbee seemed unwilling to change their own gender beliefs, they actively promoted new economic roles for their wives and children. At the Fort Adams conference, Apuckshunubee called for spinning wheels "for our young women and half breeds" to use for processing cotton. [56] The "half-breeds" represented a new Choctaw population, children of Choctaw women and Euro-American traders whose unions had been sanctioned a generation earlier as part of elite strategies to monopolize trade networks. As chiefs negotiated the new economy, they recognized that "half-breed" relatives could more easily free themselves from traditional Choctaw notions of masculinity by following the gender conventions of their Euro-American and profit-oriented fathers. At least Choctaw elites knew that American officials viewed such persons that way, and they accordingly pushed these bicultural people into new gendered roles. By 1801 trader Nathaniel Folsom reported that elite Choctaw families maintained corn and cotton plantations, and that women engaged in spinning and weaving so successfully that they were "able to clothe themselves." He credited this development to a reduction in the number of wives per elite Choctaw man and a weakening of women's dependence upon their husbands (presumably because women no longer relied on husbands to kill deer to trade for merchandise or to acquire gifts from Euro-American officials). [57]

Simultaneously, elite Choctaws fostered a new ethic of masculinity defined by individualism. Elite Choctaw families pursued economic enrichment with little regard for traditional communal obligations. Robert McClure, a bicultural Choctaw, provided one expression of this new individualism. At the Fort Adams negotiations, he urged the United States to deliver a cotton gin to the Choctaws, promising that "we, half breeds and young men, wish to go to work, and the sooner we receive those things the sooner we will begin to learn." McClure did not seek access to deer herds or enemy warriors to prove his traditional masculine bona fides. Instead he defined success as a man in the same way many white Americans did. He thanked American officials for this opportunity: "I am glad to hear it is the wish of our father, the President, to teach us to do such things as the whites can do."[58] Rising belief in individualism, as scholars of early nineteenth-century America have demonstrated, entailed new ideas about masculinity that originated in response to the emerging capitalist system of early America.[59] American agents to the Choctaws acted upon these impulses. John McKee warned Choctaw chiefs in 1800 that gifts could no longer be relied upon as a source of goods as they "offer[ed] no incitements to industry and be assured, my friends, that is the [course] from which you must derive your subsistence."[60] It fell to elite Choctaw families to decide which "incitements to industry" they should pursue. Involvement in the American market economy became a necessity, and new economic arrangements altered concepts of masculinity.

Concurrent with changing economic conditions, the United States pressured southern Indians like the Choctaws to adopt the tenets of a new "civilization" policy that contained its own definition of masculinity. The civilization policy called on Indian men to become self-sufficient small farmers with paternalistic control over their families. President George Washington promoted an end to the deerskin trade and connected it with corrupt economic dependency and an unmasculine lack of civic virtue. He questioned "whether the luxury, *effeminacy*, and corruptions which are introduced along with [trade]; are counterbalanced by the convenience and wealth which it brings with it."[61] This formulation of masculinity moved Choctaw men away from traditional forms of masculinity by encouraging them to produce renewable resources for the open market, head their households, and govern their nation. Typical of early American attitudes toward masculinity, Benjamin Franklin asserted that "every man that really is a man" acted as "master of his own family."[62] Americans viewed such labors as the moral duty of men, established by the laws of nature. Elite Choctaw men increasingly accepted this new gender arrangement as natural in the early nineteenth century.[63]

To prepare young relatives for this emergent market-oriented individualism, elite Choctaws sent them to the new missionary schools that began opening in Choctaw country in 1818. At the schools the children learned math, reading, and discipline—skills necessary in business. Boys also studied farming techniques, and girls mastered cooking, sewing, spinning, and housewifery. Of course, Choctaw women already did these things, but in this new formulation of family life and gender roles, women were no longer expected to farm. Their labor now supported a male-controlled household. The farming techniques and other skills learned by Choctaw boys prepared some of them for agriculture. But the schools trained elite Choctaw men not so much to get into the fields themselves to plant and harvest—the aversion to doing such "women's work" remained strong well into the nineteenth century—but to manage a farm where African slaves, "half-breed" men, and laborers worked the fields. In this respect, elite Choctaw men acted in ways similar to American plantation owners, and their views of masculinity followed suit. In addition, traditional Choctaw methods of education for boys, whereby elder statesmen taught history and customs in the mornings and evenings, fell into disuse by the 1820s. Middle- and upper-class Protestant Americans taught the lessons of manhood, and the future economic well-being of elite Choctaw families stemmed from American society.[64]

Those Choctaws who possessed the resources to venture into profit-generating activities did so readily. Material accumulation required capital, and only chiefs (and their families) who enjoyed established relations with traders or government officials had ready access to money, slaves, and private property. Thus only elite Choctaw families successfully participated in these new economic relationships and cultural concepts. In the Choctaw Constitution of 1826, elite Choctaws formalized their commitment to the new economy and its altered notion of masculinity. That document enhanced the authority of the lighthorse police (formed in 1820 to protect private property rights), formed a national council to make political decisions, enacted new laws protecting private property and establishing inheritance through the male line, promoted the fencing in former common lands, and discouraged polygamy. In all these ways, the 1826 Constitution brought elite Choctaw culture mores in line with those of elite American culture. Early-nineteenth-century Choctaw chiefs thus established the precedence of men over women, literate over illiterate, landowners over non-landowners, wealthy over poor, and farmers over hunters. Meanwhile, among non-elite Choctaws, the matrilineal kinship system and other traditional gender notions persisted.[65]

By the late eighteenth and early nineteenth centuries, the traditional masculine pursuits of war and hunting no longer served to promote elite status, though warfare and violence still supported certain conceptions of masculinity as they did in the larger American culture. Instead, control over access to material resources, acquisition of American-style education, possession of business acumen, and individualism became the new markers of elite Choctaw masculinity, markers tied directly to notions of masculinity held by market-oriented Americans. The challenge for elite Choctaw men in the early Republic became how to make themselves "look like men," as Chief Appapaye phrased it in 1771.[66] They had to retain access to value-laden European trade items while preserving a masculine identity, even though fundamental economic change surrounded them.

Eventually they determined that either their dependence on Europeans or their notions of manhood must be modified. Economic success became paramount, and manhood became increasingly defined through it during the early Republic.[67] The transformation of Choctaw concepts of masculinity thus became a marker of larger economic, ideological, and social shifts adopted by elites as they grappled with altered sources of power. To continue looking like men, elite Choctaw men participated in the larger American market economy, and to accommodate capitalism, they adjusted basic cultural definitions of masculinity. In the process, they demanded that "the great King [or President] be told that his Children the Chactaws look like men."[68]

## NOTES

1. Bernard Romans, *A Concise Natural History of East and West Florida*, ed. Kathryn E. Holland Braund (Tuscaloosa: University of Alabama Press, 1999), 131, 139. On southeastern Indian masculinity generally, see Charles Hudson, *The Southeastern Indians* (Knoxville: University of Tennessee Press, 1976), 267–69.

2. Works on gender among southeastern Indians include Theda Perdue, *Cherokee Women: Gender and Culture Change, 1700–1835* (Lincoln: University of Nebraska Press, 1998); Nancy Shoemaker, "An Alliance between Men: Gender Metaphors in Eighteenth-Century American Indian Diplomacy East of the Mississippi River," *Ethnohistory* 46 (1999): 239–64; and Patricia Galloway, "Where Have All the Menstrual Huts Gone? The Invisibility of Menstrual Seclusion in the Late Prehistoric Southeast," in *Women in Prehistory: North America and Mesoamerica*, ed. Cheryl Claassen and Rosemary A. Joyce (Philadelphia: University of Pennsylvania Press, 1997), 47–64. See also the important works on American Indian women in Nancy Shoemaker, ed., *Negotiators of Change: Historical Perspectives on Native American Women* (New York: Routledge, 1995); Laura F. Klein and Lillian A. Ackerman, eds., *Women and Power in Native North America* (Norman: University of Oklahoma Press, 1995); and Theda Perdue, ed., *Sifters: Native American Women's Lives* (New York: Oxford University Press, 2001).

3. Greater detail on these gender roles, spiritual power, and the role of war in Choctaw men's identity is presented in Greg O'Brien, *Choctaws in a Revolutionary Age, 1750–1830* (Lincoln: University of Nebraska Press, 2002), esp. chaps. 1 and 3. Nathaniel J. Sheidley, "Unruly Men: Indians, Settlers, and the Ethos of Frontier Patriarchy in the Upper Tennessee Watershed, 1763–1815" (Ph.D. diss., Princeton University, 1999).

4. Cyrus Byington, *Choctaw Language Dictionary*, Smithsonian Institution, Bureau of American Ethnology Bulletin 46 (Washington, D.C., 1909), 5, 170, 128, 485. The pervasiveness of these titles is apparent in a remarkable document recording the names of more than 730 Choctaw men: "A List of Towns in the Chactaw Nation with the Names of the Indians in each Town Receiving Presents at the Congress

1771–1772," British Public Record Office, *Colonial Office, Class 5: America and the West Indies,* vol. 73 (hereafter CO5).

5. James Adair, *History of the American Indians,* ed. Samuel Cole Williams (Johnson City, Tenn.: Watauga Press, 1930), 201.

6. "Hopaii," in Byington, *Choctaw Language Dictionary,* 165, 525; see also Colin G. Calloway, *The American Revolution in Indian Country: Crisis and Diversity in Native American Communities* (New York: Cambridge University Press, 1995), 220; John R. Swanton, *Source Material for the Social and Ceremonial Life of the Choctaw Indians* (Tuscaloosa: University of Alabama Press, 2001), 122–23; and Adair, *History of the American Indians,* 71.

7. Adair, *History of the American Indians,* 465.

8. Charles Stuart to John Stuart, 12 June 1770, *General Thomas Gage Papers: American Series,* vol. 94, William L. Clements Library, University of Michigan, Ann Arbor (hereafter *Gage Papers*). See also Amelia R. Bell, "Separate People: Speaking of Creek Men and Women," *American Anthropologist* 92 (1990): 336–37. For further comparative studies of manhood and the requirement that "boys must pass through testing" to become men, see David D. Gilmore, *Manhood in the Making: Cultural Concepts of Masculinity* (New Haven: Yale University Press, 1990), 11.

9. "Hunting Song," in Frances Densmore, *Choctaw Music,* Smithsonian Institution, Bureau of American Ethnology Bulletin 136 (Washington, D.C., 1943), 177.

10. Byington, *Choctaw Language Dictionary,* 268.

11. Ibid., 169, 288, 608.

12. Adair, *History of the American Indians,* 163.

13. Dunbar Rowland, A. G. Sanders, and Patricia Kay Galloway, eds., *Mississippi Provincial Archives: French Dominion,* 5 vols. (vols. 1–3: Jackson: Mississippi Department of Archives and History, 1927–1932; vols. 4–5: Baton Rouge: Louisiana State University Press, 1984), 1:33, 37.

14. Swanton, *Source Material,* 127–30.

15. Rowland, Sanders, and Galloway, *Mississippi Provincial Archives: French Dominion,* 4:16n. 3.

16. Ibid., 1:34.

17. Antonio Pace, trans. and ed., *Luigi Castiglioni's Viaggio: Travels in the United States of North America, 1785–87* (Syracuse: Syracuse University Press, 1983), 133.

18. Horatio B. Cushman, *History of the Choctaw, Chickasaw, and Natchez Indians* (1899; reprint, Stillwater, Okla.: Redlands Press, 1962), 198–99.

19. Luis LeClerc de Milford, *Memoir; or, A Cursory Glance at My Different Travels and My Sojourn in the Creek Nation,* trans. Geraldine de Courcy, ed. John Francis McDermott (1802; reprint, Chicago: Lakeside Press, 1956), 175.

20. Jean-Baptiste Le Moyne de Bienville [Governor of Louisiana] to Jerome Phelypeaux de Maurepas [Minister of Marine], 23 April 1734, in Rowland, Sanders, and Galloway, *Mississippi Provincial Archives: French Dominion,* 1:226.

21. *Nairne's Muskhogean Journals: The 1708 Expedition to the Mississippi River,* ed. Alexander Moore (Jackson: University Press of Mississippi, 1988), 46.

22. Milford, *Memoir; or, A Cursory Glance,* 175.

23. O'Brien, *Choctaws in a Revolutionary Age,* chap. 3.

24. John R. Swanton, "An Early Account of the Choctaw Indians," *American Anthropological Association Memoirs* 5 (1918): 66; "Choctaw People File," Edmund J. Gardner Papers, Gilcrease Institute of American History and Art, Tulsa, Okla.

25. Romans, *Natural History,* 72–73. See also James Hewitt to McGillivray and Struthers, 16 October 1767; Charles Stuart to John Stuart, 29 October 1767; and John Stuart to Gage, 27 November 1767, all in *Gage Papers,* vol. 72; Roderick MacIntosh to John Stuart, 16 November 1767, and John Stuart to Gage, 26 December 1767, both in *Gage Papers,* vol. 73; John Stuart to Shelburne, 7 May 1768, co5/69; John Stuart to Gage, 17 May 1768, *Gage Papers,* vol. 77; John Stuart to Hillsborough, 28 December 1768, co5/70; Adair, *History of the American Indians,* 312–14; and Greg O'Brien, "Protecting Trade through War: Choctaw Elites and British Occupation of the Floridas," in *Empire and Others: British Encounters with Indigenous Peoples, 1600–1850,* ed. Martin Daunton and Rick Halpern (Philadelphia: University of Pennsylvania Press, 1999), 155.

26. Dunbar Rowland, ed., *Mississippi Provincial Archives: English Dominion, 1763–1766* (Nashville: Brandon Printing, 1911), 238.

27. Byington, *Choctaw Language Dictionary,* 155.

28. Adair, *History of the American Indians,* 143. See also Shoemaker, "An Alliance between Men," 241, 249.

29. Rowland, *Mississippi Provincial Archives: English Dominion,* 241.

30. Nathaniel Folsom, "Discussion of Choctaw History, [1798]," Peter Pitchlynn Papers, Gilcrease Institute of American History and Art, Tulsa, Okla.

31. Ibid.

32. Dickson D. Bruce Jr., *Violence and Culture in the Antebellum South* (Austin: University of Texas Press, 1979), 70–74.

33. "Shouloustamastabe, alias Red Shoes, his Talk to the Deputy Superintendent, 4 July 1766," co5/67. On the Choctaw-Creek War, see O'Brien, "Protecting Trade through War."

34. Shoemaker, "An Alliance between Men," 245.

35. Adair, *History of the American Indians,* 463–64.

36. Eron Rowland, "Peter Chester: Third Governor of the Province of British West Florida under British Dominion, 1770–1781," *Publications of the Mississippi Historical Society,* vol. 5, *Centenary Series* (Jackson: Mississippi Historical Society, 1925), 151.

37. Paul D. Welch, "Control Over Goods and the Political Stability of the Moundville Chiefdom," in *Political Structure and Change in the Prehistoric Southeastern United States,* ed. John F. Scarry (Gainesville, Fla.: University Press of Florida, 1996), 86, 89, 91; Jon Muller, *Mississippian Political Economy* (New York: Plenum Press, 1997), esp. 55–116; Christopher S. Peebles, "Moundville from 1000 to 1500 A.D. as Seen from 1840 to 1985 A.D.," in *Chiefdoms in the Americas,* ed. Robert D. Drennan and Carlos A. Uribe (Lanham, Md.: University Press of America, 1987), 34; Timothy R.

Pauketat and Thomas E. Emerson, eds., *Cahokia: Domination and Ideology in the Mississippian World* (Lincoln: University of Nebraska Press, 1997).

38. Jerome Courtonne to William Henry Lyttelton, 17 October 1758, William Henry Lyttelton Papers, William L. Clements Library, University of Michigan, Ann Arbor.

39. Folsom, "Discussion of Choctaw History, [1798]."

40. Bruce E. Burgoyne, ed., *Eighteenth Century America: A Hessian Report On the People, the Land, the War: As Noted in the Diary of Chaplain Philipp Waldeck, 1776–1780* (Bowie, Md.: Heritage Books, 1995), 159.

41. Byington, *Choctaw Language Dictionary*, 345.

42. "Deposition of John Farrell, packhorseman in the Choctaw Nation, 4 March 1767," British Museum Additional Manuscripts, #21671, pt. 4 (photostat, Library of Congress); O'Brien, "Protecting Trade through War," 155–56.

43. James P. Pate, ed., *The Reminiscences of George Strother Gaines: Pioneer and Statesman in Early Alabama and Mississippi, 1805–1843* (Tuscaloosa: University of Alabama Press, 1998), 142.

44. This situation is summarized in O'Brien, *Choctaws in a Revolutionary Age*, chap. 5; O'Brien, "Protecting Trade through War," 149–66.

45. O'Brien, "Protecting Trade through War," 149–66.

46. O'Brien, *Choctaws in a Revolutionary Age*, chap. 5, 70–97.

47. William S. Coker and Thomas D. Watson, *Indian Traders of the Southeastern Spanish Borderlands: Panton, Leslie and Company and John Forbes and Company, 1783–1847* (Pensacola: University of West Florida Press, 1986); O'Brien, *Choctaws in a Revolutionary Age*, chap. 5.

48. Richard White, *The Roots of Dependency: Subsistence, Environment, and Social Change among the Choctaws, Pawnees, and Navajos* (Lincoln: University of Nebraska Press, 1983), 86–87; Lawrence Kinnaird and Lucia B. Kinnaird, "Choctaws West of the Mississippi, 1766–1800," *Southwestern Historical Quarterly* 83 (1980): 349–70.

49. Edward Hunter Ross and Dawson A. Phelps, trans. and eds., "A Journey over the Natchez Trace in 1792: A Document from the Archives of Spain," *Journal of Mississippi History* 15 (1953): 271. See also O'Brien, *Choctaws in a Revolutionary Age*, chap. 5.

50. Manuel Serrano y Sanz, *Spain and the Cherokee and Choctaw Indians in the Second Half of the Eighteenth Century*, trans. Samuel Dorris Dickinson (Idabel, Okla.: Museum of the Red River, 1995), 31.

51. Silas Dinsmoor to Henry Dearborn, 12 October 1805, General James Robertson Papers, Tennessee State Library and Archives, Nashville.

52. Dawson and Phelps, "Natchez Trace" 265.

53. On the Nogales land dispute, see Dawson and Phelps, "Natchez Trace"; Christopher J. Malloy and Charles A. Weeks, "Shuttle Diplomacy Eighteenth-Century Style: Stephen Minor's First Mission to the Choctaws and Journal, May–June, 1791," *Journal of Mississippi History* 55 (1993): 31–51; Lawrence Kinnaird and Lucia B. Kinnaird, "Nogales: Strategic Post on the Spanish Frontier," *Journal of Mississippi History* 42 (1980): 1–16; Serrano y Sanz, *Cherokee and Choctaw*, 36–50; Jack D. L.

Holmes, *Gayoso: The Life of a Spanish Governor in the Mississippi Valley, 1789–1799* (Gloucester, Mass.: Peter Smith, 1968), 145–53.

54. O'Brien, *Choctaws in a Revolutionary Age*, chap. 6.

55. *American State Papers: Documents, Legislative and Executive, of the Congress of the United States*, vol. 4, *Indian Affairs* (Washington, D.C.: Gales and Seaton, 1832), 662.

56. Ibid., 661.

57. Folsom, "Discussion of Choctaw History, [1798]"; see also James Taylor Carson, *Searching for the Bright Path: The Mississippi Choctaws from Prehistory to Removal* (Lincoln: University of Nebraska Press, 1999), 79–80.

58. *American State Papers*, 662.

59. See, for example, Charles Sellers, *The Market Revolution: Jacksonian America, 1815–1846* (New York: Oxford University Press, 1991), 242, 245–46; Amy Dru Stanley, "Home Life and the Morality of the Market," in *The Market Revolution in America*, ed. Melvyn Stokes and Stephen Conway (Charlottesville: University Press of Virginia, 1996), 76; and Mark E. Kann, *A Republic of Men: The American Founders, Gendered Language, and Patriarchal Politics* (New York: New York University Press, 1998), 2.

60. "Talk to the Chiefs of Choctaw Nation, 19 October 1800," John McKee Papers, Box 4, Library of Congress, Washington, D.C.

61. Washington to James Warren, 7 October 1785, in *The Writings of George Washington from the Original Manuscript Sources, 1745–1799*, ed. John C. Fitzpatrick, 39 vols. (Washington, D.C.: United States Government Printing Office, 1938), 27:17–18 (emphasis added).

62. As quoted in Kann, *A Republic of Men*, 7.

63. The best study of the early American "civilization" policy and its gender implications is Perdue, *Cherokee Women*, esp. 109–12, 189.

64. *Missionary Herald* (Boston, Mass.), 16 (1820): 417; *Missionary Herald*, 17 (1821): 49; *Missionary Herald*, 18 (1822): 152–53; Carson, *Searching for the Bright Path*, 84–85; O'Brien, *Choctaws in a Revolutionary Age*, chap. 6; Clara Sue Kidwell, *Choctaws and Missionaries in Mississippi, 1818–1918* (Norman: University of Oklahoma Press, 1995).

65. See White, *Roots of Dependency*, 127; O'Brien, *Choctaws in a Revolutionary Age*, chap. 6; Kidwell, *Choctaws and Missionaries*, 163; and Kann, *A Republic of Men*, 2–3.

66. E. Rowland, "Peter Chester," 151.

67. Dana D. Nelson, *National Manhood: Capitalist Citizenship and the Imagined Fraternity of White Men* (Durham: Duke University Press, 1998), 36.

68. E. Rowland, "Peter Chester," 151.

# Fraternity and Masculine Identity:
# The Search for Respectability among White
# and Black Artisans in Petersburg, Virginia

## L. Diane Barnes

Tracing its origins to medieval Europe, the phenomenon of the all-male fraternal society was a well-established tradition in the antebellum American South. Fraternal groups, including artisanal societies and chapters of the Freemason and Odd Fellows, united men across social, religious, and class lines. Group members' identities as men were intimately tied to, and represented through, their membership in fraternal organizations. The fraternities of white and black men in antebellum Petersburg, Virginia, sought to help members enhance their status in the community and define their masculinity. Three organizations illustrate how brotherhood bound men together in the changing economy of the antebellum South. The Petersburg Benevolent Mechanic Association was composed of upwardly mobile businessmen who aligned their fraternity with the values of planter society and regulated the behavior of participants to fit that image. The Petersburg Mechanic Association, organized by middling artisans, felt their economic position slipping in the wake of industrialization and chose to define their social status in terms of manly responsibility and in opposition to free black artisans. African American men in Petersburg faced the biggest challenges to their masculine identity through legal and institutional racism. Their Beneficial Society could do little to challenge the *Herrenvolk* democracy that placed them at the bottom of the social and economic order, yet their fraternity allowed them to stand as men within their own community and to make their own claims to respectability.[1]

Fraternalism was often grounded in exclusion. Based along gender lines, fraternal groups allowed for the construction of institutionalized power relations that made masculinity the most important framework for organizing social life.

71

This hierarchy put masculinity ahead of economics in determining social status. Through the construction of ties based on masculinity and skilled craft traditions, nineteenth-century fraternal orders managed to reduce the significance of growing class differences, offering instead gender and race as appropriate categories for organizing a collective identity.[2] The white men of Petersburg used these principles to craft a racial identity that led artisan workers and middle-class businessmen to believe they shared equal footing with local planters and elite industrialists. Indeed, more than just reflecting the South's racist attitudes, the white fraternal organizations of Petersburg artisans formed part of a larger social structure that created a *Herrenvolk* democracy based on racial separation and inequality.[3] White artisans did not, however, exert exclusive control over fraternalism in Petersburg. African American artisans and businessmen used similar organizing principles to counter white attempts to exclude them from economic opportunities and white-dominated society. Men, both black and white, used fraternal organizations to construct a masculine identity and to enhance their claims to independence and respectability.

The initial purpose of these fraternities was, however, of a more practical nature. Skilled carpenters, blacksmiths, coopers, and bricklayers formed institutes or benevolent associations to protect their interests and skills in the local economy. Based on a tradition of mutual aid, these groups often operated exclusive of political organizations such as the working men's parties that formed in the 1820s and 1830s. Mechanics' institutes and societies offered independent artisan masters and journeymen a vehicle to express their collective political ideas, including their republican ideology. Mechanics felt a strong tie to the Revolutionary republican principles upholding small producers and manufacturers as the backbone of the early Republic's economy. The growth of factories and new production methods undercut small producers and threatened their position in society. In light of increasing changes in the economy and the competition from mass-produced manufactured goods, this type of organization allowed craftsmen to persist in many areas of the nation. For those fortunate artisans who advanced in a changing economy, artisans' or mechanics' associations offered fraternal support and acknowledgment of their success. For those artisans losing status, the associations provided a tenuous safety net that might offer a small cash payment to help them get back on their feet.[4] For example, when carpenter William Wright fell on hard times in 1827, his mechanics' association provided a relief payment of ten dollars for support of his family.[5]

Like their northern counterparts, southern artisan organizations sometimes defended members' political rights, but they also pursued the unique agenda of protecting the place of white workers in a slave society. This meant advocating the value of white free labor in a region where enslaved blacks performed the bulk of manual work. In Georgia, the Savannah Mechanics Association expressed concerns particular to the coexistence of artisan workers in a plantation economy, stressing the importance of the training, skill, and dedication required in craft making, and offering benevolent relief to needy members. The group also lobbied for government relief payments after a fire destroyed many shops and businesses, and it engaged in a statewide protest against land speculation by wealthy planters.[6] The Charleston Mechanic Society, first incorporated in the 1790s, aimed to "promote the interests of the Mechanic" but made clear that only white men could join. The society provided a safety net for its members and their families. Mechanics' families received fifty dollars for "funeral arrangements." Widows and orphans qualified for assistance.[7]

In the antebellum era, as industrialization altered relationships between master mechanics and journeymen, the composition and goals of mechanics' associations shifted as well. At the end of the Revolution, skilled workers expected to advance under the traditional artisan system. Young men began training as craft apprentices at about age fourteen and at twenty-one graduated to journeyman status. After working for several years, industrious journeymen expected to become independent master craftsmen who owned their own shops and employed a new generation of apprentices and journeymen. The growth of factories and new methods of work organization in the 1830s and 1840s interrupted the artisan system, as both master mechanics and journeymen adapted to a changing economy. At times, their interests diverged: masters became merchants and manufacturers, and journeymen faced life-long wage labor. The new economic reality was a blow to journeymen's masculinity, as their ability to provide for their families became more tenuous, and opportunities for economic independence withered.

Throughout the nation, these changes led master mechanics and journeymen to form organizations independent of each other. Masters' associations grew increasingly concerned with mutual aid and fraternity, with supporting their members' upward mobility into new roles as entrepreneurs, and with cultivating their newfound middle-class respectability. While similarly interested in benevolence and mutual aid, journeymen's societies began to recognize the growing disparity of interests in the craft system. Many became trade unions as well as fraternal associations.[8] As master mechanics became entrepreneurs and strict bosses, they still collectively viewed themselves as protectors of their fellow craftsmen. Upwardly mobile men held on to their occupational ties through continued affiliation with their manual trades, but they also created a new paternal identity as protectors of all members of their craft. In this newly defined role, they justified opposition to the complaints of journeymen.[9]

Historians exploring these organizations in northern cities discovered that masters-turned-businessmen often used mechanics' associations and institutes to proclaim middle-class status and to foster bourgeois economic ideas. For example, they promoted temperance and morality among employees to increase efficiency. These masters continued to identify themselves as mechanics and remained concerned with the status of their trades. Upwardly mobile masters had significant reasons for portraying themselves as enterprising craftsmen who enhanced the productivity of their trades. First, they sought to encourage harmony in their workshop or factory, as journeymen increasingly protested over withering opportunities for their own advancement to master status. Emphasizing a more harmonious common past and continuing to call themselves mechanics, masters quelled some debate and labor unrest by setting themselves apart from merchant capitalists.[10] But at the same time, such assertions of paternal responsibility undercut the masculinity of journeymen by underscoring their dependent status as wageworkers.

Evidence from organized masters in Petersburg, Virginia, demonstrates that southern mechanics similarly shifted to protect their newly defined paternal role and middle-class status. Situated on the Appomattox River, twenty-five miles south of Richmond, Petersburg seemed destined for industrial activity. Founded in 1748 from a collection of growing settlements, Petersburg was incorporated by the Virginia General Assembly in 1784.[11] Little thought was given to planning. By 1800 it consisted of only a few muddy streets paralleling the river. Still, the town gained a reputation as a regional center for the trade and transport of tobacco. On the great plantations in the vicinity, enslaved workers produced wheat, vegetables, and, especially, tobacco. These commodities found their way to market in Petersburg. At the turn of the nineteenth century, the town's numerous tobacco warehouses formed the center of its trade. Over the next few decades, Petersburg's economy expanded beyond its tobacco warehouses. While plantation agriculture dominated the hinterland, Petersburg underwent an industrial transformation. The exceptional waterpower of the Appomattox River brought industrial developments, and by 1835, Petersburg boasted six tobacco factories, three cotton factories, two cottonseed mills, an iron foundry, potteries, and a host of small mercantile and trade establishments.[12] The Virginia General Assembly chartered the Petersburg Railroad Company in 1830. As the earliest railroad link in the state, it served not only the local market but also the region, as it reached across Virginia into North Carolina, terminating at the Roanoke River in the town of Weldon. Before 1860 five railroad links crossed at Petersburg, allowing the rapid movement of goods and people in any direction desired. As the rail hub for central Virginia, Petersburg claimed connections with Weldon, Richmond, Norfolk, City Point, and Lynchburg.[13]

Petersburg's commerce and industry attracted artisans from the surrounding countryside, the North, and even Europe. In the burgeoning city, construction of a masculine identity based on fraternity and craft pride involved men from different trades and classes but never traversed the great divide of race. Petersburg's foundries, factories, and artisan shops drew many artisans from the immediate hinterland. A majority of the town's mechanics hailed from Dinwiddie, Chesterfield, and Prince George counties, all within a few miles of Petersburg. Among these were recently emancipated African Americans who traded plantation slavery for urban work and freedom. A significant number of mechanics, however, migrated to Petersburg from outside the region. Expanding northern workshops and the changing status of journeymen and apprentices led many northern mechanics to an increasingly mobile lifestyle. As they traveled in search of work, many skilled northern workers sought employment in southern cities. European immigrant mechanics also found opportunities in southern cities. In 1860, 4 percent of Petersburg's male workforce hailed from the North, and 11 percent were born in Europe. Just over 84 percent were born in the South, 30 percent of whom were African American men.[14]

Petersburg's white master artisans formed a fraternal society in 1825, creating a special identity for its members as white working men within a slave society. On 4 January, a group of Petersburg master mechanics gathered in Richard F. Hannon's tavern to found the Petersburg Benevolent Mechanic Association (PBMA). By the third meeting of the group, the association included twenty-five local artisans; within twenty-two months, membership rose to ninety-eight. The organization formally incorporated through an act of the General Assembly in February 1826. Charter members of the association represented a wide spectrum of craft occupations: tailors, blacksmiths, carpenters, cabinetmakers, tanners, printers, weavers, bakers, and coppersmiths. Prominent craftsmen in the association also included tobacconists, masons, coach makers, shoemakers, millers, surgeons, and machinists. All believed that organization was necessary to arrest a "too general neglect which prevails among persons exercising the various mechanic arts, especially as respects the young and inexperienced, apprenticed to those arts." The PBMA placed special emphasis on aiding unemployed mechanics and their families.[15]

While the PBMA excluded African American artisans, enslaved or free, it readily accepted most European immigrants who met the other requirements. The customary denial of membership to blacks allowed white mechanics to define their status in opposition to African Americans. Although free blacks might hold the same occupations as white mechanics, for example as carpenters or blacksmiths, they would never enjoy the benefits of white mechanics' associations. The association used exclusion as a tool to reinforce the subordinate position of black men in the South.[16] In the decades before the Civil War, membership swelled to include more than 350 masters, journeymen, and other independent producers who worked with their hands, representing approximately 10 percent of the free white males in the city.[17]

The Petersburg Benevolent Mechanic Association developed a "supportive male subculture" that touted the importance of white working men in southern society.[18] This organization of several hundred skilled workers and businessmen recognized the marginal status of wage labor in the South and sought to bolster their standing by laying claim to the benefits of fraternity.[19] Even though the group included many of the most successful businessmen in the city, association members never found common ground with the planters who dominated the South. Instead they constructed ties based on images of masculinity, craftsmanship, and racial superiority, creating a social order that they believed made all white southern men equal.[20]

At the time of the organization's establishment, its members formed the core of an emerging middle class of master mechanics, businessmen, and small merchants. Although never as wealthy as the planters in the surrounding hinterland or large commission merchants in Petersburg, master mechanics of the group gained moderate amounts of property and experienced considerable business success. Many members of the association were highly skilled craft entrepreneurs who managed to accumulate and display more wealth than Petersburg's plain mechanics.[21] Embracing the "cult of respectability" that pervaded in the early national and antebellum United States, they were also status conscious men. Members of the emerging middle class found it necessary to clearly define their status as respectable members of society through engagement in proper behavior, including the consumption and display of the stylish fashions in clothing and home decoration. Because many retained ties to a heritage in the manual arts, they maintained a vested interest in elevating the status of mechanics within the community. As individuals who straddled the social division between manual and nonmanual labor, association members wanted their organization to promote their own success and to elevate the status of artisans in the South. Although the association remained committed to providing benevolent aid to needy members, most found the fraternal benefits increasingly important. Through the association's constitution they proclaimed that "[m]echanics are all of one family; like brethren, they should live together in harmony, be governed by the same rules: then, like the members of a well-ordered household, they will advance upon the stage, and become 'useful in their day and generation.'"[22]

But members were not necessarily brethren to the middling mechanics who struggled in the changing economy. Widespread ownership of slaves among members set them apart from less successful masters, journeymen, and even their northern counterparts. A survey of tax records reveals that more than

90 percent of early association mechanics owned or leased slaves for domestic or industrial labor. In 1823, seventy-nine future members of the group paid tax on an average of four slaves each. Slave-holding decreased slightly over the next decades, but a majority of members continued to enjoy the benefits of bonded labor. In 1838, 82 percent of association members held slaves, averaging six slaves each. The following decade, slave-holding rates increased to 85 percent, but individual holdings dipped to just under five slaves per slave-holding member.[23]

Although many association mechanics succeeded in business, grew comfortably wealthy, and owned or controlled enslaved workers, they could not elevate themselves in league with planters. Although they regarded themselves as the paternal guardians of their trades, their place in southern society was somewhat precariously located between elite planters and white laborers, free blacks, and the enslaved. Rooted in the mechanic arts in a slave society where common belief considered manual work degrading to white men, members cultivated a respectable image for labor and the mechanic arts in order to build their own status. The association promoted the white workingman of the South, with the keynote speaker at the 1834 annual meeting declaring that "the time is not remote when the Southern artisan will vie for intelligence and wealth with any in the world."[24]

Because of their concern for respectability, the PBMA closely regulated the behavior of members to ensure that craftsmen lived up to the group's self-image. In 1827 the organization sanctioned member William Wright for immoral and disorderly conduct. In 1839 the PBMA expelled engineer Richard Page for "deporting himself in a manner unfit for membership."[25] The group sometimes forced bonds of fraternity on members who strayed from the ideal; for example, coach maker Jedediah T. Atkinson and blacksmith Peyton Lynch were each threatened with ten-dollar fines unless they settled a bond dispute out of court.[26]

The fraternal bond brought serious obligations for society members, especially the responsibility of showing appropriate respect for fellow mechanics. When charter member Sceva Thayer was murdered in 1826, members gathered in the Blandford Churchyard and pledged a reward of $250 for the apprehension of the guilty party. Following his funeral, they placed a sealed vial in his grave containing a certificate of respect for their brother blacksmith.[27] After an 1827 proposal made by baker John Paterson, all members considered attending the funeral of a deceased colleague a manly duty. Members marched from Mechanic's Hall to the churchyard in organized procession, each wearing a black armband. When Francis G. Yancey, the organization's first head, died in 1833, the seat of the president remained "clothed in mourning for twelve months."[28]

For the most part, members remained upwardly mobile masters who found in fraternity a validation of their place in antebellum society and a collective identity as southern men. For more middling artisans, fraternal groups became more than affirmation. Fraternal organization allowed Petersburg mechanics to uphold their manhood, counter declining economic status, and thwart competition from African American workers. As their grip on independence slipped in the late antebellum era, middling white artisans organized to protect their own status and to affirm their place in the *Herrenvolk* democracy of the South.

A growing division of labor characterized the industrial development of the antebellum South. Although some industries, notably iron manufacture and textiles, depended upon machinery from an early date, most industrial growth in the South came from a reorganization of labor in tobacco manufacturing and construction trades.[29] Artisans in some areas of the South avoided the class struggles prevalent among northern skilled workers. Most regions avoided rapid urbanization and industrialization and managed to produce a more egalitarian society of white men that rooted its equality in black slave labor.[30]

Although class conflict was not a defining feature of all southern workers, this portrait does not hold true for the entire region. The situation in the upper South was more complicated, because some urban areas, including Petersburg, did experience significant population growth and a rapid increase in the city's industrial composition. As a result, class tensions divided the artisan community. Studies of Richmond demonstrate the rapid urban growth and changing configuration of the workforce that characterized the upper South's most industrial region. A major influx of immigrants and northern workers as well as an expansion of slavery in the 1850s fostered urbanization and industrial growth. For Richmond this meant flour mills, tobacco factories, and ironworks. The division of labor that evolved in the new economy meant that some occupations, such as watchmaking and silversmithing, declined as competition from northern and imported goods overwhelmed the local market. Yet at the same time, a growing need for workers in trades related to industry, such as blacksmiths and carpenters, led to increased opportunities.[31]

Like Richmond, Petersburg experienced meaningful urban and industrial development between 1820 and the Civil War. In Petersburg industrialization brought tobacco factories, textile mills, and iron foundries. The precipitate growth of the city and the concomitant changing nature of opportunities available led to new experiences for residents willing to adapt and pursue industrial work. It also created challenges as men struggled to adjust to new class structures and to redefine their masculinity. Some failed under the new system and fell into the ranks of the town's general laboring class. A significant number, more motivated or perhaps less rooted, moved on to try their luck elsewhere. But an equally important number adapted their preindustrial work cultures to the new realities of an expanding market economy, hoping to prosper as a new breed of master mechanics and entrepreneurs. These artisans fell somewhere between the rising middle class of tobacconists, master mechanics, and commission merchants in Petersburg and the manual laborers who filled a host of occupations on the lower social stratum.[32]

Most middling artisans never reached the ranks of the commercial bourgeoisie, but the changes brought by the market revolution and new relations between workers and employers in the nineteenth century created a more fluid society, leading many to believe that advancement was possible. Simultaneously, the very definition of class changed. By 1830 to be middle class meant to be without a traditionally defined social status.[33] Of course, slave ownership continued to mark middle-class status for mechanics and shopkeepers, but upwardly mobile master mechanics sometimes held dual careers, continuing some form of manual labor while building a merchant firm or business so that they could increase their slave-holdings. By 1850 more than twenty thousand southern slaveholders worked as skilled mechanics.[34]

Among the first generation born after the Revolution, the wealthy continued to monopolize societal influence and political power. In the early national era, however, democratization challenged traditional hierarchies, created new national and regional values, and increased popular participation in politics.[35] The nation celebrated the ideal of the "self-made man," even though most who experienced upward mobility enjoyed connections to the elite class.[36] Historians have long argued over the roots of the new antebellum middle class. Some suggest that the middle class that emerged in that era sprang from ideology rather than from actual physical relations of production. Other scholars argue that shopkeepers, small merchants, and manufacturers created and promoted new middle-class values to others in the community who sought self-improvement or advancement. Through evangelicalism, fraternal lodges, temperance organizations, libraries, and lectures, they imposed new standards of work discipline and personal behavior on themselves and their employees.[37]

Members of the mechanics' association closely resembled the emerging middle class depicted by these scholars. Investments in expanding shops into merchant and contracting firms led to economic and social distancing from the ranks of middling artisans. Most who joined the elite mechanics' group were not self-made men, but were instead members of a local elite whose political, personal, and business ties aided their success. Members routinely served as justices on the Petersburg Hustings Court, sat on grand juries, held local political offices and positions as militia officers, and populated the boards of educational institutions and poor relief agencies. Similar to such modern-day business organizations as the Rotary and Kiwanis, the mechanics' association promoted the mutual success of members while it celebrated and affirmed the importance of their roots in manual labor.

Many artisans who were not members of the group also aspired to improve their status. Often lacking personal connections that might boost chances for success, a number of Petersburg mechanics struggled to pull themselves out of the ranks of wage labor and to create their own identity through fraternal organization when conventional avenues, including politics, excluded them.

Although mechanics in northern states became politically active in the early Republic, Virginia mechanics did not. The freehold requirement denied the vote to those without property and kept many middling Virginia artisans out of the formal political circle until the adoption of universal male suffrage in the constitutional revision of 1851. According to Virginia law, voters were required to own twenty-five acres of land or a town lot with a dwelling. Those who boarded or who leased property could not vote.[38] In New York and other northern cities, artisans formed alliances tied to political parties. Politically expressing their interests as mechanics gave men an identity as citizens. Artisan votes often proved crucial in mayoral and other local elections. In a similar vein, the formation of the all-important General Trades' Union in Philadelphia demonstrated the vitality of politics and organization in protecting the mechanics' place in an industrializing society.[39] In northern cities, major political parties and local party organizations paid attention to the mechanic voting block because, as a numerically significant segment of the population, the mechanic vote could sway an election.

In the South, where politics remained locally based and tied to an agricultural economy, the parties typically slighted the political interests of mechanics. Politics seldom formed an avenue for protecting workers' interests and identity. Even southern states that granted white manhood suffrage from an early date precluded artisans from mustering the types of political influence their northern counterparts expressed. For example, a political division between masters and journeymen developed with the second-party system as it evolved in Georgia in the 1830s. The Whigs became the party of upwardly mobile master mechanics, while the journeymen, facing a bleak economic future, found little representation in state or local politics. The opposing Democratic Party concerned itself with agrarian and anticommerce issues and ignored the journeymen's political agenda. Although Georgia journeymen could vote in favor of legislation giving preference to white labor over slave, fear kept them from exercising that right. As opportunities for independence withered, mechanics worried that complaining might lead masters to hire slave instead of free labor.[40]

In Virginia the political situation of middling mechanics was even more dismal. Local and state politics were not strong components of mechanics' masculine identity in the antebellum era. Until 1851 white men without substantial holdings in real property remained disfranchised. Most political power was concentrated in the local courts, which became self-perpetuating bodies controlled by local elites.[41] The courts held the power of appointment for most local offices, ensuring that personal connections represented the most important qualification for officeholding.[42] Petersburg and other Virginia cities found local power vested in the Hustings Court, which met monthly to perform the tasks of city government and to deal with legal matters such as will probates, arrest hearings, small civil suits, and all criminal cases involving slaves or free blacks. Although most Virginia cities, including Petersburg, were Whig strongholds, party affiliation seldom mattered in local affairs. The master mechanics and city lawyers frequently held local office and benefited from the patronage of the Hustings Court, but few of the middling mechanics of Petersburg ever found their way into positions of power. More significantly, because many middling mechanics had no political voice and no influence on the perpetuation of the local court system, city officials seldom considered the interests of the laboring classes of Petersburg.[43]

Despite their lack of political influence in formal party structures, middling men did combine to make political statements on several occasions. As their position in society became more precarious, middling Petersburg mechanics formed a new fraternal organization to protect their interests and identity as white southern workingmen. The Petersburg Mechanic Association (PMA) was organized in the wake of economic distress that mechanics experienced after the Panic of 1857 and served as an organ for their concerns.

Advertised as a gathering to protect the interests of white labor against competition from free blacks, the first meeting of mechanics attracted so many people (as many as five hundred men, according to one account) that it adjourned and reconvened in the downtown Center Market House.[44] At subsequent meetings, the organization outlined its purpose and goals through the construction of a constitutional preamble and series of resolutions, including a statement of purpose as "elevating our mental and protecting our social condition." Although the fraternal order wanted to found a mechanics' library and lyceum, protecting their position within southern society topped their agenda.[45] Artisan workers began meeting in the late summer to create an order that would reinforce their position as white men in direct opposition to African American workers. They strenuously objected to free blacks or slaves in skilled positions or in any competition with free white labor. White Petersburg artisans used slavery and race as a standard against which to measure their fears and to assert their status as southern men.[46] Although members of the group held little hope or desire to challenge the powerful slave owners who controlled the politics and economy of the city, free blacks (nearly 18 percent of the city's population) became fair targets for white worker animosity.

Although free blacks found that racial prejudice and legal restrictions limited their ability to prosper in skilled and semiskilled occupations, the opportunities available to them in Petersburg proved to be more lucrative and less restrictive than those of skilled blacks in northern cities. African Americans made up more than half of the city's free workers. Their labors in tobacco factories, on infrastructure projects, and in skilled and semiskilled artisan occupations made important contributions to the industrial development of the town. Free blacks were most welcomed in unskilled occupations, where they consistently accounted for the majority of the city's male laborers. In 1850 free blacks constituted 70 percent of unskilled male workers; the figure dipped to 64 percent in 1860. Free blacks also made significant advances in artisan occupations, constituting 13 percent of skilled artisans by 1850. Despite an influx of immigrant and northern workers in the 1850s, the number of skilled blacks held steady through the late antebellum era.[47] Relations between black and white men in Petersburg were also generally more cordial than in northern cities. There is little evidence of racial strife and discord among workers—except in times of economic distress.

Skilled blacks in northern cities rarely worked at their chosen trades and often faced physical violence and legal proscriptions. New York City blacks found only marginal employment and legal exclusion from certain trades. Less than a third of Philadelphia's black artisans gained employment in their trades. The Mechanical Association of Cincinnati censured its president in 1830 for accepting a black apprentice.[48] By contrast, skilled blacks faced less exclusion in southern cities. Sixty percent of black artisans found employment at their trade in New Orleans and Charleston; in Baltimore nearly 20 percent of black men worked in artisan occupations. The location of black artisans in southern cities also offered more opportunities for apprenticeships, thus perpetuating the role of blacks as skilled tradesmen.[49] In Petersburg, only when financial downturns affected the economy, and especially when panic swept the country in 1857, did skilled black workers become the scapegoats of white labor. During these economic crises, whites launched campaigns to rid the city of free black artisans. But white complaints exerted little effect on the position of free black workers who formed the backbone of the unskilled workforce and were making headway into the skilled sector.

African Americans could be found in all but the most elite of artisan occupations, and quite a few black men owned successful businesses and substantial amounts of property. Mixed workshops were common: whites, free blacks, and enslaved artisans often labored in the same workplace. Yet the position of free blacks in Petersburg society, as in the rest of the South, remained precarious. Straddling the line between slavery and freedom, Petersburg's free blacks filled an important niche in the economy, but many residents remained suspicious of them. For example, the editor of the Petersburg *Daily Express* commented that "[w]ith nothing to do, and some too mean and lazy to work when they can get it honestly, this character of negroes spend their time in endless disputes, wrangles, drunken brawls, and gambling." [50] Of course most free black men were employed in honest labor, often at a wage that undercut the livelihood of white workers.

The white organizers and members of the Petersburg Mechanic Association sought to advance themselves by denigrating these free black artisans. The new fraternal organization created a racial identity that aligned members with local planters and industrialists. Although increasingly marginalized by the developing industrial economy of antebellum Petersburg, their whiteness afforded members a special wage not available to African Americans. In August 1857 organizers outlined their concerns that "a large portion of the mechanical branches of business is monopolized by a class of persons, wholly irresponsible as citizens, known as free negroes, much to the detriment of poor tradesmen of this city." They demanded justice for "families of the poor, but industrious white mechanics" and that "this serious wrong should be righted as promptly as the peculiar circumstances of the case will admit of." [51]

The PMA artisans argued that local residents should give whites preference over African Americans because of the special responsibilities white men faced as citizens. They insisted that free blacks, with no rights or responsibilities as citizens, were largely unreliable and lacked any role in sustaining the laws of the state or perpetuating community life. The association's resolutions also pointed to mechanics' special responsibilities as "men, parents and heads of growing families," claiming that their labor was as valuable to society as "any other profession of men." Spokesmen sought to align the group with white slave-holding society, claiming themselves to be "true southern gentlemen" and saying, "[W]e do not aim to conflict with the interests of slave owners, but to elevate ourselves as a class from the degrading position which competition with those who are not citizens of the commonwealth entails upon us." [52] The mechanics thus defined a southern racial and masculine identity through their new organization. They capitalized on the conception of racial inferiority outlined in planters' justifications of slavery and claimed the benefits of whiteness that southern society offered. As southern men they believed that financial prosperity, slavery, and black inferiority were intertwined. Racist assumptions permeated their culture; because most white mechanics hoped to join the ranks of slaveholders, black equality could not be permitted.[53]

Daily newspapers gave the mechanics' movement continuing coverage, printing notices of meetings, reports of activities, and resulting resolutions. The *Daily Southside Democrat* supported the mechanics' efforts to protect their economic and communal position. Editor A. D. Banks sympathized with their desires to dignify manual labor and subvert African American competition in the workplace. Banks pledged that his newspaper would "contribute actively in any legitimate way . . . to effect the desired end" and declared, "The Mechanic interest in the South is the bone and sinew of our population—one of the most powerful props of our institutions—a chief constituent of that noble and hardy yeomanry on which in the time of trial the South must mainly depend for the support and maintenance of her honor and rights."[54]

Exclusively white fraternal organizations became one more bastion of prejudice in a world where nonwhites found themselves regarded as secondary citizens or worse. Even the most successful black businessmen found living and working in Petersburg frustrating. Despite the important economic role blacks filled, southern whites were generally suspicious of the growing free population. Common white belief held that free blacks provided poor examples for enslaved workers; they could potentially ignite slave insurrections and generally threatened white rule. Upholding their manhood in a culture of institutional racism was difficult. Laws compelled Petersburg free black men to register with local authorities. They could be jailed if they failed to produce documentation of their free status. Local and state laws grouped them with the enslaved, prohibited them from educating their children, even out of state, and prosecuted them in local courts without benefit of jury trial. Local ordinances prohibited free blacks from smoking in public, and for them to keep dogs required special written permission from the mayor. Those who violated the dog ordinance faced twenty lashes as punishment.[55]

The subordinate nature of free blacks in Petersburg society and the open racism of whites gave rise to the formation of a fraternal society in the city's African American community.[56] Fraternal and mutual aid societies provided urban blacks with benefits similar to those offered by white organizations.[57] In approximately 1815 a group of economically successful black men formed the Beneficial Society of Free Men of Color of the City of Petersburg and State of Virginia. Lasting until the Civil War, this organization recognized the precarious position of free black men in the South, aimed to promote temperance and moral behavior, and offered financial relief to its members.[58] The Beneficial Society protected the interests of African Americans just as Petersburg's white fraternal organizations, including the Petersburg Benevolent Mechanic Association and the Petersburg Mechanic Association, protected their members.

Members of the Beneficial Society insisted that their prosperity rested with the "infusion of virtuous qualities" and strove for "the suppression of vice and immorality among [its] own class of people, and for the inculcation of every honest and correct principle that can render many good, respectable and happy." They hoped for alleviation of racial prejudice, that "consummate ignorance that has too long pervaded the lives of many of us," and "concluded to associate together for the ostensible purpose of administering support to each other, when in sickness or necessity."[59] If the white mechanics of the Petersburg Mechanic Association defined their masculinity in opposition to black workers, the Beneficial Society represented the black men's response to the southern society that denied them citizenship and judged them by skin color. Through fraternal association, they hoped to insulate themselves against white prejudice and attacks on their manhood.

Still, the Beneficial Society became as much an organization of elite free blacks as the Petersburg Benevolent Mechanic Association was of prominent white businessmen. As an organization of elite businessmen, the Beneficial Society reflected divisions within the black community. To be considered for membership, one had to be nominated by a current member and receive the support of two-thirds of the membership. The mandatory ten-dollar initiation fee and twenty-five cents in monthly dues effectively excluded enslaved and poor black workers. While white fraternal groups endeavored to unite men across class lines, substituting race and gender as appropriate categories of exclusion, the Beneficial Society divided African Americans according to class, excluding enslaved men.[60] Membership offered elite blacks—prominent artisans and contractors such as Henry Mason, Christopher Stevens, and Shadrack Brander and successful barbers such as Henry Elebeck and John K. Shore—the opportunity to associate with other artisans and businessmen, to form bonds that could help to advance business opportunities, and to provide moral support for black men who daily faced the racial prejudice of the dominant white community.

The benefits of membership transcended camaraderie, however. Each member was entitled to a square in the society's cemetery. The Beneficial Society made an initial purchase of land for a burial ground in 1818 and bought additional property for the same purpose in 1840.[61] The burial benefit extended to members' parents (if free), unmarried children, and brothers under age twenty-one. If a member fell ill or became disabled, he was entitled to at least $1.50 per week, providing that the society's treasury held at least $50. When a member died, his family received a one-time payment of $15, and his widow received $1 per week for as long as she remained "a prudent widow."[62]

Beneficial Society members organized "by pure and honest motives" and emphasized the importance of love for one another. In their fraternity, these men found a vehicle to edify the successful black businessman, and a safety net to protect themselves and their families from some of the brutalities of southern society. In close parallel with members of the white Petersburg Benevolent Mechanic Association, Beneficial Society members were conscious of their status and sought to protect and enhance their condition within Petersburg. But unlike the white group, the Beneficial Society became concerned with fighting racial prejudice. Distressed with the effects of the "consummate ignorance," members hoped to "surmount every impediment that may arise" and to show that they possessed "that love and fellow-feeling for each other, which nature has made the duty of every heart that is not callous to humanity." [63] They banded together and created an organization that promoted their businesses and celebrated their brotherhood. They also united to foster an image of black masculine respectability that flew in the face of racial prejudice.

Regulation of members' behavior provided an avenue to counter whites' stereotypes of free black men as idle, shiftless, and lazy. Fines were levied for drunkenness, swearing, and smoking at meetings. The society expelled members convicted of felonies, those known to participate in gambling or cockfighting, and those engaged in otherwise disgraceful behavior. Society members also felt obligated to their brethren. If one fell ill, two members were designated to sit at his bedside each night. As was the practice among members of the Petersburg Benevolent Mechanic Association, Beneficial Society members were expected to attend the funerals of deceased members to show collective respect. For the Beneficial Society, the funeral of a fellow member was an important ritual that symbolized the relations that bound them as "brothers." Failure to perform these solemn duties resulted in fines. [64]

Organized in the early antebellum era, the Beneficial Society exemplified how elite black men reacted to their exclusion from full participation in southern society through the formation of their own institutional alternatives. [65] The society had much in common with other black benevolent groups in the South, but in creating a masculine identity for members, the group created class division within the black community. To attain the desired respectability, to define a masculine identity, and to counter racial prejudice, these black men practiced their own form of discrimination, excluding black laborers and slaves from membership.

The white fraternal associations of working men in antebellum Petersburg similarly used the principle of exclusion to define a masculine identity within southern society. White men employed gender and race as organizing tools to create mechanics' associations that advanced white workingmen at the expense of African Americans. Although industrialization threatened to create a class divide, master mechanics and journeymen, as white men in southern society, always united on issues of race. White mechanics rooted their identity as men and free workers in contrast to enslaved and skilled free blacks. They claimed the special wage southern society granted them as white men, fathers, and citizens.

## NOTES

1. For studies of other southern artisans see Michele Gillespie, *Free Labor in an Unfree World: White Artisans in Slaveholding Georgia, 1789–1860* (Athens: University of Georgia Press, 2000); Johanna Miller Lewis, *Artisans in the North Carolina Backcountry* (Lexington: University Press of Kentucky, 1995); Steven Elliott Tripp, *Yankee Town, Southern City: Race and Class Relations in Civil War Lynchburg* (New York: New York University Press, 1997); and L. Diane Barnes, "Hammer and Hand in the Old South: Artisan Workers in Petersburg, Virginia, 1820–1860" (Ph.D. diss., West Virginia University, 2000).

2. Mary Ann Clawson, *Constructing Brotherhood: Class, Gender, and Fraternalism* (Princeton: Princeton University Press, 1989), 11–15.

3. Fraternal organizations were popular in antebellum Petersburg. In 1857 there were two lodges of both Freemasons and Odd Fellows, a chapter of the Sons of Temperance, a lodge of the Independent Order of Red Men, as well as the ethnic St. Andrew's Society and St. Patrick's Society; "The Benevolent Societies of Petersburg," *Daily Express* (Petersburg, Va.), 18 September 1857.

4. L. Diane Barnes, "Southern Artisans, Organization, and the Rise of a Market Economy in Antebellum Petersburg," *Virginia Magazine of History and Biography* 107 (1999): 166.

5. Board of officers minutes, 12 October 1827, Petersburg Benevolent Mechanic Association, Petersburg, Va., Records 1825–1836, Virginia Historical Society, Richmond (hereafter PBMA Records, ViHi).

6. Bruce Laurie, *Artisans into Workers: Labor in Nineteenth-Century America* (New York: Noonday Press, 1989), 98; Charles S. Olton, *Artisans for Independence: Philadelphia Mechanics and the American Revolution* (Syracuse: Syracuse University Press, 1975), 99–105; Gillespie, *Free Labor,* 39–40, 51–54.

7. *The Constitution of the Charleston Mechanic Society, Instituted at Charleston, South-Carolina, 1794* (Charleston: James and Williams, Printers, 1858), 17. The debate over the capitalistic nature of slavery and slaveholding is treated by James Oakes, *The Ruling Race: A History of American Slaveholders* (New York: Knopf, 1982); Eugene D. Genovese, *Roll, Jordan, Roll: The World the Slaves Made* (1972; reprint, New York: Vintage, 1976).

8. Sean Wilentz, *Chants Democratic: New York City and the Rise of the American Working Class, 1788–1850* (New York: Oxford University Press, 1984), 56–57.

9. Howard B. Rock, "'All Her Sons Join as One Social Band': New York City's Artisanal Societies in the Early Republic," in *American Artisans: Crafting Social Identity,*

*1750–1850*, ed. Howard B. Rock, Paul A. Gilje, and Robert Asher (Baltimore: Johns Hopkins University Press, 1995), 174–75.

10. Stuart M. Blumin, *The Emergence of the Middle Class: Social Experience in the American City, 1760–1900* (New York: Cambridge University Press, 1989), 134–36; Gary J. Kornblith, "From Artisans to Businessmen: Master Mechanics in New England, 1789–1850" (Ph.D. diss., Princeton University, 1983), 219, 224–25, 497–501; John S. Gilkeson Jr., *Middle-Class Providence, 1820–1940* (Princeton: Princeton University Press, 1986), 14–17, 95.

11. James G. Scott and Edward A. Wyatt, *Petersburg's Story: A History* (Petersburg: Titmus Optical Company, 1960), 3; Barnes, "Southern Artisans," 162.

12. "Water Power," *Niles' Weekly Register*, 23 June 1827, vol. 32, p. 275; Edward A. Wyatt, "Rise of Industry in Ante-Bellum Petersburg," *William and Mary Quarterly*, 2d ser., 17 (1937): 2–3.

13. Virginia, *Acts of the General Assembly* (Richmond: Thomas Ritchie, 1830), 58–60; Wyatt, "Rise of Industry," 5; Scott and Wyatt, *Petersburg's Story*, 94–97; Suzanne Lebsock, *The Free Women of Petersburg: Status and Culture in a Southern Town. 1784–1860* (New York: Norton, 1984); Peter C. Stewart, "Railroads and Urban Rivalries in Antebellum Eastern Virginia," *Virginia Magazine of History and Biography* 81 (1973): 5.

14. Gillespie, *Free Labor*, 167–68; Ira Berlin and Herbert G. Gutman, "Natives and Immigrants, Free Men and Slaves: Urban Workingmen in the Antebellum American South," *American Historical Review* 88 (1983): 1181; Bureau of the Census, Population Schedules, Petersburg, Va., 1860.

15. Minutes, 4 January, 15 January 1825, Petersburg Benevolent Mechanic Association Papers, 1825–1921, University of Virginia Library, Charlottesville, microfilm (hereafter PBMA Papers, ViU); Membership List, PBMA Records, ViHi; "An act incorporating the Petersburg Benevolent Mechanic Association," *Acts of the General Assembly* (1826), 80–82; Barnes, "Southern Artisans," 166–68.

16. PBMA constitution, Article II, 1826, 63, PBMA Records, ViHi. The organization maintained its ban on African American members during the entire ninety-four years of its existence. When the association was dissolved in 1919, the contents of the association's library were given to the Petersburg School Board, with explicit instructions that the materials were "for the use of white people only"; Minutes, 12 June 1919, PBMA Papers, ViU; *Charter, Constitution and By-Laws of the Petersburg Benevolent Mechanic Association . . . . Revised October, 1900* (Petersburg, Va.: Fenn and Owen, 1900), 9.

17. This figure is approximated from the 3,177 white males enumerated in the city of Petersburg in the 1850 census. The data are not broken down by age groups for urban areas in the antebellum census aggregates; see Bureau of the Census, *The Seventh Census of the United States, 1850* (Washington, D.C.: Robert Armstrong, 1853), 258; Barnes, "Southern Artisans," 168.

18. For a similar discussion of lawyers and male subcultures, see Anya Jabour, "Male Friendship and Masculinity in the Early National South: William Wirt and His

Friends," *Journal of the Early Republic* 20 (2000): 85–86. For detailed studies of southern masculinity, see Bertram Wyatt-Brown, *Southern Honor: Ethics and Behavior in the Old South* (New York: Oxford University Press, 1982); Joan E. Cashin, *A Family Venture: Men and Women on the Southern Frontier* (New York: Oxford University Press, 1991); Steven M. Stowe, *Intimacy and Power in the Old South: Ritual in the Lives of the Planters* (Baltimore: Johns Hopkins University Press, 1987).

19. Michele K. Gillespie, "Planters in the Making: Artisanal Opportunity in Georgia, 1790–1830," in Rock, Gilje, and Asher, *American Artisans*, 33–34.

20. Clawson, *Constructing Brotherhood*, 15, 131–32.

21. Wilentz, *Chants Democratic*, 36–37.

22. Blumin, *Emergence of the Middle Class*, 126–27; Preamble to the PBMA constitution, n.d., PBMA Papers, ViU.

23. Petersburg, Va., Personal Property Tax Ledgers, 1823, 1838, 1847, Library of Virginia, Richmond. Tax rolls do not offer definitive proof of slave ownership, because household heads were taxed at the same rate for slaves leased as for those owned.

24. Minutes, 13 January 1834, PBMA Papers, ViU.

25. Minutes, 9 July 1827, 8 April 1839, PBMA Papers, ViU.

26. Board of officers minutes, 30 March 1830, PBMA Records, ViHi.

27. Minutes, 1 December, 2 December 1826, PBMA Papers, ViU.

28. Minutes, 9 April 1827, 14 October 1833, PBMA Papers, ViU.

29. For important studies of mechanized industry in the antebellum South, see Charles B. Dew, *Ironmaker to the Confederacy: Joseph R. Anderson and the Tredegar Iron Works* (New Haven: Yale University Press, 1966); Tom Downey, "Riparian Rights and Manufacturing in Antebellum South Carolina: William Gregg and the Origins of the 'Industrial Mind,'" *Journal of Southern History* 65 (1999): 77–108.

30. For a case study in Georgia, see Gillespie, *Free Labor*, xviii–xix.

31. For studies of Richmond, see Werner H. Steger, "'United to Support, But Not Combined to Injure': Free Workers and Immigrants in Richmond, Virginia, during the Era of Sectionalism, 1847–1865," (Ph.D. diss., George Washington University, 1999); Gregg D. Kimball, *American City, Southern Place: A Cultural History of Antebellum Richmond* (Athens: University of Georgia Press, 2000); Midori Takagi, *Rearing Wolves to Our Own Destruction: Slavery in Richmond, Virginia, 1782–1865* (Charlottesville: University Press of Virginia, 1999).

32. Bruce Laurie, "'Spavined Ministers, Lying Toothpullers, and Buggering Priests': Third-Partyism and the Search for Security in the Antebellum North," in Rock, Gilje, and Asher, *American Artisans*, 99.

33. Karen Halttunen, *Confidence Men and Painted Women: A Study of Middle-Class Culture in America, 1830–1870* (New Haven: Yale University Press, 1982), 29.

34. Oakes, *The Ruling Race*, 57–59.

35. Joyce Appleby, *Inheriting the Revolution: The First Generation of Americans* (Cambridge: Harvard University Press, 2000), 52–55.

36. Paul E. Johnson, *A Shopkeeper's Millennium: Society and Revivals in Rochester, New York, 1815–1837* (New York: Hill and Wang, 1978), 28–32; Judith A. McGaw, *Most*

*Wonderful Machine: Mechanization and Social Change in Berkshire Paper Making, 1801–1885* (Princeton: Princeton University Press, 1987), 130–33.

37. Charles Sellers, *The Market Revolution: Jacksonian America, 1815–1846* (New York: Oxford University Press, 1991), 237; McGaw, *Most Wonderful Machine*, 265–66; Patricia C. Click, *The Spirit of the Times: Amusements in Nineteenth-Century Baltimore, Norfolk, and Richmond* (Charlottesville: University Press of Virginia, 1989), 16–18; Johnson, *Shopkeeper's Millennium*, 138.

38. Joseph Tate, *A Digest of the Laws of Virginia* (Richmond: Shepherd and Pollard, 1823), 183–84; Charles S. Sydnor, *Gentlemen Freeholders: Political Practices in Washington's Virginia* (Chapel Hill: University of North Carolina Press, 1952), 29–31.

39. Wilentz, *Chants Democratic*, 63–64, 71–72; Bruce Laurie, *Working People of Philadelphia, 1800–1850* (Philadelphia: Temple University Press, 1980), 85–104.

40. Gillespie, *Free Labor*, 141–42.

41. William G. Shade, *Democratizing the Old Dominion: Virginia and the Second Party System, 1824–1861* (Charlottesville: University Press of Virginia, 1996), 50; Richard P. McCormick, *The Second American Party System: Party Formation in the Jacksonian Era* (Chapel Hill: University of North Carolina Press, 1966), 179–80.

42. Charles S. Sydnor, *The Development of Southern Sectionalism, 1819–1848* (1948; reprint, Baton Rouge: Louisiana State University Press, 1968), 39–42.

43. Shade, *Democratizing the Old Dominion*, 50; Sydnor, *Gentleman Freeholders*, 113–14.

44. "South Ward Mechanics," *Daily Southside Democrat* (Petersburg, Va.), 27 July 1857; "Mechanics Meeting," *Daily Express*, 27 July 1857.

45. "Local Matters," *Daily Express*, 18 August 1857.

46. David R. Roediger, *The Wages of Whiteness: Race and the Making of the American Working Class* (London: Verso, 1991), 66; "Mechanics Meeting," *Daily Express*, 25 July 1857.

47. Bureau of the Census, Population Schedules, Petersburg, Va., 1850, 1860, microfilm.

48. Wilentz, *Chants Democratic*, 48n; Howard B. Rock, *Artisans of the New Republic: The Tradesmen of New York City in the Age of Jefferson* (New York: New York University Press, 1979), 224–25; Ronald Takaki, *Iron Cages: Race and Culture in Nineteenth-Century America* (1979; rev. ed., New York: Oxford University Press, 2000), 110–13.

49. Leonard P. Curry, *The Free Black in Urban America 1800–1850* (Chicago: University of Chicago Press, 1981), 35, 260.

50. "Free Negroes," *Daily Express*, 11 September 1857.

51. "Local Matters," *Daily Express*, 18 August 1857.

52. "The Mechanics' Meeting of Saturday Night," *Daily Southside Democrat*, 18 August 1857.

53. John McCardell, *The Idea of a Southern Nation: Southern Nationalists and Southern Nationalism, 1830–1860* (New York: Norton, 1979), 75–76; Oakes, *The Ruling Race*, 130–32.

54. "The Mechanics' Meeting Saturday Night," *Daily Southside Democrat*, 19 August 1857.

55. Ira Berlin, *Slaves without Masters: The Free Negro in the Antebellum South* (New York:

Vintage, 1974), 185–86, 327–33; "Ordinance Concerning Dogs," *Daily Express*, 15 July 1857.

56. For discussions of African American benevolent and fraternal organizations, see Berlin, *Slaves without Masters*, 308–13; Christopher Phillips, *Freedom's Port: The African American Community of Baltimore, 1790–1860* (Urbana: University of Illinois Press, 1997), 170–75.

57. With its large free black population, for example, Baltimore counted a significant number of benevolent groups. Some black-sponsored mutual aid societies guaranteed fee-paying members support during times of illness and death. Others including mental improvement societies, lyceums, and bible study groups aimed to promote the intellectual, cultural, and moral development of black Baltimoreans. The Prince Hall Masons, a black Masonic organization begun in the Revolutionary era, and a black chapter of the Odd Fellows were also prominent in antebellum Baltimore. Phillips, *Freedom's Port*, 170–75; Clawson, *Constructing Brotherhood*, 132–33.

58. Luther Porter Jackson, *Free Negro Labor and Property Holding in Virginia, 1830–1860* (New York: D. Appleton-Century, 1942), 162–63; Constitution, Rules and Regulations of the Beneficial Society of Free Men of Color, Petersburg, Va. (as revised 2 August 1852), Colson/Hill Papers, Virginia State University, Petersburg (hereafter ViSU).

59. Constitution, Beneficial Society, Colson/Hill Papers, ViSU.

60. Ibid.; Berlin, *Slaves Without Masters*, 312–13.

61. Jackson, *Free Negro Labor*, 162–63.

62. Constitution, Beneficial Society, Colson/Hill Papers, ViSU.

63. Ibid.

64. Ibid.

65. Phillips, *Freedom's Port*, 170–73; Joe William Trotter Jr., *Coal, Class, and Color: Blacks in Southern West Virginia, 1915–32* (Urbana: University of Illinois Press, 1990), 209–12.

# Belles, Benefactors, and the Blacksmith's Son: Cyrus Stuart and the Enigma of Southern Gentlemanliness

## Craig Thompson Friend

In early March 1828 Cyrus Stuart reflected upon the southern belles who lived in and around his hometown of Pendleton, South Carolina: "I find that they are best pleased when they think their acquirements and experience superior to those with whom they may converse. And as I have some appetition to ingratiate myself in the favours of the ladies, I must affect to be more ignorant than what I realy am." It was a predictable reply of a young southern man who was trying to meet the expectations of gentlemanliness as defined in *Lord Chesterfield's Advice to His Son on Men and Manners,* a popular guide to genteel masculinity in the early American Republic. "You must look into people as well as at them," Chesterfield had written. "Search, therefore with the greatest care, into the characters of all those whom you converse with: endeavour to discover their predominant passion, their prevailing weaknesses, their vanities, their follies, and their humours." Stuart aspired to join the ranks of southern gentlemen, but his decision to feign ignorance in order to allure southern belles (and therefore to enter the ranks of the South's elite) would undermine his efforts in the end. The story is in his diary, initiated a month earlier on his twentieth birthday, when he cracked the spine of a journal. He would never fill all its pages. Yet, while brief, the diary reveals much about southern masculinities from the perspective of one who desired upward mobility, coveted the status of gentleman, and thought that marriage into planter society would facilitate both.[1]

Some may argue that the journal of one young South Carolinian, however interesting, cannot bear the interpretive weight. Of course historians have turned regularly to the diaries and personal testimonies of specific individuals for broader cultural commentary. While such materials often fill volumes, smaller evidentiary foundations (particularly letters) have been employed as well to draw broad conclusions about early Americans. The challenge in unveiling Stuart's construction of his masculinity lies not in the brevity of his diary but in his own obscurity. Unlike what we know about southern men like William Byrd, William Wirt, and James Henry Hammond, nearly everything we can discern about Stuart's life derives from his own hand. Additionally, intimate records of the thoughts and experiences of less genteel southerners are rare, especially those of young men eager to meet the standards established by plantation society but falling woefully short.[2]

This essay is not meant to be a study of an entire culture. It is, instead, a story of how one young man struggled to rise through the genteel stratifications of the early-nineteenth-century South and how that quest affected his construction and eventual reconstruction of masculinity. In some regards, this study responds to historian Kenneth A. Lockridge's suggestions about the evolution of genteel masculinity in the South. Lockridge once concluded that in the colonial generation of would-be southern gentlemen who were "most vulnerable to failure. . . . we should see the highest degree of frustration, and of misogynistic rage."[3] By the 1820s physical distance no longer posed the serious obstacle to "peripheral would-be gentlemen" of the South as it had to colonial men who sought entry into the genteel ranks of the British empire. Increasingly it was the establishment of higher standards of behavior and background by the planter class that separated certain young southern men from the opportunity of gentlemanliness. Hobbled by the disadvantages of youth and class, Stuart was particularly situated to fail in this regard. While his diary entries repeatedly relate frustration, however, he did not direct his anger at women, as Lockridge found among aspiring colonial southern gentlemen. Rather, Stuart complained about and denounced wealth, which he interpreted as the foundation of the ideal patriarchal model.

Even as he criticized planter pretensions and advantages, he desired to join planter society. Yet he could not: he was the son of a blacksmith who lost his family early in life; he lacked the background and demonstrated little of the behavior expected of would-be patriarchs; he faced and usually failed tests of courtship, education, and self-esteem created by planter society to distinguish men of moral worth from those of less deserving character. The status of gentleman eluded him, and he never wielded political, social, or economic power. Still he continued to aspire to a gentlemanly status that was available only within the planter class. He consciously elected not to identify with either the southern yeomanry or a class of professional townspeople, always hoping that his education and his ability to move within planter social circles would make him deserving. Cyrus Stuart was a young man with dreams that would go unfulfilled.[4]

On a chilly day in early February, seated by the window in his room at Sarah Lorton's boarding house, Cyrus Stuart began his diary. He was very much alone. His mother had apparently died at his birth in 1808. Ten years later, a disgruntled customer murdered his father, a local blacksmith. As reported by the local press, "the ball entered the body below the right nipple, and passed out below the left; he died a short time afterwards." Sometime thereafter, his brother John migrated from Pendleton for newly available lands in Tennessee. So Stuart had no family, and he was also without friends. Although he convinced himself that he could not relate to the planters' sons with whom he attended school, he did make acquaintance with a Mr. Dupont. In late March the two attended the circus, but the relationship proved either brief or insignificant, for no other reference appears in the diary. Stuart acknowledged no other as a social peer. Living at Lorton's boarding house, enrolled in the local academy, and serving as a teaching assistant to the headmaster, Cyrus Stuart was, indeed, alone in Pendleton.[5]

From his isolation, Stuart watched and commented on the southern society in which he lived. Because of his education, he associated with planters' sons in the classroom and with planters' daughters at social events. He sought social guidance in the pages of gentility literature, developing through his readings an appreciation for the art of gentlemanliness. He wrote in his journal about themes that permeated gentleman's literature in antebellum America and would have concerned any American youth with the leisure to contemplate identity: awkwardness, bashfulness, good breeding, graces, worldly knowledge, dignity of manners, gentleness, moral character, oratory, vanity, virtue, seeking out good company, and employment of time. He also invested far more time and energy in reading, writing, and oratory than most southerners and imagined his intellectual skills sufficient substitutes for a lack of familial lineage and social graces. But within the planters' world, aspiration and education could never supplant good breeding. Stuart's intelligence permitted him to mingle with the planter class, but without a family to model gender, sexual, and patriarchal relations, he failed miserably in joining that class.

In many regards, Stuart exemplified a distinctive model of southern masculinity, one that arose within the stratified atmosphere of the Old South, as individuals who lacked the gentility to hobnob with the elite attempted to do so anyway. In a society in which even the ambitions of planters' sons were suppressed through ritual, it is not surprising that a young man like Stuart had difficulty fully grasping the demands of southern manhood.

That Stuart had access to planter society at all might seem surprising. Southern society, however, awkwardly blended the aristocratic and the common. From their stagecoaches, visitors remarked on the stark contrasts between the columned mansions of cotton plantations and the wooden shacks of cracker culture, between the crinoline dresses of planters' daughters and the country linen blouses of farm girls, between the honorable violence of genteel duels and the bawdy brutality of yeoman eye-gouging matches and drunken brawls. Genteel and vulgar were not necessarily antithetical, for there were conventions of honor, mastery, and whiteness that permeated white southern society and bound genteel people to the plain folk, ultimately defining political participation, class identity, familial and communal relations, and gender roles.[6]

Still, the genteel maintained a social distance from common whites by combining "moral uprightness with high social position," as historian Bertram Wyatt-Brown phrased it. As a small but significant portion of the southern population, the planter elite embellished its role through grace, religiosity, gentleness of manners, and a determination to pass the legacies of honor and refinement along to their children. Wealthier southerners hired tutors to teach classical languages and literature to their sons, and French, drawing, and needlepoint to their daughters. Gentility became the discriminating characteristic of a leisurely planter class.[7]

For that reason, other members of southern society who had sufficient leisure and wealth—merchants, cotton factors, educators, ministers, and doctors—coveted and pursued refinement, blurring the distinctions between genteel and common, and making social status less certain and more easily contested. These townspeople profited by catering to genteel tastes; concurrently, they sought to mimic the ostentatious lifestyles of the planter class. Those who were able rode about in carriages, wore expensive and imported clothes, and constructed opulent homes in which they entertained. To match the refinement of planter residences, professional townsfolk arranged their communities and homes according to contemporary ideas about urban gentility. By 1860 the southern village became the economic, political, even spiritual center of southern life: "Our bodies are in the country, our souls in town," proclaimed the South's leading circular, *DeBow's Review*.[8]

Many residents of Pendleton took full advantage of this quest for gentility. Merchants and tavern keepers eagerly advertised the trappings of refinement they could offer. William Robertson wished to "inform the public and particularly those Gentlemen from the Lower Country" of his boarding house. Taylor and Cherry's mercantile promoted its "elegant assortment of Lady's, Gentlemen's, and Children's Fashionable Hats" recently arrived from Philadelphia. Sitting on store shelves, the material culture of gentility was available to anyone who had enough money.[9]

In the southern town, then, existed great opportunities for social mimicry, mobility, and dissension. Although their educations and manners often exceeded those of the wealthiest of planters, more prosperous citizens of these communities teetered tenuously between the aristocratic and the plain, crippled by their marginalization by the former and their own indifference to the latter. Cyrus Stuart defined himself as such a person. He was no visionary who subverted the status quo or trumpeted an alternative construct of southern life. Historically he was a nobody, one of the faceless thousands who wandered the same streets, ate at the same taverns, and worshiped the same God as the renowned men and women whose names adorn countless histories of the Old South.[10]

By the 1820s South Carolina's planter class had impressed itself strongly on Old Pendleton. Originating in the 1790s as a courthouse village that awakened once or twice a month when the circuit justice arrived, Pendleton inauspiciously sat in the foothills of the southern Appalachians, where "the mountains from Mrs. Lortons window [were] the most beautiful sight" Stuart had ever seen. The upcountry of South Carolina offered little in the way of transportation and market connections requisite to town-building. Pendleton, like so many of the villages of the backcountry, was not only a market town and a stop along a stage route but also the judicial center of its respective district. South Carolina's judicial system remained so unsettled during the late eighteenth century, however, that Pendleton did not begin to develop until 1798. By 1806 New England tourist Edward Hooker described the village as "pleasantly situated over a cluster of little stony hills, . . . laid out in four squares—[with] ten or twelve good houses (some of which are large and handsome) a strong stone gaol, and an old Court House."[11]

Pendleton's days as a sleepy upcountry village were few. By the early 1800s news of the region's scenic and healthful environment summoned waves of lowcountry planters who, fleeing the vernal threats of malaria along the seaboard, relocated to the upcountry and lounged in vacation mansions throughout the summer before returning to coastal estates with the first frost. "The society of our neighborhood was most of families from a warmer climate," recalled one of the guests, Mary Ester Huger, "people of means who bought or built summer homes scattered around the Village of Pendleton from one to six or eight miles." Throughout the summer, "a frequent intercourse of visits & dinner parties" occupied the days and evenings of these lowcountry visitors. Men whose family names dominated the history of South Carolina—Huger, North, Pinckney, Dart, Bishop, Gaillard, and Smith—led the annual migration. Additionally, a cluster of upcountry "families of respectability," as Edward Hooker described them, arose in Pendleton's hinterlands. Patriarchs like Andrew Pickens Sr., John C. Calhoun, and Robert Anderson worked to create their own indigenous planter society in this remote corner of the state. By the 1820s, as Stuart came of age, the two groups merged into South Carolina's ruling class.[12]

As throughout the South, slave-holding supported the wealth and gentility of planters. But in this hilly, remote part of the state, the institution was paltry. By 1790 less than 19 percent of Pendleton District's population was black, and the pattern moderated only slightly over the next thirty years: 11.4 percent in 1800, 15.4 percent in 1810, and 18.1 percent in 1820. Pendleton ranked as South Carolina's most racially homogenous district throughout the antebellum era. Yet slave ownership remained *a*, if not *the*, defining factor in social status. Of fifteen families that constituted the core of Pendleton's societies and churches by 1810, twelve lived beyond town limits, and only six owned fewer than twelve slaves (which in itself was a significant holding for the district).[13]

This was the Pendleton into which Cyrus Stuart was born. Most planter families that lived in the area had little vested interest in the sleepy village of the up-country, dedicating their attention to the slave-produced, staple-crop economy of the lowcountry. The limited social and political life in Pendleton could not compare with that of Charleston, the grand dame of South Carolina society. Lowcountry planters, nonetheless, dictated Pendleton's development and over the first two decades of the nineteenth century transformed the village from an unremarkable backcountry judicial center to a premier planters' resort. The Pendleton of 1828, the year in which Stuart penned his diary, was alien to his fond and probably whitewashed memories of its more rudimentary years. Reflecting on the village's transformation, Stuart wrote regretfully, "I have often thought that a village life was far preferable to a rural one, but experience teaches me the contrary." A Sunday school society, a social library, a Bible society, a female scholarship society, and the Pendleton Farmers' Society began with the blessings and patronage of the planters. In the late fall and throughout the winter, when the lowcountry planters returned with their families to the coast, the societies and other institutions such as the Hopewell-Keowee Presbyterian Church and St. Paul's Episcopal Church closed or reduced their operations. There was little doubt about whom the churches and societies served.[14]

The institution that brought the most acclaim to Pendleton society and most obviously served the interests of the planter class was the Pendleton Male Academy. Founded in 1825 to prepare planters' sons for admission to South Carolina College, the academy attracted students from throughout the state to its well-equipped classroom and substantial endowments. Henry K. McClintock assumed the headmastership and implemented a curriculum that emphasized classical and military education, the type of program that the school's trustees— John C. Calhoun, Thomas Pinckney, Francis K. Huger, David K. Hamilton— and other wealthy Carolina planters sought for their sons. Beyond education, academic life served a parental role comparable to father-son relationships that instilled social values and distilled career decisions. The Pendleton Male Academy contributed to the socialization process by providing institutional expressions of paternalism and a framework for cultural transmission. Fathers or guardians maintained control over the process by holding trusteeships or by making conspicuous contributions to the academy's coffers, and exerted their control by hiring faculty, setting rules for student behavior, and overturning faculty decisions on discipline and advancement. Consequently, even in their absence, fathers made certain that the academy and the college provided paternal direction and controls necessary for their sons' success in southern society.[15]

Academy education, therefore, held promise for marginal young men like Stuart. In fact, we know that Stuart hoped to use the academy as a substitute for absent parents and insufficient lineage, since he planned to emulate the life and success of politician George McDuffie. It is somewhat interesting that Edgefield District's McDuffie, not Pendleton planter and academy trustee John C. Calhoun, served as the young man's role model. Calhoun's and Stuart's paths must have crossed at least once. Calhoun enjoyed quizzing the academy's graduates at commencement ceremonies, and both Stuart and Calhoun attended St. Paul's Church. Calhoun inhabited a different South, however. He inherited his wealth and social position from an elite upcountry family and, in 1824, after years in the U.S. Congress, became vice president to John Quincy Adams and then to Andrew Jackson. Stuart—and McDuffie—in contrast, had origins in the South Carolina backcountry. McDuffie was also the son of a blacksmith, and at one time, his political and social future appeared as dubious as Cyrus saw his own. Sponsored by the elite Calhouns, McDuffie made his reputation in an Edgefield District academy, gained political and social stature, and became a U.S. congressman in 1828. He even practiced law in Pendleton for a brief time, so he may possibly have met Stuart. His accomplishments testify to the opportunities within southern culture for one to rise above humble origins.[16]

Like McDuffie, then, Stuart enjoyed access to a local academy that filled educational and social voids of his life. With a benefactor from a local planter family, Stuart reasonably imagined he could reach the same heights as McDuffie. Stuart's animosity toward the academy's headmaster, however, injured his chances. Expressing his anger at McClintock's "partiality" to the other students, Stuart wrote, "my hair rises on my head, and apparently stands erect, my passions enkindle and my blood boils along my arters and reverberates with incredible rapidity." By April 1828 the tension between the two men increased so much that Stuart complained that McClintock upset him so that he could "scarcely continue to go to school with him." Also, daily interaction with the sons of wealthy planters increasingly impressed upon the blacksmith's son the glaring differences in worldviews: "I hear the boys express their sentiments upon different subjects, with Whom I did disagree in almost every instance." The strain between teaching assistant and headmaster became unbearable, and the chasm between teaching assistant and students grew unbridgeable.[17]

McClintock certainly contributed to the situation. Despite increased enrollments, some trustees believed him to be an ineffectual headmaster. Upon entering West Point and achieving some academic success, Patrick Calhoun received a letter from his somewhat relieved father, John C.: "when I reflect how imperfectly prepared you were . . . I ought to be satisfied." Unhappy with McClintock's curriculum, Francis K. Huger withdrew both his sons from the academy and refused to send his daughters to the Pendleton Female Academy, an 1827 auxiliary that prepared girls for southern motherhood. Pressures on McClintock to appease the wealthy supporters of the academy would have made Stuart's attitude toward the other students an unwelcome distraction to the headmaster.[18]

Stuart's years as an orphan made him too independent to engage in a relationship with any surrogate father. In his mind, and contrary to southern conventional wisdom, a patriarchal figure was no longer needed for his personal development and achievement. Southern culture expected the family to prepare a son or daughter for his or her respective role in society. Parents guided children in decisions of career, marriage, and education; children responded with deference and eagerness to fulfill their parents' plans. Stuart lacked that advantage. He described himself as "a poor orphan boy, whose education was egregiously neglected at the most susceptible period of life." Distressed over the absence of a family, he resented the academic institution designed to supplement it.[19]

A substitute camaraderie did form in Stuart's relationship with patron James Overton Lewis, the son of Colonel Richard Lewis, a wealthy planter whose exploits in the Revolutionary War and participation in North Carolina's Constitutional Convention made him somewhat of a local celebrity. James was in a position to pay some of Stuart's tuition and to provide, as described by Stuart, "all the good advice which thou thought requisite to guide me in the ways of men." His use of the familiar "thou" suggests that he was comfortable with the relationship, and James's sisters, Sarah Ann and Lindamira, became the early focus of Stuart's affections. Consequently he spent many hours at the Lewis plantation, just east of Pendleton.[20]

Like George McDuffie's, Stuart's connections to a planter family and his attendance at the local academy evidenced a window of opportunity for non-planters into elite culture. Stuart's desire and ability to participate in planter society, however peripheral, was not unique. Pendleton's society was not a closed, static world: in Pendleton, and throughout the South, movement in and out of the planter class was not inconceivable.[21]

As he turned twenty, Stuart actively sought to join that class, despite the problems at the academy. On 19 February 1828, he read *Lord Chesterfield's Advice to His Son on Men and Manners* and "thought it a very good book indeed." Since the late 1700s, Chesterfield's work had become increasingly popular in American society. The volume instructed young men on "honour, virtue, taste, fashion" and, according to the subtitle, promised to be adaptable to "every Station and Capacity." While he never again mentioned the book by name, Stuart's abridgments of Chesterfield's maxims appear throughout the rest of the diary.[22]

Particularly in its discussion of "company," *Lord Chesterfield's Advice* exerted a significant influence on the young man. After his day at the circus with Mr. Dupont, Stuart reported the following:

> I returned home, where I found the house crowded with younkers, enjoying themselves with reciprocated jokes and puns. We then went to supper, where I saw impoliteness by people who were good scholars, farmers, and citizens, but unacquainted with the rules of politeness, some appeared to eat with the gulosity of an esurian Tiger and them sitting at the table eructing in the most disgusting manner. I saw some of the most flabulent coxcombs, that I ever saw before, who said that they were fond of praise, fricasse, gallimafry & such things, which I doubt they ever saw and only said so to make the people believe they were gentlemen & very erudite.

The depiction echoed Chesterfield's warning that "horse-play, romping, frequent and loud fits of laughter, jokes, waggery, and indiscriminate familiarity, will sink both merit and knowledge into a degree of contempt. They compose at most a merry fellow, and a merry fellow was never yet a respectable man."[23]

Stuart determined instead to heed another of Chesterfield's counsels: "Above all things, endeavour to keep company with people above you; for there you rise as much as you sink with people below." Beyond his visits to the Lewis plantation, Stuart engaged members of planter society on a regular basis. Yet he did so with some contempt as well. His critique of the boisterous and ill-mannered "younkers" seemed mild compared to his commentary on plantation society. Of lowcountry planters, he wrote, "When they first come here the people think them the literate, but I do not, it is only because they have better society and habituates themselves to converse in company more." On a gathering at William Hunter's plantation, he observed "some thing new to me, (i.e.) the jest of the rich are ever received with applause howsoever inspired they may be." Even the Lewis family did not escape his criticism: "I observed how influential men of high rank and wealth are, even when their talents are inferior to the ordinary."[24]

Stuart's meager station as a blacksmith's son inhibited his ability to identify with the rich world of the planters. "There is one consoling benison attendant on poverty, that the rich are prohibited from," he reassured himself, "that is the kingdom of heaven." The conflict between acquiring earthly treasures and assuring eternal life boiled inside Stuart. Contemplating his desire to become a successful lawyer, he queried, "is it not aborring . . . to accumulate great wealth, for which [I] must inevitably barter my soul[?]" But upon returning one evening from yet another plantation, in a moment of despair, he lamented, "O! what a pitty it is that the two things Poverty and Pride should ever be united, they so crucify the feelings." Of course his condemnations of wealth were only partially sincere, for he continued to desire the status and opportunities of the elites. Only in self-pity could he envision himself better than those he envied. More important, his criticisms of the planter class suggest that while some upwardly aspiring southern men expressed frustrations in misogynistic and racist language, at least some couched their anxieties in antiwealth rhetoric.[25]

In the late 1820s, antagonisms against the wealthy were taking a particular political tone in South Carolina and throughout the United States. Two groups had come to dominate South Carolina politics: lowcountry planters controlled the more conservative factions in the state; upcountry planters represented the state in national politics. Indeed, Pendleton's own John C. Calhoun led the upcountry crowd, which included George McDuffie. In his diary, Stuart rejected not only the social pretensions of these planter factions but their political dominance as well. "What is the race of mankind, but one family widely scattered upon the earth? All men by nature are brothers, and should be naturally endeared to each other by a brother's love": this idealistic egalitarianism stood in diametric opposition to the patriarchal politics of the plantation South, and despite the implications, he aligned himself more closely to the radical discourse of Jacksonian democracy. Adopting a folksy tone that seems oddly out of place in the diary of one who considered himself well read and well spoken, Stuart punned,

A cobweb pair of breeches, a porcupine saddle, a long journey, and hard trotting horse to the enemies of Gen. Jackson.

May a limb of the huge hickory of the west fall upon Adams, and crush him to the clay from whence he came.

May the wheels of government never cease to run for want of a hickory axletree, nor its progress *again* be retarded by the clay of Kentucky.

This adulation of Jackson is a bit perplexing when considering Stuart. The folksiness of the conundrums hints that despite his aspirations to gentlemanliness he was not so far removed from the common folk of upcountry South Carolina.[26]

Despite having one foot on the threshold of the planter's world, then, Cyrus Stuart could neither consciously or subconsciously escape his cultural heritage so easily, making it awkward for him as he courted Pendleton's daughters. Marriage offered middling men a chance to rise in southern society. Stuart proved unable to exploit this opportunity. Almost without exception, the women he met became "superhuman" so that he stumbled in speech and eventually left their company feeling a fool. Hence their own deficiencies in etiquette often worked against them. This curse, this inability to approach elite white women comfortably, became fixed in Stuart's psyche. Early in February 1828, he wrote, "Now Flattery, with its silver tone, insidious smile and heartless scatters with unsparing hand its poisoned arrows where ever they may prove effectual to the attainments of its objects. Solomon says that 'a flattering mouth worketh ruin.' I think on itself, for out of the abundance of the heart the mouth speaketh, therefore, the heart must be replete with flattery and a heart full of flattery is like the house founded on the sand, which was overthrown when the winds and storms came." His desperate need for intimacy nonetheless consumed Stuart's attentions. Within months, he abandoned completely his denouncement of flattery as a sinful and ruinous practice, resolving "to flatter every girl that I meet or converse with."[27]

Flattery, however, was not one of Chesterfield's precepts, and Stuart's praise of its usefulness highlights an important spin in his construction of masculine identity. There was a moment that inspired this shift from denouncing flattery to espousing it. In mid-February Stuart met a "charming nymph" at a local store. Following Chesterfield's counsel, he engaged in "that fashionable kind of *small talk* or *chit-chat*, which prevails in all polite assemblies, and which, trifling as it may appear, is of use in mixed companies, and at table." But the young woman "commenced conversation and spoke with such facility and force, grace and refinement, that [Stuart] was astonished and determined to go directly home and read the newspapers."[28]

Unable to comprehend the independent mind of this southern daughter, Stuart resolved to resort to cajolery. In the diary, he began to present himself as a slight cad whose talents at flattery cut against the grain of gentlemanliness. Again, he stumbled as he tried to court the planters' daughters. But he faced a situation with which he had little experience; he was not prepared for the levels of freedom granted young plantation women in the realm of courtship. It was a status that they could never recapture; and courtship was the one activity involving men that women largely controlled. Most took advantage of the opportunity to rise above their subordinate social and familial positions, usually employing fickleness, flirtation, and rejection to express their freedom. Lindamira

Lewis, for example, made "remarks and observations" behind Stuart's back that "were intended to cast ridicule on [him], as an opportunity presented of her making a display of her wit." Even a planter's son, self-conscious of his own position, could be unsteadied by the coquetry and rebuffs. But for one like Stuart, on the margins of planter society, such actions could be paralyzing, as when he bumbled in conversation with Mary Margaret Taliaferro, "alluring both in her features and manners." Later, in his diary, he painfully recalled, "as flattery was my trade, and I practiced it with the greatest ease imaginable, I thought I could insinuate myself into her favour, this I only hoped, for none ever had a better nack of hoping than I have, but soon perceived from the cold water that she threw on me, that I would have to travel an immense distance before I could reach the climate of her favour."[29]

The independence that young women demonstrated in their dealings with Stuart also suggests that society extended some latitude to its youth. Courtship was, like other social events, a public affair. In the evening hours, "gentlemen escort the ladies almost continually. The ladies carress and flatter the gentlemen . . . enjoying themselves in the best manner." In Pendleton, possibly because it came only once every fourth year, 29 February was the night on which "the ladies have the right and liberty of going to see their beaux." The public nature of courtship allowed guardians to oversee the rituals of romance and to ensure the continued good character of their children. Premarital sex was not uncommon within the planter class, but young women were unwise to "give loose reigns to their brutal lust," as Stuart put it. Intense intimacy during courtship threatened ladies' virtue and discretion. It was a concern reiterated by Stuart who, perhaps subconsciously, exposed the contradiction between gentlemanliness and cadishness, virtue and vice when he wrote that "any girl who will yield to man's colloquing flatteries becomes a compatible subject for their scoff and ridicule." The very flattery to which he pledged his efforts demonstrated a lack of good breeding among young men and a threat to the good reputations of young women.[30]

This inability to appreciate the nature of southern belles partially derived from Stuart's lack of parents and older siblings who typically advised young men on love, relationships, and sexual interactions. His only training for life came from the all-male academy. As Chesterfield explained, learned men "cannot have the easy and polished manners of the world, as they do not live in it." Since family proved so essential to the emotional and mental development of southern youth, the reasons for Stuart's particularly inept courtship become clearer.[31]

Through "epistolary affairs," planter society offered young people like Stuart an opportunity to conquer timidity and enhance reputations. Courtships by correspondence temporarily removed the pressures of tête-à-tête relationships. In his love letters, Stuart conversed with the objects of his affections without suffering embarrassment. He confided in Rebecca Benson that "to break the long cherished affiance would break my tender, amorous heart." His correspondence with a "Dulcinia" in Georgia elicited "a billet in which she declared that there was a deep and eduring affection in her heart toward [Stuart], which time would never erase." Yet, without recording a reason, he did not pursue this opportunity, although he admitted that "it made [his] heart dilate with unutterable joy." [32]

Men and women appreciated epistolary revelations of feelings, and Stuart became quite adept at humorous, passionate, and melodramatic openness. The knowledge of a courtier's intentions or a belle's feelings helped establish the relationship in its initial stages. As historian Steven Stowe explained, "courtship was joined, a lover was caught up in a ritual almost like a paradox: one had to risk the game, guide it, cherish it, all the while searching for the single player who would free one from it." Stuart's difficulty lay in his inability to guide the game. Although he could reveal his feelings to any woman and establish the relationship, he did not know what to say next. On 8 March, he visited the plantation home of Rebecca and Sarah Whitner, "two of the most beautiful, bewitching, elegant, etherial-minded girls every sent below the clouds." He quickly realized that Rebecca was far more educated than he, and resolved "to study more than I have done heretofore and go back and see if she will excel me as far as she did this time." Unable to rely on substance in his blooming relationship with Rebecca Whitner, Stuart once again fell back upon "[f]lattery—of which it has been allowed by the best connoisseurs that their sex could digest a double draught." But flattery was a digression in the romance ritual, entrenching Stuart in the flirtatious stage of courtship. [33]

Stuart remained smitten with Whitner, whom he originally met in late February when both attended a quilting bee in Lorton's boarding house. "A perfect paragon for angelic indeed," she flirted with him and tried to persuade him to quilt alongside the women. He coyly responded that he needed a thimble but had unsuccessfully searched the village for one. Although he "extended resons sufficiently potent to satisfy any rationly lady," she insisted until he agreed to participate. The episode must have bothered him a bit, for that evening he again penned in his journal a critique of planter society, this time directing his comments toward the gathered ladies: "[they] direct their conversation merely because they are opulent, yet I care not a groat, for I fancy as good as they." Then, in April, he poured out his emotions in an eighteen-verse poem for Whitner that included a proposal of marriage:

Say charming, true-love wilt thou be
My comforter and mate,
And if thou wilt I'm sure that we
Our lives felicitate
    Consent fair nymph I do implore
    And let me not thy loss deplore.

Whitner never responded to the offer. Indeed, Whitner never married. Her decision to remain single further hints of the power of the unmarried woman. The prolongation of courtship, even the avoidance of marriage, allowed women continued independence and self-determination.[34]

The trials of young adulthood, his failures at courtship, his social awkwardness, and his lack of friends and family overwhelmed Stuart, and he retreated to his diary. More than a record of his daily life, the diary was a stage on which Stuart rehearsed his aspirations and failures, often by relating dreams. Describing one dream sequence, he wrote, "[after being elected to an office] of very considerable distinctions, I joined in the holy bonds of matrimony, and O! delicious thought, I lay my neck upon her arms, and put my arm around her and reveled there with sweet kisses on her ruby lips, until We were both overcome by Morpheus. Yet, I woke alone, isolated, and still in celibacy." There is a tragic element to Stuart's inability to portray romantic intimacy as anything other than illusory. His knowledge of it was limited to the gentlemen and gentlewomen caressing in the moonlight whom he observed from his boarding room window.[35]

The "fair nymphs" of plantation society remained beyond Stuart's embrace, and once again he blamed wealth: "This is a cryptic reason to me, that wealth is preferred by almost all the girls." Unfortunately, he remained impoverished. Although he occasionally accompanied young ladies to and from church, escorted them on walks, and visited their homes, Stuart never exceeded the playful flirtations of early courtship. Rather than showering his female acquaintances with gifts, Stuart relied on expressions of flattery and intimacy that, in a world where women could expect similar behavior in their homosocial relationships, proved unexceptional and ultimately counterproductive.[36]

Initiation into southern manhood, as Stuart discovered quickly and painfully, was a complex process. Without family, wealth, and social and courtship skills, he aspired to a status that for him would require extraordinary effort and luck. He recognized and resented the advantages enjoyed by his fellow students—all planters' sons—who aroused his "feelings so much that they often make [his] body quiver, just on contemplating the unjustness of a Preception so partial to the opulent." Unable to relieve the social pressures he so keenly felt and the social distance he faced, Stuart became absorbed in his studies and in his diary. In contrast to plantation men for whom honor, mastery, and gentility shaped self-esteem and identity, Stuart decided to bury his nose in books: "nothing yields one so much happiness pure, holy, and unalloyed as Learning." In a way, by making this decision, Stuart emulated other town professionals, particularly lawyers, whose masculine identities were derived from educational achievement.[37]

The heart of southern education, and the method by which Stuart hoped to finally prove himself, was oratory. Throughout the South, oratorical and literary associations formed at colleges and academies. "Oratory, or the art of speaking well, is useful in every situation of life, and absolutely necessary in most," proclaimed Chesterfield. "A man cannot distinguish himself without it, in parliament, in the pulpit, or at the bar." The advice no doubt appeared especially compelling to a young man desperately seeking distinction. He acknowledged in his diary how inspired he felt by the public speaking skills of men like George McDuffie and Henry Clay. Hoping to follow in their paths, he joined the Phileuphemion Society of Pendleton Academy and attended weekly meetings, reveling in the recitations of the classics and belles lettres. Orations were not merely speeches, however, but were moments in which the speaker commanded respect by revealing his wisdom, virtue, and personality in a public show of masculinity. Stuart saw oration as an opportunity to increase his stature, hoping to satisfy "an insatiable desire to acquire a facility in public speaking"; he vowed to "attend to reading, conversation and reflection for reading enriches the memory, conversation polishes the mind, and reflection forms the judgement."[38]

By July 1828, when Stuart moved from Pendleton to Elberton, Georgia, he was actively pursuing gentlemanliness through oratory. Although he ceased his diary entries in early June 1828, he did record a copy of a speech he delivered to the Elberton Phileuphemion Society. Even on this occasion, however, when social acceptance depended upon the power of his oration, Stuart stumbled: "I have not given the subject the reflection due the importance which it merits," he apologized in the first sentence. He never completed a second speech.[39]

In Elberton he attached himself to the plantation of Richard Fortson, tutoring the nephew, Jesse Marion Fortson. In return, the elder Fortson paid for Stuart's schooling in the last months of 1828 and first nine months of 1829. Stuart's possessions at the time—a bottle of ink, twenty-six books and an empty journal, an inkstand and paper, and a trunk—suggest his roles as plantation tutor and continuing student. His wardrobe, in contrast, reflected the sartorial style of an aspiring gentleman. He owned a pair of boots and a pair of shoes, a blue frock coat, a brown dress coat, a black vest, two pairs of pantaloons, one pair of drawers, two shirts, socks, a morning gown, one pair of gloves, two hats, and suspenders.[40]

It is unclear what Stuart would have accomplished in Elberton. In October 1829, at age twenty-one, he died. Doctor T. F. Gibbs, giving no details, assigned his death to an extended illness. Twenty months after Stuart celebrated his twentieth birthday by breaking the spine of a journal to record his dreams and anxieties, Elbert County's sheriff sold the young man's possessions, including the diary, to pay medical and internment fees.[41]

In his short life, Cyrus Stuart studied advice books, courted planters' daughters, worked to improve his education and oratory skills, and wrestled with the ideological questions that arose as a boy of humble origins sought to become a genteel man. The enigma of southern gentlemanliness was not so difficult to unravel, and Stuart seemed to grasp its essence when he wrote of his lack of money and his inability to substitute education for the good breeding requisite to planter life. But he was born a blacksmith's son, and in his self-deprecating view of southern life, Stuart struggled with the notion that education, moral character, friendship, and virtue could change his situation. While planter society offered many opportunities for Stuart to elevate his station and to enter the genteel world, his insecurity and self-doubt undermined his aspirations. Although he saw the ideal before him, he could not succeed in the testing—he experienced conflict in the academy, was rebuffed in courtship, stumbled in oration, was unable to overcome self-doubt, and failed to separate illusion from reality.

In his 7 June entry, Stuart recorded an anecdote about a young women who gave in to her beau's carnal lusts to "complete a union between her and her lover," only to be abandoned after the tryst. As "withering and lingering years steal away the rose from the cheek of beauty," she abided with a broken heart, hoping to erase the memories. Likewise, Cyrus Stuart gave himself over to a quest to join genteel society, only to have his spirit broken by the rituals of gentlemanliness. In the end, like his fictive young woman, Stuart's soul pined as well—"until its gentle spirit bid adieu to the treacheries of Earth and flit away to the bosom of its God."[42]

NOTES

For their thoughtful suggestions and critiques of this manuscript, the author thanks Carole Adams, Rose Beiler, Toby Ditz, Lorri Glover, Shirley Leckie, Greg Massey, Theda Perdue, and Steven Stowe. For their assistance with research, the author thanks Michael Kohl of the Clemson University Special Collections, the staff of the Pendleton District Historical and Recreational Commission, Peggy Johnson of the Elbert County Public Library, Karen Ellenberg, and Diane Svarlien.

1. Diary of Cyrus Stuart, 8 March 1828, Special Collections, Clemson University, Clemson, S.C. (hereafter SCCU); *Lord Chesterfield's Advice to His Son on Men and Manners: or, a New System of Education; in which the Principles of Politeness, the Art of Ac-*

quiring a Knowledge of the World, with every Instruction Necessary to Form a Man of Honour, Virtue, Taste, and Fashion, are Laid Down in a Plain, Easy, Familiar Manner, adapted to every Station and Capacity. The Whole Arranged on a Plan Entirely New (New Brunswick, N.J.: Abraham Blauvelt, 1801), 75. I have elected to leave original spelling and grammar unaltered. Only when a quotation required elaboration for understanding did I include editorial remarks.

2. In his study of women's courtship in the southern planter class, Steven M. Stowe distilled a great deal of information from a limited number of letters, most written from one perspective; see "'The *Thing* Not Its Vision': A Woman's Courtship and Her Sphere in the Southern Planter Class," *Feminist* Studies 9 (1983): 113–30. For studies dependent on longer diaries and collections of letters, see Drew Gilpin Faust, *James Henry Hammond and the Old South: A Design for Mastery* (Baton Rouge: Louisiana State University Press, 1982); Kenneth A. Lockridge, *The Diary, and Life, of William Byrd II of Virginia, 1674–1744* (Chapel Hill: University of North Carolina Press, 1987); Anya Jabour, *Marriage in the Early Republic: Elizabeth and William Wirt and the Companionate Ideal* (Baltimore: Johns Hopkins University Press, 1998).

3. Kenneth A. Lockridge, *On the Sources of Patriarchal Rage: The Commonplace Books of William Byrd and Thomas Jefferson and the Gendering of Power in the Eighteenth Century* (New York: New York University Press, 1992), 104. Also see Kenneth A. Lockridge, "Colonial Self-Fashioning: Paradoxes and Pathologies in the Construction of Genteel Identity in Eighteenth-Century America," in *Through a Glass Darkly: Reflections on Personal Identity in Early America*, ed. Ronald Hoffman, Mechal Sobel, and Fredrika J. Teute (Chapel Hill: University of North Carolina Press, 1997), 274–339.

4. Bertram Wyatt-Brown, *Southern Honor: Ethics and Behavior in the Old South* (New York: Oxford University Press, 1982); E. Anthony Rotundo, *American Manhood: Transformations in Masculinity from the Revolution to the Modern Era* (New York: Basic Books, 1993); Robert Griswold, *Fatherhood in America: A History* (New York: Basic Books, 1993); Matthew Basso, Laura McCall, and Dee Garceau, eds., *Across the Great Divide: Cultures of Manhood in the American West* (New York: Routledge, 2001).

5. *Pendleton Messenger*, 12 August 1818; Diary of Cyrus Stuart, 3 March, 24 March 1828.

6. Richard L. Bushman, *The Refinement of America: Persons, Houses, Cities* (New York: Knopf, 1992), 392, 398; Wyatt-Brown, *Southern Honor*, 88–89.

7. Wyatt-Brown, *Southern Honor*, 88–89. The theme of gentility permeates southern history, historiography, and culture. The South was "traditionally genteel," wrote Richard Bushman in his study of gentility in early America; Bushman, *The Refinement of America*, 390. Beginning with W. J. Cash's exploration of the southern character in 1941, historians have faced the past having to account for its aristocratic obsession with gentility; see Cash, *The Mind of the South* (New York: Knopf, 1941); Clement Eaton, *The Growth of Southern Civilization, 1790–1860* (New York: Harper, 1961); Richard Beale Davis, *Intellectual Life in Jefferson's Virginia* (Chapel Hill: Uni-

versity of North Carolina Press, 1964); William R. Taylor, *Cavalier and Yankee: The Old South and American National Character* (New York: Braziller, 1961).

8. Bushman, *Refinement of America*, 390–91; *DeBow's Review* 29 (1860): 613–14.

9. *Miller's Weekly Messenger* (Pendleton, S.C.), 16 January, 2 May 1808.

10. Lacy K. Ford Jr., *Origins of Southern Radicalism: The South Carolina Upcountry, 1800–1860* (New York: Oxford University Press, 1988), 89; David R. Goldfield, *Cotton Fields and Skyscrapers: Southern City and Region, 1607–1980* (Baton Rouge: Louisiana State University, 1982), 32; Orville Vernon Burton, *In My Father's House Are Many Mansions: Family and Community in Edgefield, South Carolina* (Chapel Hill: University of North Carolina Press, 1985), 28; Michael Steven Hindus, *Prison and Plantation: Crime, Justice and Authority in Massachusetts and South Carolina, 1767–1878* (Chapel Hill: University of North Carolina Press, 1980), 5–9; Hurley Badders, *Pendleton Historical District: A Survey* (Pendleton, S.C.: Pendleton District Historical and Recreational Commission, 1973), 23.

   For an excellent study of the significance of villages and towns to the primarily rural South, see Darrett B. Rutman and Anita H. Rutman, "The Village South," in *Small Worlds, Large Questions: Explorations in Early American Social History, 1600–1850*, ed. Darrett B. Rutman (Charlottesville: University Press of Virginia, 1994), 231–72. Also, Joan N. Sears, "Town Planning in White and Habersham Counties, Georgia," *Georgia Historical Quarterly* 54 (1970): 23–25; Lisa C. Tolbert, *Constructing Townscapes: Space and Society in Antebellum Tennessee* (Chapel Hill: University of North Carolina Press, 1999).

11. Diary of Cyrus Stuart, 6 March 1828; J. W. Babcock, ed., "Diary of Edward Hooker, 1805–1808," *American Historical Association Proceedings* (Washington, D.C.: Government Printing Office, 1897), 902.

12. Lawrence Fay Brewster, *Summer Migrations and Resorts of South Carolina Low-Country Planters* (Durham: Duke University Press, 1947), 1–2; "Reminiscences," Mary Ester Huger File, SCCU; Babcock, "Diary of Edward Hooker," 902; Rachel N. Klein, *Unification of a Slave State: The Rise of the Planter Class in the South Carolina Backcountry, 1760–1808* (Chapel Hill: University of North Carolina Press, 1990), chap. 8.

13. Julian J. Petty, *The Distribution of Wealth and Population in South Carolina* (Columbia: South Carolina State Council for Defense, 1943), app. F. Between 1800 and 1820 Pendleton District's slave-holding households increased by less than 3 percent. Of the 833 slaveholders in Pendleton District in 1820, 560 owned no more than 5 slaves. Less than 1 percent, or 33 families, owned at least 20 slaves. Although indicative of the opportunity generated by the cotton boom of the early 1800s, the established planter elite gained the most from the expansion of cotton and slaves; see Lacy K. Ford, "Yeoman Farmers in the South Carolina Upcountry: Changing Production Patterns in the Late Antebellum Period," *Agricultural History* 60 (1986): 23.

14. Diary of Cyrus Stuart, 17 March 1828; Ford, *Origins of Southern Radicalism*, 65–66; Sarah Edith Ann Smith Mills Reminiscences, SCCU.

A comparison of memberships in the bible society, the Sunday school society, the female scholarship society, and the social library evidences a core of fifteen prominent families in Pendleton's societal life whose relationships, as Darrett Rutman wrote about early American communities, "were multistranded in the sense that one dealt with the same group of 'others' over and over again and in a variety of ways"; Rutman, "Community: A Sunny Little Dream," in Rutman, *Small Worlds, Large Questions*, 293. Those families, determined by their participation in two or more organizations, were the Lewis (47 slaves), Anderson (39), Pinckney (33), Story (24), Dart (20), Cherry (18), Whitner (18), Gaillard (15), Harris (12), North (8), Benson (5), Grisham (3), Sharpe (0), Ross (unknown), and Walker (unknown) families; compiled from *Federal Census 1820: South Carolina*, Pendleton District; Caroliniana Committee, *Records of the Pendleton Sunday School Society, 1819–1824* (Columbia: University of South Caroliniana Library, 1936); Pendleton Social Library Society, SCCU; Addie S. Vance, comp., *Pendleton Female Academy, Pendleton, S.C.* (Columbia: Work Projects Administration, 1936); and *Pendleton Messenger*, 18 October, 13 September 1820.

15. *Miller's Weekly Messenger*, 1 October 1807; Edgar W. Knight, *Public Education in the South* (Boston: Ginn, 1922), 75–77; Contract with headmaster, Dr. James H. Saye Papers, SCCU; John C. Calhoun to Sylvanus Thayer, 28 July 1828, *The Papers of John C. Calhoun*, ed. Robert Meriwether, 11 vols. (Columbia: University of South Carolina Press, 1959), 10:405; Bertram Wyatt-Brown, "The Ideal Typology and Antebellum Southern History," *Societas* 5 (1975): 5–28; Jon L. Wakelyn, "Antebellum College Life and the Relations between Fathers and Sons," in *The Web of Southern Social Relations: Women, Family, and Education*, ed. Walter J. Fraser Jr., R. Frank Saunders Jr., and Jon L. Wakelyn (Athens: University of Georgia Press, 1985), 111; Joseph F. Kett, *Rites of Passage: Adolescence in America, 1790 to the Present* (New York: Basic Books, 1977).

Pendleton Male Academy had its origins in the Pendleton Circulating Library Society, a social organization formed in 1808 to supply literature to its members. In 1811 the South Carolina legislature authorized the library to raise funds through a lottery of public lands in Pendleton. Although in 1814 the library commissioners received permission to reform the library into a school, it was not until 1825 that the state incorporated the Pendleton Male Academy; see Albert Glenn, "The Pendleton Male Academy," 1967, SCCU.

16. Goodman G. Griffin to John C. Calhoun, 13 April 1822, *Papers of John C. Calhoun*, 7:31; John Niven, *John C. Calhoun and the Price of Union: A Biography* (Baton Rouge: Louisiana State University Press, 1988), chaps. 1–3; Burton, *In My Father's House*, 67.

17. Diary of Cyrus Stuart, 15 March, 22 April, 2 June 1828. A complete list of Stuart's fellow students is not extant. Among the schoolboys of 1828 were Andrew Pickens Calhoun (son of John C. Calhoun), Joseph Galuchat, Cleland Kirloch Huger (son of Francis K. Huger), Peter Charles Gaillard (son of James Gaillard), and William Henry Drayton Gaillard (son of Peter Gaillard). All except Calhoun came from

coastal South Carolina to study in Pendleton; Academies File, Pendleton District Historical and Recreational Commission, Pendleton, S.C.

18. John C. Calhoun to Patrick Calhoun, 9 June 1841, *Papers of John C. Calhoun,* 15:559; Niven, *John C. Calhoun,* 222; Mary Stevenson, ed., *The Recollection of a Happy Childhood* (Pendleton, S.C.: Foundation for Historic Restoration in Pendleton Area, 1976), 22; Vance, *Pendleton Female Academy,* 1; Glenn, "The Pendleton Male Academy," 4; "Reminiscences," SCCU. For the changing purpose behind women's education in the late 1820s South, see Anya Jabour, "'Grown Girls, Highly Cultivated': Female Education in an Antebellum Southern Family," *Journal of Southern History* 64 (1998): 23–64.

19. Diary of Cyrus Stuart, 8 February 1828.

20. R. W. Simpson, *The History of Old Pendleton District* (Covington, Tenn.: Bradford, 1970), 166–67; Diary of Cyrus Stuart, 4 April 1828.

21. James Oakes, *The Ruling Race: A History of American Slaveholders* (New York: Knopf, 1982), 67.

22. Diary of Cyrus Stuart, 19 February 1828; *Lord Chesterfield's Advice,* title page.

23. Diary of Cyrus Stuart, 24 March 1828; *Lord Chesterfield's Advice,* 99.

24. Diary of Cyrus Stuart, 10 February, 19 May 1828; *Lord Chesterfield's Advice,* 20.

25. Diary of Cyrus Stuart, 26 February, 10 March, 20 May, 23 May 1828.

26. Diary of Cyrus Stuart, 1 March 1828, "conundrums"; Bushman, *The Refinement of America,* 390; Robert V. Remini, *Henry Clay: Spokesman for the West* (New York: Norton, 1988), 315; Harry L. Watson, *Liberty and Power: The Politics of Jacksonian America* (New York: Hill and Wang, 1990), chaps. 1–2. For an analysis of South Carolina's political culture in the late 1820s, see Ford, *Origins of Southern Radicalism,* esp. 120–27.

27. Diary of Cyrus Stuart, 7 February, 7 April 1828.

28. Diary of Cyrus Stuart, 13 February 1828.

29. Guion Griffis Johnson, "Courtship and Marriage Customs in Antebellum North Carolina," *North Carolina Historical Review* 8 (1931): 384; Steven M. Stowe, *Intimacy and Power in the Old South: Ritual in the Lives of the Planters* (Baltimore: Johns Hopkins University Press, 1987), 128; Rotundo, *American Manhood,* 111–16; Catherine Clinton, *The Plantation Mistress: Woman's World in the Old South* (New York: Pantheon, 1982), 61–63; Ellen K. Rothman, *Hands and Hearts: A History of Courtship in America* (New York: Basic Books, 1984), 41; Diary of Cyrus Stuart, 11 February, 24 February 1828.

30. Oakes, *The Ruling Race,* 60; Rothman, *Hands and Hearts,* 22–26, 42–43; Diary of Cyrus Stuart, 27 May 1828. For a brief discussion of premarital sexual relationships within the planter class, see Johnson, "Courtship and Marriage Customs," 392–93.

31. Diary of Cyrus Stuart, 29 February, 12 May 1828; *Lord Chesterfield's Advice,* 19.

32. Stowe, "'The *Thing* Not Its Vision,'" 119; Diary of Cyrus Stuart, 18 February, 19 February 1828; Simpson, *History of Old Pendleton,* 216.

33. Stowe, *Intimacy and Power,* 93; Diary of Cyrus Stuart, 8 March 1828.

34. Diary of Cyrus Stuart, 26 February, "A Piece sent to Miss Rebecca Whitner," dated April 1828; Simpson, *History of Old Pendleton*, 170; Rothman, *Hands and Hearts*, 31–35.

35. Diary of Cyrus Stuart, 13 May 1828.

36. Stowe, *Intimacy and Power*, 96; Stowe, "'The *Thing*, Not Its Vision,'" 119–23; Diary of Cyrus Stuart, 29 May 1828.

37. Diary of Cyrus Stuart, 16 February, 9 April 1828.

38. Wyatt-Brown, *Southern Honor*, 92–94; Diary of Cyrus Stuart, 22 February, 27 February, 21 March 1828; Edward R. Crowther, "Holy Honor: Sacred and Secular in the Old South," *Journal of Southern History* 58 (1992): 617–36; *Pendleton Messenger*, 25 April 1821; Kenneth S. Greenberg, *Masters and Statesmen: The Political Culture of American Slavery* (Baltimore: Johns Hopkins University Press, 1985), 12–13.

39. Diary of Cyrus Stuart, "Speeches to the Phileuphemion Society, Elberton, Geo."

40. Elbert County Will Book N, Court of Ordinary Mixed Records, Elbert County Court House, Elberton, Ga.; Elbert County Will Book 1830–1835, Office of the Probate Judge, Elbert County Court House, 119–20.

41. *Pendleton Messenger*, 28 October 1829; Elbert County Will Book 1830–1835, 119–20.

42. Diary of Cyrus Stuart, 17 June 1828.

# Being Shifty in a New Country: Southern Humor and the Masculine Ideal

*John Mayfield*

Let me introduce you to some shifty characters. Consider Ned Brace, respectable citizen of antebellum Georgia, circa 1830. Brace dressed well, spoke good English, and made friends easily. He was also a practical joker extraordinaire who lived "only to amuse himself with his fellow-beings," especially "the fop, the pedant, the purse-proud, [and] the over-fastidious."[1] Brace delighted in tormenting landladies, Frenchmen, and preachers. "He could assume any character which his humour required him to personate, and he could sustain it to perfection." Then there was Ovid Bolus of Alabama. This caretaker of the law, this genius among solicitors "was a natural liar, just as some horses are natural pacers, and some dogs natural setters."[2] Bolus lied in the Romantic tradition; his "lying came from his greatness of soul and his comprehensiveness of mind. The truth was too small for him." Or there was Captain Simon Suggs, of the Tallapoosa Volunteers. Suggs never paid for a drink or a meal, never actually paid for anything at all. He was absolutely democratic in his approach to his fellow human beings: everyone was fair game for a bilking. He got along fine. "It is good to be shifty in a new country," he explained.[3] All these men are perfectly believable, perfectly straightforward in their bent way, and perfectly southern. Each is the creation of a humorist.

The humor of the Old South is full of such characters—ostensibly gentlemen but changelings and liars underneath. Each had a counterpart in real life. For his book *Georgia Scenes* Augustus B. Longstreet modeled Ned Brace on a friend. Ovid Bolus personified the lawyers that Joseph G. Baldwin parodied in *Flush Times of Alabama and Mississippi*. Simon Suggs was the alter ego of Johnson J. Hooper, a lawyer and journalist and all-around bad boy from lower

Alabama. Even the humorists themselves were shifty characters. Longstreet and many others used pseudonyms, as did Mark Twain. One way or another, they dealt in what Hooper called the "counterfeit presentment."[4]

Traditional models for the antebellum southern male do not usually extend to practical jokers, liars, and horse thieves. Southern men, the legend goes, were supposed to be aloof, fixated on honor, prone to violence, and generous to a fault. They focused, as historian Kenneth Greenberg has argued, on "the surfaces of things," the symbolic code of manners and behaviors that served as an indicator of social status and, in gendered terms, manliness. This symbolic code was remarkably complex. Southern men wore the family name like a badge; they left manual labor to the help; they treated each other to drinks; they idealized white women. They also cosigned loans they often could not afford, drank themselves into stupors, bet the farm on horses, and indulged their lusts in the slave quarters. They bristled when anyone questioned their sincerity, and they simply would not abide being called liars. (John Randolph once flatly announced to a visitor that he was "not at home." He could not admit that he had forgotten the appointment.) Young men might prove their manhood through fighting, horse racing, gambling, swearing, drinking, and wenching, while older men mellowed into courtly incarnations of generosity, civic responsibility, and integrity. All these postures were designed for public appraisal, and maintaining a good name was a given. To "unmask" a gentleman, to play him for a fool, invited violence. Ambiguity or a sense of irony was supposedly alien to his nature.[5]

Literary incarnations of the southern gentleman, the "serious" ones anyway, exhibit the same tendencies. The long romances of William Gilmore Simms or William Alexander Caruthers usually contained sharply drawn battles between good and evil, personified by radically opposite representations of manhood. To modern eyes, conflicts between high-browed, clear-eyed, finely formed heroes and oily, shifty scoundrels may seem simplistic and stereotypical, but a skilled writer could fashion these manly stereotypes into powerful cultural expectations. Stereotypes, critic Jane Tompkins writes, "are the instantly recognizable representatives of overlapping racial, sexual, national, ethnic, economic, social, political, and religious categories; they convey enormous amounts of cultural information in an extremely condensed form." That said, the manly ideal in antebellum southern fiction is a cavalier hero who exists, says Michael Kreyling, "without irony."[6] He is always open, always noble, and always gets the girl. He is also fairly dull and one-dimensional; the most interesting characters in these novels are usually women and frontier scouts.

Humor deals in stereotypes too, but it inverts them.[7] Humor is under no obligation to be edifying. It takes conventional ideals, especially gendered ones, and tests them mercilessly. Humor can also model alternative ideals. We might

expect southern humor to center on race and poverty—the flip side of the genteel ideal—and much of it does. But often southern humor focused on gentlemen or men on the make. Ned Brace and Ovid Bolus were white men up the social scale, and Simon Suggs was a con man. The humorists who created these
and other characters took the southern male's obsession with honor, openness,
and fearlessness and inverted it. More, they substituted alternative manly models couched in terms of deceit, masking, role-exchange, guile, and negotiation,
and they did it in ways that made these masculine traits seem oddly admirable.

Guile and negotiation are terms of the marketplace, and their presence in humor signifies a deep fascination in southern culture with the market and the
types of men who competed there. The Old South was a diverse place; alongside
slaves and planters, it harbored people in small towns, professionals of one sort
or another, settlers, and speculators—plus bankers, traders, lawyers, and the in-
evitable swindlers and charlatans. All—with hardly a voice raised in protest—
believed in getting rich and moving upward. In manly terms, they favored the
entrepreneur and his ethic of self-interest, individualism, and constant, limitless
mobility.

The diverse, mobile South is too often overlooked. It is easy to forget, for
example, that in 1800 the only southern states west of the Appalachians were
Kentucky and Tennessee and that settling and organizing the southern frontier
took another half-century. Large chunks of Alabama, Mississippi, and Georgia
belonged to the Indians until Andrew Jackson drove them out in the 1830s; as
late as 1860 the settled parts of Texas and Florida were mainly coastal plains. Although slavery and the plantation system dominated southern culture, most
southerners were not slaveholders. They were free whites, arguably as politically
progressive as northerners and more so than most Europeans. Between 1790
and 1860 every southern state except South Carolina extended the franchise to
any white male who could mark a ballot, and for a time during the 1830s and
1840s, party competition in the South grew as spirited and as divisive as in any-
place else. Southerners argued passionately over railroads, banks, canals, paper
money—whatever would make them rich. They also moved constantly. "The
new country seemed to be a reservoir," wrote Joseph Baldwin, "and every road
leading into it a vagrant stream of enterprise and adventure."[8] Here was a land
for the entrepreneur and his business ethic; here was a land, simultaneously, for
the planter and his traditions.

There was no clear line between the two. Planters were capitalists and entrepreneurs, just as speculators and lawyers shared planter ideas about hierarchy
and paternalistic control. In many ways, planters subscribed to the progressive
impulse. Many had started life in modest circumstances. They valued self-
improvement, progress, and freedom—so long as it was white freedom built on

a foundation of black slavery. Conversely, the slaveless entrepreneurs of the South as often as not wanted to become planters, and they were certainly not interested in liberalizing race relations. Yet the two groups differed, and their manly ideals were always a little incongruent.

Therein lies the humorous potential. The tensions evident in these manly ideals created the raw materials for humorists. We can conceive of the market (or the plantation or the courtroom for that matter) as a place, as an economic process, and as a set of behaviors—all of which favor certain manly qualities and frown on others. Upon these values stand the future of any ruling class's claims to legitimacy and authority. Who should lead? What should they achieve? How should others hold them accountable? Equally important, how do you pose such questions?

Voicing criticism is a sensitive undertaking in societies where public image is important, and the capacity for extremely violent behavior lies close to the surface. Offending someone in the antebellum South was a rather simple task, particularly when manliness was at issue, so southerners tended to be polite and indirect. At the same time, the South was changing rapidly, and perceptive southerners needed ways of reacting without giving offense. In certain ways the antebellum South resembled Tudor England. Both were societies in flux. Both invited introspection and self-criticism. Both could be hard on dissenters. Both needed ways to test values and to offer criticism without risking a violent reaction. As Jean-Christophe Agnew has argued, the Elizabethan theater offered a fine way to stage, literally, the aspects of deceit, cunning, negotiation, and duplicity inherent in a commercializing society such as Tudor England.[9] Not for nothing did Shakespeare use masks and double identities, "counterfeit presentments." Where Elizabethans used the stage, antebellum southerners turned to humor.

Southern humor is a rich field.[10] Much of it appeared after 1820 in the form of wild tales about bear-eaters and ripsnorters on the southern frontier—just the sort of thing that made David Crockett famous and mythologized Mike Fink. By the 1840s the tales were a staple item in sporting magazines such as New York's *Spirit of the Times,* and tale-telling had been turned into a minor art form by the southern gentlemen who relished it. Masculine imagery in these stories tended to be rough. A gentleman often began the story in his own cultured voice, then assumed the rough dialect of some alligator man whose chief purpose was to gouge eyes, chew off ears, and drink whole barrels of whiskey for sport. Such men are folk heroes from the margins of civilization, and their relation to genteel storytellers is problematic. Some argue that the gentlemen narrators who described these characters may have used them as whipping boys to demonstrate the inferiority of the uneducated mob. To "look down on the spectacle of life with tolerantly superior amusement, was immensely reassuring to would-be sophisticates," observes Kenneth Lynn, one of the storytellers' most perceptive critics.[11] To take another perspective, gentlemen may have gloried in the violence of not-so-gentle men because their own proper lives were so limited and confined.[12] Either way, the very presence of these rough men and their rough masculinity suggests that alternative manly ideals were a normal part of southern intellectual discourse.

At the other end of the social scale were the patrician and the entrepreneur.[13] Humor that focused on these manly ideals was more traditional, even if it occasionally borrowed characters or dialect from the bear-eater school. The locations were more likely to be the plantation, the courtroom, or the small town rather than the woods or the frontier, and characters spoke or misspoke accordingly. Where the yarnspinners tended to write newspaper filler, more genteel humorists produced longer and more unified works. Longstreet and Baldwin, among others, collected their stories into books. Hooper, on the other hand, introduced Simon Suggs through a fake campaign biography, and John Pendleton Kennedy wrote a comic novel. These men were deeply thoughtful, self-conscious artists who took humor seriously. Their art voiced a subtle but sustained appraisal of the South's masculine ideals and a deep sense of ambivalence. In their works cavaliers and con men confront each other with no sure winner.

Humorists were likely to be marginal men; they lived on the cusp between the hierarchical demands of a conservative, slave-holding society and the mobile promises of an expanding economy. Usually they were lawyers or journalists; a few held political office, and some owned slaves. Hardly any could be called a planter. From the margins, they developed a peculiar perspective on southern manliness. Their humor is quietly subversive of the gentleman planter, whom they found surprisingly limited and weak. "With Poe," writes critic Jesse Bier, "these southern writers were the first informal school to protest a growing nineteenth-century prettification of life, most absurdly realized in the South. . . . [T]he wellspring of their energies was more than a simple irreverence, it was contempt and covert hostility for a veritable system of falsifications, of which 'moonlight and magnolias' of the old slavocracy remains the apotheosis in our history."[14] They were also fascinated with entrepreneurs and self-made men but unsure of the new generation's worthiness and masculinity. Humor let them explore the issue.

Three works are suggestive. John Pendleton Kennedy's *Swallow Barn* (1832), Augustus B. Longstreet's *Georgia Scenes* (1834), and Joseph Glover Baldwin's *Flush Times of Alabama and Mississippi* (1853) are very different books, yet each is in some way a reaction to the market process, or lack thereof, in southern culture. Each is an exercise in masculine image-making and image-mocking. Taken together, they show a fairly rapid evolution away from the patrician ideal and toward the entrepreneur. All demonstrate ambivalence and uncertainty.

John Pendleton Kennedy's *Swallow Barn* serves as a kind of touchstone for gauging the extent of this evolution.[15] Kennedy began writing *Swallow Barn* in late 1829, before Nat Turner's rebellion, before nullification, and before Virginians rejected the idea of gradually abolishing slavery in their constitutional revisions of 1831. It is a carefully crafted work, especially for a "first novel." But then again, as Kennedy noted, it is not quite a novel, but maybe a "book of travels, a diary, a collection of letters, a drama, and a history."[16] *Swallow Barn* has been treated as a fond look at a patrician paradise—organic, self-sufficient, hierarchical, traditional, and genteel. It is that as well as a subtle satire of patrician culture gone stale, isolated, trivial, and backward. This first of the great comic narratives uses a Yankee outsider, Mark Littleton, as a narrator. Littleton is obviously a surrogate—a counterfeit, if you will—for Kennedy. By using an outsider for the narrative voice, Kennedy can put maximum distance between himself and the Virginia gentry he describes and turn the whole thing into a sort of English comedy of manners—amusing but not threatening.[17]

Kennedy was himself distanced from southern society; in many ways, he barely lays claim to being "southern" at all. "Born and educated in Baltimore," writes historian Vernon Parrington, "he was a son of the borderland, with strong ties of kinship and love that drew him to the Old Dominion, and even stronger ties of intellectual, social and financial interests that drew him towards Philadelphia and New York. Saratoga and Newport."[18] Kennedy's father emigrated from northern Ireland to Philadelphia shortly after the Revolution, later set up a copper business in Baltimore, and impulsively married a Virginia girl of great beauty and forceful intelligence. In his youth Kennedy frequently visited his mother's kin, who furnished him with models for the characters in *Swallow Barn*. Kennedy's relatives were genteel people in an idyllic environment, and in many ways he adored them. He made his life and fortune, however, in Baltimore.

There he became, in his own way, a model for the American self-made man. John Pendleton Kennedy toyed with several careers in his life: lawyer, businessman, politician, and writer. He was good at all of them, yet he was not *born* into any of them. What characterizes his life is an easy sociability combined with shrewd intelligence and great ambition that propelled him up the social ladder. He married well, wrote novels, history, and biography, and patronized Edgar Allan Poe. He also made money, became a fixture in Maryland politics, and supported the Whig Party and the Union. As a member of the House of Representatives, he persuaded Congress to help finance Samuel Morse's experiments with the telegraph. As secretary of the navy, he sent Commodore Perry to open Japan to American shipping. As a unionist, he complained to a South Carolina friend in 1860 that what the country needed was a "real gentry" North and South who could unite "with their kindred classes 'across the line,' to inspire a national esteem for the elegancies of character, love of what is good, scorn for what is base, purity of taste, and contempt of all make-believe."[19]

How surprising, then, that his first book was a gentle but wicked send-up of the Virginia gentry and its "elegancies of character." As a comedy of manners, *Swallow Barn* is a book of poses, deeply concerned with stereotypes and their meanings. Kennedy spent a good part of the book simply sketching personalities, everyone from lawyers to field hands. His focal point, however, is the icon of southern manhood, the Virginia gentleman. The master of the plantation is Frank Meriwether, "the very model of a landed gentleman," and what we get in Meriwether is a pretty passable image of republican manhood. He is a tall, finely browed lover of horses and old books, a man who indulges his children and dominates his neighbors, who gathers visitors around him like ducklings on a pond. "A guest is one of his daily wants."[20] Meriwether is opinionated, self-sufficient, and a master of his realm.

But there is something anachronistic, even frivolous about Meriwether and his ilk. He is "a man of superfluities," observes Littleton; there is less to him than meets the eye. Meriwether has been through all the proper schoolings. As a young man he got a gentleman's background in law, "for during three years he smoked segars in a lawyer's office in Richmond," wore "six cravats" and "yellow-topped boots," "ate oysters," and read a little Blackstone on the side. Whether he actually learned anything is not, for him, an issue. After that he married well and took possession of his wife's estate, Swallow Barn, by paying off "some gentlemanlike incumbrances which had been sleeping for years upon the domain" (27). For his efforts Meriwether assumed the right to be adored. Opinions flow out of him like "a full stream irrigating a meadow, and depositing its mud in fertilizing luxuriance." "The solitary elevation of a country gentleman, well to do in the world, begets some magnificent notions," notes the narrator. "He becomes as infallible as the Pope; gradually acquires a habit of making long speeches; is apt to be impatient of contradiction, and is always very touchy on the point of honor" (35). These are phrases that might apply to William Byrd or John Randolph, and there is hardly a better portrayal of the country gentleman elsewhere in southern literature, humorous or not.

Meriwether's patrician qualities set the pace (a slow one) for the community around him. Visitors come and go for weeks at a time; his daughter dallies with a handsome cousin by making the latter act like a knight-errant and go falconing with a hapless bird that, on close inspection, looks much like a chicken hawk. A central issue in the book is a pointless lawsuit over a worthless piece of land; the suit has preoccupied Meriwether's neighbor for decades. Law is a point where the interests of the community and the wants of the individual compete for supremacy. In *Swallow Barn* the community clearly dominates. The lawsuit becomes a stage set, a mock trial, that allows Kennedy to introduce variations on the gentlemanly theme. We get puffed-up lawyers and hangers-on who muddy their boots and wax poetic over a shred of land "not worth a groat" (149). It is not even a real legal action; Meriwether has rigged the outcome so that his neighbor's sense of honor will be preserved, which, in a community where order is everything, is essential.

Besides, these were not lawyers in any contemporary sense of the term. They represented the public side of the Virginia gentleman, the part of the patrician ideal that presumably fought the Revolution and wrote the Constitution out of sheer noblesse oblige. In *Swallow Barn,* however, the lawyer-gentleman appears as superfluous as the planter. Worse, from the viewpoint of southern masculinity, he may be effeminate. One example, Singleton Oglethorpe Swansdowne, is, to the women, "an elegant, refined, sweet-spoken, grave, and dignified gentleman" and, to the men, "the most preposterous ass—the most enormous humbug—the most remarkable coxcomb in Virginia." It is hard, says the narrator, "to tell the counterfeit from the real in these things" (113). Swansdowne's major shortcomings are a tendency to write bad poetry and bore people to sleep. Still, he charms the credulous. "It can be nothing but his modesty," swoons an adoring girl, "that keeps him in the background now. He never would have been beaten three times for Congress, if he had not been so diffident" (298–99).

The better example is Philpot Wart, who troops around the countryside with his law books and his dogs and approaches all life—especially legal affairs—like a foxhunt. As with all successful southern gentleman, Wart's claim to fame rests on military honors. During the War of 1812 he commanded a company of men who stayed resolutely upstream a hundred miles from the British and guarded the "hen-roosts along the river" (186). Was it dangerous? asks a dinner companion. "Tolerably severe," replied Philly, "while it lasted. It rained upon us nearly the whole way from here to Norfolk, and there was a good deal of ague and fever in the country at that time, which we ran a great risk of taking" (343). It is hard to tell if Wart is being facetious or dead serious, and it takes a minute for Kennedy's humor to come through. But in that one sly twist Kennedy cuts through generations of southern militarism from the colonial wars all the way to "Colonel" Sanders.

It is this sheer pointlessness, this insularity, that makes Swallow Barn, the plantation, a flawed ideal. There is no life to it. As critic Leo Marx argued years ago, it is the presence of the machine—the train chugging through a corner of the landscape painting—that somehow makes the garden more interesting.[21] There is no train, no capitalist force, running through Swallow Barn. The very absence of market energies renders the patrician head of the plantation naive, something of a simpleton. Meriwether, observes the narrator, "thinks lightly of the mercantile interest, and, in fact, undervalues the manners of the large cities generally. He believes that those who live in them are hollow-hearted and insincere."[22] Of course they are, at least outwardly, but city folk at least go places. Meriwether stays home. "I don't deny that the steamboat is destined to produce valuable results," he orates to no one in particular, "—but after all, I much question . . . if we are not better without it. . . . This annihilation of space, sir, is not to be desired. . . . Virginia was never so good as when her roads were at their worst."[23]

As Jan Bakker has observed, Mark Littleton's ironic take on this insularity marks a turning point in the southern pastoral. "As in James Dickey's *Deliverance*, in *Swallow Barn* the city becomes the secure, desirable place. It becomes an urban *locus amoenus* that offers the sojourner in the garden an image of salubrious human activity and refuge to counterbalance the lethargic, progress-denying life in fiction of southern plantation idyll."[24] What is remarkable from the historian's perspective is that Kennedy had produced a sustained and commercially successful satire of the patrician ideal at almost the very moment that a self-conscious southern "nationalism" began to raise its profile.

It is tempting to write Kennedy off as a border southerner, given his Baltimore roots and his unionist sympathies. But two other writers, Longstreet and Baldwin, were indisputably southern—nullifiers, no less. These writers moved away from the comedy of manners and wrote stories in which the patrician became increasingly involved in the action and, thus, in subverting his own image. Baldwin and Longstreet created what the Russian formalist critic Mikhail Bakhtin has called a dialogic possibility—the presence of multiple voices within the tales, voices that offer up different perspectives and create an internal tension within the story. Or, to borrow a phrase from Eliot Oring's wonderful analysis of Israeli humor, the incongruities in their humor offered "two independent perspectives . . . in the definition of a single situation."[25] Longstreet and Baldwin spoke dialogically in two voices, one belonging to the patrician, the other to the entrepreneur, and the satire is on both.

The dialogic possibility is most evident in Longstreet's *Georgia Scenes*. In this uneven yet often brilliant series of sketches, the narrator is a gentleman—two of them, in fact—who move into the action directly. The device gives Longstreet an authorial cloak, as Littleton did for Kennedy, but the use of two aliases means that the narrator's stance is less fixed. Moreover, these narrators are native southerners, not Yankee imports. They are literate and capable of writing good prose, and most of their stories deal with ordinary, middle-status white southerners, most of them town folk. Longstreet's two aliases are also familiar with no'counts, charlatans, and white trash, and they speak the language. They are negotiators, double agents perhaps, between a stable, patrician ideal and one that is assertive, unformed, yet definitely powerful.

Longstreet's double agents derived from his own experience. Like Kennedy, he was not born to wealth; like Kennedy, he had northern connections. His parents moved to Augusta, Georgia, from New Jersey, where his father had been an unlucky inventor of sorts (he claimed a steamboat and a cotton gin, but too late). His father, in fact, may have been exceptional only in his speculations and dreams, yet he and Longstreet's mother sent their son to the best schools they could afford. At Moses Waddel's academy in Willington, South Carolina, across the Savannah River from Augusta, young Longstreet boarded with George McDuffie—who later became a senator and governor of South Carolina and a fierce nullifier. He also came to know John C. Calhoun, the very architect of southern nationalism. From there Longstreet spent two years at Yale and then studied some law in Litchfield, Connecticut. After that, he read law for a few years and, again like Kennedy, married up, to a young woman whose dowry included thirty slaves.[26]

Longstreet could have parleyed his wife's estate into a plantation and adopted the planter's life. But he was too much his father's son, and he diversified, buying and selling real estate, practicing law, serving as a judge, and editing a newspaper that staunchly advocated nullification. When his young son died, he also took up religion and worked for a time as a Methodist minister. After 1837 he turned to higher education and served as the president of four colleges, including the University of South Carolina.

It was a life of constant invention and reinvention, as if the father had passed his tinkering tendencies on to the son. Longstreet, however, combined his creativity with a tough, shrewd business sense. He invested skillfully, sued his debtors when necessary, and when times turned temporarily bad, sold all his wife's slaves and never bought another. Such attitudes and actions did not fit the mold of a southern gentleman, who was supposed to be profligate, intemperate, and paternalistic to the point of ruination. Not Longstreet. He was a "Georgia Yankee," in Parrington's words, "with an emotional religion that took comfort in discovering that God was always on his side of any controversy."[27] Thus he embodied two prime traits of the successful Victorian male: a skinflint's eye for the market and a tendency to moralize.

He brought both traits into *Georgia Scenes,* a little book that began as news-paper sketches in the early 1830s and came out in book form in 1835 and again in 1840. Longstreet never wrote anything better. Some critics have regarded *Georgia Scenes* as a prime example of frontier, or Old Southwest, humor. The book has frontier elements, certainly, mostly in its use of dialect and rough char-acters. But *Georgia Scenes* centers on town life in northeastern Georgia, hardly a frontier in 1835. The tales range over all social classes and both sexes and include cracker ferrets such as Ransy Sniffle ("height, five feet nothing, average weight in blackberry season, ninety-five") and the nouveau riche with their irritating tendencies to market their children socially and to skip out on their creditors.[28] The frontier is never very far, to be sure, but it is actually a frontier between re-spectability and chicanery, and that is where the market comes in.

Where the market was a distant outside force in *Swallow Barn,* it moves ag-gressively into *Georgia Scenes* as a set of manly characteristics. Two central char-acteristics of market behavior are competition and deception. Buyers and sellers compete for the best deal; each holds back some of the truth. In societies where the organic integrity of the community comes first, neither competition nor de-ception may be much valued, although both naturally exist. The organic ideal, however, lost ground during the antebellum years to what one historian has called a "middle-class ideology of competitive individualism," which itself is an "ideology of manhood."[29] In *Georgia Scenes* the ideology of competition trans-lates into an endless variety of games—practical jokes, sporting events, fights, gander-pulls, horse trades, and politics. To be a man is to win, simple enough.

Or is it? The competitive ideal in the South was too clouded by class and gen-tlemanly status to be pure, and there was always apprehension that all this indi-vidualism might get out of hand. Critic Scott Romine has argued that Longstreet tried to mediate a "middle ground between oligarchy and populism that defined public life in the antebellum South"—to have a cultivated narrator play with the lowlifes but ultimately reassert gentlemanly authority over them.[30] There is some evidence for that in *Georgia Scenes,* especially at the ends of certain stories where the narrator, having described page after page of high jinks, concludes on a moral trope. "The Fight," for example, is a classic story in which two coun-try boys kick the stuffings out of each other. The narrator, Hall, details every bloody ear and gouged eye in exquisite detail, then ends with a bit of optimistic moralizing: "Thanks to the Christian religion, to schools, colleges, and bene-volent associations, such scenes of barbarism and cruelty . . . are now of rare occurrence."[31]

Well, maybe, but crackers are not the only men in need of redemption in *Georgia Scenes.* Longstreet was too tough minded to ignore the fact that much of what passed for gentility in the South was actually new money putting on airs. The genius of his little book lies in its ability to pair highbrow and lowbrow competitions and games and to expose the nonsense in both. For every fight scene, there is a duel; for every gander-pull, there is a foxhunt; for every redneck talking trash, there is a blue blood singing off-key Italian arias. Longstreet's narrators are double agents here, lampooning both social sets by merely quoting them. In no case does the patrician or his republican ethic redeem the situation, and the masculine ideal remains unstable.[32]

The deceptions and masquerades that form so much of the comedy in *Georgia Scenes* exaggerate the instability. *Georgia Scenes* is full of cons, gags, role switching, and deceits; there is even a nice touch of cross-dressing and transvestism. All these behaviors reflect the deceptions of the marketplace. But therein lies a problem. Deception may be a useful tool in the competitions of the market and politics, but is it manly? Longstreet's answer is again ambiguous.

Consider "The Horse-Swap." On court day, the one time of the month when a southern village could guarantee an audience, two men trade nags. What would ordinarily be a simple commercial transaction becomes—in Longstreet's skillful hands—a dissertation on market behavior. "I'm the boy," says one to the crowd, "perhaps a *leetle,* jist a *leetle,* of the best man at a horse-swap that ever trod shoe leather." The language is necessarily hyperbolic. Who would listen to a tight-lipped salesman? He is offering "Bullet," a spindly runt that looks like a dwarf giraffe with a double-curve tail. The horse is, without a doubt, "the best piece of *hoss*flesh in the thirteen united univarsal worlds."[33] Bullet spends his time being skittish and touchy. If the trader can palm this thing off, he can trade anything.

He does, but not to his satisfaction. A dry old farmer takes up the challenge with an old nag named Kit. Kit is, shall we say, placid. Not even a rifle blast next to the ears ruffles his composure. The trader is interested, then challenged, and after an elaborate ritual, he parleys Bullet and three dollars for Kit. The deal done, the saddle blanket comes off Bullet's back to reveal the source of the horse's skittish spirit: a large and sickening sore. One up for the trader. "I'm a man," he gloats, "that, when he makes a bad trade, makes the most of it until he can make a better" (29). Fair enough, but he has just acquired a horse that is placid because it is stone deaf and blind. One up for the farmer. "You are a *leetle* the best man at a horse-swap that I ever got hold of," mocks the farmer (31). He pockets his money and takes his horse.

The intriguing thing about the story is why anyone would want either horse in the first place. One is blistered; the other is deaf as a post. In Georgia, however, the scenario makes perfect sense if we consider that the whole scene is literally played for the public. It is a sort of folk theater. The horse trader operates from a base of values different than that of the Yankee peddler or the confidence man. The fictional peddler is a tight-lipped miser who sells junk and then moves on. The con man bilks and leaves town one step ahead of the sheriff. The southern horse trader, however, operates wholly in the public light. His game requires an audience.

The audience is key to the southern quality of the story, indeed of all Longstreet's work. In a society that valued honor and reputation above all, manliness was always on public display. In one-on-one competitions involving business, the winner had to beat his opponent and humiliate him openly. The idea that bilking someone in front of an audience might also invite a whipping made up part of the game. Honorable men were supposed to be indifferent to danger. Again, Longstreet had merged two ethics, two masculine ideals.

Longstreet completed the merger in the final story, "The Shooting-Match." Here Longstreet abandoned his perch as observer and moved directly into the action and into the role of deceiver. It is a turning point in the southern humorous tradition as important as Frank Meriwether's lifeless insularity is to the pastoral. The action begins simply enough with a comic effort to establish identity. Longstreet's narrator Hall is out among the country folk, ambling his horse through Upper Hogthief, Georgia, on his way to business somewhere. He meets one of the natives, and we get this exchange: Says the local, "It seems to me I ought to know you." "Well, if you *ought*," replies the narrator, "why *don't* you?" The other man digs in. "What *mout* your name be?" he asks. "It *might* be anything," says the gentleman, correcting the redneck's English, but it "*is* Hall." "Pretty digging!" came the retort. "I find you're not the fool I took you to be" (197–98).

The verbal horseplay is a particular kind based on market behavior. Longstreet's gentleman here has stepped out of his ascribed role and entered one based on negotiation, hidden realities, and exchange: classic market behavior. His wordplay, he admits, is "borrowed wit; for I knew my man, and knew what kind of conversation would please him most" (197–98). He cannot distance himself from these common men; rather, he must play by their rules in order to establish his legitimacy with them. He borrows his wit from the marketplace.

The game quickly turns to a test of manhood. The redneck recognizes Hall from years back, when the latter was a gifted kid who shot a bull's-eye in a shooting match. A "chance shot," says Hall truthfully, but the plain man insists that he join him at yet another contest. After several pages of the most wonderful theatrics on the etiquette of a country competition, Hall gets manned with a gun so heavy he can barely lift it. He "wabbles" it around, literally aimlessly, squints his eyes, and lets it go off on the downswing. Incredibly Hall not only hits the target, he gets second place. He is both surprised and thrilled. "'Second best!' exclaimed I, with uncontrollable transports." Then he sees possibilities in the situation and changes tone. "'Second best!' reiterated I, with an air of despondency" (212). Many of the crew know a charlatan when they see one, but a "decided majority . . . were clearly of opinion that I was serious; and they regarded me as one of the wonders of the world" (213). They give him a side of beef, which he promptly gives away. Later on, they make polite inquiries about the possibility of Hall's running for office. "If you ever come out for anything," says one, "jist let the boys of Upper Hogthief know it, and they'll go for you to the hilt" (214).

Longstreet's second-best shot fused two manly ideals. As a patrician, he has behaved impeccably and has demonstrated unassuming modesty. He retains a certain aloofness but properly defers to his constituents' demands. He gives back his prize—gifts being a gentleman's prerogative. He is honorable and honored. Hall has also triumphed in a competition, acquired a reputation for being sharp, used his very truthfulness as a form of deceit, and emerged as a common man's hero. He has bargained a lucky shot and a side of beef for all the adulation he could want, and he could win office now on the strength of his competitive skills. It is unlikely that he could have done so as a mere patrician. He is a "counterfeit presentment" of the most ambivalent kind, capable of being all things to all people. It is that very ambivalence that makes *Georgia Scenes* as fine a piece of southern fiction as anything written before the war.

The ambivalence in southern humor evolved into a kind of astonished self-awareness as the genre moved west. The narrator, in turn, evolved from observer to participant to victim. Joseph G. Baldwin's *Flush Times* is both descriptive satire and autobiography, and the suckers in it are almost always gentlemen-patricians like Baldwin, who offers himself as the biggest sucker of all. This deeply personal, self-effacing approach was completely outside the stance that male southerners, authors or not, were supposed to take. Baldwin literally and figuratively "unmasked" himself, gave himself the lie, and reduced the Virginia patrician to a helpless anachronism.

Baldwin almost fit the role of southern gentleman.[34] Born in 1815 in the Shenandoah Valley (the same area where Kennedy's kinfolk lived), Baldwin came from an old, respectable Virginia family that traced its English heritage to the twelfth century and its American one to seventeenth-century Connecticut. He got a good classical education, but not from school, and studied law in the offices of an uncle. Baldwin carried his Virginia roots throughout his mobile life. A Virginian, he wrote, "never gets acclimated elsewhere; he never loses citizenship to the old Home. . . . He may breathe in Alabama, but he lives in Virginia."[35]

This sentimental vision fit the aristocratic ideal perfectly, but Baldwin's real life refuted it at every step. His proud family heritage was built on industry, not on slaves and tobacco; Baldwin's grandfather and father operated cotton and woolens mills near Winchester. Baldwin may have even been born at one of them, the oddly named Friendly Grove Factory. He never went to college, never took the grand tour of Europe, and in fact dropped out of school at fourteen. But he was bright, organized, and ambitious, and he loved law. (Unlike Frank Meriwether, Baldwin studied to learn. By the time he died in 1864 he had helped codify the statutes of two wildly disorganized states, Alabama and California.) At the age of twenty-one, suffering from restlessness and a failed romance, he threw a few law books into his saddlebags and rode west to Alabama and Mississippi.

He might as well have traveled to another continent. The new states of the frontier South were so unlike Virginia that Baldwin felt like Marco Polo among the Chinese. In contrast to the rather settled, homey world of the Shenandoah Valley, Alabama was a land of constant motion. Baldwin arrived precisely at the moment when land speculation had gone wild. Andrew Jackson had sent the Cherokees and Choctaws down the Trail of Tears, threw their ancestral lands on the market at $1.50 an acre, and then promptly rearranged the money supply so that hundreds of banks sprang up overnight, printing bills and issuing credit on little more than a promise and a prayer. "Under this stimulating process," Baldwin wrote, "prices rose like smoke. Lots in obscure villages were held at city prices; lands, bought at the minimum cost of the government, were sold at from thirty to forty dollars an acre, and considered dirt cheap at that. . . . Society was wholly unorganized: there was no restraining public opinion: the law was well-nigh powerless—and religion was scarcely heard of except as furnishing the oaths and *technics* of profanity."[36] It was, in other words, an entrepreneur's nirvana, and it called for new men to take command.

Where Longstreet approached market behavior through games and competitions, Baldwin used the law, itself an elaborate competition and, some would say, game.[37] Land speculation in the 1830s transformed the law in two important ways. First, it turned law away from a discipline that reflected the republican order and virtue and made it an instrument of competing interests. By 1850, argues legal historian Morton Horwitz, law had turned itself into an instrument of commerce and development. "Law, once conceived of as protective, regulative, paternalistic and, above all, a paramount expression of the moral sense of the community, had come to be thought of as facilitative of individual desires and as simply reflective of the existing organization of economic and political power."[38] Second, speculation changed the role of the lawyers themselves. As historian Robert A. Ferguson notes, the lawyer ceased being a spokesman for the whole community and became "a narrower agent of competing concerns. As the increasingly technical representative of vested interests, he found less and less reason to function as the ideological guardian of his culture."[39] The law became a commodity, and lawyers turned into salesmen.

*Flush Times* is a comic history of the transformation, one that Baldwin used industrial and marketing metaphors to detail. Newcomers to the bar were entrepreneurs, men "armed with fresh licenses which they had got gratuitously;" they hawked law like snake oil, "standing ready to supply any distressed citizen who wanted law, with their wares counterfeiting the article."[40] Old-timers, however, formed a kind of capitalist elite. Keeping the law "as a close monopoly," they had "conned the statutes for the last fifteen years" for obscure precedents and rulings, which they sprang on their younger colleagues like traps. They were "perfect in forms and ceremonies—very pharisees . . . 'but *neglecting judgment and the weightier matters of the law.*'" New or old, members of the legal profession approached their craft as an industrial process. "They seemed to think that judicature was a tanyard—clients skins to be curried—the court the mill, and the thing 'to work on their leather' with-*bark:* the idea that justice had any thing to do with trying causes, or sense had any thing to do with legal principles, never seemed to occur to them once" (54–55).

The masculine ideal evolved, and Kennedy's Frank Meriwether and Longstreet's Mr. Hall gave way to Ovid Bolus. Where the Virginia gentleman made his reputation on restraint and honor, Bolus made his on exploitation and chicanery. Bolus took the qualities of a gentleman, ran them through a speculator's rose-colored glasses, and distorted them. A gentleman's strict probity and consistency—which one would ordinarily associate with truthfulness—became for Bolus an absolute consistency in lying. He never told the truth, ever. "Indeed," observed Baldwin, "sometimes his very silence was a lie" (6). A gentleman was generous; so was Bolus. "Bolus was no niggard. He never higgled or chaffered about small things. He was as free with his own money—if he ever had any of his own—as with yours. If he never paid borrowed money, he never asked payment of others" (7). He was the hail-fellow par excellence, telling stories on himself and others, treating the saloon to a round of drinks and putting it all on his "account"—then using his legalese and his charm to strip the suckers of every hard-earned dollar in their pockets. He was gallant with women, provided they had rich fathers, yet never took one to the altar in order to preserve her name. He was the con man's Homeric hero, and the only time he stepped out of character was when he went after pickings that were *too* easy, rather like "setting a trap for a pet pig." Baldwin could only speculate that Bolus's lapse was a sign of ambition. He was "on the lift for Texas, and the desire was natural to qualify himself for citizenship" (11).

Bolus was a scoundrel, but Baldwin's fascination with him displayed a certain admiration for the sheer authority and sense of command that such a man—or manly ideal—could assemble. An expanding, commercializing economy could not operate on gentlemanly poise and absolute frankness. Baldwin may not have entirely approved of the shift, but at least he had the candor to admit that the southern gentleman was an anachronism.

This frankness was most evident in a wry, self-effacing chapter that stood as a kind of sociological primer on southern manly ideals. "How the Times Served the Virginians" essentially closed the circle begun in *Swallow Barn*. Where Mark Littleton had stood apart from Frank Meriwether and gently mocked him, Baldwin's voice here was clearly autobiographical—narrator and author have become one at last—and yet the message is very much the same: the Virginia gentleman is doomed. His qualities are a familiar catalogue of republican virtue; he has a great sense of place, is "magnanimous," patriotic, soft-spoken, a natural leader. "Eminently social and hospitable, kind, humane, and generous is a Virginian," Baldwin writes, "at home or abroad . . . . [T]hey necessarily become well mannered, honorable, spirited, and careful of reputation, desirous of pleasing, and skilled in the accomplishments which please" (79–80).

In short, they were lost souls. The speculative, credit-crazed frenzies on which the market economy thrived were toxic to the patrician, who lived by a kind of anticapitalist ethos. In the old state, Baldwin writes, the gentleman might start "the business of free living on a capital of a plantation and fifty or sixty negroes" and hold out, with the "aid of a usurer, and the occasional sale of a negro or two . . . until a green old age." In the new economy, no such luck. "All the habits of his life, his taste, his associations, his education—every thing—the trustingness of his disposition—his want of business qualifications—his sanguine temper—all that was Virginian in him, made him the prey, if not of imposture, at least of unfortunate speculations. Where the keenest jockey was often bit, what chance had *he*?" (92–93).

In Baldwin's hands, the South took on a carnival atmosphere, a Mardi Gras of social relations in which bottom became top and vice versa. "The old rules of business and the calculations of prudence were alike disregarded, and profligacy, in all the departments of the *crimen falsi,* held riotous carnival" (85). "Shylock himself," Baldwin added, "couldn't live in those times, so reversed was everything." The rapid intrusion of market values and the simultaneous deflation of patrician ideals unsettled everything. "Nobody knew who or what they were," Baldwin concluded, "except as they claimed, or as a surface view of their characters indicated" (88–89).

So who should they be? Two serious essays in *Flush Times* suggest an answer.

A short essay on Francis Strother, who was commissioned to reorganize Alabama's chaotic state bank, portrayed a rather flinty lawyer whose personal habits would have cheered John Calvin himself: "He loved labor for its own sake the way some men love ease," wrote Baldwin, and he meant it as praise. (254) A longer piece on Sargeant S. Prentiss was more ambivalent. Prentiss, a Maine-born attorney, Whig congressman, notable orator, and frequent duelist who burned out at age forty-two, got all the loving phrases associated with patrician ideal: He was sociable, generous, gifted at oratory, guileless, a veritable Byronic genius if you like Romantic poetry or a Prince Hal if your tastes run to Shakespeare. Baldwin went on for pages like this, but stopped to meditate on Prentiss's weaknesses, which were his very patrician qualities. He was, in fact, too gifted, too amiable, too high-spirited and generous. "Prentiss lacked regular, self-denying, systematic application," warned Baldwin in a straightforward lecture to his readers. "He accomplished a great deal, but not a great deal for his capital" (218). In that final assessment, Baldwin had in effect abandoned Virginia and its gentlemen forever. He had interpreted the manly ideal in terms of the stock market. Not long after writing *Flush Times,* Baldwin put his own capital to work and sailed for California.

By itself, humor does not direct social change. Humor does, however, engage social change intellectually, and it has a unique way of rephrasing social and cultural assumptions. The masculine imagery in southern humor is a case in point. Antebellum southern culture may have been patriarchal, but the very existence of alternative masculinities in southern humor is itself an indication that "patriarchy" was a shifting concept. For a time, during the 1830s and 1840s, the ideal of the republican gentleman coexisted with that of the self-made man and go-getter. The coexistence, however, was uneasy. Antebellum southerners never fully abandoned the republican gentleman and never fully endorsed the man of enterprise. It was this paradox, this sense of ambivalence, that made the humor of the Old South so fresh.

The freshness did not last. It is notable that Baldwin's book, published in 1853, is among the last sustained efforts to explore patrician and entrepreneurial ideals in humor before the Civil War. During the growing tensions of the 1850s, and certainly after the war years, southern humor either lost its edge and became quaint "local color" or, in the single instance of George Washington Harris and his Sut Lovingood stories, went off into genuinely creative anarchism.[41] After the war, the ambivalent and ironic perspective on the patrician-entrepreneur duality collapsed under the weight of the myth of the Lost Cause. The need to justify the plantation, to sentimentalize the lost world of the gentleman and his lady, overwhelmed the reality of the antebellum South and homogenized it into a legacy of cavaliers on horseback and ladies in crinoline.[42]

In the ultimate irony, Frank Meriwether and the denizens of Swallow Barn became objects not of satire and fun, but ancestor worship.

## NOTES

1. Augustus B. Longstreet, *Georgia Scenes* (1840; reprint, Nashville: J. S. Sanders, 1992), 32.
2. Joseph G. Baldwin, *The Flush Times of Alabama and Mississippi: A Series of Sketches* (1853; reprint, Baton Rouge: Louisiana State University Press, 1987), 3.
3. Johnson Jones Hooper, *Adventures of Captain Simon Suggs, Late of the Tallapoosa Volunteers* (Tuscaloosa: University of Alabama Press, 1993), 12.
4. Ibid., 8.
5. Kenneth S. Greenberg, *Honor and Slavery: Lies, Duels, Noses, Masks, Dressing as a Woman, Gifts, Strangers, Humanitarianism, Death, Slave Rebellions, the Pro-Slavery Argument, Baseball, Hunting, and Gambling in the Old South* (Princeton: Princeton University Press, 1996), 25, 32. On honor and southern chivalry, see also Bertram Wyatt-Brown, *Southern Honor: Ethics and Behavior in the Old South* (New York: Oxford University Press, 1982); Dickson D. Bruce Jr., *Violence and Culture in the Antebellum South* (Austin: University of Texas Press, 1979); Steven M. Stowe, *Intimacy and Power in the Old South: Ritual in the Lives of the Planters* (Baltimore: Johns Hopkins University Press, 1987); Bertram Wyatt-Brown, *The Shaping of Southern Culture: Honor, Grace, and War, 1760s–1880s* (Chapel Hill: University of North Carolina Press, 2001).

   For other discussions of manhood, especially southern manhood, see Anne Goodwyn Jones and Susan V. Donaldson, eds., *Haunted Bodies: Gender and Southern Texts* (Charlottesville: University Press of Virginia, 1997); John Mayfield, "'The Soul of a Man!': William Gilmore Simms and the Myths of Southern Manhood," *Journal of the Early Republic* 15 (1995): 477–500; Ted Ownby, *Subduing Satan: Religion, Recreation, and Manhood in the Rural South, 1865–1920* (Chapel Hill: University of North Carolina Press, 1990); Nicholas W. Proctor, *Bathed in Blood: Hunting and Mastery in the Old South* (Charlottesville: University Press of Virginia, 2002). See also Peter G. Filene, *Him/Her/Self: Gender Identities in Modern America*, 3d ed. (Baltimore: Johns Hopkins University Press, 1974); David G. Pugh, *Sons of Liberty: The Masculine Mind in Nineteenth-Century America* (Westport, Conn.: Greenwood Press, 1983); E. Anthony Rotundo, *American Manhood: Transformations in Masculinity from the Revolution to the Modern Era* (New York: Basic Books, 1993); and the study by David Leverenz, *Manhood and the American Renaissance* (Ithaca: Cornell University Press, 1989).
6. Jane Tompkins, *Sensational Designs: The Cultural Work of American Fiction, 1790–1860* (New York: Oxford University Press, 1985), xvi; Michael Kreyling, "The Hero in Antebellum Southern Narrative," *Southern Literary Journal* 16 (1984): 3–20. For similar perspectives, see Theodore L. Gross, *The Heroic Ideal in American Literature* (New York: Free Press, 1971); Louis D. Rubin Jr., *William Elliott Shoots a Bear: Es-*

*says on the Southern Literary Imagination* (Baton Rouge: Louisiana State University Press, 1975); Lewis P. Simpson, *The Dispossessed Garden: Pastoral and History in Southern Literature* (Athens: University of Georgia Press, 1975); J. V. Ridgely, *William Gilmore Simms* (New York: Twayne, 1962).

7. Humor theory is a rich field. For a sampling, see Elliott Oring, *Jokes and Their Relations* (Lexington: University Press of Kentucky, 1992); the essays in Robert W. Corrigan, ed., *Comedy: Meaning and Form* (Scranton: Chandler, 1965); Paul E. McGhee, *Humor: Its Origin and Development* (San Francisco: Freeman, 1979); Wayne C. Booth, *A Rhetoric of Irony* (Chicago: University of Chicago Press, 1974); plus the classics, Sigmund Freud, *Jokes and Their Relation to the Unconscious,* trans. James Strachey (New York: Norton, 1963), and Henri Bergson, *Laughter,* trans. Cloudesley Brereton (New York: Macmillan, 1928).

8. Baldwin, *Flush Times,* 83. The modernity of the antebellum South is one of the most debated subjects in southern history and will probably remain so. Studies that accentuate traditional and premodern characteristics in southern culture include the works cited in note 5, above. Eugene Genovese's many influential works have acknowledged the capitalistic tendencies in southern society, but on the whole, they are subsumed within a planter-nonplanter dichotomy best described as paternalistic, hierarchical, and organic. This view tends to limit the competitive and mobile tendencies among southerners; see *The Slaveholders' Dilemma: Freedom and Progress in Southern Conservative Thought, 1820–1860* (Columbia: University of South Carolina Press, 1992); "Yeoman Farmers in a Slaveholding Democracy," *Agricultural History* 49 (1975): 331–42; *The Political Economy of Slavery* (New York: Pantheon, 1961). James Oakes, however, leads a school that emphasizes the entrepreneurial ambitions of the southern bourgeoisie, a group that included professionals, townfolk, and most small-to-medium slaveholders; see his *The Ruling Race: A History of American Slaveholders* (New York: Knopf, 1982); see also Laurence Shore, *Southern Capitalists: The Ideological Leadership of an Elite, 1832–1885* (Chapel Hill: University of North Carolina Press, 1986). The best intellectual historian writing from this perspective is Michael O'Brien; see *Rethinking the South: Essays in Intellectual History* (Baltimore: Johns Hopkins University Press, 1988). Other works on southern mobility, the impact of the market, and such topics include (but are decidedly not limited to) Bradley G. Bond, *Political Culture in the Nineteenth Century South: Mississippi, 1830–1900* (Baton Rouge: Louisiana State University Press, 1995); Lacy K. Ford Jr., *Origins of Southern Radicalism: The South Carolina Upcountry, 1800–1860* (New York: Oxford University Press, 1988); Steven Hahn, *The Roots of Southern Populism: Yeoman Farmers and the Transformation of the Georgia Upcountry, 1850–1890* (New York: Oxford University Press, 1983); J. William Harris, *Plain Folk and Gentry in a Slave Society: White Liberty and Black Slavery in Augusta's Hinterlands* (Middletown, Conn.: Wesleyan University Press, 1985); John C. Inscoe, *Mountain Masters: Slavery and the Sectional Crisis in Western North Carolina* (Knoxville: University of Tennessee Press, 1989).

9. Jean-Christophe Agnew, *Worlds Apart: The Market and the Theater in Anglo-*

*American Thought, 1550–1750* (New York: Cambridge University Press, 1986); see also Mikhail Bakhtin, *Rabelais and His World*, trans. Helene Iswolsky (Cambridge: MIT Press, 1968).

10. There is a huge body of work on southern humor. For a sampling, see Jesse Bier, *The Rise and Fall of American Humor* (New York: Holt, Rinehart and Winston, 1968); Walter Blair, *Native American Humor* (1937; reprint, San Francisco: Chandler, 1960); Hennig Cohen and William B. Dillingham, eds., *Humor of the Old Southwest*, 2d ed. (Athens: University of Georgia Press, 1975); Michael Fellman, "Alligator Men and Cardsharpers: Deadly Southwestern Humor," *Huntington Library Quarterly* 49 (1986): 307–23; M. Thomas Inge, ed., *The Frontier Humorists: Critical Views* (Hampden, Conn.: Archon, 1975); Kenneth S. Lynn, *Mark Twain and Southwestern Humor* (Boston: Little, Brown, 1959); Constance M. Rourke, *American Humor: A Study of the National Character* (1931; reprint, New York: Harcourt Brace Jovanovich, 1959); M. Thomas Inge and Edward J. Piacentino, eds., *The Humor of the Old South* (Lexington: University Press of Kentucky, 2001).

11. Lynn, *Mark Twain and Southwestern Humor*, 6. See also Fellman, "Alligator Men."

12. Lynn's critics are many and vocal. See especially the essays in Inge and Piacentino, *Humor of the Old South*.

13. These groups have been studied but not with the same relish as the study of the frontier humorists. See Edd Winfield Parks, "The Three Streams of Southern Humor," *Georgia Review* 9 (1955): 147–59; Susan Kuhlmann, *Knave, Fool, and Genius: The Confidence Man as He Appears in Nineteenth-Century American Fiction* (Chapel Hill: University of North Carolina Press, 1973); Christopher Morris, "What's So Funny? Southern Humorists and the Market Revolution," in *Southern Writers and Their Worlds*, ed. Christopher Morris and Stephen G. Reinhardt (College Station: Texas A&M University Press, 1996), 9–26; Mary Ann Wimsatt, *The Major Fiction of William Gilmore Simms: Cultural Traditions and Literary Form* (Baton Rouge: Louisiana State University Press, 1989). An extremely provocative piece on the relation between humor and slavery is Johanna Nicol Shields, "A Sadder Simon Suggs: Freedom and Slavery in the Humor of Johnson Hooper," *Journal of Southern History* 56 (1990): 641–64.

14. Bier, *Rise and Fall*, 63.

15. John Pendleton Kennedy, *Swallow Barn; or, A Sojourn in the Old Dominion*, ed. Lucinda H. MacKethan (1852; reprint, Baton Rouge: Louisiana State University Press, 1986).

16. Ibid., 11.

17. On authors and "authorial cloaks," see Wayne C. Booth, *The Rhetoric of Fiction* (Chicago: University of Chicago Press, 1961); Louis D. Rubin Jr., *The Teller in the Tale* (Seattle: University of Washington Press, 1967).

18. Vernon Louis Parrington, *Main Currents in American Thought: An Interpretation of American Literature from the Beginnings to 1920*, 3 vols. (New York: Harcourt, Brace, 1927, 1930), 2:46. Works on Kennedy include Charles H. Bohner, *John Pendleton Kennedy: Gentleman from Baltimore* (Baltimore: Johns Hopkins University Press,

1961); J. V. Ridgely, *John Pendleton Kennedy* (New York: Twayne, 1966); and interesting chapters in Jan Bakker, *Pastoral in Antebellum Southern Romance* (Baton Rouge: Louisiana State University Press, 1989); O'Brien, *Rethinking the South;* Thomas Brown, "John Pendleton Kennedy's *Quodlibet* and the Culture of Jacksonian Democracy," *Journal of the Early Republic* 16 (1996): 625–44; Jay B. Hubbell, *The South in American Literature, 1607–1900* (Durham: Duke University Press, 1954).

19. To Judge G. S. Bryan of South Carolina, 12 January 1860, quoted in Hubbell, *South in American Literature,* 487.

20. Kennedy, *Swallow Barn,* 32–33. Hereafter cited in text.

21. Leo Marx, *The Machine in the Garden: Technology and the Pastoral Ideal in America* (New York: Oxford University Press, 1967).

22. Kennedy, *Swallow Barn,* 35.

23. Ibid., 72–73.

24. Bakker, *Pastoral in Antebellum Southern Romance,* 49. See also Ridgely, *John Pendleton Kennedy.*

25. Elliot Oring, *Israeli Humor: The Content and Structure of the Chizbat of the Palmah* (Albany: State University of New York Press, 1981), 125; see also Oring, *Jokes and Their Relations;* Ken Hirschkop and David Sheperd, eds., *Bakhtin and Cultural Theory* (Manchester, Eng.: Manchester University Press, 1989); Aileen Kelly, "Revealing Bakhtin," *New York Review of Books,* 24 September 1992, 44–48.

26. Studies on Longstreet include Kimball King, *Augustus Baldwin Longstreet* (Boston: Twayne, 1984); John Donald Wade, *Augustus Baldwin Longstreet: A Study of the Development of Culture in the South* (New York: Macmillan, 1924); Oscar Penn Fitzgerald, *Judge Longstreet: A Life Sketch* (Nashville: Publishing House of the Methodist Episcopal Church, South, 1891); James R. Scafidel, "The Letters of Augustus Baldwin Longstreet" (Ph.D. diss., University of South Carolina, 1976); and James E. Kibler's fine introduction to the modern edition of Longstreet, *Georgia Scenes.*

27. Parrington, *Main Currents,* 2:168.

28. Longstreet, *Georgia Scenes,* 55.

29. Leverenz, *Manhood and the American Renaissance,* 4.

30. Scott Romine, *The Narrative Forms of Southern Community* (Baton Rouge: Louisiana State University Press, 1999), 34. Romine's argument is reminiscent of Lynn's in many ways. See also Keith Newlin, "*Georgia Scenes:* The Satiric Artistry of Augustus Baldwin Longstreet," *Mississippi Quarterly: The Journal of Southern Culture* 41 (1987–88): 21–37.

31. Longstreet, *Georgia Scenes,* 64.

32. John Mayfield, "The Theater of Public Esteem: Ethics and Values in Longstreet's *Georgia Scenes,*" *Georgia Historical Quarterly* 75 (1991): 566–86.

33. Longstreet, *Georgia Scenes,* 24. Hereafter cited in text.

34. Studies of Baldwin include James Justus's excellent introduction to *Flush Times* in the 1987 edition; Samuel B. Stewart, "Joseph Glover Baldwin" (Ph.D. diss., Vanderbilt University, 1941); Benjamin Buford Williams, *A Literary History of Alabama: The Nineteenth Century* (Cranbury, N.J.: Associated University Presses, 1979), 82–

95. See also Philip D. Beidler, *First Books: The Printed Word and Cultural Formation in Early Alabama* (Tuscaloosa: University of Alabama Press, 1999), 87–101.

35. Baldwin, *Flush Times,* 73.

36. Ibid., 84.

37. Mary Ann Wimsatt, "Bench and Bar: Baldwin's Lawyerly Humor," in Inge and Piacentino, eds., *Humor of the Old South,* 187–98.

38. Morton J. Horwitz, *The Transformation of American Law, 1780–1860* (Cambridge: Harvard University Press, 1977), 253.

39. Robert A. Ferguson, *Law and Letters in American Culture* (Cambridge: Harvard University Press, 1984), 202.

40. Baldwin, *Flush Times,* 52. Hereafter cited in text.

41. John Mayfield, "George Washington Harris: The Fool from the Hills," in *The Human Tradition in Antebellum America,* ed. Michael A. Morrison (Wilmington: Scholarly Resources, 2000), 229–43.

42. Caroline Gebhard, "Reconstructing Southern Manhood: Race, Sentimentality, and Camp in the Plantation Myth," in Jones and Donaldson, *Haunted Bodies,* 132–55.

# The Absent Subject: African American Masculinity and Forced Migration to the Antebellum Plantation Frontier

*Edward E. Baptist*

In 1849 Francis Burdett, a white Mississippian who caught runaway slaves for a living, wrote to a planter employer: "I caught one fellow that has not been home for more than two year, him & two women were in a cave in sight of Vicksburg. He was wild & fought like a hero."[1] Burdett's "fellow" had defied a white society that said African Americans should be enslaved. Risking his life, the runaway had, "like a hero," refused to submit—at least for a while. His response to the violence inflicted on black bodies, communities, and spirits implied one set of beliefs about what it meant to be a man. His beliefs about masculinity and his response to the violence inflicted by whites differed from those of another enslaved man on the plantation frontier, one Joe Kilpatrick. During the 1830s, in a slave cabin on a plantation near Tallahassee, Florida, Kilpatrick quietly raised a boy named George Jones as his adopted son. Jones had been separated from his parents at the age of five, while Kilpatrick had been sold south away from his daughters, Lettice and Nellie. Kilpatrick never saw the two again, but when Jones grew up, married, and had children, he named his own daughters Lettice and Nellie, after the sisters he had never seen. Kilpatrick saw freedom in 1865 and was able to watch his granddaughters grow, but even thirty years of endurance could not win him another look at the Lettice and the Nellie whom he had lost.[2]

How did these men understand what their actions, and the outcomes of their actions, related or did not relate about their identities? One fought; slavery's white agents defeated him. The other seemingly surrendered. In light of the things done to each man, and the ways in which he responded, did each consider himself masculine? Joe Kilpatrick was a role model for George Jones, but

136

was he a model of manhood? And what about the two sets of Lettices and Nellies and their mothers? Or the two women caught with the "hero" in the Mississippi cave—who would they deem manly? Finally, was masculinity even a central pillar of identity for both the "hero" and Joe Kilpatrick? These questions would be difficult enough to answer, even if historians could still discuss slavery as an implicitly static world characterized by the master–slave relationships of the long-settled plantations of the Chesapeake and Carolinas. But the massive geographical and demographic expansion of slavery that took place between the founding of one slaveholders' republic in 1789 and the attempted creation of another in 1861 complicates all pictures of slavery in the United States. Over those seventy-odd years, the forced migration of at least one million enslaved African Americans dominated and reshaped the lives of southern slaves.[3] For the hundreds of thousands of enslaved men moved across space, like the "hero" and Joe Kilpatrick, westward expansion exacerbated the dilemmas of manhood. Forced migration affected men in specific ways, imposing new forms of physical and psychic violence intended to emasculate them.[4]

The masculinity of men like Joe Kilpatrick and the nameless "hero" was a crucial issue in the cultural politics of the preemancipation United States. The denial of black manhood was central to white manhood, American nationalism, and class relations. In fact, concepts of white manliness that structured households, animated political conflict and consensus, and authorized violence depended on the disempowerment of blackness. By claiming manly self-restraint, in supposed contrast to the alleged profligacy of slaves and free men of color, the Irish and others became white. The ability to exercise violence, often sexual in nature, against women of color made other males into dominating white men. The nation's growing strength made white men in both the North and the South feel powerful, but many proclaimed that republican freedom for whites would collapse if black men became the political and social equals of white citizens. Confederate yeomen seceded in order to form a nation that would protect their manly rule over households that included enslaved dependents. The absence of black manhood helped make white men into the active citizens who constituted a republic. In southern and northern communities, the everyday presence of males without rights allowed those with rights to congratulate themselves and to believe that their own manly commitment to republican freedom justified the difference.[5]

According to the grammar of American manhood, enslaved men were not men at all. They could do none of the things that made white males men. Whites denied African American men the fruits of their labors, seized their possessions, destroyed their marriages through sale and forced migration, and prevented them from raising their own children. Black men did not participate in electoral politics and deployed violence in public only at the risk of massive, summary retaliation. Racist myths and minstrel shows branded the image of the African American male on the white mind as the embodied antithesis of self-restraint.[6] And the "failure" of enslaved men to seize freedom and equality—despite the immense forces that prevented them from doing so—was interpreted as evidence of their unfitness. After all, whites argued, if enslaved men were real men, they would never have submitted to slavery, manhood's inversion.[7]

African American abolitionists in the North fretted that the relative paucity of rebellions by enslaved males confirmed that they were not, in fact, real men. In the first half of the nineteenth century, free black authors shared the belief that to be a man, one must rebel against attempts to enforce slavish submission, even if the result was the loss of one's life. Only thus could one maintain the dignity necessary to be a fully individual human being, a citizen, or even a Christian—terms that they gendered as male by equating them with the roles of father, husband, and citizen.[8] In 1829, David Walker, a free advocate of revolutionary resistance, argued that black men needed to prove to American whites "that [black men] are MEN[,] and not *brutes*" who "will stand still and let another man murder him," much less passively allow someone to kill "mother, wife, and dear little children." Haiti, for Walker, was "the glory of blacks and the terror of tyrants," because the Haitians "are men who would be cut off to a man, before they would yield to the combined forces of the whole world." Haiti, born in a successful slave rebellion against the French and British empires, was the first black republic in the Americas. Haitians, who in Walker's rhetoric were apparently all male, preferred to die rather than to live in slavery.[9] Although they won their political freedom by overthrowing French colonial power, what was more important was their willingness to die for their freedom. Walker feared that many enslaved males in the United States preferred living in slavery to dying while resisting domination: "I know that there are a great many *swell-bellied* fellows among us, whose greatest object is to fill their stomachs. Such I do not mean— I am after those who know and feel that we are MEN." For Walker, manhood and freedom were inseparable. Dying to prove one's hold on heroic manhood was better than living in slavery. A "swell-bellied fellow" who refused to fight to the death deserved his emasculating enslavement. He "ought to be kept with all his children or family, in slavery, or in chains, to be butchered by his *cruel enemies*."[10]

Perhaps it should come as little surprise that in the nineteenth century many free African American writers accepted the white assumption that only those males who resisted enslavement unto death were real men. Yet oddly enough, those shared beliefs continue to echo in present-day understandings, both academic and popular, of slavery and masculinity. For scholars of nineteenth-century black masculinity and resistance, Frederick Douglass has served as a paradigmatic model of the fugitive who freed himself.[11] While enslaved in Maryland, Douglass refused to submit to a beating from a locally notorious "slave-breaker," Edward Covey. Later he escaped to freedom. Looking back, Douglass insisted that his willingness to risk death in the confrontation with Covey made him a man and claimed that his resistance at that moment was the foundation of both his escape from slavery and his subsequent free life. Like white men, Douglass insisted on control over his life and a unity to his self that did not quite exist, even in the world of his autobiographical text.[12] Douglass's conception of his own masculinity, of course, was not founded on the fictions of dominance over households and bodily invulnerability on which southern slave owners constructed their own identities. But Douglass, Walker, and many other free black men agreed with fugitive ex-slave Lewis Clarke, who said to approving white Northern audiences, "A SLAVE CAN'T BE A MAN."[13]

Slavery's assault on manhood haunted those who escaped its clutches and, indeed, has continued to haunt American memory long after the peculiar institution ended. This has been true for both popular and academic narratives of enslavement. Even though historians have not used the terms of masculinity as explicitly as Walker, Douglass, and Clarke, "resistance" has often served as a code word for manhood. Proving or disproving that significant resistance existed pervades modern scholarship on American slavery.[14] Thankfully, in their pioneering work, women's historians have used gender to reveal assumptions and to transform the understanding of slavery. Feminist scholars have demonstrated that, because women rebelled against slavery, resistance and manhood could hardly be synonymous. Their explorations of the ways in which gender roles shape lives have exposed the complexity and power of ideas about femininity and masculinity.[15] Lewis Clarke said one thing to his white audience. But he knew from experience that there were other ways to be a man, and perhaps even more ways to be Lewis Clarke.

Men such as Joe Kilpatrick, swept up in the headlong expansion of the plantation system to the Old Southwest, had little opportunity to repeat Frederick Douglass's heroic negation of white manhood's claims over his body. Moved from the Chesapeake and Carolinas to the plantation frontier by slave owners and traders, driven ever farther from the free states, they seldom could escape. Instead they endured new and varied forms of physical and psychological violence, assaults that specifically targeted any sense of the self as manly. And most of those taken would not escape before the end of slavery to tell and reshape their tales in ways familiar and palatable to white audiences. Some records that survive, however, detail the memories of such men and women. Among the former slaves interviewed in the 1930s by employees of the New Deal Works Projects Administration were hundreds of ordinary survivors of southwestern slave labor camps. Records left by migrant white planters also contain glimpses of enslaved African Americans' actions and echoes of their words. Through these sources we can see how men enslaved on the plantation frontier weathered the defeats and humiliations that marked them as the antitheses of whiteness and masculinity.[16]

The pressures of slavery grew greater for African American men taken south and west by slave traders and migrant planters. For instance, contemporary white and black accounts, as well as interviews with former slaves, depict the plantation frontier as a place where whites inflicted increased physical violence on blacks. Enslaved people in the Southeast imagined the frontier as a place of brutal punishment. New migrants soon saw that reality, if anything, exceeded myth. Shortly after his North Carolina–born slaves arrived in Alabama, Paul Cameron recorded that one of his men, Toney, ran away. Some men who were having a foxhunt caught him shortly afterward. As Cameron put it: "They escorted him home, with the *entire pack* of hounds, to the horror of all the plantation. I hope it will have a good effect." Southwestern planters were not the only ones who hunted runaways with dogs, but such methods were clearly atypical in the North Carolina Piedmont from which Cameron's slaves hailed. In 1849, as if it was a matter of course in his neighborhood, Mississippi planter Everard Baker "[h]ad a sham negro chase with Todd's pups" one evening. A few months later, the same Todd and his pack "chased one of his negroes through my yard tonight."[17]

What mattered, as Paul Cameron noted, was not the fierceness of the dogs, but their power to instill fear. White folks seemed to relish the intimidation that the threat of dog-hunting created. "When you went to bed at night," remembered Scott Bond, an ex-slave from Mississippi, "you could hear them blood hounds . . . You could hear them running colored people. The white folks said that the music they made was the sweetest music in the world." William Gale wrote that when his slaves learned that the body of their murdered runaway compatriot Henry had been recovered from the Big Sunflower River, they began to behave "remarkably well." And whites took pleasure in this intimidation. An Alabama woman "declare[d] that it did her good to see [her husband] beat the boys," which he did "with a hand saw and with hickories."[18]

White men who moved south and west in these years were already a violent lot, and it is unlikely that the conflicts among them made anyone more placid and forgiving. As J. S. Short noted from Alabama in 1837, "The people are getting all most desperate—more shooting and killing each other here than you have any idea of. I have seen more people tried for their lives—since I have been in Livingston—than I ever have in No. Ca[rolina]."[19] These irritable, violent men surely were less than calm when they encountered enslaved migrants who resisted the stringent new work regimes imposed on them by boom-time cotton production. According to Short, Wash, enslaved on an Alabama plantation, complained to the overseer that "he had never done the same kind of work that he has to do here." A. K. Barlow wrote back to North Carolina from Mississippi that because "negroes does twice as much work here as negroes generally do in N.C.," his enslaved workers ran away, feigned sickness, and "Every Thing else that the Devil and their own Ingenuity could Invent." Migrant slave owners thus appreciated overseers who adeptly used sudden and extreme violence to compel labor and cow resistance. One Mississippi owner wrote that "even those overseers who leave Carolina with good names are influenced by the barbarian overseers in this country, who consider that the more they kill the higher their reputation is advanced, and the higher their wages will be raised." Another linked the rate of profit per hand to the abuse and murder of workers: "I have endeavored to find out the real profits of cotton-planting—and so far, as I can form an opinion, it ranges between three and four hundred dollars, although many persons make more, they are real negro-killers." [20]

Violence, murder, and terror enabled white settlers to extract labor from black folks, cotton from that labor, and profit from that cotton. While planter men asserted the ability to use violence against others to retaliate against insults and threats to their power, and while both they and yeomen claimed that the right to retaliate against violence was essential to their manhood, enslaved men could do neither. [21] To fight back against physical assault invited death. That is what an enslaved "boy" in Mississippi found out in 1854 when he stabbed a white man named Hugh Hardin. "Hardin then shot at him but missed—then drew his knife and stabbed the boy 25 times. He stabbed the boy four times on the head breaking his skull." Ann Clark of Texas remembered her enslaved father's attempt to claim the untouchability coveted by white men: "My poppa was strong. He never had a lick in his life . . . but one day the marster says, 'Sir you got to have a whoppin'.' And my poppa says 'I never had a whoppin and you can't whop me.' And the marster says, 'But I kin kill you,' and he shot my poppa down." [22]

Enslaved African American men were also forbidden to protect or control the female members of their families—a circumstance enforced, as ex-slaves and black abolitionists noted, by the law of southern slavery. [23] As historians have long noted, white men's ability to invade black families with sexual violence was constant. The physical and emotional costs of that threat were immense for enslaved women throughout the South, but on the plantation frontier, rape and sexual abuse were apparently even more frequent than in the old states. Forced migration removed women from the families, friends, and (in some cases) white allies who might have protected them from or mitigated the effects of white male attacks. The frontier states contained far more white men than women, and their new plantations proved perfect sites for white predators to ambush their prey. Some even bought enslaved women specifically to abuse them sexually.[24]

The slave trade, in particular, exposed black women to sexual brutality and exacerbated the infiltration of sexual imagery into American discussions of black women. True, abolitionist critiques revealed much about bourgeois whites' anxieties when they depicted the auction block as the site of exposure, taunting, and sexual coarseness, yet their picture of the auction seems on the mark when one reads the writings of slave traders like Alexander Boyd, who wrote in 1858 that his sale of "negroes" would include "intertainment for all who wish to patronize me." Traders like R. C. Ballard, Isaac Franklin, and John Armfield incessantly discussed the rape of mulatto (or even "white") female slaves and graded the looks of every female slave whom they mentioned. The auction of women, reported former slaves, "excited the attention" of spectators, and sexual banter and forced disrobing "intertained" white men.[25]

Whether increased sexual assault was the result of forced migration or simply became more public in the slave trade, its effect on enslaved men was devastating. Men saw the rape and insult of their wives, mothers, sisters, and daughters, and stood powerless to stop it. Whites used sale and transportation, and the varied degradations they implied, to humiliate enslaved black women: Isaac Williams, a former slave, recalled that when his mother was sold from Fayetteville, North Carolina, to a "speculator" taking a gang of slaves to Alabama, local whites said, "Good enough for her . . . she's always held her head too high." By exercising authority and sexual violence against enslaved women, white men underlined the powerlessness of African American men to control and protect their households. Nor could enslaved men stop planters from separating spouses, parents and children, and siblings.[26]

Ex-slaves noted that sexual assault suggested other ways in which forced movement to the plantation frontier unmanned (at least in white terms) enslaved men. White men, they argued, raped black women for two strangely intertwined purposes: pleasure and the creation of new commodities. As Geneva Tonsill put it, "Lots of the girls was being sold by their master who was their father." John White of Texas remembered that his owner did not mind selling his own children: "No difference if it was his own flesh and blood if the price was right!" Carrie Mason "heared tell of a white man what would tell his sons ter 'go down ter dem nigger quarters an' git me mo slaves.'" "He would sell his own children by slave women" was a Tennessee man's depiction of the typical owner; "[j]ust since he was making money." Rapes that created more property to be sold in the market were a double assertion of white manhood and a double denigration of black manhood. Assaults and sales took place as white men increasingly linked their own gendered identity to the ability to hold and manipulate property as a commodity in a market. Men bought, moved, and sold things, and those who did not were not men. Thus market success, built with the bodies of black people, allowed white males to assert that they were men. They triumphed with profits and anxiously reexamined their identities when panics, bank crashes, and depressions led to their own "embarrassment."[27]

At the same time, the nature of the plantation frontier kept black men from carving their own independence within the market. Enslaved men in the tidewater regions could sometimes cultivate small-scale cotton and corn patches or pursue handicrafts. In the eastern slave states, this enabled some men to create a little financial autonomy, but such activities proved more difficult in the new frontier regions.[28] Moreover, the slave and cotton markets were making it clearer than ever that by monetizing human beings, white men could become wealthy and powerful. Enslaved men became, as historian Walter Johnson has argued, the pieces of white men's new worlds. "I [will]," wrote one planter moving westward to Alabama, "dispose of some negroes to live on." Enslaved people, male and female, became equivalent to pieces of paper and abstracted sums of money. They were the objects of white male subjects whose manipulations of commodities made them men in the market and through the market. And as the actual building blocks, the objects manipulated by white men in their construction of a southwestern plantation empire, enslaved men were denied the opportunity for male self-creation in the marketplace.[29]

Formerly enslaved people remembered and understood the beliefs and desires that had made the manipulation of African Americans as financial objects so common. "In slavery," said one, "niggers and mules was white folks' living." "'Sho' I like my niggers,'" Nancy Williams remembered her owner saying, "'dey's money to me.'" Another white family supposedly sold a slave in order to send their son to medical school, making the enslaved person into a building block for his evolution into a professional, independent man. Enslaved people remembered white men taunting, warning, and threatening African Americans with their status as commodities, mere objects traded by free subjects. "Every slave," recalled Isaiah Butler, "know what 'I'll put you in my pocket, sir!' meant"—to convert the slave into cash money by selling him or her into the domestic slave trade.[30] There could perhaps be no more obvious statement of white men's ability to create their own manhood by manipulating enslaved people— by crumpling, folding, enclosing, and dealing away their lives. To end with "sir" stated with precise irony that black men were not worthy of the respect that the honorific ironically implied. Owners assumed that enslaved people understood the logic of pocket conversions well enough to fear what the slang suggested. Ubiquitous fiction held that the ability to commodify others meant that one was a man, and that to be commodified meant that one was not.[31]

In forced migration, African American men were thus more than ever the objects of whites' manipulations and desires. Previous social structures and beliefs about morality crumbled, and the desire for profit reorganized the ways in which people saw—or were forced to see—the world.[32] As bees follow the queen, so the lure of King Cotton drew masses of white migrants to the west and south. In the process, plantation owners and other whites haphazardly created a geographically, culturally, and socially new South. At first, the communities and states that grew from the settlement of the frontier were unstable, riven with conflict among white factions and classes. But as time went on, relationships among white men stabilized, becoming more egalitarian and even placid. The South became, in a sense, "Old."[33] Even as life for whites settled (until they destroyed their own peace through the onset of civil war), life for the enslaved swept up in the migration continued to resemble that of refugees or prisoners during a massive war. The disruption of forced migration was evident in every region touched by the domestic slave trade. Still, in the face of chaos and the concerted efforts of whites to prove that a slave could not be a man, enslaved males refused to accept white definitions of their own inadequacy.

Some enslaved African American males measured masculinity in ways that paralleled the standards held by free northern African Americans like Frederick Douglass. These men, like the hero caught by Francis Burdett, resisted enslavement by running away, fighting, and defying white authority on the frontier. Some escaped to the caves and woods of the old Southwest. Although a few runaways did find in Native American groups some sort of free status, many of the black folks associated with the Choctaw, Creeks, or other groups had been sold to them by planters or slave traders. The most successful runaways were ex-slaves of white pioneers who had lived on a succession of settlement frontiers. These folks knew the terrain of contact zones between European and Native Americans. Later arrivals in the Southwest were usually lifelong field hands from long-settled districts of the Chesapeake and the Carolinas. As rebellious as they might have been—southwestern planters perpetually feared that sellers were sending them slaves exiled for their roles in revolts and conspiracies—very few became successful maroons.[34]

The accounts of planters who moved to the old Southwest bristle with individual enslaved men who tried to escape. William, a North Carolina man taken to Alabama by his owner Fabius Haywood, ran away to the plantation of Fabius's brother John, claiming that the overseer worked the slaves on Sundays and at night. Dick, a man who in 1853 lived on a Louisiana plantation, once told his white overseer Henry Shaw that "he hates to have the name of being caught." To be caught meant harsh punishments and a return to submission. To be caught was also to lose a challenge to white men, as Dick understood it. He would "have the name" of one whose new humiliation was known even by those who did not see him dragged back to the plantation in ropes, coated in sweat and blood, mud and dog saliva.[35]

Runaway men like Dick often interpreted their efforts to escape as a struggle with whites over manhood, and whites concurred. In Alabama, a bondman of Joseph Labrenty took to the woods in an effort to force Labrenty to sell him back to North Carolina. Labrenty fumed hysterically that he would never let a mere slave compel his behavior, claiming that he would rather do a slave's labor than fulfill a slave's demands: "I would go into the woods and mall [sic] rails for the next twelve months to pay the reward to have him shot. I am so provoked with the villain that I would almost prefer anything being done to giving up to the rascal and selling him in Fayetteville." He preferred to reassert his authority by killing the man: "I wish to god that I could get within 40 yards of him with a double barrelled & if I should not stop him I am much mistaken." The need to dominate enslaved men and defeat their resistance surpassed even their value in one's pocket. "As to giving up to him," wrote Labrenty, "or regarding his threats, I am solemnly determined to spend double his value to conquer him, and I prefer to hear that he is dead rather than taken one cent less than a thousand dollars for him."[36]

In most cases capture or death quickly "conquered" men like Labrenty's "villain." Twenty-year-old Dread ran away in 1857. Whites hunted Dread all over northeastern Louisiana, and in February they found him on Walnut Bayou. They shot him and brought him back wounded to Elcho plantation, where he died ten days later. The outcome of Dick's capture also underlines the difficulty for most African American men of navigating a pathway between submission and death. Shaw, the overseer, caught Dick hiding under his own (Dick's) house: "I put him in the stocks and give him 100 licks with a strop Sunday morning give him another hundred and this morning I give him a hundred more and put him to work." After these brutal punishments, Dick seemingly gave up his struggle for manhood: "He ses he is mistaken in himself he is not as smart as he thought. . . . He ses I have learned him something." After a series of brutal beatings, Dick bent to the overseer's will, admitting that he was "caught," submissive to a man who "learned" him corporal lessons like a child or a beast.[37]

Dick was neither Nat Turner nor Frederick Douglass. He was willing to take risks, to come close to death to keep the stigma of being "caught" from his name, but he was not willing to die. Plainly, he did not achieve what author Tzvetan Todorov, in a different context, defines as heroism: a willingness to die for abstracted ideals like glory, honor, and freedom. Todorov's study of concepts of twentieth-century concentration camps and gulags began with uprisings against the Nazis in Warsaw. There he found heroic resistance that would have pleased

David Walker. The Jewish rebels of 1943 and the Polish rebels of 1944 argued that one must be willing to die for the value of freedom: "people must die so that moral and political values can survive." "To the hero," in fact, argued Todorov, "death has more value than life"—at least more than life under conditions in which one cannot claim freedom. Those who put survival ahead of freedom were unworthy of respect from themselves or from others and, in fact, did not value anything more than staying alive. Men who believed in such standards yet failed to resist domination to the death would consider themselves humiliated. And perhaps, if they lived in a society that associated manhood with both independence and the domination of women, they would also feel themselves feminized. In short, if the central pillar of a man's identity was heroic masculinity, failure to resist domination would lead to the collapse of his identity.[38]

Yet, speaking in a time when many Americans defined males who failed to exhibit heroic resistance as unmanly, ex-slaves would have agreed that in surrendering, Dick made the only possible choice. "I was a fighter," said one man, and "he couldn't whip me unless I was tied. . . . [But] I had to let him tie me, 'cause he had a gun." "I have heard a heap of people say they wouldn't take the treatment what the slaves took," said another, "but they woulda took it or death." WPA narratives from ex-slaves shaped by forced migration recount few tales of successful heroic male resistance. The real threat of death made talk of heroic behavior, to say nothing of its execution, a serious proposition. And heroism's negative consequences even lasted long after death. In the midst of a social world atomized and then reshaped by forced migration, resistance to the death meant not only physical but also social, psychic, and historical destruction. A Louisiana ex-slave told of a young man, bought for his fine physique, who refused to plow. He had never done such coarse labor in the southeastern states. His new master forced him to dig a deep hole, made the young man stand in it, and shot him. Such deaths underlined not the glories of resistance, but the power of the master. Heroic or otherwise, such outcomes did not even provide lessons to family members, who never learned of their loved ones' fates.[39]

Those dragged west and south in the grip of migrant slave owners and traders had to abandon as futile, at least for the present, dreams of escape, violent resistance, and revolution. The power of the forces that took them to the frontier broke community and family bonds, destroying much of the organizational footing for heroic resistance.[40] But what standards for male behavior, besides the hero, could sustain men's identities in the extreme circumstances experienced by those driven to the slave labor camps of the plantation frontier? Let us take a hint from Todorov, who contrasted the ideal of the "hero" with the "ordinary virtues" displayed by victims who helped others in the camps and gulags to survive within those inescapable collective traumas. While heroes die for such objectives as freedom, respect, masculinity, or independence, men who displayed ordinary virtues did not actively seek death in the quest of liberation. Todorov identified two kinds of ordinary virtue that also flowered in the course of forced migration in the United States: dignity and caring. Enslaved men displayed dignity by subjecting their own acts to a higher moral code. They also carried out acts of caring. And while Western societies have traditionally associated heroism with masculinity, and caring with femininity, it does not follow that enslaved men considered caring feminine. Although depicted as objects stripped of claims to masculinity, many enslaved men stubbornly demonstrated through acts of caretaking and dignity that they believed that their own lives and identities mattered, and that they had choices and will.[41]

Like their ancestors ripped from Africa, who built new generations on the shores of Carolina and the Chesapeake, survivors of forced migration to the southwestern plantation frontier became husbands, friends, and fathers once more. Peter Carter, for instance, was sold to Florida at the height of the 1830s cotton boom, when he was almost forty. He left behind a family of children that included his namesake son in Halifax County, North Carolina. In Florida, in his fifties, he built another household when he remarried and fathered at least three children. John Walker, separated from his first wife in Culpeper County, Virginia, by his owner's migration southward in 1835, waited years before he remarried. But when he did so, in his fifties, he adopted the two young children of his new wife, Jane. Carter and Walker did not choose to seek heroic deaths. Instead, they accumulated new relationships, obligations, and ways in which to care for others.[42]

Joe Kilpatrick, Peter Carter, and John Walker cared for others, helping them survive the disruptions of forced migration. The caretaker role was essential for the survival not only of others but also of themselves. Such obligations, after all, required caretakers to stay alive in order to fulfill them. Charles Ball, sold from Maryland to frontier Georgia in the first decade of the 1800s, depicted the husband of a woman named Lydia as a sorry excuse for a man. Lydia's husband, a native African, sat and moped over his changed condition, slowly declining. Ball, who had contemplated suicide after being separated from his family, had a different reaction to his own defeat, his own deeper enslavement. He assisted the family in whose cabin he was lodged, and also served as a foster father to a four-year-old boy: "He was of the same age with my own little son, whom I had left in Maryland; and there was nothing that I possessed in the world, that I would not have divided with him, even to my last crust."[43]

Enslaved men in the midst of forced migration attempted to maintain or rebuild the bonds of families, to supply their needs, and to guide the young. Like Bob, a man taken by William Bryarly from Virginia to Mississippi, some also sought to reunite with those left behind in the southeastern states. Bryarly agreed that Bob might marry but forbade him to marry off the plantation. In that case, Bob suggested that perhaps when Bryarly returned to Virginia, he would buy Bob's old love, Pillar, who belonged to one Colonel Bell. Since Bob's forced migration, Pillar had borne twins (not Bob's children), but Bob still hoped to reunite with her. His request confused his owner. Why would a man want to be reunited with a woman who had not waited for him? Bob's concept of manhood comprehended deeper, stronger emotions than Bryarly could understand.[44]

Long after emancipation, formerly enslaved men tried to reunite the parted strands of kinship. Providing for those whom they could not hope to protect mattered to them. Twelve years after slavery ended, Alabama's Jack Hannibal wrote to his former owner, asking for assistance in recovering his scattered family: "[P]lease be so kind to write to Florida to my two sisters to let them know where I am. . . . Do you know if my brother Ben is still living?" He described his family in Alabama—his first and second wives, his son who had died at the age of six, and his living children. He was proud to tell their story to one at least partly responsible for banishing him from the fields of his childhood. His manhood did not center on his authority over dependents, but rather on his efforts to fulfill his obligations to the ones he loved. In fact, he was making a place for those still lost, if only they could be found: "Please write to my two sisters in Florida that if they are not doing well . . . I am now doing like Joseph of old, preparing corn now for them if they should come out."[45]

Jack Hannibal did not compare himself to "Joseph of old" to evoke the masculine dominion of the patriarchs Abraham or Jacob, masters of flocks, slaves, and wives. Hannibal's biblical model was instead a man disinherited by violence and sold off to slave traders.[46] Similar indignities had been inflicted on Hannibal. But in Hannibal's story, as in that of the male archetype whom he claimed, a man was more than what was done or not done to him. Here was a clear contrast with the assumptions of heroic masculinity. The past with its horrors had happened, and no one could change it. Now Hannibal sought his sisters, so that he might provide for them, recompose a household, and rebuild from loss. Hannibal described his accomplishments as designed for the specific purpose of reuniting and caring for his sisters.[47] He believed they survived, somewhere in a South devastated by the tumult of forced migration and war. Such men derived their sense of self from their ability to endure, to build and rebuild, and to lend their strong endurance to others.

Of course, men like Joe Kilpatrick and Jack Hannibal could not forget the losses they had suffered. In the names they gave their children, they remembered those who had died and those from whom they were separated. Green Davidson, taken to Tallahassee from North Carolina, named his daughter Betsey, after a sister driven to Georgia. Robert Henry, removed to Florida as a boy in 1830, named his son Sam, after a brother and father in Middlesex County, Virginia. Isaac Davis, born in South Carolina, also ended up in Florida, where he raised a son named Arch, after his father and brother in South Carolina, and a daughter, after his sister Peggy, who had been moved to Texas. Both these children were in time "carried to Texas." Just as pointed was the name that Charles and Sally of William Cabell's Mississippi plantation gave to their daughter—Liberty. There were also Mourning, Silence, and Maryland, a boy named after his parents' home.[48] Other slaves changed their own names to memorialize the past from which they had been torn: Mandy Jones's father changed his last name from that of his Mississippi owner Stewart to Jones, that of the Maryland planter from whom he had been sold at the age of ten. Such names, and the stories that surely went with them, passed on visions of survivors' lost families, communicating an understanding of the past that warned children that white people felt justified in inflicting incredible physical and psychic injuries on black people.[49]

The damage done by forced migration was serious and could destroy both body and soul. "When you was sol'," said one ex-slave from Virginia, "hit was de end of you. Dey carry you away down South," and to those left behind, you might as well have been dead. So men fought against an understandable tendency toward despair, in themselves and in others. But they could not fight by fighting. Instead, for instance, in the face of a white society that divided black husbands from black wives, created a sexually exploitative slave trade, and ripped children from parents, African American men cared for their female counterparts in important ways. Men helped women to survive, perhaps finding meaning in their own lives by protecting those of others. Some relationships were sexual or marital, but other bonds of solidarity emerged as well.[50] Young Lucy Thurston was sold from Kentucky and her mother to Covington, Louisiana. Put to swinging a hoe in the cotton fields, she moved like an automaton, disinterested in life. She could have wilted and died, but the men working with her in the fields helped her to save herself. The "people" in the fields sang, and the one that she remembered touching her was the raucous, distinctively male song of praise for female spirit "Liza Jane." Day after day, joyous tunes like "Liza Jane," and no doubt also sad ones, sounded deep the well of her sorrow. One day they found its floor, and she rose back up out of the pit. She opened her mouth, and rekindled life rang out: "I got happy and sang wid de res'."[51]

Of course, in some slave households of the plantation frontier, men did not emphasize caring but sought to establish their own authority and dominance.[52] Such an approach followed conventional ideals of masculinity. But there was another ideal at work as well, another side to the roles of husband, father, brother, and friend. In the plantation frontier, black men who wanted to be fatherly, brotherly, caring, and dignified needed not the strength to dominate so much as the ability to suffer and wait. Men even helped others who experienced the ultimate loss of control: death resulting from planters' attempts to live out their own dreams of wealth. In 1833 planter William Harriss moved his slaves from eastern North Carolina to his new plantation in Tipton County, Mississippi. The migrants included two men named Aaron and Nat and a boy named Bartlet. All three, separated from family members, lived in a cabin together. Shortly after the slaves had begun to clear and plant the fields, sickness broke out on the plantation. Bartlet, Aaron, and Nat fell ill, and all three "thought that they would die." Aaron died within two days. Bartlet struggled in and out of consciousness for three weeks, hallucinating, saying that "[h]e wanted to see his mama and his dady." His parents were not there, but he had Nat, who cared for Bartlet despite his own illness. Nat "would often sing a little and would pray and would ask Bartlet to pray also, but Bartlet told him that he did not know how to pray." So Nat prayed for the semiconscious boy, singing to comfort him. The boy died. Nat recovered. Nat had served Bartlet as foster father, brother, friend, guiding and guarding the boy's spirit as they faced death together in the cabin.[53]

Like Joe Kilpatrick, Jack Hannibal, and thousands of other men, Nat was a caretaker who helped others endure that which they could not overcome. In the roles of husbands, friends, fathers (symbolic or biological), brothers, and sons, black men mapped out caretaking in both practice and rhetoric. Christianity certainly served as a rich source for language and models of male caretaking, as in the case of Jack Hannibal. Indeed, the situation in which forced migrants found themselves was so apocalyptic that for many the only way to describe their plight was through dramatic religious language and visions. One formerly enslaved woman remembered a dream that seemingly conflated the road southwest with the road to and through hell: "I was traveling along a big road. Down on each side I saw the souls in torment." Like those on the road southwest, in their despair "[t]hey were saying 'Oh, how long?' I met on the road a great host, some walking, some on mules, going down to hell."[54]

Hell began on the path southwest, and the new slave labor camp was its deepest circle; the devil was the slave trader or new master. Salvation came to many in dreams in which loved ones who remained in the east spoke of conversion. The dreams counseled them to escape despair by turning toward religion: "I was sold into slavery," recalled one man who took such spectral advice, "and sent to Mississippi to work on a cotton plantation. Even there I prayed." Parting words could serve the same function as visions and dreams. Another man, sold in South Carolina to a slave dealer, was allowed to say good-bye to his father. At their parting, the older man said, "Whatever you do, treat people right; respect the old; go to [religious] meetings; and if you never more see us in this world, meet us in heaven." Taken to Louisiana, he met a master "who was a devil on earth," a man who made him realize that "[u]p until the time I was sold down in Louisiana I didn't know what hard times was." Times were so difficult, in fact, that seventy years later he recalled that he "just gave up all earthly hopes and thought all the time about the next life." [55]

Rhetorical focus on the next world was a way to avoid complete despair, but to survive in body and spirit, men had to take some action in this world. Indeed, prayer and conversion were important actions, responses to the traumas of forced migration, choices that sought to emphasize ordinary virtue rather than heroic resistance and self-destruction. Even in retrospect former slaves did not argue that it was easy to choose the path of endurance and survival. But those who reconceived the traumas of forced migration as the occasion for religious transformation made a choice that one should not write off as having solely personal repercussions. Many men also remembered religious conversion as a turning away from old patterns of manhood that they later came to believe had been destructive — drinking, fighting, running away. The theology and the process of religious commitment led many men to reach out, to assert obligations to others, to become caretakers. Men remembered, for instance, that their conversions called them to preach to other enslaved people. They offered their own testimony to clear common ground, to build new relationships among diverse and often unrelated people in the slave labor camps of the plantation frontier. [56]

Religion also offered enslaved people a vocabulary by which to understand and criticize whites. Christian blacks privately rebuked white people, especially white males who could not put aside violent, exploitative definitions of masculinity long enough to behave in ways that enslaved people considered Christian. Some argued that it was impossible for any whites to be Christians in practice so long as slavery existed. A formerly enslaved man named Charlie claimed that his master admitted that he had beaten Charlie simply because he had the power to do so. And yet, after slavery, Charlie, like many other African Americans, attempted to forgive whites for their moral weaknesses and failures. He reportedly said to his former owner: "I would have fought for you because I am a man among men." Charlie offered, in retrospect, to extend his protection, his forgiveness — elements more reminiscent of caretaking than of heroic manhood, despite his example of manly violence. Indeed, said Charlie, a mixture of caretaking and physical courage made him a man. But despite his reaching out to his former owner, Charlie never received equivalent respect from the ex-master. This failure reflected for Charlie not on his own manhood but on the still misshapen identity of the former slave owner, and so Charlie said to him: "You ain't right yet, Marster." [57]

No matter what they did to bolster their own sense of manhood, enslaved men still had to suffer from the behavior of white men who were far from "right." Conversion to Christianity or other behaviors that focused on maintaining one's own dignity still left caretakers vulnerable. Choosing whether to protect self or others forced some men to make no-win choices. In Alabama, Cato Carter, both the favorite slave and the nephew of Oll Carter, faced a difficult decision. Oll gave Cato a gun and told him to go out in the field and kill an enslaved man who had been mistreating the mules. Cato protested, but Oll insisted, leaving Cato with a painful choice. So Cato went to the field with the gun and said to the other enslaved man: "You has got to leave this minute, and I is too, 'cause I is s'pose to kill you, only I ain't and Massa Oll will kill me." The two men crawled through a fence into the woods and ran away. "I hated to go," recalled Carter in the 1930s. He had risked not only relative comfort but also personal safety and his attachment to his family by disobeying his owner and running away. "But today I is an old man and my hands ain't stained with no blood." Dignity triumphed. But other ex-slaves wondered whether forced submission had not taken away their will, stealing their dignity little by little with each death evaded. No wonder then that some men, looking back, regretted not choosing death, the glorious end of heroic masculinity. Robert Falls said, "If I had my life to live over . . . I would die fighting rather than be a slave again." Yet, Falls added, "In those days us niggers didn't know no better." Still, his own father was a famous fighter who resisted until threatened with sale from his family.[58] Death or division from one's family were the only realistic ends to such resistance that most of the enslaved could see.

For men enslaved on the plantation frontier, the struggle to maintain a self based on ordinary virtues was so fraught with contradictions to existing models of manhood that one might even wonder whether this identity was specifically masculine. Did caretaking men believe that their behavior made them men first and foremost, or that it made them good fathers, brothers, husbands, and friends? Did they strive to be good men or good Christians; to protect their manhood or their souls? If manhood was not foremost in their minds, can we measure their identities in terms of "masculinity"? Further complicating the issue was the emergence, from the chaos of forced migration, of a third mode of men's behavior. This new ideal was hardly heroic in the classical sense, but in it men clearly defined themselves as men first, ahead of other aspects of their identities. They now simply used a different, more ambiguous definition of manhood than the one offered by heroic resistance.

Forced migration closed the possibility of life within the more established communities and kin networks of the southeastern states, but for some men, it opened opportunities for new, more individualistic expressions of quasi-independent manhood. New chances emerged, in fact, from the landscape of white greed. At the peaks of economic booms, frantic planters eager to expand production paid exorbitant prices not only to buy but also to rent slaves. In Mississippi, in 1836, one planter paid two hundred dollars for each enslaved man whom he could hire for ten months. In the same year, a white woman reported that sawyers were hiring for two dollars a day, meaning that they would earn in a week what white laborers to the east made in a month. Migrant slave owners, eager for hard cash, hired out enslaved men as laborers, wagon drivers, and sawyers, and many allowed the workers to keep part of their hire as incentive. Of course, more than financial reward might have motivated a man like Harry, enslaved in Kentucky, who asked Thomas Gale to send him south to Mississippi to work as a wagoneer for Josiah or Robert Gale. Wagon driving gave a man freedoms denied to most of the enslaved, including physical mobility and a respite from the oversight of whites. While many enslaved African Americans objected strenuously to being moved south and west, Harry, imagining some degree of independence (however narrow) on the frontier, asked to go.[59]

"Root, hog, or die" went a saying in the expanding American empire, and in a purportedly African American song found scribbled in one planter's papers. White mythology about the frontier proclaimed that young men who threw off the shackles of established society and headed west had to root or die. Yet the ones who survived earned the psychic freedom of the self-constructed individual as well as other rewards. The song, which featured an enslaved man who also proclaimed, "I'm de chief cook, de bottle washer / Captain ob de waiters," may have been a white fantasy about what blacks sang. Or the song may have been a white transcription of something that blacks sang, or even some combination of the two. In any case, this version of "Root, Hog, or Die" contained some interesting lines.

The narrator depicted forced migration as a rude instruction to the limits of black men's lives in a world twisted by white force: "Oh white folks I hab crossed de mountains / How many miles I didn't count 'em / Oh, I'se left de folks at de old plantation / An' come down here for my education." "Down here" on the frontier, where planters applied brutal force to extract cotton from black labor, the narrator learned how things worked: "De first dat I eber got a licken / Was down at de forks ob de cotton picken." The Southwest was famed for the savagery of its punishments of the enslaved, and this may have been a "licken" that made any previous lashings seem like nothing. This singer brought southwest a new understanding—"I'm right from Old Virginny / Wid a packet full of news,"—of how he was accounted: "I'm worth a thousand dollars / As I stand here in my shoes." Accepting the way in which that valuation constrained his choices, he came to believe that his old values and relationships were irrelevant and that he would have to live in the new ones with no recourse to outside standards: "Makes no bit ob difference / To either you or I / Big pig, little pig, / Root, hog, or die." No matter what ties he wanted to preserve, they would be broken. No matter his dreams of constrained fatherhood or patriarchy, he could not preserve them. Rooting for oneself was unlikely to unearth anything on which to found a stable household or a durable freedom, if that was what one sought. If he wanted anything of his own, he must dig it out by himself, for himself, within slavery. Thus, he was left with one highly individualistic imperative: "Root, hog, or die." [60]

The best one could get might, in fact, be the chance to keep rooting. Few exemplified this rootless digging better than a man named Alfred. Enslaved first to a North Carolina woman, Alfred was sent to his owner's son-in-law in Alabama, a Mr. Sexton. Sexton hired Alfred to a local tavern keeper and then gave him a pass to hire himself out for the balance of 1844. Pass in hand, Alfred first went to an Alabama resort area. Finding bleaker prospects there than he had hoped, he moved on—without permission—to Lauderdale Springs in Mississippi. Sexton was at first certain that Alfred had absconded, but when Alfred returned, he gave Sexton all the money from his hire—"much to [Sexton's] relief and [Alfred's] honour." In a world that refused to admit that black men could have "honour," Alfred carved out his own version, one that even Sexton dimly recognized. Soon he traveled the area's waterways as a cabin servant on steamboats. His owner back in North Carolina liked the deal, for she and Sexton profited from Alfred's labors. Now, however, they could no longer hold the everyday violence of the plantation over his head. Alfred enjoyed the arrangement so much that he even refused an opportunity to go back to North Carolina, declining a return to his family that would also have meant returning to the master's gaze. [61]

Alfred's sense of manhood was not rooted in community, family, or a quasi-revolutionary ideology of resistance. Alfred was interested in none of those. Perhaps, however, he was not unusual. An unknown number of young men like Alfred traced the rivers and towns, roads and backwaters of the cotton frontier, trying to carve chips of individual freedom from the surface of the hard white empire—even if they had to do so by being chief cook and bottle washer. Some survived, and some even thrived. Some ran away, like "Owen's Rozier" who was hired to various planters in Mississippi by the agents of an absentee North Carolina planter and eventually "stole Mr. Howard's mule and carried him down below Carrolton and sold him." Taking the money, Rozier slipped from one degree of quasi-freedom into a deeper one. But to gain the opportunity to "take care of themselves," he, with Alfred and so many others, left behind family and other permanent attachments. [62]

Such men rejected identification with a coherent community bound by common interests. We can see this suggested in the experiences of William Wells

Brown, a fugitive slave who claimed that before his escape he worked first for a slave trader and later as a servant on a Mississippi steamboat. Brown preferred these kinds of work to hard labor in the field. Although he found distasteful many elements of his employment under the slave trader, he received in return a kind of mobility that he enjoyed. He was willing, if not eager, to black the gray hair of the older slaves for sale. Brown's travels eventually helped him to plan his escape. They also gave him the confidence and, perhaps, the amoral manipulativeness of others that enabled him on one notable occasion to pass on a whipping. Given a note to take to the jailer in Vicksburg, the then-illiterate Brown walked down to the docks and asked a sailor to read it to him. Upon being told that it requested the jailer to whip the bearer, Brown found an unsuspecting enslaved man who, equipped with less guile and less experience, accepted both the note and Brown's request to pick up a trunk at the jail. He went to the jail and received Brown's whipping. While Brown later felt guilty about the trick he had played, his experience taught him to reject the ideals of dignity and caring in order to protect himself. One can see that the very process of forced migration allowed some men to root up the prizes of an individualized manhood. Their way of being in the world did not create an alternative or antithesis to white domination. Indeed, rooting for oneself meant that at times one had to act directly against other enslaved people.[63]

On the frontiers of slave society, many enslaved men found that the formula of manhood that suited their situations and desires the best was confrontational yet elusive. Such men were again and again defeated by the white regime, but never quite checkmated. Such men usually avoided the life-or-death stands taken by men like Frederick Douglass—and others whose names we do not know because they were less successful. They escaped confrontation without giving the outward evidence of utter compliance that white men wanted to see. Overseer Henry Shaw bragged to his employer that he had symbolically and physically beaten Dick—the runaway from R. C. Ballard's Outpost plantation who hated to "have the name of being caught"—into a state of submission. "He is not as smart as he thought. I put him in the stocks and give him 100 licks with a strop[,] Sunday morning give him another hundred[,] and this morning I give him a hundred more and put him to work. He ses I have learned him something." Shaw clearly thought that he had "learned" Dick who was in charge and that in the future Dick would acknowledge his authority.[64]

Under torture, Dick said the magic words that made Shaw happy for a time. The overseer then asserted that he had "broken" Dick, but the slave had in effect signed surrender papers that meant nothing for the future. That summer and fall, as Shaw desperately drove the workers of Outpost plantation to gather the cotton crop, Dick aided other runaways and then ran himself. By January

Dick was negotiating with Shaw, visiting the quarters at night, and passing on the message that he wanted to meet with the absentee plantation owner Ballard. Dick refused to learn the "lessons" that Shaw sought to teach him. Who had the name of being "caught"—and who was being taught—now?[65]

Shaw's attempt to negotiate with Dick revealed a slowly growing understanding that an enslaved man who feigned surrender again and again, and who escaped again and again, was operating under a code of manhood that made him hard to defeat. In February 1854 a man with dogs caught Dick and brought him back to Outpost. Shaw ignored his earlier pledge not to punish Dick until they could both speak with Ballard. But he did not repeat the ordeal of three hundred lashes that he had given Dick the previous year. Instead he gave the runaway only a "sound paddling."[66] Shaw was realizing the frustration involved in trying to punish a man whose present defeat and physical humiliation did not promise future submission.

Dick and similar men accepted certain losses when they decided to define themselves as outsiders, individualistic rebels and outlaws, men who said "no" to every conventional expectation of manhood. They sought separation at the cost of close relationships. Dick was unreliable, and unsurprisingly he and his wife had a troubled marriage. She felt so little loyalty to him that she sometimes blamed him for her own actions. Men like Dick were likely to be sold away from family and friends. And they were perhaps least committed to carrying out obligations of relationship to others. A Tennessee ex-slave remembered with disgust her brother Henry Halfacre, a rebellious man who beat up an overseer and ran away, calling him "such a scoundrel" because he lived with several women and refused to support his children.[67]

Alfred, Dick, William Wells Brown, Henry Halfacre, although quite different from one another other, chose in their various ways one option: that of living on the outside of all communities. Each rejected the ideal of caretaking, and while men like Alfred and Dick rooted hard, they rooted for themselves alone. Seeking freedom from the plantation frontier's worst impositions, they rejected the ties of marriage, parenthood, and friendship. For them, each tie to another enslaved person could bring tremendous loss and pain. Investing oneself in caretaking manhood made one vulnerable to the assaults of slave owners. Caretakers worked all their lives to provide for those with whom they had forged new bonds. But, in an instant, an owner could decide to boil down those new relationships for the profits they would render—in the form of thriving, or at least surviving, black bodies—in the cauldron of the market.

Outsiders rejected caretaking and dignity. They gave up the ordinary virtue that would have held them to a standard of moral principles and self-sacrifice for others. Instead, they chose, not so much survival, but the chance to attain a sliver of independence, a piece of individuality. They did not internalize shame, since they understood that honor on white terms was impossible; many enslaved African American men saw little in white manhood that was worth imitating. Therefore, such men rejected both the white ideal of dominant manhood and the black ideal of the caretaker. Dissociating themselves, like Dick, from all defeats, they lied without compunction, resisted humiliation almost to the breaking point, and then ignored it when it occurred. Manifestations of new masculinity, recorded in the images of the bad man, the outlaw, and the shameless and aggressive trickster-slave, grew more common in the migrations that made the slaveholders' empire.[68]

Men who rooted hard for themselves created on the plantation frontier an individualistic, self-regarding African American masculinity. Like white manhood, the new ideal was restless and contradictory. Yet those who lived out the new identity were ciphers to whites, not rebels but individualistic semioutlaws who provided a slippery, mocking force that would-be masters could not pin. Men's attempts to realize the ideal produced real consequences in the lives of others, because creating this self required selfishness. In the context of a bourgeois white man's life, selfishness would have been not only acceptable (and not seen as selfishness) but supported by the legal, economic, and cultural weight of a society set up to realize the dream of masculinity. Such a man could support the fiction of his coherent self through his ability to carry out his wishes on the substrate of family, employees, property, and politics, in buying and selling in the market, or even on the bodies of his slaves. The law prohibited men like Dick and Alfred from carrying out such activities. To support their own fiction of a self that did not surrender, that could not be hurt, enslaved men had to resort to a different kind of selfishness. They abandoned shame; they abandoned women and children; they abandoned honesty. Or perhaps one could say that they exploited what they abandoned—like Dick, they feigned shame to trick masters; like Henry Halfacre, they used women and left children to avoid attachments.

Such behaviors were not previously unknown in the Southeast, but in the course of forced migration they became more common and were celebrated as ways in which to be a man. The ideal man was a rebel who was not a significant threat to slave owners' power, a resister who always ran away to snipe at white authority another day, a liar whose unwillingness to be possessed was his core truth. This ideal has had powerful effects. In these rebels, we can see the first hints of later migrants and wanderers—black men who, even after emancipation, sought their masculine identity neither as patriarchs nor as race men (alternative postemancipation archetypes of African American masculinity). Instead, rejecting both white authority and the commitment to caretaking that would have that fixed them in one place, easy targets for that authority, they strove to live as individuals.[69] In the forced migration to the plantation frontier, radically individualistic men pioneered a quintessentially modern identity, one shaped under the pressures of migration, the dissolution of family ties, and quasi-industrialized production. As time went on, their views metastasized into those of the outlaw, the gambler, the traveling man, and the wandering blues guitarist, men whose ambiguous dealings with both the devil and women became self-celebrated legend. All traced their points of origin to the costly creativity of men like Alfred, Henry, and Joe. So modern, malleable, and attractive is this particular style of male blackness that tables have turned, and whites have been trying to commodify and imitate it since at least the early twentieth century.[70]

For over a century, many African American intellectuals have criticized the outlaw version of black manhood and its myriad offshoots for its emphasis on individualism and its destructive effects. Looking back at slavery, these thinkers have, instead, valorized rebellion. But in so doing, they have implicitly or explicitly agreed with the nineteenth-century whites who believed that blacks who did not rebel in some way were absent all traces of manliness.[71] In this, they concur with the scholars whose standard of "resistant" masculinity and heroism has excluded manhood from the history of slavery; it is a subject defined by the absence of heroic masculine subjects.

Most enslaved African American men could not seize one ounce of freedom, steal one gram of independence, or force whites to treat them with respect. Men like Joe Kilpatrick, however, did not believe that resistant, heroic manhood was the only way to construct and enact their identities. In traders' droves and in slave labor camps of the southwestern frontier, the strong faced evidence of their own inability to control their lives, and men who prided themselves on taking care of others lost their families. In the face of grim realities, most of these men did more than merely survive. By living out the ordinary virtues of dignity and caring, Joe Kilpatrick and others gathered the lost around themselves, built and rebuilt families, and passed on lessons. They did not conform to the requirements of the types of masculinity we are likely to recognize, whether white domineering honor, or black heroic resistance. Perhaps we simply cannot see their way of being as masculinity, given our cultural blinders. Perhaps ordinary virtues were simply another path to a different definition of manhood.

One could argue, however, that ordinary virtues are not specifically masculine and that men thought of their actions as evidence not only of their manhood but also of their personhood and their souls. Although enslaved men seem to have connected caretaking to their social and cultural roles as husbands and fathers, which are obviously male roles, they may not have emphasized caretaking as masculine. The classical male "subject," the idea that there should be some dominating, impenetrable core of a man's identity, was thus absent from that way of being. And if masculinity did not serve as the core of their identities, perhaps it should not serve as a centerpiece to our understanding of how enslaved men defined their successes and failures. For most enslaved men on the plantation frontier, masculinity was indeed an absent subject. Still, the quest to enact ordinary virtues produced a coherent identity, whether specifically male or not. Because we have for so long questioned the manhood of enslaved men, perhaps it would be only fair for us to consider whether they, were they here today, might not question present-day America's apparent standards of masculine behavior. Why, they might ask, do many choose to base normative understandings of manhood not on the ways of ordinary virtue, but either on the ultimately false claims to impenetrability of heroism or on the selfishness of outlaw manhood? Indeed, these forms of identity may well look more like those espoused by white "masters" than those of caretakers. Perhaps even the quest to find masculinity in the past serves in perverse ways to normalize the oppressions and fictions that domineering forms of masculinity inflict on others, and on the self. Could it be that the enslaved and former enslaved might tell us that we still "ain't right yet?"

NOTES

The author would like to thank Jennifer Ratner-Rosenhagen, Phillip Troutman, and the editors of this volume for useful comments and criticism, as well as Stephanie Baptist and Fred D'Aguiar for interesting conversations on masculinity.

1. Francis Burdett to R. C. Ballard, 3 July 1848, folder 130, R. C. Ballard Papers, Southern Historical Collection, University of North Carolina (hereafter SHC).

2. George Jones, application 1184, Register of Signatures of Depositors in Branches of the Freemen's Savings and Trust Company, 1865–1874, Tallahassee, Fla., 25 August 1866–15 June 1874, National Archives Microfilm Series (NAMS) M816, roll 5 (hereafter RSD).

3. Authors of older works on slavery, including the sequence of synthetic books published in the 1950s, 1960s, and 1970s, do not make forced migration a central part of their argument: Eugene Genovese, in *Roll, Jordan, Roll: The World the Slaves Made* (New York: Vintage, 1974), says little on the subject (the domestic slave trade is mentioned on pages 419, 453, and 625, and masters' migrations are not discussed); Kenneth Stampp, *The Peculiar Institution* (New York: Knopf, 1956), 239–78, discusses the slave trade, but not masters' migrations; Stanley Elkins, *Slavery: A Problem in American Intellectual and Institutional Life* (Chicago: University of Chicago Press, 1959), mentions the domestic slave trade twice (53, 211). Both Leslie Howard Owens, *This Species of Property: Slave Life and Culture in the Antebellum South* (New York: Oxford University Press, 1976), 173–91, and John W. Blassingame, *The Slave Community: Plantation Life in the Antebellum South*, 2d ed. (New York: Oxford University Press, 1979), 173–76, discuss the interstate slave trade and family separations, as does as Herbert Gutman, in *The Black Family in Slavery and Freedom,*

*1750–1925* (New York: Pantheon, 1976). Gutman's is the only synthetic work on American slavery to discuss extensively the outcomes of slave migration, as he does with his work on plantation communities in transition (144–84). Much early debate, following the pattern of abolitionist critique, centered on the issue of family separations in the domestic slave trade: Frederic Bancroft, *Slave Trading in the Old South* (Baltimore: J. H. Faust, 1931); Winfield Collins, *The Domestic Slave Trade of the Southern States* (New York: Broadway, 1904); Robert Fogel and Stanley Engerman, *Time on the Cross: The Economics of American Negro Slavery* (Boston: Little, Brown, 1974), 42–58; Herbert Gutman and Richard Sutch, "The Slave Family: Protected Agent of Capitalist Masters or Victim of the Slave Trade?" in *Reckoning with Slavery: A Critical Study in the Quantitative History of American Negro Slavery*, ed. Paul A. David et al. (New York: Oxford University Press, 1976); Herbert Gutman, *Slavery and the Numbers Game: A Critique of "Time on the Cross"* (Urbana: University of Illinois Press, 1975), 106–7. More recent works have expanded discussion on the slave trade: Michael Tadman, *Speculators and Slaves: Masters, Traders, and Slaves in the Old South* (Madison: University of Wisconsin Press, 1989); Walter Johnson, *Soul by Soul: Life in the Antebellum Slave Market* (Cambridge: Harvard University Press, 1999); Phillip D. Troutman, "Slave Trade and Sentiment in Antebellum Virginia" (Ph.D. diss., University of Virginia, 2000). Other works, most of them also relatively recent, have begun to reexamine the scope and effects of forced migration, often in a local context. See Ann Patton Malone, *Sweet Chariot: Slave Family and Household Structure in Nineteenth-Century Louisiana* (Chapel Hill: University of North Carolina Press, 1992); Allan Kulikoff "Uprooted Peoples: Black Migrants in the Age of the American Revolution, 1790–1820," in *Slavery and Freedom in the Age of the American Revolution*, ed. Ira Berlin and Ronald Hoffman (Charlottesville: University Press of Virginia, 1983), 143–71; Steven Miller, "Plantation Labor Organization and Slave Life on the Cotton Frontier: The Alabama-Mississippi Black Belt, 1815–1840," in *Cultivation and Culture: Labor and the Shaping of Slave Life in the Americas*, ed. Ira Berlin and Philip D. Morgan (Charlottesville: University Press of Virginia, 1993), 155–69; Allan Kulikoff, *The Agrarian Origins of American Capitalism* (Charlottesville: University Press of Virginia, 1992), 226–63; Joan E. Cashin, *A Family Venture: Men and Women on the Southern Frontier* (Baltimore: Johns Hopkins University Press, 1994), 49–51; Gail S. Terry, "Sustaining the Bonds of Kinship in a Trans-Appalachian Migration, 1790–1811: The Cabell-Breckenridge Slaves Move West," *Virginia Magazine of History and Biography* 102 (1994), 455–76; Brenda Stevenson, *Life in Black and White: Family and Community in the Slave South* (New York: Oxford University Press, 1996), 218–25; Don H. Doyle, *Faulkner's County: The Historical Roots of Yoknapatawpha* (Chapel Hill: University of North Carolina Press, 2001), 128–31, 145–46; Edward E. Baptist, *Creating an Old South: Middle Florida's Plantation Frontier before the Civil War* (Chapel Hill: University of North Carolina Press, 2002).

4. Tadman, *Speculators and Slaves*, 303, produced the best estimate that we have of the number of slaves taken in the domestic slave trade, estimating that at least six hun-

dred thousand forced migrants went with slave traders. Historians disagree about whether the domestic trade selected for sex: Tadman, *Speculators and Slaves*, 26–30, 66–70; Troutman, "Slave Trade and Sentiment," 65. The big commercial traders may have taken more men than women. From 1831 to 1834, R. C. Ballard shipped more than a thousand slaves to Isaac Franklin, and Ballard's records of shipments show that 59 percent were male; R. C. Ballard and Co. Invoice Book, folder 417, volume 2; R. C. Ballard and Co., Slaves Bought, 1832–1834, folder 420, volume 4; [Enclosures in volume 4], folder 421, all R. C. Ballard Papers, SHC.

5. On race and masculinity in the antebellum United States, see Dana D. Nelson, *National Manhood: Capitalist Citizenship and the Imagined Fraternity of White Men* (Durham: Duke University Press, 1998); Stephanie McCurry, *Masters of Small Worlds: Yeoman Households, Gender Relations, and the Political Culture of the Antebellum South Carolina Low Country* (New York: Oxford University Press, 1995); Noel Ignatiev, *How the Irish Became White* (New York: Routledge, 1995); David R. Roediger, *The Wages of Whiteness: Race and the Making of the American Working Class* (London: Verso, 1991); Craig Wilder, *A Covenant with Color: Race and Social Power in Brooklyn* (New York: Columbia University Press, 2000); Edward Baptist, "'Cuffy,' 'Fancy Maids,' and 'One-Eyed Men': Rape, Commodification, and the Domestic Slave Trade in the United States," *American Historical Review* 106 (2001): 1619–60; E. Anthony Rotundo, *American Manhood: Transformations in Masculinity from the Revolution to the Modern Era* (New York: Basic Books, 1993); Michael Kimmel, *Manhood in America: A Cultural History* (New York: Free Press, 1996); François Furstenburg, "Beyond Freedom and Slavery: Autonomy, Virtue, and Resistance in Early American Political Discourse," *Journal of American History* 89 (2003): 1295–1330. For earlier episodes in the creation of these identities through the use of race and manhood, see Kathleen M. Brown, *Good Wives, Nasty Wenches, and Anxious Patriarchs: Gender, Race, and Power in Colonial Virginia* (Chapel Hill: University of North Carolina Press, 1996); Carroll Smith-Rosenberg, "Dis-Covering the Subject of the 'Great Constitutional Discussion,' 1786–1789," *Journal of American History* 79 (1992): 841–73; Mechal Sobel, *Teach Me Dreams: The Search for Self in the Revolutionary Era* (Princeton: Princeton University Press, 2000); Gail Bederman, *Manliness and Civilization: A Cultural History of Gender and Race in the United States, 1880–1917* (Chicago: University of Chicago Press, 1995).

6. See Eric Lott, *Love and Theft: Blackface Minstrelsy and the American Working Class* (New York: Oxford University Press, 1993); Robert Reid-Pharr, "Tearing the Goat's Flesh: Homosexuality, Abjection, and the Production of a Late Twentieth-Century Black Masculinity," *Studies in the Novel* 28 (1996): 372–94. Henry L. Gates, *Figures in Black: Words, Signs, and the "Racial" Self* (New York: Oxford University Press, 1987), and Paul Gilroy, *The Black Atlantic: Modernity and Double Consciousness* (Cambridge: Harvard University Press, 1993) concur with Reid-Pharr that the black self has been conceptualized, in Reid-Pharr's words, as "an inchoate, irrational nonsubject, as the chaos that both defines and threatens the borders of logic, individuality, and basic subjectivity" (373).

7. For white reasoning, see Furstenburg, "Beyond Freedom and Slavery"; Jim Cullen, "'I's a Man Now': Gender and African American Men," in *A Question of Manhood: A Reader in U.S. Black Men's History and Masculinity*, ed. Darlene Clark Hine and Earnestine Jenkins, vol. 1, *"Manhood Rights": The Construction of Black Male History and Manhood, 1750–1870* (Bloomington: Indiana University Press, 1999), 489–501; W. E. B. DuBois, *Black Reconstruction* (New York: Russell and Russell, 1935), 110; Michael Hatt, "'Making a Man of Him': Masculinity and the Black Body in Mid-Nineteenth-Century American Sculpture," *Oxford Art Journal* 15 (1992) 21–35. Even for many of the whites who supported black freedom, only the self-sacrifice of black men on the ramparts of Fort Wagner in 1863 would show that African American soldiers deserved the title of "men."

8. James O. Horton and Lois Horton, "Violence, Protest, and Identity: Black Manhood in Antebellum America," in Hine and Jenkins, *A Question of Manhood*, 382–98; Henry Highland Garnet, "Speech before the National Convention of Colored Citizens. Buffalo, New York, 16 August, 1843," in *The Black Abolitionist Papers*, ed. C. Peter Ripley, 5 vols. (Chapel Hill: University of North Carolina Press, 1985–92), 3:403–12; David Leverenz, *Manhood and the American Renaissance* (Ithaca: Cornell University Press, 1989), 108.

9. David Walker, *David Walker's Appeal to the Coloured Citizens of the World*, ed. Peter Hinks (University Park: Pennsylvania State University Press, 2000), 23, 28, 32.

10. Quotations from Walker, *Appeal*, 14–15, 18. For the wider agreement of large segments of the antebellum free black community with the ideas of manhood enunciated by Walker, see Horton and Horton, "Violence, Protest, and Identity"; Peter Hinks, *To Awaken My Afflicted Brethren: David Walker and the Problem of Antebellum Slave Resistance* (University Park: Pennsylvania State University Press, 1997); Richard Yarborough, "Race, Violence, and Manhood: The Masculine Ideal in Frederick Douglass's 'The Heroic Slave,'" in *Frederick Douglass: New Literary and Historical Essays*, ed. Eric Sundquist (New York: Cambridge University Press, 1990), 166–88. There is an astonishing correspondence between these ideas and those of the most un-Africanist of thinkers, Hegel; see G. W. F. Hegel, *The Phenomenology of Mind*, trans. J. B. Baillie (New York: Harper and Row, 1967), 233, and Alexandre Kojève, *Introduction to the Reading of Hegel: Lectures on the Phenomenology of Spirit*, trans. James H. Nichols Jr. (Ithaca: Cornell University Press, 1980). Hegel's discussion of the struggle unto death has exerted a powerful influence upon latter-day interpreters of slavery, including Orlando Patterson, who, in *Slavery and Social Death: A Comparative Study* (Cambridge.: Harvard University Press, 1982), argued that the slave was "socially dead" and "natally alienated," a perpetual outsider in society (7–8, 35–76).

11. William L. Andrews, *To Tell a Free Story: The First Century of Afro-American Autobiography, 1760–1865* (Urbana: University of Illinois Press, 1985), 127; Leverenz, *Manhood and the American Renaissance*, 108–34; for paradigmatic status see Charles J. Heglar, *Rethinking the Slave Narrative: Slave Marriage and the Narratives of Henry*

*Bibb and William and Ellen Craft* (Westport, Conn.: Greenwood Press, 2001), 16–22; Kenneth S. Greenberg, *Honor and Slavery: Lies, Duels, Noses, Masks, Dressing as a Woman, Gifts, Strangers, Humanitarianism, Death, Slave Rebellions, the Proslavery Argument, Baseball, Hunting, and Gambling in the Old South* (Princeton: Princeton University Press, 1996), 35–37.

12. For Douglass's movement toward a "whiter" masculine self-representation, in the sense of a greater dependence on claims to self-control and other-dominance as a component on the sense of self and manhood, see Leverenz, *Manhood and the American Renaissance*, 108–34; Robert Reid-Pharr, *Conjugal Union: The Body, the House, and the Black American* (New York: Oxford University Press, 1999).

13. Lewis Clarke, in *Slave Testimony: Two Centuries of Letters, Speeches, Interviews, and Autobiographies*, ed. John W. Blassingame (Baton Rouge: Louisiana State University Press, 1977), 152. For the contradictory nature of mastery (and self-mastery too, perhaps), see Hegel, *Phenomenology of Mind*, 236–37, and Kojève, *Introduction to the Reading of Hegel*, 46–47. Some argue that masculinity in all cultures takes the form of an attempt to impose a false unity on disparate selves, control over the uncontrollable, a final answer to persistent questions of achievement and identity; see Elisabeth Badinter, *X/Y: On Masculine Identity* (New York: Columbia University Press, 1995); Sigmund Freud, "Fetishism," in *The Standard Edition of the Complete Psychological Works of Sigmund Freud*, ed. James Strachey (London: Hogarth Press, 1953), 21 : 152–58; Sigmund Freud, "The Sexual Aberrations," in Strachey, *Standard Edition*, vol. 7, esp. 152–55. For southern white men and their contradictions, see Bertram Wyatt-Brown, *Southern Honor: Ethics and Behavior in the Old South* (New York: Oxford University Press, 1982); Edward Baptist, "Accidental Ethnography in an Antebellum Southern Newspaper: Snell's Homecoming Festival," *Journal of American History* 84 (1998): 1355–83; Johnson, *Soul by Soul;* David R. Roediger, *Black on White: Black Writers on What It Means to be White* (New York: Schocken, 1998). On sexual coercion as a component of mastery and masculinity, see Sharon Block, "Lines of Color, Sex, and Service: Comparative Sexual Coercion in Early America," in *Sex, Love, Race: Crossing Boundaries in North American History*, ed. Martha Hodes (New York: New York University Press, 1999), 141–63, esp. 143–48; Baptist, "'Cuffy'"; for male-on-male rape by owners, see Harriett Jacobs, *Incidents in the Life of a Slave Girl* (Boston, 1861), 288–89. Political and social conflict with lower-class white men forced many planter men to find ways to balance the ideal and the actual, especially after the 1830s: see J. Mills Thornton III, *Power and Politics in a Slave Society: Alabama, 1800–1860* (Baton Rouge: Louisiana State University Press, 1978); Baptist, *Creating an Old South;* McCurry, *Masters of Small Worlds*, 128–29. Some planters never adjusted to relative democratization: see Drew Gilpin Faust, *James Henry Hammond and the Old South: A Design for Mastery* (Baton Rouge: Louisiana State University Press, 1982), 131–33. White women were more easily controlled, in theory, given the legal, economic, and cultural authority given to white men by marriage: Victoria Bynum, *Unruly Women: The Politics of Social and Sexual Control in the*

*Old South* (Chapel Hill: University of North Carolina Press, 1992); McCurry, *Masters of Small Worlds*, 171–207.

14. For years racist white vernacular historiography, black shame about the past, and white academic historiography agreed in assuming that the lack of revolution also meant a deeper moral or other failing of character among the enslaved. Frequently this was expressed in the language of masculinity. Stanley Elkins argued that slavery's traumas infantilized black males, shaping them into childlike and decidedly unmanly "Sambos." Herbert Aptheker, John Blassingame, and Herbert Gutman redeployed black men as men—as revolutionary rebels, protoblack nationalists, and fathers— who fit into patterns that would have been comforting to nineteenth-century free northern blacks. Meanwhile Eugene Genovese emphasized that the antebellum southern lower classes, both black and white, never led a social revolution that challenged the terms dictated by the planter class. That absence showed that both groups had been swindled into willing submission; Blassingame, *Slave Community;* Elkins, *Slavery;* Gutman; *Black Family;* Genovese, *Roll, Jordan, Roll.* See also the critiques of Genovese's assumptions about manhood in his analysis of slave Christianity and his approval of the "forcefulness" of the planter class: Clarence E. Walker, *Deromanticizing Black History: Critical Essays and Reappraisals* (Knoxville: University of Tennessee Press, 1991), 68–72. More recently, Darlene Clark Hine and Earnestine Jenkins argue in their summary of twenty-three articles about African American men before 1873 that the most salient characteristic of masculinity in slavery is that the experience of enslavement "provoked" among black men a "resistant masculinity." That perhaps only three of these twenty-three articles actually discuss the forms of masculinity "provoked" by the experience of slavery, suggests the difficulty in forcing experience into this template. Hine and Jenkins are determined to find evidence of "resistant" masculinity, but how can we define masculinity that might not always be able to resist? "Black Men's History: Towards a Gendered Perspective," in Hine and Jenkins, *A Question of Manhood*, 1–60; quotation, 57. Critiques of the valorization of revolution by historians include Johnson, *Soul by Soul*, 186–88, and James Scott, *Domination and the Arts of Resistance: Hidden Transcripts* (New Haven: Yale University Press, 1990).

15. Pioneering works on the history of women in American slavery include Deborah Gray White, *Ar'n't I A Woman? Female Slaves in the Plantation South*, 2d ed. (New York: Norton, 1999), 27–46; Angela Y. Davis, *Women, Race and Class* (New York: Vintage, 1981), 3–29; Stevenson, *Life in Black and White;* Stephanie Camp, "Viragos: Enslaved Women's Everyday Politics in the Old South (Ph.D. diss., University of Pennsylvania, 1998); Hortense Spillers, "Mama's Baby, Papa's Maybe: An American Grammar Book," *Diacritics* 17 (1987): 65–81; Catherine Clinton, "Caught in the Web of the Big House: Women and Slavery," in *The Web of Southern Social Relations: Women, Family, and Education*, ed. Walter J. Fraser Jr., R. Frank Saunders Jr., and Jon L. Wakelyn (Athens: University of Georgia Press, 1985), 19–34; idem, *The Plantation Mistress: Woman's World in the Old South* (New York: Pantheon, 1982), 212–13, 220–21; Saidiya Hartmann, *Scenes of Subjection: Terror, Slavery, and Self-*

*Making in Nineteenth-Century America* (New York: Oxford University Press, 1997), 79–112; Patricia Gordon, ed., *Discovering the Women in Slavery: Emancipating Perspectives on the American Past* (Athens: University of Georgia Press, 1996), 47–60; Thelma Jennings, "'Us Colored Women Had to Go through a Plenty,'" *Journal of Women's History* 1 (1990): 45–74; and Nell Irvin Painter, "Soul Murder and Slavery: Toward a Fully Loaded Cost Accounting," in *U.S. History as Women's History: New Feminist Essays*, ed. Linda K. Kerber, Alica Kessler-Harris, and Kathryn Kish Sklar (Chapel Hill: University of North Carolina Press, 1995), 125–46; Leslie Schwalm, *"A Hard Fight for We": Women's Transition from Slavery to Freedom in South Carolina* (Urbana: University of Illinois Press, 1997); Marli F. Weiner, *Mistresses and Slaves: Plantation Women in South Carolina, 1830–1880* (Urbana: University of Illinois Press, 1998); Nell Irvin Painter, *Sojourner Truth: A Life, a Symbol* (New York: Norton, 1996); David Barry Gaspar and Darlene Clark Hine, *More Than Chattel: Black Women in the Americas* (Bloomington: Indiana University Press, 1996); Elizabeth Fox-Genovese, *Within the Plantation Household: Black and White Women of the Old South* (Chapel Hill: University of North Carolina Press, 1988). See the historiographical discussion in Michele Mitchell, "Silences Broken, Silences Kept: Gender and Sexuality in African-American History," *Gender and History* 11 (1999): 433–44.

16. The witness of the ex-slaves, if we read carefully, can tell us much about the ways in which they remembered the ideas that helped shape their years of enslavement. This is the case even though recent historians and literary critics have almost completely dismissed the WPA narratives. Some argue that the age of the interviewees, the race (white) and power of the interviewers (many were prominent in the communities in which interviewees lived, some were children of the ex-slaves former owners, and so on) taint these sources. See the introduction to Blassingame, *Slave Testimony*, xliii–lxii; Johnson, *Soul by Soul*, 8–11, 226n. 24; and Donna J. Spindel, "Assessing Memory: Twentieth-Century Slave Narratives Reconsidered," *Journal of Interdisciplinary History* 27 (1996): 247–61. However, see the discussion of both complexities and possibilities in Sharon Ann Musher, "Contesting the Way 'The Almighty Wants It': Crafting Memories of Ex-Slaves in the Slave Narrative Collection," *American Quarterly* 53 (2001): 1–31. Yet nineteenth-century narratives by former slaves also have "problems." Fugitive slave narratives published before the Emancipation Proclamation are disproportionately from slaves who grew to adulthood in, and escaped from, the upper South and so cannot tell us all that we want to know about the plantation frontier. Even when African Americans achieved freedom, their words fell into, were shaped by, and recorded within the white debates that treated slave masculinity as an object. So Frederick Douglass learned, forcing him into a new, continued struggle against a different kind of bondage; William S. McFeely, *Frederick Douglass* (New York: Norton, 1991); Waldo E. Martin Jr., *The Mind of Frederick Douglass* (Chapel Hill: University of North Carolina Press, 1984); and Sterling Bland, *Voices of the Fugitives: Runaway Slave Stories and their Fictions of Self-Creation* (Westport, Conn.: Greenwood Press, 2000). Despite the difference in social power between white in-

terviewers and elderly black interviewees in the WPA interviews, ex-slaves often slipped in critiques of whites—or even overtly rebuked locally powerful whites for attempting to tint the history of enslavement in warm paternalist hues. Laura Stewart of Georgia constructed her words as a corrective to white mystifications: "In spite of what *white ladies* say in de papers . . . I can 'member slaves being sold at markets, outside," in Augusta, where she lived. When read collectively, the narratives reveal in their common themes and tropes a tradition of criticism that may have been formed around the campfires of slave traders and which was clearly passed on in the slave cabins of the plantation frontier; George Rawick, gen. ed., general introduction, *The American Slave: A Composite Autobiography*, suppl., ser. 1 (Westport, Conn.: Greenwood Press, 1979), 11:xxxix, and Edward E. Baptist "'Stol' and Fetched Here': The Creation of a Vernacular History by Enslaved Migrants to the Old Southwest" (paper presented to Southern Historical Association, Louisville, Ky., November 2000). As Susan Merritt, an ex-slave from Texas, insisted, age was not always a barrier to recalling early, formative experiences: "I couldn't tell how old I is, but does you think I'd ever forget them slave days?"; Susan Merritt, in *American Slave*, 5.3 (Texas), 75; Laura Stewart, in *American Slave*, suppl., ser. 1, 4.2 (Georgia), 593; *American Slave*, 18 (Tenn.), 141–42.

17. Paul Cameron to Duncan Cameron, 2 December 1845, folder 973, Cameron Family Papers, SHC; Everard Green Baker Diary, 23 March 1849 and 27 September 1849, folder 2, Everard Green Baker Papers, SHC; C. Steele to Samuel S. Boyd, 7 June 1847, folder 112, R. C. Ballard Papers, SHC; *American Slave*, 18 (Tenn.), 256; John Hope Franklin and Loren Schweninger, *Runaway Slaves: Rebels on the Plantation* (New York: Oxford University Press, 1999), 160–64.

18. *American Slave*, suppl., ser. 2, 1 (Arkansas), 33; William Dudley Gale to Anne Gale, 8 April 1844, folder 3, Gale and Polk Papers, SHC; interview with Samuel Scomp, 1826, in Blassingame, *Slave Testimony*, 180–81.

19. J. S. Short to T. P. Westray, 1 August 1838, folder 5, Battle Family Papers, SHC.

20. L. A. Finley to Caroline Gordon, 17 February 1853, folder 10, Gordon-Hackett Papers, SHC; A. K. Barlow to James J. Philips, n.d., folder 1, Ivan P. Battle Papers, SHC; J. S. Haywood to G. W. Haywood, 1 December 1837, folder 151, Haywood Papers, SHC; P. A. Bolling to Edmund Hubard, n.d., folder 72, Hubard Family Papers, SHC.

21. Whites in Tennessee called men who would not fight in response to an insult "Poke-easy"; Blassingame, *Slave Testimony*, 157.

22. E. G. Baker Diary, 2 June 1854, folder 2, Everard Green Baker Papers, SHC; Ann Clark, in *American Slave*, 4.1 (Texas), 223–24; *American Slave*, 18 (Tenn.), 77, 95, 296.

23. William Craft, *Running a Thousand Miles for Freedom; or, The Escape of Ellen and William Craft from Slavery* (London: W. Tweedie, 1860), 14–15.

24. For purchases specifically for the purpose of this form of exploitation, see Richard Macks, in *American Slave*, 16.3 (Maryland), 54; also 18 (Tenn.), 251–52; Rosa and Jack Maddox, suppl., ser. 2, 7.6 (Texas), 2531; Mary Reynolds, 8.7 (Texas), 3292; Julia Williams, 16.4 (Ohio), 104; Charles Perdue, Thomas Barden, and Robert

Phillips, eds., *Weevils in the Wheat: Interviews With Virginia Ex-Slaves* (Charlottesville: University Press of Virginia, 1992), 250; Blassingame, *Slave Testimony*, 362, 400. Melton A. McLaurin, *Celia: A Slave* (Athens: University of Georgia Press, 1991); L. R. Starks to R. C. Ballard, 5 February 1833, folder 10; P. B. January to R. C. Ballard, 28 October 1854, folder 217; P. B. January to R. C. Ballard, 29 November 1854, folder 219. Ballard Papers, SHC.

25. A. D. Headen to Archibald Boyd, 24 October 1858, Archibald Boyd Papers, Rare Book, Manuscripts, and Special Collections Library, Duke University. (hereafter Duke); James P. Franklin to Messrs. R. C. Ballard and Co., 27 March 1832, folder 5; Isaac Franklin to R. C. Ballard, 29 January 1833, folder 10; Isaac Franklin to R. C. Ballard, 25 December 1833, folder 12; and Bacon Tait to R. C. Ballard, 25 November 1838, folder 25, Ballard Papers, SHC; interview with Tabb Gross and Lewis Smith, 1861, in Blassingame, *Slave Testimony*, 347; Perdue, Barden, and Phillips, *Weevils in the Wheat*, 48–49; Stevenson, *Life in Black and White*, 236–37; Mary Reynolds, *American Slave*, 5.3 (Texas) 243–44.

26. Isaac Williams, *Aunt Sally; or, The Cross the Way of Freedom. A Narrative of the Slave-Life and Purchase of the Mother of Rev. Isaac Williams, of Detroit* (Cincinnati: American Reform Tract and Book Society, 1858), 102; Blassingame, *Slave Testimony*, 362, 400.

27. *American Slave*, suppl., ser. 1, 4.2 (Georgia), 373; *American Slave*, 7.1 (Oklahoma), 325; *American Slave*, suppl., ser. 1, 4.2 (Georgia), 423; American Slave, 18 (Tenn.), 298; Blassingame, *Slave Testimony*, 400–402, 422, 505. For whites' confessions that they believed in such strangely intertwined relationships, see Jesse Cage to Thomas Cotton, 27 August 1839, folder 28, Ballard Papers, SHC; Baptist, "'Cuffy,'"; Joan Dayan, *Haiti, History, and the Gods* (Berkeley: University of California Press, 1995), 197–99; and Johnson, *Soul by Soul*. For masculinity and markets, see the implications of Edward Balleisen, *Navigating Failure: Bankruptcy and Commercial Society in Antebellum America* (Chapel Hill: University of North Carolina Press, 2001).

28. Solomon Northup, *Twelve Years a Slave. Narrative of Solomon Northup, a Citizen of New-York, Kidnapped in Washington City in 1841 and Rescued in 1853, from a Cotton Plantation near the Red River in Louisiana* (Auburn, [N.Y.]: Derby and Miller; Buffalo: Derby, Orton and Mulligan; London: Sampson Low, Son and Company, 1853), 108, 194–96, reported that many enslaved people transported to Louisiana cotton and sugar plantations had to work on Sundays and nights to obtain necessities such as meat (202–4). Independent production or small-scale marketing and "internal economies" could make a difference in the lives of the enslaved; Roderick McDonald, *The Economy and Material Culture of Slaves: Goods and Chattels on the Sugar Plantations of Jamaica and Louisiana* (Baton Rouge: Louisiana State University Press, 1993); Larry Hudson, *To Have and to Hold: Slave Work and Family Life in Antebellum South Carolina* (Athens: University of Georgia Press, 1997); Larry Hudson, ed., *Working toward Freedom: Slave Society and Domestic Economy in the American South* (Rochester, N.Y.: University of Rochester Press, 1994); Ira Berlin and Philip D. Morgan, eds., *The Slaves' Economy: Independent Production by Slaves*

*in the Americas* (London: Frank Cass, 1991); Dylan Penningroth, "Slavery, Freedom, and Social Claims to Property among African Americans in Liberty County, Georgia, 1850–1880," *Journal of American History* 84 (1997): 405–35.

29. Quotation from J. G. Rowe to James C. Cole, n.d., folder 14, Cole-Taylor Papers, SHC; Johnson, *Soul by Soul*, 78–116; Alexander Allen to G. W. Allen, 29 December 1849, folder 2, G. W. Allen Papers, SHC.

30. *American Slave*, 18 (Tenn.), 298; Perdue, Barden, and Phillips, *Weevils in the Wheat*, 318; *American Slave*, 18 (Tenn.), 129; *American Slave*, 2.1 (South Carolina), 158.

31. *American Slave*, 7.1 (Oklahoma), 89; *American Slave*, 8.2 (Arkansas), 206; *American Slave*, 8.3 (Mississippi), 1170; Perdue, Barden, and Phillips, *Weevils in the Wheat*, 180, 21, 215; Blassingame, *Slave Testimony*, 155, 163, 263–64.

32. Cotton booms often displayed "irrational exuberance," to use Alan Greenspan's language, and cruelty, but also badly reformulated economic structures and moral and social conventions; Richard Dunn, *Sugar and Slaves: The Rise of the Planter Class in the English West Indies, 1624–1713* (Chapel Hill: University of North Carolina Press, 1972); James, *Black Jacobins;* Robin Blackburn, *The Rise of New World Slavery: From the Baroque to the Modern, 1492–1800* (London: Verso, 1997); Edmund S. Morgan, *American Slavery, American Freedom: The Ordeal of Colonial Virginia* (New York: Norton, 1975).

33. Baptist, *Creating an Old South;* Christopher D. Morris, *Becoming Southern: The Evolution of a Way of Life, Warren County and Vicksburg, Mississippi, 1770–1860* (New York: Oxford University Press, 1995); Daniel Dupre, *Transforming the Cotton Frontier: Madison County, Alabama, 1800–1840* (Baton Rouge: Louisiana State University Press, 1997); Thornton, *Power and Politics;* Sarah P. Russell, "Cultural Conflicts and Common Interests: The Making of the Sugar Planter Class in Louisiana, 1795–1853," (Ph.D. diss., University of Maryland, 2000).

34. For runaways and Native Americans, see Franklin and Schweninger, *Runaway Slaves*, 87–89, 112–16. Kenneth W. Porter, *The Negro on the American Frontier* (New York: Arno, 1971), 182–358, has a different view. For southwestern whites' fears, see Adam Rothman, "The Expansion of Slavery in the Deep South, 1790–1820," (Ph.D. diss., Columbia University, 2000); Isaac Franklin to R. C. Ballard, 28 February 1831, folder 1, Ballard Papers, SHC; Alex Bontemps, *The Punished Self: Surviving Slavery in the Colonial South* (Ithaca: Cornell University Press, 2001); Ira Berlin, *Many Thousands Gone: The First Two Centuries of Slavery in North America* (Cambridge: Harvard University Press, 1998).

35. J. S. Haywood to G. W. Haywood, 21 June 1837, folder 150, Haywood Papers, SHC; H. Shaw to R. C. Ballard, 15 March 1853, folder 188, R. C. Ballard Papers, SHC.

36. Joseph H. Labrenty to John Waddill, 22 September 1836, folder 6, Elijah Fuller Papers, SHC.

37. Elcho Plantation Account Book, 1857, page 134, folder 453, R. C. Ballard Papers, SHC; Franklin and Schweninger, *Runaway Slaves;* H. Shaw to R. C. Ballard, 15 March 1853, folder 188, R. C. Ballard Papers, SHC.

38. Tzvetan Todorov, *Facing the Extreme: Moral Life in the Concentration Camps*, trans. Arthur Denner and Abigail Pollak (New York: Metropolitan Books, 1996), 8, 10; Todorov analyzes moral life among the prisoners of the concentration camps of the Nazis and the Soviets. The apt criticisms of Stanley Elkins's misuse of early analyses of concentration-camp psychology to create his famed "Sambo thesis" do not apply here; for criticism of Elkins, see Ann J. Lane, ed., *The Debate Over Slavery: Stanley Elkins and His Critics* (Urbana: University of Illinois Press, 1971). Elkins's argument that moral life in concentration camps and on cotton plantations were the same, which would supposedly produced similar personalities in reaction to similar conditions—i.e., the *Kapo* and the Sambo. In contrast, Todorov and I are both writing about how people understood the ethics of actions taken in response to morally wrong deprivations of freedom.

39. *American Slave*, 18 (Tenn.), 95, 296; "Mrs. Webb" interview, in Ronnie Clayton, ed., *Mother Wit: The Ex-Slave Narratives of the Louisiana Writers' Project* (New York: P. Lang, 1990), 209.

40. This ideal of heroic revolution as the true measure of resistance—and, in the assumption of many, of manhood—has stunted good scholarship, according to Michael P. Johnson's rebuke to previous scholarship on the Vesey conspiracy scare. Denmark Vesey's conspiracy, a rebellion plotted in Charleston, South Carolina, in 1822, has been one of the major historiographical examples of large-scale slave resistance in U.S. history; see Michael P. Johnson, "Denmark Vesey and His Co-Conspirators," *William and Mary Quarterly*, 3d ser., 58 (2001): 917–75; and the responses (and his counterresponse) in "Forum: The Making of a Slave Conspiracy, pt. 2," *William and Mary Quarterly*, 3d ser., 59 (2002): 135–201. See the extensive scholarship cited by Johnson that addresses the Vesey conspiracy.

41. Todorov, *Facing the Extreme*, 15–24.

42. Peter Carter, RSD 359; John Walker, RSD 377. Others, like William Stephens, who left nine children in North Carolina, remarried but did not have any other children in the Southwest; RSD 634. Herbert Gutman's analysis of Mississippi freedpeople's registration of their marriages with the Union Army in 1864–65 found a large number of remarried men, who had been separated by force (most likely via migration) from earlier spouses; see Gutman, *Black Family*, 145–55.

43. Charles Ball, *Slavery in the United States: A Narrative of the Life and Adventures of Charles Ball* . . . (New York: John S. Taylor, 1837), 263–65, 275. See the exegesis of Ball's account in Bruce, *Origins of African American Literature*.

44. Wm C. Bryarly to Samuel Bryarly, 17 February 1848, folder 1844–1858, Samuel Bryarly Papers, Duke. Meanwhile, told that he "would be able to get another wife in Georgia," Charles Ball eventually escaped, not once but twice, to return to his Maryland family; Ball, *Slavery in the United States*, 36.

45. Jack Hannibal to Dear Mistress, 9 August 1878, Jack Hannibal Letter, Duke.

46. In contrast, some earlier planters exulted in comparing themselves to patriarchal masters from Genesis; see William Byrd II to Charles, Earl of Orrery, 5 July 1726, in

"Virginia Council Journals, 1726–1753," *Virginia Magazine of History and Biography* 32 (1924): 27; and Rhys Isaac, *The Transformation of Virginia, 1740–1790* (Chapel Hill: University of North Carolina Press, 1982), 39–40.

47. Nor were his siblings the ones who had sold him into the slave trade—although some enslaved African American men did find themselves in such a situation; see *American Slave*, 18 (Tenn.), 86: "I was mighty near Joseph and my half-brother sold me."

48. Green Davidson, RSD O.A. [original application series] 135; Robert Henry, RSD O.A. 273; Isaac Davis RSD 351; Isaac Foster, RSD 660; Jesse Courtney, RSD 902; Green Monroe, RSD 910; Mortgage of William S. Cabell and William Spotswood Cabell to Morton, Pleasants, and Company, 1842, folder 1, Thomas Bibb Papers, Duke; Thomas Bray to O. Fields, 10 June 1823, Obadiah Fields Papers, Duke; Jos. Sheppard to Jas. and John Sheppard, 17 September 1843, James Sheppard Papers, Duke; *American Slave*, 6.1 (Alabama), 168; Gutman, *Black Family*, 124, 128.

49. *American Slave*, suppl., ser. 1, 8.3 (Mississippi), 1240; Mia Bay, *The White Image in the Black Mind : African-American Ideas about White People, 1830–1925* (New York: Oxford University Press, 2000); Baptist, "Stol' and Fetched Here.'" Such naming practices differed from the more stable naming patterns found on long-established lowcountry plantations; Cheryll Ann Cody, "There Was No 'Absalom' on the Ball Plantations: Slave-Naming Practices in the South Carolina Low Country, 1720–1865," *American Historical Review* 92 (1987): 563–96.

50. Perdue, Barden, and Phillips, *Weevils in the Wheat*, 71.

51. *American Slave*, suppl., ser. 1 , 10.5 (Mississippi), 2113. One visitor who described southwestern women in the fields as automatons was Frederick Law Olmsted, *The Cotton Kingdom: A Traveller's Observations . . .* ed. Arthur M. Schlesinger Sr. (New York: Modern Library, 1984), 451–52. Some forced migrants did not survive the separation from their loved ones; *American Slave*, 2.2 (South Carolina), 235.

52. Christopher Morris, "Within the Slave Cabin," in Christine Daniels and Michael Kennedy, eds., *Over the Threshold: Intimate Violence in Early America* (New York: Routledge, 1999), 268–85. For the ideas of free black men in the North about male dominance, see James O. Horton, "Freedom's Yoke: Gender Conventions among Antebellum Free Blacks," *Feminist Studies* 12 (1986): 51–76, for the ideas of free black men in the North about male dominance.

53. William Harriss to Thomas Harriss, 29 April 1833, folder 1795–1834, Thomas Whitmel Harriss Papers, Duke.

54. *American Slave*, 19 (Tenn.), 98–99.

55. *American Slave*, 19 (Tenn.), 19, 23. Salvation from the east (which of course has other symbolic references in Christian and in African American visions as well), in *American Slave*, 19 (Tenn.), 24, 33, 37, 64, 81, 154; visions of family, in *American Slave*, 19 (Tenn.), 43, 45–46, 71, 95; *American Slave*, 19 (Tenn.), 162–65.

56. *American Slave*, 19 (Tenn.), 104–45.

57. Ibid., 124, 165, 175. In his telling, Scott Bond, who had been moved with his enslaved mother to Arkansas, eventually went back to Mississippi to see if he could help his *white* father; *American Slave*, suppl., ser. 2, 1 (Arkansas), 34–37. For Christianity as

a source of critique, see Bay, *White Image*, 178–83. Genovese, *Roll, Jordan, Roll*, argues that Christianity's critique of masters was less significant than its role in helping the enslaved to identify with their owners. This author simply does not see such a pattern in evidence in the WPA narratives. Even documents like Jack Hannibal's letter use the common ground of Christianity in an instrumental sense, attempting to talk whites into acting in *blacks'* interests.

58. *American Slave*, 4.1 (Texas), 12–13, 16, 208–9.

59. T. J. Brownrigg to Richard Brownrigg, 29 January 1836, folder 4, Brownrigg Papers, SHC; Sarah Amis to Mrs. Hugh Johnston, 22 December 1836, folder 40, Elizabeth Blanchard Papers, SHC; Thomas Gale to Josiah Gale, 22 August 1833, folder 2, Gale and Polk Papers, SHC.

60. "Root, Hog," n.d., James B. Bailey Papers, SHC. For the southwest as a rumored site of white savagery, see *American Slave*, 18 (Tenn.), 202–3, 256. For white beliefs about the frontier as a site where white men transformed themselves into patriarchs and leaders, see Richard Slotkin, *The Fatal Environment: The Myth of the Frontier in the Age of Industrialization, 1800–1890* (New York: Atheneum, 1985).

61. A. R. Sexton to Ann Thomas, 7 March 1844; A. R. Sexton to Ann Thomas, 20 November 1844; Ann Thomas to Anna Fuller, 24 April 1847, all in Fuller-Thomas Papers, Duke.

62. Mary Bartlett to William Blanks, 14 December 1841, Mary Blanks Papers, Duke; William Wells Brown, *Narrative of William Wells Brown*, in *Slave Narratives*, ed. William Andrews and Henry L. Gates (New York: Library of America, 2000), 409; W. Jeffrey Bolster, *Black Jacks: African American Seamen in the Age of Sail* (Cambridge: Harvard University Press, 1997).

63. William Wells Brown, *The Black Man, His Antecedents, His Genius, and His Achievements* (New York: T. Hamilton, 1863), 19–26; William Wells Brown, *Narrative of William Wells Brown, an American Slave, Written by Himself* (Boston: Anti-Slavery Office, 1847), 34–57. Brown came to be a "Negro antithesis who defies all the norms of respectability"—including those of his own people; Andrews, *To Tell a Free Story*, 145. J. D. [Jacob] Green, *Narrative of the Life of Jacob Green, a Runaway Slave, from Kentucky, Containing an Account of His Three Escapes, in 1839, 1846, 1848* (Huddersfield, Eng.: Henry Fielding, 1864), not only claimed to have played the same trick as Brown, but was in general a trickster who worked against both whites and blacks. Also see William Hayden, *Narrative of William Hayden, Containing a Faithful Account of His Travels for a Number of Years, Whilst a Slave, in the South* (Cincinnati: William Hayden, 1846), and Troutman, "Slave Trade and Sentiment." Recent scholarship has challenged the simplistic ideal of a protonationalist or collective community identity among the enslaved. See Stevenson, *Life in Black and White;* Penningroth, "Slavery, Freedom"; Evelyn Brooks Higginbotham, "African-American Women's History and the Metalanguage of Race," in *Feminism and History*, ed. Joan W. Scott (New York: Oxford University Press, 1996), 183–208; and Nell Irvin Painter, "Soul Murder and Slavery," 125–46.

64. H. Shaw to R. C. Ballard, 14 March 1853, folder 188, Ballard Papers, SHC.

65. H. Shaw to R. C. Ballard, 12 July, 17 July, 31 July 1853, folder 195; H. Shaw to R. C. Ballard, 24 September 1853, folder 198; H. Shaw to R. C. Ballard, 13 November 1853, folder 200; H. Shaw to R. C. Ballard, [clearly fall 1853], folder 205; H. Shaw to R. C. Ballard, 15 January 1854, folder 206; H. Shaw to R. C. Ballard, 24 January 1854, folder 207, Ballard Papers, SHC.

66. H. Shaw to R. C. Ballard, 18 February 1854, folder 209, Ballard Papers, SHC.

67. H. Shaw to R. C. Ballard, 12 July 1853, folder 145, Ballard Papers, SHC; *American Slave*, 18 (Tenn.), 77, 246.

68. For "rough" masculine culture among African American men in the Old Southwest, see Charles Thompson, *Biography of a Slave, Being the Experiences of Charles Thompson . . .* (Dayton, Ohio: United Brethren, 1875), 49. Hints of such behaviors appeared before slavery expanded to the southwestern states, but they flowered in the massive expansion of slavery that followed American independence. Cf. Bontemps, *The Punished Self.* Patterson and Wyatt-Brown described the "shameless slave" personality as a permanent condition, one with little evidence of oppositional behavior, rather than as a momentary tactic. Shamelessness, of course, was defined by the master class, which could not easily understand those to whom shame did not stick; see Patterson, *Slavery and Social Death*, 196–97. Meanwhile, discourse in enslaved families and communities reinforced suspicion of white claims to masculinity; Bay, *White Image;* Roediger, *Black on White.*

69. For discussions of postemancipation evolutions of African American male identity, see Lawrence Levine, *Black Culture and Black Consciousness: Afro-American Folk Thought from Slavery to Freedom* (New York: Oxford University Press, 1977); Marcellus Blount and George Cunningham, *Representing Black Men* (New York: Routledge, 1996); David Marriott, *On Black Men* (New York: Columbia University Press, 2000); and Hazel Carby, *Race Men* (Cambridge: Harvard University Press, 1998).

70. In the predictable transformation of masculinist ghetto music, fashion, slang, and sports trends into campus fashions lie white attempts to appropriate identities whose ancestors were first played out by Alfred, Dick, and William Wells Brown. Numerous commentators on the racial politics of popular culture have investigated this strange and commodified relationship between lure and longing that we see in many white (especially white male) attitudes toward individualistic black men; see David Shields, *Black Planet: Facing Race during an NBA Season* (New York: Crown, 1999); Robert Cantwell, *Bluegrass Breakdown: The Making of the Old Southern Sound* (Urbana: University of Illinois Press, 1984); Lott, *Love and Theft;* William Pinar, *The Gender of Racial Politics and Violence in America: Lynching, Prison Rape, and the Crisis of Masculinity* (New York: P. Lang, 2001); Nathan McCall, *Makes Me Wanna Holler: A Young Black Man in America* (New York: Vintage, 1994); and idem, *What's Going On: Personal Essays* (New York: Random House, 1997). The saga of white masculinity and its anxieties about race, individuality, and black insolence in the late nineteenth and twentieth centuries is beginning to be told in various places, although a good place to begin is Bederman, *Manliness and Civilization.* White male

anxiety has at several points in the years since emancipation (including the present day) become perceived as a national crisis; Susan Faludi, *Stiffed: The Betrayal of the American Man* (New York: Morrow, 1999), Sally Robinson, *Marked Men: White Masculinity in Crisis* (New York: Columbia University Press, 2000); Pinar, *Gender of Racial Politics.*

71. W. E. B. DuBois, *The Souls of Black Folk* (1903); reprint, New York: Signet, 1995), 199–203. For recent reconsiderations, see Ellis Cose, *The Envy of the World: On Being a Black Man in America* (New York: Washington Square, 2002); Phillip Brian Harper, *Are We Not Men: Masculine Anxiety and the Problem of African-American Identity* (New York: Oxford University Press, 1996); Orlando Patterson, *Rituals of Blood: Consequences of Slavery in Two American Centuries* (New York: Civitas/Counterpoint, 1998).

# "Stout Chaps Who Can Bear the Distress": Young Men in Antebellum Military Academies

*Jennifer R. Green*

Your son and my cousin has acted like a MAN," Citadel senior John Wylie reported in July 1854 of his kinsman and fellow South Carolina Military Academy cadet, Lafayette Strait.[1] Wylie wrote to his uncle and aunt that their son Strait, despite his suspension and resignation, had remained true to the ideas about manhood he learned at the military academy. The Citadel administration suspended Strait for permitting an unauthorized cadet meeting while on guard duty, but Strait insisted he had done no wrong and resigned rather than accept censure. The cadet evidently rejected the advice that his cousin gave him two years before his trouble; Wylie had urged Strait to maintain his "honor as a man" and to use *"Iron-Will"* to adapt to the contradictory impulses of traditional southern male independence and military academy duty.[2] Military school environments required cadets, like these two young men, to balance the submission that discipline required with their desire to act independently. Wylie declared Strait a "man" because he embodied the cadets' model of manhood, merging independence and submission, accepting hierarchy, employing self-discipline, and displaying military deportment.

Strait's departure from the Citadel indicated the difficulty in reconciling the conflicting ideals of manhood within the military school situation. Cadets imbibed and refined their parents' advice, their schools' regulations, the southern elite ideal, and national trends. The study of young men in military academies demonstrates that no monolithic conception of manhood existed among southern youth of the late antebellum period. Leaving their parents' advice and homes for military school, young men formed their vision of manhood in a primarily male environment, defining themselves in opposition to females and blacks.

174

Successful cadets moderated the traditional southern manhood, defined by mastery and independence. Their conception of manhood addressed the contradictory impulses of southern independence and of military academy submission. They also recognized the importance of a man's hierarchical status but modified elite male goals of wealth, honor, and mastery over slaves, replacing the standards of valuation with ones they could attain, such as self-discipline, education, and industry. Their new ideal, in fact, mirrored some nineteenth-century national trends, including the promotion of industry, religiosity, and temperance. Furthermore, the cadets' male archetype displayed their physicality though military spectacle and culminated in professional responsibility. Cadets blended these expectations into a vision of manhood centered on self-discipline.

Private and state military schools such as those attended by Wylie and Strait spread throughout the South in the 1840s and 1850s.[3] The institutions represented both the educational experimentation of the era and a particular response to the specific problems of southern education. Before the Civil War, almost one hundred private and state-funded military academies opened after the founding of the Virginia Military Institute in 1839. More than eleven thousand young men between the ages of thirteen and twenty-two made their way through these schools.[4] While operating with military discipline and uniforms, private and state military academies shared *no* connection with and offered *no* entry into the armed forces.

Since southern states failed to fund public school systems in the antebellum years, military academies offered a secondary education to non-elite young men. The academies rejected the classical education of Greek and Latin prevalent at colleges. Military schools' curricula of mathematics, science, and modern languages permitted parents unable to afford tutors—or their sons' time away from labor—to enroll the boys in military programs with academic standards much lower than those of colleges. The scientific content also made the curricula more practical, closer to vocational education than intellectualism. Such families also benefited from funding at the nine state academies, including the Virginia Military Institute and South Carolina Military Academy, which provided free tuition for at least one boy from each of the state's counties. Military academies, then, encouraged non-elite parents with professional ambitions for their sons to educate the young men appropriately. Few graduates went on to run plantations, instead they turned to professional careers in the law, medicine, and education.[5] Such opportunities for men of middling rank—without slaves and plantations but with military education—helped shape a distinctive ideal of manhood in the South.

Once at the academies, boys slowly developed into young men, in an era when no strict boundaries between adolescence and manhood existed. The meanings given to gender fluctuate for the people of any time and varied significantly in the antebellum era, ranging between southern rugged manhood and the self-restrained, entrepreneurial model of the North.[6] These southern cadets, maturing from boys to men, strove to achieve a male ideal from a variety of influences—parents, school, peers, and society—as did their peers at nonmilitary academies and colleges. Military academies played a significant role in re-shaping these non-elite ideals of manhood. The nonplanter origins and the particular setting of the military school led cadets to combine these factors into a gendered worldview that originated in their regional location and class status.

Cadets consciously reacted to the most prescient cultural message they received about male identity in the antebellum South: the issue of honor. Although historians often use honor to explain southern masculinity, it should instead be seen as one component of manhood. As an essential feature of manhood, honor both dictated behavior and was reinforced by elite principles of masculinity.[7] Slave-holding necessitated the ability to command dependents, and displaying honor demonstrated such mastery. Aggressive physical displays and the refusal to accept, or at least a willingness to defend against, insult marked southern honor. Traditional elite manhood required self-presentation that illustrated independence and mastery, while maintaining the public face of honor and status in the social hierarchy.[8]

The preeminent authority on southern honor, historian Bertram Wyatt-Brown, stated that children had to display "a military submissiveness" to their fathers as "part of the training in honor," but after reaching adolescence "defiance lent stature to the planter's son and gave confidence in leadership."[9] Deference to fathers, however, rarely translated to schoolmasters. From adolescence to adulthood, southern manhood stressed independence. Both antebellum writers and present-day historians often described the raucous behavior of elite southern adolescents. Most southern colleges suffered at least one student riot in the antebellum years, and a University of Virginia student even shot a professor. This conception of rugged manhood also meant that elite youths drank, gambled, and demanded that others treat them as independent men of honor.[10] This elite southern view offered a foundation for cadets' ideals, but manhood, at least for non-elite cadets, also entailed values connected to self-discipline.

Once a young man enrolled in a military academy, his parents allowed him to grow independently; they gave advice more often than directives. Sixteen-year-old Leeland Hathaway, for example, discovered that he had to stand behind his own decisions. Distraught by his homesickness, Hathaway ran away from the Western Military Institute and returned home. His father, although disappointed with his son's flight, gave the cadet shelter. Beyond expressing his disapprobation, the father demanded nothing from his son, which forced Hathaway to make his own decision to return to school.[11]

Indeed, lacking control over their sons' lives, parents exerted limited influence in cadets' day-to-day behavior. The father of another Western Military Institute cadet remained encouraging but critical: "I only regretted that while you was so near having a perfect record you was not quite able to have it completely unexceptionable."[12] The father lamented the situation but refrained from criticizing the poor performance or ordering better performance. Parents wanted sons to demonstrate good character, and that expectation probably underlies why parents sent their sons to military academies to become men.[13] The specific qualities of that ideal varied by individual, of course; all parents hoped their boys would grow into men without failings.

The institutional structure of military schools worked to break cadets' lingering ties to both parental authority and independence. Upon entering the academy, the cadets took an oath to obey school regulations, above even parental directions. "When a cadet enters the Institute," the state military academy of Virginia explicitly ordered, "he enters the service of the State under the military command of those appointed to govern it and that he is not subject to the independent controll of his parent except in subordination to the law and authority of the Institute."[14] In the state-funded institutions, this pledge reminded young men of their responsibility to guard state armories housed in military academies. Essentially, schools employed cadets as guards in exchange for education.[15] Entering a workforce beyond the family home not only distanced cadets from their parents in more than a physical way, but also moved cadets' responsibilities and experiences beyond their parents' domain and into military institutions.

For most adolescents, moreover, young men's values centered in peer-based groups. Cadets stepped into the first stage of manhood, developing from boyhood to adolescence and leaving home for a state of semidependence in either apprenticeship or schooling.[16] As cadets left their parents and parental control behind, socialization occurred in a clearly defined male space. Every military school and almost every college in the nation employed and enrolled men exclusively. Military academies usually restricted females from their campuses; cadets at the state military institute in Virginia described admiring the superintendent's wife from afar, lacking other female presence. While all visitors were limited, meeting female relatives, or even girls attending local schools, could take place only beyond school walls. This environment was neither uncommon nor unsurprising, since secondary schools facilitated male adolescents' entrance into manhood. Regulations kept cadets scheduled twenty-four hours a day, so other than for classroom recitations, cadets spent little time with adults. At military institutions, the young men lived together (often four to a room), ate together, supervised each other, and spent their waking hours primarily with other cadets.[17]

Within this male atmosphere, cadets defined themselves in contrast to what they perceived as the basic nature of women and of blacks. Largely because of women's dependence on men, the cadets conceptualized them as opposite to men. While they made allowances for the powers that their mothers possessed, cadets' perceptions of women remained consistent with traditional southern views. Essays by cadets James Morrison and Joseph Carpenter at the Virginia Military Institute in the 1850s, for example, described women as passive, men's first teacher, men's temptation, and chaste mothers. At the Citadel, in the same decade, Lafayette Strait compared marrying a woman to buying a horse. Most cadets believed that a male remained independent after marriage, while a female became a wife and mother. They defined an adult man by his own character, and a woman by her relationship to others.[18]

Cadets' humor and play stressed their opposition to feminine dependency. One Georgia Military Institute cadet told his parents that his roommates called him by "the euphonious name of Chloe"; the student considered being labeled a female so ridiculous that he construed it as a joke rather than an insult to his honor.[19] Further reinforcing the distinction between masculine and feminine, other jests affirmed the more physical and competitive aspects of male youth—for example, hazing and fighting—that reinforced the cadets' manhood. Cadets engaged in physical tussles, threw "missiles," tied other cadets up and dunked them in water, and employed mental challenges, such as putting new cadets on "trial" for nonexistent crimes.[20] Such actions echoed southern trends of male competition and aggression. Still, cadets' behavior was only a faint echo of southern rugged masculinity; in contrast to their elite contemporaries in colleges, they seldom physically challenged their professors.

Even more explicitly than they asserted the independence that women lacked, cadets rejected the dependency that characterized blacks' lives. Young men adopted the master class's view of black inferiority and white superiority as components of southern non-elite manhood. One rare comparison to a black was made when Citadel cadet Lafayette Strait described himself "as well and hearty as any Quarter darkie."[21] Comparison between the cadet and a slave centered on physical condition and did not imply any other likeness. More often, cadets used racialized rhetoric common in the antebellum South to describe their own sense of dependence. Young men refused to be treated like "slaves."[22] The complaints targeted a range of situations, from inappropriate comments by professors to the requirement that state scholarship recipients teach for two years after graduation. "The Institute should not seek to make slaves of its graduates," one state-funded Virginia Military Institute alumnus protested when he could not find a teaching job at a desired salary.[23] In many regards, the military academy constrained cadets, reducing their autonomy, but the majority of cadets reconciled that position with independence so that they were not subservient like wives or slaves, at least in the cadets' minds.

Even as they retained adolescent desires to leave their semidependent status behind and assume an independent male prerogative, cadets began to balance independence and submission. Cadets, dreaming of independence, named as their role models southern politicians and military leaders. For example, a Citadel graduate speaking before the alumni association on "the profession of arms" named Generals George Washington, Winfield Scott, and Andrew Jackson as his role models. Jackson, he felt, was a "true man," because he was "independent, fearless, self-willed," and self-educated.[24] Other archetypes commonly listed were John C. Calhoun, Henry Clay, Patrick Henry, Thomas Jefferson, and James Madison. Cadets appreciated these prominent men for their patriotism, autonomy, energy, and, as sectional tensions intensified, their southernness. Occasionally, Napoleon received credit as a republican and military genius.[25] Those who ranked high on the cadets' lists projected precisely what the cadets wanted for themselves: education, independence, social influence, integrity, and military competence.

In contrast, most military school superintendents rejected the cadets' fantasies of autonomy and stressed only obedience or self-discipline. Virginia Military Institute superintendent Francis H. Smith, for example, specifically said that one goal of the military academy was to instill in young men a sense of self-control. In an 1856 speech, he portrayed the perfect Virginia Military Institute cadet as the man who practiced self-restraint: a cadet must be put "constantly upon his guard—to make him watch against trifling indiscretions." Likewise, "Military institutions educate also through the control and subordination they teach," an orator told the same cadets in the same year.[26] The message focused on submission to authority, particularly through self-monitoring. "I would counsel the governed habitually . . . to hold it more honorable and manly to submit occasionally to individual wrong," an 1854 orator told the Citadel students; "as cadets of a military academy, subordination and submission to discipline are peculiarly your duty."[27] The central message of military education, then, had become the observance of obedience. Clearly, submission to duty and authority marked the adolescent's experience at a military academy.

Institutions promoted deference and duty as goals for their students. Academies wanted to reduce the temptations that many antebellum Americans thought plagued colleges. Part of the military academies' message attempted to modify the expectations of the elite, slave-holding culture. For example, an 1855 article in the *Nashville Union and American* promoted the newly incorporated Western

Military Institute and lamented that in the South blacks performed the labor, which made it "extremely difficult for [white] parents to exercise controlling restraints over youth." A military academy remedied this problem: the imposition of military discipline worked as an antidote to lax child-rearing. The trustees at the University of Nashville acknowledged that discipline problems existed, because "the Students in our Southern Colleges are as a matter of fact *boys* and not young men." Trustees voted to work with the Western Military Institute to alleviate this predicament, challenging the more traditional view of students as young men of honor and promoting a military model of men as subordinate to self-discipline.[28]

In an academy environment, discipline was crucial: too much autonomy led to ungovernable youths, and submission made schools run smoothly. Notwithstanding this operational benefit, educators endorsed the idea that submission could be manly. Military academies, including the Western Military Institute, promoted a "manly character" of morality and inner-directed obedience. According to the Georgia Military Institute, the qualifications for such character included "self-reliance, coolness, deliberation and judgement, promptness and subordination which such [a military] education bestows."[29] Representing similar sentiments in his first speech before the literary societies, the Citadel superintendent Francis W. Capers said that the goals of the school were to teach cleanliness, regular habits, exercise, and morality (particularly as discipline against bad habits).[30] A decade later, in 1857, a speaker at the Citadel told the cadets to "practice the virtues of sobriety, industry and integrity."[31] Military school administrations consistently valued submission and self-discipline over traditional southern honor.

Cadets and military educators frequently indicated that military academy manhood entailed submission. Western Military Institute promoted this goal in the *Nashville Union and American* article about the school, presenting the qualities of "obedience, subordination and deference to authority, which constitute a sound basis for good citizenship" for southern white men.[32] These youths were not the independent or authoritative men who ruled on plantations. They resisted elite southern men who said that to "submit" was to act as (or to be) a slave.[33]

Cadets, thus, needed to balance the competing values advanced by their region and by their institutions. They had to restrain independence and submit to the rules if they wanted to remain at their schools. As military academies circumscribed the rugged excesses of southern adolescence, the students themselves adopted more restrained behavior and accepted limits on their freedom. To earn diplomas, cadets reconciled the southern ideal of independence with the military academy's call for submission. "Construct [a] code to regulate your actions," one valedictorian told his peers at the Citadel.[34] This code, he suggested, defined an inviolate self that accepted the authority of others and internalized institutional rules. When homesick cadet Leeland Hathaway ran away from the Western Military Institute, he "had intended to be manly [but] had only played the baby."[35] Because he had not followed the appropriate internal directive, he judged his action as not worthy of a man.

After all, these adolescents aspired to independent manhood, even as they negotiated obedience to parents, teachers, and administrators. They were accustomed to the conflict and eager to resolve it. They tried to act independently, but self-discipline forced them to submit to regulations. At least one educator explored the tension between autonomy and subordination that cadets needed to reconcile. "The young man, who has been taught from his cradle, to reverence parental authority, and to respect Bible truth, and has learned that subordination to government does not involve meanness and cowardice," wrote professor D. H. Hill, "will be distinguished by a manly, upright and honorable deportment throughout the whole of his college career."[36] Hill, who started the North Carolina Military Institute five years after this comment, easily combined manhood, physical bearing, and deference. After opening his academy, however, Hill refined the relationship between submission and manhood, separating from manliness the "habits of order and system" that military academies taught. "Manliness and independence" were even more highly prized than these habits.[37] Daily interactions at the North Carolina Military Institute transformed Hill's views on manhood; he found that manliness required both submission and independence. Cadets internalized military discipline and submission and at the same time kept the southern man's demand for and their youthful desire for independence.

Ironically, their autonomy allowed them to *choose* to submit.[38] The central tenet of military discipline necessitated submission to duty and authority. The key to maintaining these rigorous ideals lay in cadets' self-discipline. In general, when institutions or cadets listed the traits that they considered beneficial, they focused on self-control and desired a definition of manhood based on self-restraint. The ideal fit nicely with the military disciplinary system that regulated every aspect and hour of their lives. The cadets' own ideals dovetailed with those of Hill, who believed that a combination of submission and independence was central to manliness. Cadets considered the messages of their parents, southern gender expectations, national trends, and the demands of the military institutions, and chose self-discipline. In accepting self-discipline and submission, cadets constructed an alternative version of manhood that derived from the military academy setting.

In addition to balancing submission and autonomy, cadets crafted their manhood by modifying another traditional southern principle. Elite southern men displayed their honor and believed that they presided over the social hierarchy. Historian Christopher J. Olsen explains that southern white males evinced the hierarchical tendencies of southern society.[39] Military academy men accepted this prevalent idea of hierarchy. Moreover, because they lacked the resources to compete with the established elite social rank—kin, slaves, land, and classical education—cadets began to evolve their own qualifications for status. Their redefinition developed out of their positions as nonplanters and reflected a hierarchy of cadet corps military rank, which was assigned without consideration of external variables.[40] Cadets' manhood centered on balancing submission and independence, hierarchy, self-discipline expressed in specific qualities, military spectacle, and career responsibility.

When cadets expressed the specific characteristics of manhood and adulthood, they described the traditional southern masculine ideal of hierarchy, but their ranking was based on standards different from those of the elite. Cadets and academy speakers defined the most important traits of manhood so that cadets could raise their status in a society where the demarcations of rank were often unclear.[41] Cadets' non-elite status made their position precarious and necessitated that rank be determined by qualities other than land and slave ownership. *"Indomitable energy* of *purpose,* and *firmness* and *decision of character,"* cadets at the Rappahannock Military Institute were told, "are the qualities which can alone elevate a man above a common level."[42] While it highlighted energy and decision making, this statement acknowledged that antebellum southern men believed in a hierarchy of men, so that a cadet could aspire to be "a man, in the highest, truest, noblest sense of the term!"[43] Citadel cadets learned to become "gentlemen of high tone and the purest sense of honor" through their military education.[44] A cadet would attain the highest rank among men, it appeared, by demonstrating decisive behavior. Cadets thus validated the southern white idea of manhood based on hierarchy but adapted the values to their circumstances.

Military school students redefined the southern belief in male hierarchy through scientific education more than through classical refinement. As members of the minority of antebellum southerners who achieved secondary education, cadets unsurprisingly presented their ideal of a true man as a man of letters, a man with knowledge of the world around him, especially of science, which was preeminent in military academy curricula. "My earthly ambition is to be a profoundly learned man," one cadet wrote his guardian in 1848. Similarly, a decade later, another cadet at the Virginia Military Institute described gaining intellectual improvement as his "laudable ambition."[45] Education and knowledge provided a way to gain status as a man. Thus, performing well at a military academy raised cadets' social status as non-elite men.

Idealizing self-discipline encouraged military academy males to espouse both hierarchy and submission. Other traits that cadets valued—industry, fortitude, frugality, religion, and temperance—derived from that principle. For example, the acceptance of hard work reflected changes in attitudes toward southern manhood. Often excoriated by planters as being the lot of slaves, industry became a central tenet of military academy cadets' manhood in the 1850s. Parents, students, and teachers agreed that life meant strife and that the expenditure of energy in the fight through life led to success. "Duty calls," the 1857 Citadel valedictorian told his classmates, by which he meant young men must now enter the larger world and accept its demands.[46] All antebellum schools, particularly military academies, taught students to do their duty. In the classroom, many schools used the recitation method, where students memorized the textbook and recited it back to the teacher. Good grades depended on accurate recitation, not on creativity. At military academies, nineteenth-century pedagogy prepared a young man for the larger duties of life (whether to be a citizen soldier or to succeed in a career).

Hard mental and physical work formed the foundation of the cadets' standards. Their belief in their own labor reflected the widespread drive for industry in antebellum America.[47] Cadets shared the national concern over inactivity and its result, dissipation. Industry was the cadets' antidote to idleness, but as one Rappahannock cadet put it, when too successful and wealthy, citizens faced the same problem—idleness.[48] Military academies used discipline and schedules to minimize the opportunity for indolence. After a tour of military institutes, University of Mississippi president F. A. P. Barnard reported to the university's trustees that the schools used "surveillance" to take away "idleness."[49] Likewise, the Western Military Institute's 1848 catalog stated that "idleness . . . [was] regarded as contrary to the rules."[50] One of the reasons for military discipline, then, was to promote industry and, in turn, morality.

Alongside industry, cadets pursued fortitude. "The military is truly hard," Cadet Lafayette Strait boasted, "but fortunately I am so constituted as to withstand all of its hardships."[51] Since southerners perceived life as strife, cadets unsurprisingly felt it their duty to "struggle on manfully" through the hardships that a military education brought.[52] A Virginia Military Institute cadet considered the importance of the topic in a poem:

> It's all for improvement, these little things come.
> Endurance the lesson we wish to impress
> So let every kind parent keep babies at home
> And send us stout chaps who can bear the distress.[53]

Exhibiting fortitude as "stout chaps," which included describing the hardships they overcame, demonstrated cadets' status.

Indeed, enduring the hard work of military discipline gave young men credit for masculine fortitude. Western Military Institute student Leeland Hathaway described this feeling in his memoir: "The military instruction and discipline were copied rigidly from that maintained at West Point and went far to giving that physical culture which should always go hand in hand with the training of the mind. Much of [the] manly part rank and I graduated with good credit in all branches of study." [54] By doing well at a military academy, Hathaway thought he outperformed the best young men. He envisioned his status as higher in the male hierarchy through attention to the traits he and his cadet peers identified as important to manliness: duty, industry, fortitude, and military conduct.

In their letters home, by stressing their industry and fortitude, cadets reassured their parents that they had imbibed good moral characteristics. Many also described themselves as frugal, a consequence partially of the academies' regulations restricting money usage. Their parents certainly approved of frugality as a reflection of self-discipline against extravagance and a value directly related to the cadets' middling status. Few cadets enjoyed either a great deal of spending money or access to unlimited resources. [55] Frugality, same as the other traits that cadets advanced, illustrated self-discipline's central position in the cadets' manhood.

Additionally, manhood at military academies reflected a religious context that encouraged self-discipline. Christianity played a significant role in the lives of many nineteenth-century southerners, including cadets. Evangelical denominations, especially Methodists and Baptists, increased membership throughout the South after 1800. Their influence began to shape southern manhood, because evangelicals contradicted elite manhood, demanding that their adherents demonstrate self-restraint in public and reject drinking, gambling, and other displays of rugged manhood. [56] Even as cadets expressed religiosity and self-discipline, however, they did not necessarily subscribe to evangelical denominations. Military academy students and professors appreciated religiosity, though more often as Episcopalians and Presbyterians than as evangelical Methodists and Baptists. While military schools often refused to endorse specific denominations, they stressed moral training and required cadets to attend church. At the Virginia Military Institute, the senior class had mandatory Bible recitations on Sundays. Reports of church attendance and Bible recitations assuaged national concerns about the moral direction of academy learning and reflected the cadets' acceptance of self-restraint. [57]

Some young men reconsidered the states of their souls and converted or became born again while at an academy. They desired to be religious men and to behave according to religious tenets. "I am much impressed this day with the sinfulness of the life I am leading, and have resolved to try and improve," one Hillsboro Military Academy cadet wrote. "May God give me grace to sustain this resolution." [58] Similarly, soon after his Virginia Military Institute graduation, while teaching at a school with a cadet corps, Robert Gatewood's conversion compelled him to give at least 10 percent of his salary to charity. "May I be just, firm, fearless, yet merciful—acting always in love—prompt and decided in action, and my every action be well weighed before acted," Gatewood prayed; "this can only be done by following the precepts of the word of God and by Prayer to Him for Guidance." [59] Religion became a guiding principle for some cadets, and its prevalence suggests an environment that fostered religious conviction.

Among many cadets, the next logical step was a rejection of sin, in particular the consumption of alcohol. Students from various academies, including the four largest military academies—the state academies in Virginia, Georgia, South Carolina, and Tennessee's Western Military Institute—founded temperance societies. "All the young men here have joined the Temperance Soc but myself," a Western Military Institute cadet wrote to his father, "and they have begged me so much to join that I concented." [60] Indeed, entire classes of cadets pledged to abstain from alcohol. [61] At the Rappahannock Military Institute, Leonard Slater turned in a composition on the perils of drinking, condemning it generally as the "worst of evils" and concluding that it could lead wealthy men to crime. Institutional support must have existed for him to feel comfortable handing in that topic to his professor, who happened to be a Virginia Military Institute graduate. [62] Administrative approval of temperance efforts also existed at the state military academy in South Carolina. [63] Antialcohol pledges at military schools were in distinct contrast to the drinking that remained part of traditional southern manhood. Many cadets rejected college "student debauchery," what historian Daniel Kilbride describes as "an important element of upper-class identity," in order to embrace manhood with self-discipline. [64]

The religious and temperance mood at the schools led a few cadets to swear off other negative behaviors including cursing and tobacco use. "I Solemnly pledge my honor as a man and Cadet of the Arsenal Academy Columbia That I will neither swear, smoke tobacco, or use it in any of its forms before the thirteenth day of September 1854," pledged Lafayette Strait. Similarly, at the state military academy in Virginia, a cadet promised to use no tobacco products until the age of twenty-five. [65] Abstinence from tobacco was less recorded than temperance, but both preferences reflected evangelical impulses in the South and, more specifically, cadets' desire for manhood based on self-discipline. Self-restraint centered in all these traits suggests that the military school environment encouraged young southerners to adopt some characteristics often identified with northerners. Cadets focused on self-discipline as they negotiated the different strains of masculinity in antebellum America.

Beyond these traits connected to self-discipline, cadets used military performance to represent themselves as men. Many cadets expressed positive attitudes toward the military component of their schooling.[66] Cadets wrote proudly of their uniforms, modeled after those of United States Military Academy at West Point, and the associated aura of manliness as the most impressive aspect of military education.[67] Uniforms distinguished cadets from other men, bringing honor and respect. One Virginia Military Institute alumnus working as a teacher, for example, criticized his school's "very stupid ideas on military discipline" as it failed to adequately drill and teach tactics; most important, he complained, the students "never had a uniform."[68] He stressed that military discipline and its desired result remained incomplete without accompanying appearance and behavior.

Cadets displayed their uniforms and military aspect when the public attended drills and when cadets went to public events. The young men received commendation for appearing in uniform as military representatives of their state and station.[69] Drills and parades gave them a chance to flaunt their training and physical prowess. "We passed a School House where the *scholars* were at play," said a Virginia Military Institute cadet, preening in a march before other young men, "and we perfectly amazed them by the glitter of our guns and bayonets, and our military display."[70] This cadet felt superior to scholars, analogous to elite young men at colleges and regular academies. Thus, as cadets incorporated military spectacle into their male archetype, they replicated both southern honor (hierarchy and public display) and the self-discipline they found so important at military academies.

The military system required cadets to maintain military demeanor, endorsed in their society as both a man's public honor and a male physicality associated with militarism. The father of Western Military Institute cadet Joel Scott, for instance, repeatedly encouraged his son to gain military carriage.[71] Cadets like Joel Scott had their own reasons for desiring the behavior. They believed that military training brought good health and that upright posture indicated manners and refinement. Drilling made a youth "walk strait so that he looks like somebody," commented one Citadel cadet.[72] The "somebody" epitomized the high male status, military bearing, and appearance of status and manners that cadets associated with manliness.

Of course, military display reflected traditional southern men's concern with the public display of honor, but the act of wearing a uniform carried more significance—it represented actual duties and responsibilities. The duties were not those of soldiers, since military academies *rarely* produced active soldiers in the United States military (less than 4 percent of matriculants in the antebellum years). As part of their responsibilities, however, cadets replicated the behavior of militias or of soldiers at drill. Even a traveler passing through Lexington, Virginia, in 1852 noted the "military might" of the Virginia Military Institute cadets, connecting the sight of the school with "war."[73] The cadets would have happily accepted this judgment and the status that it gave them. Part of this appreciation reflected the militaristic spirit of southern manhood in general. Historians have portrayed the South as prone to violence and martial spirit, which it exhibited specifically in military schools.[74] In actuality, uniforms and physical activities manifested the educational and disciplinary benefits of military education more than its martial content.

Finally, military conduct satisfied the desire for self-discipline. People incorrectly focused on the *"mere drill and uniform"* of military institutions, wrote Citadel superintendent Capers.[75] These physical manifestations reflected something much more important: the development of young men. Cadets became men—educated and self-sufficient—at military academies. The physical self-regulation demonstrated an internalized acceptance of discipline that reflected externally in the cadets' performance. A militaristic appearance was part of the cadets' redefinition of manhood, rooted in an inner-directed sense of duty, discipline, and submission, and the status that these qualities gave young men. It symbolized the industry and fortitude that the cadet maintained during his education. This centrality of self-discipline and submission constructed a different gender identity for thousands of young men in the Old South.

Beyond hierarchy, submission, self-discipline, and military display, the cadets' transition to adulthood entailed "taking upon ourselves the responsibilities of manhood," as a valedictorian at the Citadel put it.[76] Near the age of twenty-one, apprentices typically came into their own, and society recognized them as men. At the same age, most military academy graduates entered manhood through the start of a career, "the very beginning of your days of manhood," said an uncle of Micah Jenkins, a recent Citadel graduate.[77] The shift to manhood was marked by the move from the physicality of boyhood to the career and intellectual status by which men judged each other.[78] The responsibilities that men had in adulthood mirrored the duties of cadet life, necessitating the values, including subordination to authority, that they had learned in the military academy. Military education, then, developed the appropriate self-discipline for career-minded non-elite cadets, the majority of whom did not have plantations waiting for them and, consequently, went on to work as teachers, lawyers, and doctors before the Civil War.[79]

"Perhaps it is even time, for us to think, what is to be, the place and manner of the study of my profession," an eighteen-year-old Virginia Military Institute cadet wrote to his guardian. Despite being a year away from graduation, he tried to decide whether to pursue a university degree, but placed the issue in his guardian's and mother's hands. "I press an early decision," he encouraged, "because I have no desire to waste a moment, after I leave here."[80] The cadet focused on his prospects after graduation. Leaving the academy was an important transition in his life. Other cadets echoed this view, including a young man who, writing to his father, said, "The time will soon come when it will be my duty to select a profession—or occupation."[81] Another cadet at the state military academy of Virginia, Robert Simpson, also understood that graduation meant entering the adult world. "I am of an age to choose a profession for life," he declared.[82] Along with his father and many of his peers, Simpson chose to teach.

Young men in the 1840s and 1850s found their own way to manhood in a time of changing gender definitions. Cadets modified the southern elite ideals of hierarchy and honor to include the values of evangelicalism, self-discipline, and, primarily, military education. Military academies demanded that southern nonelite cadets espouse submission in their lives, and the cadets responded positively. Cadets balanced submission with their impulse toward independence, claiming to assert autonomy by internalizing deference. In conjunction with this balance, they adopted the ideal of self-discipline in the form of industry, fortitude, frugality, religiosity, and temperance. As they defined manhood within the military academy, they negotiated countervailing forces. The self-regulated manhood that they achieved was both predicated on and reflective of their integration of the military school environment, national values, and southern culture.

NOTES

The author would like to thank Nina Silber, Lou Ferleger, and the editors of this volume for their comments and suggestions.

1. John D. Wylie to Aunt [Isabella Strait], 14 July 1854, South Caroliniana Library, University of South Carolina (hereafter SCL). For the details of the event, G. Lafayette Strait to Father, 12 July 1854, SCL. Before 1865, the South Carolina Military Academy consisted of the Arsenal Academy in Columbia and the Citadel in Charleston.

2. John D. Wylie to G. Lafayette Strait, 25 December 1852, SCL.

3. Before the Civil War, American education lacked standardized terminology. The differences between a college (or university) and an academy (or institute) were often hazy. The term "academy" usually meant a private preparatory school, but could also refer to higher education. Both types were typically the final stage of a young man's

education. This article uses the words "academy" and "institute" interchangeably and employs "college" for all B.A.-granting institutions, including universities. On military schools, see Rod Andrew Jr., *Long Gray Lines: The Southern Military School Tradition, 1839–1915* (Chapel Hill: University of North Carolina Press, 2001), esp. chap. 1.

4. Bruce Allardice, "West Points of the Confederacy: Southern Military Schools and the Confederate Army," *Civil War History* 43 (1997), 321, estimates that twelve thousand military academy alumni entered the Confederate army. Calculations from my data indicate that at least eleven thousand young men attended military schools in the antebellum period. These figures exclude the U.S. service academies.

5. The majority of individuals under investigation were neither slave owners nor yeomen; Jennifer R. Green, "Books and Bayonets: Class and Culture at Antebellum Military Academies" (Ph.D. diss., Boston University, 2002), chaps. 1, 5.

6. E. Anthony Rotundo, *American Manhood: Transformations in Masculinity from the Revolution to the Modern Era* (New York: Basic Books, 1993), introduction, chaps. 1, 3; Michael Kimmel, *Manhood in America: A Cultural History* (New York: Free Press, 1996), pt. 1. On developing southern manhood, see John Mayfield, "'The Soul of a Man': William Gilmore Simms and the Myths of Southern Manhood," *Journal of the Early Republic* 15 (1995): 477–500; Peter S. Carmichael, "Eager Confederates" (paper presented at the Southern Historical Association Annual Conference, New Orleans, La., November 2001); Anya Jabour, in "Masculinity and Adolescence in Antebellum America: Robert Wirt at West Point, 1820–1821" *Journal of Family History* 23 (1998), 394, 399, analyzes parental influence on one southern adolescent at West Point and locates a tension between southern honor and the family's residence in a border state. On masculinity, see David D. Gilmore, *Manhood in the Making: Cultural Concepts of Masculinity* (New Haven: Yale University Press, 1990).

7. See Edward L. Ayers, *Vengeance and Justice: Crime and Punishment in the Nineteenth-Century American South* (New York: Oxford University Press, 1984), esp. 24; Bertram Wyatt-Brown, *Southern Honor: Ethics and Behavior in the Old South* (New York: Oxford University Press, 1982); Bertram Wyatt-Brown, *The Shaping of Southern Culture: Honor, Grace, and War, 1760s–1880s* (Chapel Hill: University of North Carolina Press, 2001); Elizabeth Fox-Genovese, *Within the Plantation Household: Black and White Women in the Old South* (Chapel Hill: University of North Carolina Press, 1988), esp. chap. 4; Steven M. Stowe, *Intimacy and Power in the Old South: Ritual in the Lives of the Planters* (Baltimore: Johns Hopkins University Press, 1987), chaps. 1, 3; Christopher J. Olsen, *Political Culture and Secession in Mississippi: Masculinity, Honor, and the Antiparty Tradition, 1830–1860* (New York: Oxford University Press, 2000); Nicolas W. Proctor, *Bathed in Blood: Hunting and Mastery in the Old South* (Charlottesville: University Press of Virginia, 2002), esp. chap. 3; Mayfield, "'Soul of a Man.'"

8. Kenneth S. Greenberg, *Honor and Slavery: Lies, Duels, Noses, Masks, Dressing as a Woman, Gifts, Strangers, Humanitarianism, Death, Slave Rebellions, the Proslavery Argument, Baseball, Hunting, and Gambling in the Old South* (Princeton: Princeton

University Press, 1996); Wyatt-Brown, *Southern Honor;* Stowe, *Intimacy and Power,* esp. chap. 1.

9. Wyatt-Brown, *Southern Honor,* 157, 163. On youth and honor, see Joseph F. Kett, *Rites of Passage: Adolescence in America 1790 to the Present* (New York: Basic Books, 1977), chap. 1; Robert F. Pace and Christopher A. Bjornsen, "Adolescent Honor and College Student Behavior in the Old South," *Southern Cultures* 6 (2000): 9–28.

10. In contrast with college riots, protests at antebellum military academies usually consisted of walkouts or petitions to the administration. Pace and Bjornsen, "Adolescent Honor," esp. 12–13, 19–21; Daniel Kilbride, "Southern Medical Students in Philadelphia, 1800–1861," *Journal of Southern History* 65 (1999): 697–732.

11. Leeland Hathaway, memoir, Southern Historical Collection, University of North Carolina (hereafter SHC). On the decreased role parents played, see Stephen M. Frank, *Life with Father: Parenthood and Masculinity in the Nineteenth-Century American North* (Baltimore: Johns Hopkins University Press, 1998), esp. chap. 2; Rotundo, *American Manhood,* esp. 62–71; Michael Zuckerman, "Penmanship Exercises for Saucy Sons: Some Thoughts on the Colonial Southern Family," *South Carolina Historical Magazine* 84 (1983): 152–66; Shawn Johansen, *Family Men: Middle-Class Fatherhood in Early Industrializing America* (New York: Routledge, 2001), esp. 133–36.

12. Robert Scott to Joel Scott, 31 October 1853, Department of Library Special Collections, Manuscripts, Western Kentucky University (hereafter WKU).

13. For example, John Winn to Philip Winn, 8 January 1841, Special Collections Library, Duke University (hereafter Duke); E. C. Finney to Francis H. Smith, 8 May 1847, 30 June 1848; Edmund Ruffin to Francis H. Smith, 25 April 1851, Preston Library, Virginia Military Institute Archives (hereafter VMI).

14. Order #14, 27 January 1860, *Order Book 31 July 1858–31 December 1860,* VMI.

15. Even young men who paid their own tuition worked as guards and accepted the duties and responsibilities that came with the job.

16. Studies generally consider adolescence as the ages between fifteen and twenty-five, especially while attending academies, colleges, and apprenticeships. Kett, *Rites of Passage,* 36; Frank, *Life with Father,* 49, 196 n. 75; Rotundo, *American Manhood,* 20–21; Jabour, "Masculinity and Adolescence," 404. On the increased role of peers, see Rotundo, *American Manhood,* esp. 62–71; Patricia Cline Cohen, "Unregulated Youth: Masculinity and Murder in the 1830s City," *Radical History Review* 52 (1992), 46.

17. See, for example, *Catalogue and Regulations of the Western Military Institute at Georgetown, Kentucky* (Cincinnati: Herald of Truth Printers, 1848); *Regulations of the Georgia Military Institute, Marietta, Georgia* (n.p.: January, 1853); *Regulations of the Military Academies of South Carolina* (Columbia: R. W. Gibbes, 1858).

18. James H. Morrison, "Woman's Character," essay, 3 December 1857; Joseph H. Carpenter, diary, 1853, VMI; G. Lafayette Strait, "The disappointed Bachelor," essay, [23 February 1854], SCL. For similar ideas in a speech to cadets, Albert Pike, *An Address Delivered by Albert Pike* (Little Rock: William E. Woodruff, 1852), 8.

19. Theodore Fogle to Father and Mother, 16 August 1852, Richard Woodruff Library, Department of Special Collections, Emory University (hereafter Emory).

20. Charles Derby to Father, 9 May 1846; Philip A. Fitzhugh to Patrick Fitzhugh, 28 December 1844; Joseph Chenoweth to Father, 28 September 1855; Henry T. Lee to Fellows, 15 July 1844, VMI; Hathaway, memoir; John Henry Custis to unknown, 17 May 1861; Henry K. Burgwyn to Anna Burgwyn, 12 August 1860, SHC; John Edward Dodson to Harriet Cogbill, 8 May 1863, Virginia Historical Society (hereafter VHS); Beverly Stanard, *Letters of a New Market Cadet*, ed. John G. Barrett and Robert K. Turner Jr. (Chapel Hill: University of North Carolina Press, 1961), 43. Jabour, "Masculinity and Adolescence," 409, describes the 1820s West Point subculture as fraternal and competitive.

21. G. Lafayette Strait to Jacob F. Strait, 25 January 1853, SCL.

22. G. Lafayette Strait to Father and Mother, 7 February 1854; G. Lafayette Strait to Aunt Amanda [Wylie], 7 February 1854, SCL.

23. William Lee to Francis H. Smith, 23 March 1854; Timothy Thorp to Francis H. Smith, 9 March 1841, VMI.

24. John Thomas, *On the Profession of Arms* (Charleston, S.C.: Walker, Evans, 1859), 16. "Western Military Academy," *Nashville Union and American*, 14 February 1855, 2, also promoted Andrew Jackson as a role model.

25. Edwin Heriot, *The Polytechnic School* (Charleston: Walker and James, 1850), 19–20; George Rumbough, "Graduating Speech," 4 July 1856; Joseph Chenoweth to Father, 21 February 1857, VMI; John Hankins to Father and Mother, 1855, VHS.

26. Francis H. Smith, *Introductory Address to the Corps of Cadets of the Virginia Military Institute, on the Resumption of Academic Duties* (Richmond: MacFarlane and Fergusson, 1856), 11; Lawrence Massillion Keitt, *Address before the Two Literary Societies of the Virginia Military Institute* (Richmond: MacFarlane and Fergusson, 1856), 15.

27. Richard Yeadon, *Address, on the Necessity of Subordination, in our Academies and Colleges, Civil and Military* (Charleston, S.C.: Walker and James, 1854), 17–18, 20.

28. *Nashville Union and American*, 2; Meeting Minutes, vol. 2, 9 March 1855, Vanderbilt University Archives (hereafter Vanderbilt); Kett, *Rites of Passage;* Pace and Bjornsen, "Adolescent Honor," 13.

29. Georgia Military Institute, *Report by the Board of Visitors of the Georgia Military Institute, To his Excellency, Howell Cobb, Governor of the State of Georgia For 1853*, 11, Duke.

30. Francis W. Capers, *State Military Academies* (Charleston, S.C.: Tenhet and Corley, 1846), 19. Capers moved consecutively from superintendencies at the state military academies in South Carolina, Kentucky, and Georgia between 1843 and 1862.

31. James D. Tradewell, *Address on the Study of the Federal Constitution Delivered before the Polytechnic and Calliopean Societies of the Citadel Academy* (Charleston, S.C.: Walker, Evans, 1857), 33.

32. *Nashville Union and American*, 2. See also "Military Institute," *Gleason's Pictorial Drawing-Room Companion*, 1 January 1853, 16; *Regulations of the Georgia Military Institute*, 20, stated that "obedience and subordination are essential to the purposes of this institution."

33. Fox-Genovese, *Plantation Household;* Steven Kantrowitz, *Ben Tillman and the Reconstruction of White Supremacy* (Chapel Hill: University of North Carolina Press, 2000), 23.

34. W. M. Tennent, "Valedictory before the Calliopean," speech, [1857], SCL.

35. Hathaway, memoir, SHC.

36. D. H. Hill, *College Discipline* (Watchman Office, 1855), 9.

37. D. H. Hill, *Essay on Military Education* (Daily Bulletin Office, 1860), 9.

38. See, for example, John D. Wylie to G. Lafayette Strait, 19 August 1852, SCL.

39. Olsen, *Political Culture,* 25–26. Wyatt-Brown, *Southern Honor,* chaps. 3, 14, 15, also describes hierarchy as a facet of southern honor.

40. *Regulations of the Military Academies of South Carolina,* 14, states, "No difference shall be made in the treatment, or in the duties required, between the [tuition paying and scholarship] Cadets; nor shall any distinction between Cadets be known in the Academy, other than that arising from merit."

41. Rotundo, *American Manhood,* 65–66, 69–70, contends that competition among young men was part of youth culture. He does not suggest that manhood entailed competition among all men for status. This aspect of the cadets' lives derived from the hierarchical nature of southern elite honor.

42. G. W. Lewis, *Address Delivered Before the Literary Society and Students Generally of the Rappahannock Academy and Military Institute* (Washington: Gideon, 1852), 9.

43. Joseph H. Chenoweth to Father, 21 February 1857, VMI.

44. Samuel McGowen, *An Address Delivered before the Polytechnic and Calliopean Societies of the State Military Academy* (Charleston, S.C.: Edward C. Councell, 1851), 20.

45. Samuel Garland to Samuel Garland, 12 January 1848, VHS; Joseph Chenoweth to Father, 21 February 1857, VMI. Also see, Heriot, *Polytechnic,* esp. 21; Pike, *Address,* 5–6. Certainly, many educated men found the military academies' scientific education less reputable than a college's classical curriculum, but any secondary education elevated cadets above yeomen. The practical education of the military schools aided alumni in attaining careers.

46. William Tennent, "Valedictory," speech, [1857], Citadel Archives and Museum (hereafter CIT). Similarly, the Honorable Willoughby Newton, *Virginia and The Union* (Richmond: MacFarlane and Fergusson, 1858), 31.

47. Increasingly throughout the nineteenth century, self-control helped middle-class northerners promote their ideals and social reforms. Frank, *Life with Father,* 116; Mary Ryan, *Cradle of the Middle Class: The Family in Oneida County, New York, 1790–1865* (New York: Cambridge University Press, 1981), 161; Richard L. Bushman, *The Refinement of America: Persons, Houses, Cities* (New York: Knopf, 1992), esp. 64–65, 319–26; Mayfield, "'Soul of a Man,'" esp. 481, 497, 499.

48. The Rappahannock cadet's comments also inherently criticized the wealth of the gentry; Leonard Augustus Slater, essay book, 11 December 1850, VHS. Similarly, Edmund Ruffin to Francis H. Smith, 8 February 1851; Robert H. Simpson to Francis H. Smith, 24 February 1852, VMI.

49. F. A. P. Barnard, *Report on the Organization of Military Academies* (Jackson, Miss.: Cooper and Kimball, 1861), 14; also see Hill, *College Discipline.*

50. *Catalogue . . . of the Western Military Institute,* 22.

51. G. Lafayette Strait to Catharine Baskins, 15 April 1853, SCL.

52. John D. Wylie to Aunt, 29 February 1852, SCL.

53. Edward C. Shepherd, diary, 1855, VMI.

54. Hathaway, memoir, SHC. Hathaway attended both Western Military Institute and Kentucky Military Institute.

55. See, for example, Mary Lee to Francis H. Smith, 4 December 1852; R. D. Powell to Francis H. Smith, 16 August 1845, VMI; Francis H. Smith to John Winn, 29 February 1840; John Winn to Philip Winn, 16 November 1840, Duke; Frederick Bryan to Mother, 25 February 1861, North Carolina State Archives; Joel Scott to Robert Scott, 24 October 1853, WKU.

56. Christine Leigh Heyrman, *Southern Cross: The Beginnings of the Bible Belt* (New York: Knopf, 1997), esp. chap. 5; Olsen, *Political Culture,* 23–24; Carmichael, "Eager Confederates." Wyatt-Brown, *Southern Honor,* 146, notes that evangelicals often believed in self-discipline in contradistinction to other southerners. On Methodism's challenges to southern manhood in an earlier period, see Cynthia Lynn Lyerly, *Methodism and the Southern Mind, 1770–1810* (New York: Oxford University Press, 1998). The writing of the only confirmed Jewish cadets examined here addressed issues in the same manner as their peers. Albert Moses Luria Papers, North Carolina State Archives; Solomon Jacobs, student file, VMI; Miriam G. Moses Cohen Papers, SHC.

57. Some alumni became Baptists after the Civil War, but the existent records make it problematic to determine cadets' antebellum denominational affiliations. Philip Winn to John Winn, 14 December 1839, Duke; Order #19, 4 November 1844, *Order Book 1839–1852;* William Green to Capt. Duff Green, 10 September 1843, VMI; Claudius Fike to Parents, 20 April 1862; G. Lafayette Strait to Sallie Strait, 9 January 1853, SCL; 28 April 1858, WMI *Order Book,* Vanderbilt; Virginia Literary, Scientific and Military Academy *Catalogue.* January 1841, American Antiquarian Society. Jabour, "Masculinity and Adolescence," 401–2, notes that West Point cadet Wirt's mother promoted "the lessons of evangelical Christianity" and that he promised religiosity.

58. William Calder, diary, 31 March [1861], Duke. For cadet diaries and letters on church attendance, see Eugene F. Cordell, diary, 1859, Duke; Carpenter, diary; Robert Gatewood, diary; Walter W. Williams, diary, VMI; Gratz Cohen to Parents, 28 July 1862, SHC; Theodore Fogle to Father and Mother, 16 August 1852, Emory.

59. Gatewood, diary, 14 April 1850, 30 November 1851, VMI.

60. Joel Scott to Robert Scott, 24 October 1853, WKU. Other cadets supporting temperance included Philip A. Fitzhugh to Patrick Fitzhugh, 28 December 1844, VMI; Theodore Fogle to Mother, 9 July 1852, Emory; John D. Wylie to Aunt Hannah, 11 June 1852; G. Lafayette Strait to Mother, 16 March 1853, SCL; John Scott to Lucinda Henry, 16 July 1850, VHS; Thomas Hart Law, *Citadel Cadets: The Journal*

*of Cadet Tom Law* (Clinton, S.C.: PC Press, 1941), 7 June 1857. On temperance, Barton J. Bledstein, *The Culture of Professionalism: The Middle Class and the Development of Higher Education in America* (New York: Norton, 1976), 153–55; Rotundo, *American Manhood*, 72; Frank, *Life with Father*, 26, 30.

61. November 1848, Western Military Institute's Order Book, Vanderbilt; Order #12, 5 September 1857, Order #131, November 1858, Order Book, VMI. This type of pledge is documented in the only existent order books; many more cadets at other academies may have made similar pledges.

62. Slater, 18 December 1850, VHS.

63. G. Lafayette Strait to Mother, 16 March 1853, SCL.

64. Kilbride, "Southern Medical Students," 723.

65. G. Lafayette Strait, n.d., SCL; Henry Burgwyn to Anna Burgwyn, 14 December 1856, SHC; Burgwyn's inclusion of the age implied that he felt that adult men could use tobacco, and twenty-five must have appeared to be the age of majority to the fifteen-year-old.

66. Thomas, *Profession of Arms*, 1–23; John D. Wylie to G. Lafayette Strait, 27 April 1855, SCL; Gratz Cohen to Solomon Cohen, 10 June 1862, SHC; William Terrill to Francis H. Smith, 3 December 1857, George Porterfield student file, VMI. Of course, a few cadets disliked the military or, in particular, the military component of their academies. This negative response reflected that neither military honor nor militarism was fully accepted throughout the South.

67. See Stapleton Crutchfield, speech, 4 July 1855, VHS; W. R. Wiggins to Theodore Kingsbury, 23 December 1846, SHC; William DuBose, "Soldier, Philosopher, Friend, Awakener of the Undying Good in Men," memoir; Claudius Fike to G. A. Fike, 12 February 1862, 20 April 1862, SCL. Catlett Fitzhugh Conway, "Autobiography," typescript, ca. 1911, VHS, described in minute detail the uniform and military operations as a cadet at Culpeper Military Academy.

68. Charles Denby to Francis H. Smith, 28 January 1851, VMI.

69. On militias and uniforms, James B. Whisker, *The Rise and Decline of the American Militia System* (Cranbury, N.J.: Associated University Presses, 1999), chap. 7; John Hope Franklin, *The Militant South: 1800–1861* (Boston: Little, Brown, 1960), 167–68, 176–78, 184–85; Wyatt-Brown, *Southern Honor*, 10, 418–19.

70. Philip C. Gibbs, diary, 21 March 1851, VMI. See also Egbert Ross to Emma Ross, 21 October 1860, SHC; Seaborn Montgomery to Julia Montgomery, 23 September 1863, Duke.

71. Robert W. Scott to Joel Scott, 27 September 1853, 31 October 1853, WKU. See also Thomas, *Profession of Arms*, especially 21; Pike, *Address*, 20; Eagleswood Collegiate and Military Institute, *Catalog*, [1861], American Antiquarian Society, Worcester, Massachusetts.

72. G. Lafayette Strait to Aunt [A. S. Wylie], 21 January 1852 [1853], SCL. On refinement in the North and South, see Bushman, *Refinement of America*, esp. 238–447; Kilbride, "Southern Medical Students."

73. Curran Swaim, diary, 24 August 1852, VHS; Green, "Books and Bayonets," app. 2. By the time southern military academies opened, militias had ceased to be a vital force in society; Whisker, *American Militia*, chap. 7; Dickson D. Bruce Jr., *Violence and Culture in the Antebellum South* (Austin: University of Texas Press, 1979), 166–69.

74. At the center of this debate are Franklin, *Militant South*, and Marcus Cunliffe, *Soldiers and Civilians: The Martial Spirit in America, 1775–1865* (Boston: Little, Brown, 1968), esp. chap. 10. Dickson D. Bruce Jr. stated that military academies "probably did not . . . have any special appeal in the South"; Bruce, *Violence and Culture*, chap. 7, quotation 171. Andrew, *Long Gray Lines*, 1–3.

75. Capers, *State Military Academies*, 8–9.

76. George G. Wells, "Valedictory Addresses Delivered by Cadet G. G. Wells," 1862, CIT. This graduate wrote during the Civil War, when most of his graduating class were asserting their manhood by marching off to war.

77. Joseph Jenkins to Micah Jenkins, [1856], SCL. Jenkins and a fellow Citadel graduate founded Kings Mountain Military Academy in 1855.

78. Ages based on Frank, *Life with Father*, 13. Joseph Kett suggests that middle-class or upwardly mobile youth entered manhood when they broke into their professions. Southern men started working in their professions earlier than men in other regions; for example, 72 percent of southern doctors started practicing before they were twenty-five (compared with 59 percent for the entire United States), and most lawyers started in their early twenties; Kett, *Rites of Passage*, 35. Rotundo, *Manhood*, 70; Green, "Books and Bayonets," chap. 5, app. 2.

79. Slightly more than 65 percent of fathers and 74 percent of military academy alumni pursued nonagricultural professions; Green, "Books and Bayonets," chap. 1, app. 2.

80. Samuel Garland to Samuel Garland, 12 January 1848, VHS.

81. Joseph Chenoweth to Father, 21 November 1858, VMI.

82. Robert H. Simpson to Francis H. Smith, 9 January 1850, VMI.

# "Commenced to Think Like a Man": Literacy and Manhood in African American Civil War Regiments

*Heather Andrea Williams*

During the Civil War, literacy, already a prized but rare commodity among enslaved African Americans, became an essential component of emancipation as black men, women, and children prepared themselves to take on new identities as free people. Whether they envisioned the coming of freedom as a mass exodus from bondage or as an individual escape, enslaved people often imagined how they would choose to live in freedom. As they escaped from slavery, enlisted in the Union army, or took on the status of "contrabands," African Americans articulated demands for land, political agency through the vote, and education.

In slavery, the very act of learning to read constituted a secret form of resistance, but upon emancipation freedpeople transformed the act of becoming literate from a clandestine occurrence into one of life's necessities. As the momentum toward freedom built during the Civil War so did the quest for literacy. Realizing that illiteracy would severely constrict their success as a free people in a literate society, many newly freed people latched on to the spelling book as both a symbol and tool of liberation. Acquiring literacy in conjunction with freedom potentially opened access to democratic political activity, which in turn held the promise of enabling former slaves to help shape the society that had hitherto considered them chattel—insurgent chattel, but chattel just the same. With the coming of war, African Americans sought to enter the public sphere as individuals distinct from owners. They were on the verge of being counted for the first time as citizens, not as part of an owner's inventory for tax assessment or as a percentage of a man for political apportionment. Illiteracy, they knew, would impede the fulfillment of their ambition for full political participation.[1]

Both African American men and women aspired to self-determination and political participation. In the middle of the nineteenth century, however, civic participation remained a deeply gendered notion, with public power and political participation reserved for white men. In a world that denied suffrage and civic independence to even the most privileged white women, black women could scarcely anticipate inclusion. The greatest hope of political inclusion rested in African American men. Knowing this, and understanding as their ancestors had in earlier wars the relationship between military service, freedom, and citizenship, enslaved and free black men hammered away at the federal government to accept them as soldiers. Military service, black men hoped, would serve as a launching pad for political rights. For the first two years of the war the United States government refused to arm black men. In the face of impending defeat, it finally relented in 1863.[2]

Once admitted into military service for the Union, black men determined not only to liberate themselves and fellow blacks but also to become literate. Those black soldiers and black chaplains who were already literate men emerged as leaders of an incipient educational movement among freedpeople. As such, they advocated increased educational opportunities for fellow soldiers as well as for the larger freed population. In addition, some black soldiers helped to build schools for African Americans. Always, they linked literacy to freedom and the achievement of full manhood.[3]

This essay engages the links that African American men made between manhood and literacy. Their conceptions of manhood were neither monolithic nor static; their definitions included power, self-determination, and the ability to provide for and protect families and communities.[4] For many soldiers, literacy provided an important means toward achieving these varied measures of manhood. But neither literacy nor freedom guaranteed equal treatment. As they sacrificed to achieve freedom and to attain literacy, black men contended with attacks on both their humanity and their manhood. While abolitionists such as Frederick Douglass and Henry McNeal Turner challenged black men to go to war and thereby prove their manhood, powerful northern white men assailed enlisted black men's character and intellect. White men's feelings of superiority over black men did not disappear when black men picked up arms; both southern and northern whites clung to the biases they used to distinguish themselves from African Americans. Thus white Union officers issued commands and assessed African Americans' competence on the basis of racialized notions of capacity rather than on individual ability. Black soldiers were in a sense wedged between the exhortations of Frederick Douglass and the judgments of Thomas Wentworth Higgenson, a white colonel of an African American regiment, who gazed admiringly at black soldiers' musculature even as he demeaned their intellect.

The life of Elijah Marrs illuminates the movement of former slaves into military service, into literacy, and into leadership. It exposes the tensions that arose for adult males who, regardless of their courage, or skill, or respect within the community of their peers, did not consider themselves fully men, since they were denied the rights that society bestowed upon white men. Marrs's own narration of his life, supplemented by documents including his military service record and Freedmen's Bureau records, provides rich insights into a young man working to liberate himself both physically and emotionally. For Marrs, literacy, freedom, and manhood were intimately intertwined. His ability to read and write constituted an important element of his self-concept within his community of slaves. As he adjusted to life as a free man and as a soldier, Marrs grappled with the substance of this new freedom and wondered when he would achieve full status as a man. He and other soldiers, including John Sweney, along with black chaplains such as Henry McNeal Turner, perceived a fundamental kinship between literacy and the duties of free men. They and other African American men used the tragic circumstances of the Civil War to prepare themselves to serve their communities.

The Emancipation Proclamation in January 1863 freed the slaves in territories under Confederate control and announced the Union's intention to enlist black soldiers. Five months later, the War Department created a Bureau of Colored Troops, and the Union finally accepted African American men as soldiers. Thus, when in September 1864, Elijah Marrs walked away from the Shelby County, Kentucky, farm where he worked alongside thirty other enslaved people, instead of seeking protection as a contraband of war, he marched toward enlistment as a soldier in the Union army. At age twenty-three, Marrs set out to claim his freedom by taking up arms against slavery.

When Elijah Marrs decided to enlist, he did not go alone. He spent the daylight hours rounding up a network of "old comrades" to join him on the march to Louisville, twenty miles east of Shelby. As night fell, twenty-seven men met Marrs at a local black church. There, they elected him their captain.[5] Choosing Marrs was a logical move for a number of reasons. His physical stature alone would have marked him as a leader. At five feet, ten inches, he was nearly a head taller than most of the men around him.[6] More important, because Marrs was a literate man, others in the slave community in Shelby had long recognized him as a leader. Indeed, the farm on which he lived served as a secret "general headquarters for the negroes," where Marrs read newspapers to gathered slaves, provoking angry whites to brand him the "Shelby County negro clerk." When black men, including Marrs's older brother, Henry, began enlisting in the army, Marrs continued to read letters that they sent home to illiterate family members, despite his owner's warnings against such actions. "The colored soldiers had confidence in me," Marrs recalled, "and knew that their letters would be faithfully delivered." [7] Finally, the men chose Marrs as their captain because he conceived of and activated their collective movement toward freedom.

Even as the men met to map out the route to Louisville, however, Marrs's capacity for leadership met its first test as a rumor spread that "the rebels were preparing to make a raid upon the church." Shouting at the backs of men who fled, over the screams of women in the church, and beyond his own terror at the prospect of a rebel raid, Marrs beseeched the men to remain: "If we staid at home we would be murdered; that if we joined the army and were slain in battle, we would at least die in fighting for principle and freedom." [8] Marrs's words to his men persuaded them to maintain their resolve to enlist in the army. They marched through the night, armed with "war clubs and one old rusty pistol," leaving the main road when they arrived at a notorious area "through which the colored people seldom passed with safety." As the sun rose on Marrs's band, they reached the recruiting office in Louisville. Everyone enlisted with the exception of one boy who was too young. They arrived just in time. By noon, their owners reached Louisville in pursuit of their former slaves—now soldiers in the Union army. The former slave owners returned home empty handed. [9]

Elijah Marrs and more than two dozen black men from Shelby joined a growing number of men who escaped slavery by enlisting in the military. In his autobiography, Peter Bruner, an ex-slave in Kentucky, recalled his own persistence in attempting to enlist: "The officers asked me what I wanted there and I told them that I came there to fight the rebels and that I wanted a gun. When I had run off before and wanted to go in the army and fight they said they did not want any darkies, and that this was a white man's war. After I had been there about a week they make up a regiment and called it the Twelfth U.S. Heavy Artillery." Bruner and sixteen other escaped slaves enlisted at the same time. [10] Black enlistment varied from state to state, depending on the number of African American residents and their legal status. Northern states, whose small black populations were already free, offered up fewer recruits than border states such as Kentucky and Missouri, where the Emancipation Proclamation left slavery intact. Enlistment in the military became an escape hatch for thousands of black men in these loyal slave states. In fact, Kentucky, with 5 percent of the black men in the country, provided 13 percent of the black men who enlisted nationwide. More than half of Kentucky's enslaved men between the ages of eighteen and forty-five enlisted. [11]

Freedom was a multidimensional process for Elijah Marrs. He began his movement toward freedom when he decided to leave Shelby to enlist in the army. Marrs's legal transition from slavery to freedom occurred in the few moments it took him to muster into the service. However, the emotional transition to feeling free proved a greater challenge for the vulnerable, displaced young man who had left behind the security of family and high status within the slave community.

In his autobiography, published in 1885, Marrs adopted patriotic and biblical imagery to convey this shift from feeling like a slave to feeling like a free man. During his first nightmare-filled, homesick night in camp, Marrs realized that although he had gained freedom from his master, he had incurred new obligations to perhaps an even more demanding master: the army. At roll call the following morning, he coaxed himself to accept his soldier status: "I can stand this said I, and like a man, with cup, pan, and spoon, marched up to the window and received my rations. It is true I thought of my mother's sweet voice when she used to call me to dine, but 'pshaw!' said I, 'this is better than slavery, though I do march in line to the tap of the drum.'" Then, finding inspiration in the national symbols all around him, Marrs appropriated the language that white colonists had used to assert themselves as free and independent men, "I felt freedom in my bones, and when I saw the American eagle, with outspread wings, upon the American flag, with the motto, 'E Pluribus Unum,' the thought came to me, 'Give me liberty or give me death.' Then all fear banished. I had quit thinking as a child and had commenced to think as a man." [12]

Marrs's previous identity as a slave centered on his literacy and the service it enabled him to provide to fellow slaves. He spent much of his early life inadvertently preparing for the pivotal moment when he led his peers into the military service of the Union; he had learned to read and write. "Very early, in life," he remembered, "I took up the idea that I wanted to learn to read and write. I was convinced that there would be something for me to do in the future that I could not accomplish by remaining in ignorance. I had heard so much about freedom, and of the colored people running off and going to Canada, that my mind was busy with this subject even in my young days" (11–12). It is perplexing to consider what would cause an enslaved child to think that he would have important things to do, and what would propel him to make the link between education and effectiveness. Nevertheless, like Frederick Douglass, Elijah Marrs dated his desire for literacy to childhood; and like Douglass he drew inspiration from stories of other slaves escaping to freedom. As did many other slaves, Marrs "sought the aid of the white boys" to teach him. He practiced his lessons by reading the newspapers and the addresses on letters he collected for the "white people" during daily trips to the post office (12).

Some time after Marrs learned to read, Ham Graves, an old black man on the Robinson farm, opened a school that met at night. Graves taught Marrs to write. Marrs, too young to realize that he was leaving evidence of his illicit behavior, practiced writing all over the farm: "on every gate-post around the stables, as on the plow-handles, you could see where I had been trying to write" (1–12). After Marrs joined the church and was baptized, his owner, Jesse Robinson, permitted him to attend Sunday school. There his teacher allowed him to read the Bible. Both his owner and Sunday school teacher forbade Marrs to write, however. According to Marrs, "We had to steal that portion of our education, and I did my share of it I suppose" (15).

Marrs's literacy afforded him elevated status within the community of slaves in Shelby. As he constructed an identity as a free man, his identity again rested on his literacy. However, one particularly painful incident threatened that status. Shortly after enlisting, Marrs developed "a reputation as a writer," and many of his fellow soldiers asked him to draft letters to their families. What Marrs had been obliged to do in secret while a slave, he now did openly as a soldier. When the regiment's officers discovered that Marrs was "skilled in the use of the pen," they sought him out and found him "surrounded by a number of the men, each waiting his turn to have a letter written home." Satisfied that they had found a "penman," the officers promoted Marrs to duty sergeant.[13] He accepted the position with the understanding that he would receive "personal instruction in army tactics" to enable him to fulfill his new role. The new sergeant was sorely disappointed when, some days later, his commanding officer ordered him to take a squad of men to clear ground for the erection of barracks. Despite his promotion and literacy, Marrs, like most black soldiers, found himself relegated to the most grueling, distasteful tasks of war.[14]

Marrs's treatment by Union officers highlights the duality of African American experience. Slaves in Shelby and black soldiers in his regiment considered Marrs a valuable asset whose skills enhanced their well-being. Within these two communities, he was well respected and appreciated. In contrast, much as his owner had, his Union commanders used him for labor as they needed him, whether the labor required skill or not. Insulted by orders to perform manual labor, Marrs reflected on the disparity between his actual situation and his long-nurtured notions of freedom. "While I felt myself a free man and a U.S. soldier," he complained, "still must I move at the command of a white man, and I said to myself is my condition any better now than before I entered the army? But the idea would come to me that I was a soldier fighting for my freedom, and this thought filled my heart with joy. I thought, too, that the time will come when no man can say to me come and go, and I be forced to obey."[15]

Marrs was not alone in his understanding of this hopeful equation of soldiering and manhood. Frederick Douglass and other black abolitionists issued an urgent manifesto to black men in 1863 in which they made the same linkage. "Men of Color To Arms! To Arms," their recruitment broadside called, imploring black men to fight for the Union to gain their freedom and to prove their manhood. "Our enemies have made the country believe that we are craven cowards, without souls, without manhood, without the spirit of soldiers. Shall we die with this stigma resting upon our graves?" it asked. "Shall we leave this inheritance of Shame to our children? No! A thousand times NO! Let us rather die freemen than live to be slaves." In exchange for a display of manly courage, the abolitionists promised free and enslaved black men a new social order. "A new era is open to us," they pledged; "for generations we have suffered under the horrors of slavery, outrage and wrong; our manhood has been denied, our citizenship blotted out, our souls seared and burned, our spirits cowed and crushed, and the hopes of the future of our race involved in doubt and darkness." The recruiters promised, "Our relations to the white race are changed. Now therefore is our most precious moment. Let us rush to arms." [16] Douglass expounded on the sentiments expressed in the recruitment broadside in an article published in his newspaper, *Douglass' Monthly*. In his enumeration of nine responses to the question "Why should a colored man enlist?" Douglass argued that enlistment would benefit the esteem of each black soldier. "Decried and derided as you have been and still are, you need an act of this kind by which to recover your own self-respect," he told his audience. Black men sometimes measured their own worth according to the opinions of their enemies, he argued, and therefore underestimated their self-worth. "You owe it to yourself and your race to rise from your social debasement, and take your place among the soldiers of your country, a man among men," Douglass argued. [17]

But the abolitionists' promises remained unfulfilled, and Elijah Marrs's freedom and manhood remained tenuous. Becoming a soldier freed him from the physical grasp of his owner, but the owner still held a legal claim over him. He picked up arms, but his commanding officer now ordered him to pick up a shovel. Enlistment in the army, instead of allowing him to fully exercise his freedom, imposed new constraints on him that insulted his standing in the black community and prevented him from using his own judgment and fulfilling his own desires. Although Marrs believed that literacy elevated him, white officers relegated him to menial labor, a stinging reminder of slavery. He now imagined a new meaning for freedom: equality with white men. It was no longer sufficient not to be owned by white men; Marrs wanted to escape their domination entirely. He longed to be "a man among men."

Another black soldier, Alexander Newton, similarly understood that freedom might not mean equality. Although born to a free mother in New Bern, North

Carolina, Newton early encountered the affronts of slavery through the experiences of his enslaved father. "I learned what slavery was," he recalled, "I felt its curse in my bones and I longed for an opportunity and the power to play the part of a Moses in behalf of my people. I suppose that this was the wild dream of every child born during slavery." Tired of obeying white employers' orders, Newton left North Carolina and moved to Brooklyn, New York, in 1857 at the age of twenty. There he joined his mother who, with the help of abolitionists, collected money to purchase his father's freedom. Newton returned south for the first time as a soldier in the Twenty-ninth Regiment Connecticut Volunteers. Stationed in Beaufort, South Carolina, Newton found himself "in the full realization of what it meant to be again in the South, not a cringing black man, but a proud American soldier with the Union and Old Glory behind, before, over and under me."[18]

For Newton, as for Elijah Marrs and thousands of other black soldiers, military service held the promise of transforming the social order. Newton recalled that General Rufus Saxton, an early and steadfast advocate for the enlistment of African American troops, advised the black soldiers, "'Boys, if you want to make good soldiers you must look a white man straight in the face and let him know that you are a man.' This gave us fresh courage to press forward as soldiers to a certain victory."[19] Saxton's injunction presaged the social structure that many black men sought. Saxton had in mind facing Confederate white men as equals. However, once a black man considered himself equal to one white man, it would not be long before he considered himself equal to all white men, whether from the South or the North. Before Elijah Marrs ever faced a Confederate soldier, he questioned his unequal stature in contrast with white northern Union officers and wanted to be considered equal to them.[20]

While Marrs struggled for equality and the achievement of his vision of manhood, he returned to the methods that had previously defined him as a leader among slaves. He continued to write letters for fellow soldiers, and while stationed at Camp Nelson, Kentucky, he began to teach as well. He and Sergeant Major George Thomas formed classes among the men, and they taught vocal music and the rudiments of English grammar while in camp.[21] By teaching, Marrs hoped to pass on his skills and to bolster his self-respect. The greatest boost to his esteem came, however, when he was assigned to supervise contraband women and children in Bowling Green. According to Marrs, his officers finally recognized his efficiency as a sergeant and ordered him to report for "assignment to more important duties." Hundreds of women and children whose husbands and fathers had enlisted were driven from their homes by angry owners and flooded into the camp seeking protection.[22] The camp also promised liberation. "All they had to do was to get there and they were free," Marrs wrote.[23]

Setting up headquarters in the black Methodist church, Marrs provided these contrabands with rations. He held authority to "punish the unruly" and to set up a system of government. Marrs's confidence blossomed as he supervised the women and children. "They looked to me as if I were their Saviour," he wrote. "Whatever happened in camp to disturb or annoy them, the story was at once detailed to me, and I was expected to remedy every evil." He even instituted a court of sorts, in which he could sit as "judge, examine witnesses, and condemn the guilty to such punishment as in my judgement the offense deserved; as a rule, that was the last of it." [24] Lacking full equality with white men, Marrs enjoyed the opportunity to exert power over African Americans.

To some extent, Marrs positioned himself as a man by exercising authority over black women. [25] In essence, he stood as the proxy head of a large household, much as white planters imagined themselves patriarchs over households that included slaves. As such, he could assert a claim to one of the attributes of manhood that white men jealously guarded in the antebellum South. His perceived role as a savior to black women was part of a shift in power relations between black men and women, with men cast as liberators and the women who had labored beside them for generations cast as dependents. [26] Hidden from history, however, are the women's reactions to these new power arrangements. One can safely speculate that not all women appreciated Marrs's role as provider, judge, and jury in that time that historian Laura Edwards described as replete with contention over sex roles. For his part, Marrs took pride in his new role and the degree of manhood that it conferred upon him. Although his newfound manhood operated within limited boundaries—he could not, for example, exert authority over white men, women, or children—for the moment, he deemed power over members of his own group sufficient. [27]

Although initially frustrated in his desire to achieve a sense of freedom, independence, and authority in the military, Elijah Marrs eventually achieved the stature he coveted. Without doubt, Marrs's ability to read and write launched his movement up the military ranks. At the same time that Marrs struggled to find his identity as a free man, his enlistment in the army freed him to display literacy he formerly hid in the slave quarters.

Within the military structure, other black soldiers and officers urged the government to provide teachers and books for black soldiers. They, too, discerned a clear relationship between literacy, leadership, and manhood. For example, ex-slave and first sergeant John Sweney advocated black education. In a letter asking the Freedmen's Bureau to establish a school for his regiment, Sweney articulated black soldiers' desire for education, predicted that many soldiers would become community leaders after the war, and declared a wider African American intention to be self-supporting. Sweney learned to read and write in slavery and, as Elijah Marrs did, likely secured his promotion to first sergeant because he could perform clerical duties. The morning reports for Company F of the Thirteenth Regiment carry Sweney's daily count of officers, enlisted men, and serviceable weapons, endorsed by his slowly etched signature.[28] In his new position in the military hierarchy, Sweney wrote to the Freedmen's Bureau out of self-conscious duty to the other men of his regiment and the larger black population of Kentucky. Although his punctuation and spelling demonstrated the flaws of the self-taught, his reasoning was flawless.

Sweney wrote, "Sir, I have the honor to call your attention To the necessity of having a school for The Benefit of our regiment We have never had an institution of that sort and we Stand deeply inneed of instruction the majority of us having been slaves We wish to have some benefit of education To make of ourselves capable of business in the future." Sweney anticipated that to lead their communities he and other African American men serving in the military would need education. He was determined to help build self-supporting African American institutions. "We have establesed a literary Association which flourished previous to our march to Nashville," he continued. "We wish to become a People capable of self suport as we are Capable of being soldiers." Then, in his role of advocate for the soldiers of his regiment and the larger communities from which they came, Sweney explained, "My home is in Kentucky where Prejudice regns like the mountain Oak. I had a leave of absence a few weeks a go on a furlough and it made my heart ache to see my race of people there neglected And ill treated on the account of the lack of Education being incapable of putting Their complaints or applications in writing For the want of education totally ignorant of the Great Good Workings of the Governement in their behalf."[29]

By noting what he deemed the ignorance and neglect of fellow blacks in Kentucky, Sweney made an explicit link between education and empowerment. Once they learned to read, the black men of Kentucky would understand the workings of the government and would petition for their rights. Further, in his request for a school for the regiment, Sweney intimated that the regiment's education could not be contained. Literacy would spread to blacks in Kentucky and in the other states from which the soldiers hailed. Sweney ended his letter with a nod to the beneficence of the white officers in charge of his regiment and a proposal for implementing a coherent, regiment-wide system of education. "We as soldeirs," he wrote, "Have our officers who are our protection To teach how us to act and to do But Sir what we want is a general system of education In our regiment for our moral and literary elevation."[30] John Sweney, who likely learned to read and write in secret, now publicly asserted the civil rights that education enabled black people to claim. Further, he insinuated that it was the government's duty to protect those rights by at least providing resources.

Other black men joined Sweney in appealing to the government to provide educational resources for black soldiers. Henry McNeal Turner, one of only a few African American chaplains serving in the Civil War and a future bishop of the African Methodist Episcopal Church, took up black soldiers' demands for education. He beseeched his superior officers to provide much needed teachers and books. When the Civil War began, Turner was pastoring Israel African Methodist Episcopal Church in Washington, D.C., a congregation with several hundred members.[31] He used his prominence in Washington to recruit black men into the Union army. To reward Turner's efforts, President Lincoln appointed him the first African American chaplain in the United States army in September 1863.[32]

Bold and contentious, Turner demanded books for black soldiers. Frustrated by the army's recalcitrance, he even attempted to bargain for education in exchange for promotions. Unlike John Sweney, Turner felt no need to avow the goodness of white officers. Enslaved until he enlisted in the army, Sweney was well versed in public transcripts that demanded deference and loyalty be exhibited when blacks addressed whites.[33] Turner, in contrast, emitted a self-confidence that emanated from his pride in being born free. Elijah Marrs questioned when he would feel like a free man, whereas Henry McNeal Turner reveled in his freeness, regarding it as the core of his being. Unlike Marrs, Turner did not have to wait for the day when he could assert his freedom or his manhood. He had always known freedom and drew on the confidence this status provided him, whether interacting with blacks or whites.

Turner's obligatory monthly reports to the adjutant general of the United States army in the first year of his chaplaincy affirmed that the moral character of his regiment fared no worse than any other, and he regretted that frequent engagements with the enemy precluded regular religious services.[34] He did not mention education. In June 1865, however, after the regiment, the First United States Colored Troops, settled on Roanoke Island, North Carolina, in quarters that afforded them "favorable conveniences," he reported that the regimental church met regularly, and then took up the question of education for the black soldiers. Turner reported that he had "constantly kept the subject of education before [the] soldiers," and that they had advanced well even under the conditions of war. However, all progress reached a virtual standstill because he could not supply the heavy demand for books among the men. His tone turned scornful when he told his superior officer that if his repeated requests for a leave of absence had been granted, he would have purchased books for the men, even at his own expense. Instead, they had none. Hundreds of books he had previously provided to the soldiers were destroyed in their knapsacks when their boat sank in the Cape Fear River. Turner mockingly hoped that it would not be "an outrage upon the right of petition" to request the government's help in procuring educational supplies.[35]

Like Sweney, Turner linked education to good citizenship, and he contended that the army owed it to these troops to prepare them for meaningful participation in the new America that the war would create. Turner requested a large number of advanced spelling books because many of the troops "who can read and write some, need to be much better drilled in spelling." Negotiating for five hundred spelling books, he challenged military powers to reward the men of his regiment for their "bravery, courage and invincibleness" in the face of the enemy. "I claim this favor for my regiment," he declared, "upon the ground that she is the mother of colored Troops, and that in nine battles, regardless of skirmishes, she has never faltered, given way, or retreated unless ordered by the General Commanding. I challenge mortal man to stain her career with one blot of cowardice." Then he made the same linkages that Sweney did, asserting that the spelling books were necessary "as a means to make brave soldiers, good and intelligent citizens."[36] According to Turner, the soldiers had proven themselves men through their bravery; now they must become literate in order to exercise the prerogatives of civic manhood.

When by August 1865 Turner's regiment had still not received the books, he again solicited the adjutant general. He hoped to shame the army when he wrote, "The progress which the soldiers are making in trying to acquire an education, surpasses the most sanguine expectation. It is indispensable however that I renew my application, asking that you have my Regiment furnished with five hundred advanced spelling books. The soldiers themselves pay all the expenses incurred by the employment of teachers." In Turner's estimation, the men had done all they could by having an intense desire to learn, and by paying teachers from their own pockets. Still, they saw no alternative but to rely on the government to send them spelling books. The final twist came when Turner attempted to hold the army accountable for discriminating against black soldiers. He proposed to trade medals for spelling books, arguing that as the Union refused to promote or commend black soldiers for gallantry, it should at least supply them with the books necessary to "improve their minds."[37]

Turner made no attempt to veil his cynicism. He had worked to recruit African American soldiers for the Union army but grew frustrated in his efforts to provide his men with one of the things they needed and wanted most. On their behalf he proposed this sneering trade of medals for books. Evidence does not reveal whether the regiment ever received the advanced spelling books Turner sought. By the end of August, however, he reported that instead of only one regimental school there were several company schools in operation, "employing the leisure hours of all the soldiers who are off duty." According to Turner, "the men learn with flattering success. I have never seen the fruits of my labor so visibly as I do now since I have held my position."[38]

Henry McNeal Turner, Elijah Marrs, and John Sweney constituted part of the patchwork of educational resources available to illiterate African American soldiers. Like their civilian counterparts in contraband camps and freedmen's villages, these men believed that learning to read and write was essential to their performing new roles as free men. But black men's assertions of manhood were by no means uncontested, for even as black soldiers established schools and taught one another, powerful white men questioned black men's capacity for learning and for leadership. As black men fought to throw off the mantle of slavery, they entered a world in which many whites maintained long-held notions of white racial superiority and black inferiority. For example, Thomas Wentworth Higgenson, a widely published author and commander of the First South Carolina Volunteers, a regiment of black men, questioned black soldiers' manhood and at times even their humanity. Higgenson lauded African American soldiers' dedication to becoming literate; "their love of the spelling-book is perfectly inexhaustible." However, his language betrayed paternalism when he described the men "stumbling on by themselves, or the blind leading the blind, with the same pathetic patience which they carry into everything." Higgenson did not limit his observations to education. He found the black soldiers peculiar as he attempted to fit them into his own experiences and worldview.[39]

Black soldiers' efforts to achieve literacy and thereby to prepare themselves for civic participation as free men could not spare them from this powerful white northerner's scrutiny and judgment. A native of Massachusetts, Higgenson had never seen so many African Americans and spent much of his time in the regiment trying to categorize the men. Poking and prodding, examining and measuring, Higgenson's curiosity mirrored that of many northerners who found themselves face to face with the slaves and former slaves they had previously only read about. In pseudo-scientific manner, he assessed size, speech, intelligence, and ability, as he attempted to fathom the nature of these men. Nothing escaped his scrutiny: how they walked, how musical they were, how rhythmic, how quickly they learned. He wrote in his camp diary of the sudden transformation of men from slaves into soldiers. He viewed them as representing "a race affectionate, enthusiastic, grotesque, and dramatic beyond all others." Fascinated by the men's color, he commented that they "all looked as thoroughly black as the most faithful philanthropist could desire; there did not seem to be so much as a mulatto among them." And he was taken with these black men's bodies, noting, "To be sure they often look magnificently to my gymnasium-trained eyes; and I always like to observe them when bathing,—such splendid muscular development, set off by that smooth coating of odipose tissue which makes them, like the South Sea Islanders, appear even more muscular than they are. Their skins are also of finer grain than most of the whites, the surgeons say, and certainly are smoother and far more free of hair." But Higgenson thought he found a vulnerability that offset these seeming physical advantages. He reckoned that "their weakness is pulmonary; pneumonia and; pleurisy are their besetting ailments; they are easily made ill." Although Higgenson acknowledged that whites frequently became ill in the hot season, he held on to his assessment that blacks possessed weaker constitutions than whites. He insisted that his "conviction of the physical superiority of more civilized races [was] strengthened on the whole, not weakened, by observing them." He did, however, believe that black soldiers were equal or superior to whites when it came to military drill and duty.[40]

In contrast to Elijah Marrs and John Sweney, who pursued literacy for black soldiers as a means of moving them from historical positions of subservience, Higgenson's conception of black manhood required black men to be humble and deferential. A self-described abolitionist who lionized the radical abolitionist John Brown, he thought it the business of white northern men like himself to educate these childlike "young barbarians" to manhood.[41] Higgenson compared the demeanor of the black soldiers he met in the South with that of free black men in the North and was relieved that, although the southern men were courteous to each other, he as yet saw "none of that upstart conceit which is sometimes offensive among free negroes at the North, the dandy-strut. This is an agreeable surprise, for I feared that freedom and regimentals would produce precisely that."[42] Higgenson was surprised to detect among the men a determination to become self-reliant. He found that "as one grows more acquainted with the men, their individualities emerge"; he found, "first their faces, then their characters, to be as distinct as those of whites." And as the men increasingly became distinct individuals to Higgenson, he learned of "the desire they show to do their duty, and to improve as soldiers; they evidently think about it, and see the importance of the thing; they say . . . white men cannot stay and be their leaders always and that they must learn to depend on themselves, or else relapse into their former condition."[43] These men, whom Higgenson saw as at once docile, barbaric, and childlike, were using education and military service to prepare themselves for leadership.

Despite any desire by Higgenson and other white men to constrain them, black soldiers throughout the South stepped out of their place in the social order. They marched away from slavery and, on the streets of the South, began to act in ways that disrupted southern and northern white expectations. A teacher in Pine Bluff, Arkansas, reported seeing many of his soldier-students "stand guard with book in hand." This was an astounding phenomenon in states that still officially prohibited black people from learning to read or write.[44] Rev.

Joseph Warren, superintendent of colored schools for the Department of Tennessee, commented on black soldiers' commitment to become literate. Many soldiers attended the schools Warren ran, learning lessons alongside children and other adults. "One of the most gratifying facts developed by the recent change in their condition," Warren wrote, "is, that they very generally desire instruction, and many seize every opportunity in intervals of labor to obtain it. I saw a small detachment of infantry soldiers, who had previously been unable to secure any attention from a teacher, placed within reach of a mission family. The soldiers had not been there an hour when those not on sentry duty had, of their own motion, procured spelling-books, and begged one of the ladies to aid them occasionally; they soon were busily at work on the alphabet." Emboldened by their uniforms, black men not only felt free to approach white "ladies" in the street but also felt secure in publicly professing and displaying their imminent literacy.

Informal schools, although rarely documented, nonetheless played an important part in fulfilling black soldiers' desire to become literate and to confirm their manhood. Warren reported on soldier self-help strategies within camp: "I find that in the colored regiments the men often find assistance from their comrades. A chaplain of one of these regiments, who has done very much for his charge, tells me that they have done more for one another."[45] Within Union regiments, black soldiers held to a strong sense of community and prepared one another to become leaders once the war ended. Literate men such as Elijah Marrs and John Sweney taught men in their regiments. Other soldiers taught as they learned, sometimes substituting for absent missionary teachers or assisting teachers in classrooms.[46] A nighttime study session of black soldiers profoundly affected the life of the young runaway slave John McCline. At eleven, McCline escaped from the Clover Bottoms Plantation near Nashville, Tennessee, to work in a white Union regiment that marched by the plantation. The regiment assigned him the care of the quartermaster's mules. One night, while stationed in Chattanooga, McCline wandered off from his regiment and stumbled upon a camp of black troops, the first he had ever seen. Entranced by the sight, he went to investigate: "Going up a light rise where stood several large square tents," he later recalled, "I stopped, and was cordially invited to enter. There were four or five in the great tent, and to my great surprise, some were reading, and others writing. All were neatly dressed and looked so nice in their uniforms." This scene fell far beyond anything the young boy had ever imagined. Black men in uniforms with polished shoes, engaging in what had until recently been a prohibited activity—reading. So impressed was McCline that he soon tried to emulate this new personification of black manhood. He obtained a Webster's speller and requested spelling lessons from a member of his regiment. After the war, McCline attended a school for freedpeople and in time became a teacher in a freedpeople's school.[47]

As Elijah Marrs and his men stepped into their Union blues and picked up army issued rifles, the insults and indignities of slavery followed them. Marrs knew that by enlisting he had earned his freedom and thus eluded the physical grasp of his former owner. He probably did not know that in bargains struck by Lincoln, Radical Republicans in Congress, and the governor of Kentucky, the Union government had agreed to compensate slave owners for each slave who enlisted in the army. Lincoln initially resisted enlisting slaves from the border states, fearing that arming the "property" of loyal slaveholders might drive them into the Confederacy. In 1861, fearing a domino effect in which losing one loyal state to the Confederacy would lead to the loss of others, Lincoln predicted that "to lose Kentucky is nearly the same as to lose the whole game."[48] Ultimately, however, the exigencies of war necessitated using slaves and former slaves as soldiers. Lincoln and Congress then agreed to compensate loyal slave owners three hundred dollars for each of their slaves who enlisted. Elijah Marrs numbered among the thousands of men for whom slave owners sought compensation, casting a shadow of ownership over them even after they fought to gain freedom.

Neither literacy nor military service prevented the persistent legal denigration of African American men. On 10 December 1866, more than two years after Marrs enlisted and eight months after he mustered out of the service, Marrs's former owner filed a claim with the War Department "For Compensation For Slave Named Elijah Marrs." Jesse Robinson swore an oath of loyalty to the United States and attested that, as he owned Elijah Marrs's mother when Elijah was born, Elijah had belonged to him since birth. Robinson averred that at the time of enlistment, Marrs was worth eight hundred dollars. He entered a claim for three hundred dollars, the maximum amount allowed by the government. Elijah Marrs was not a party to this transaction. It was a matter between the slaveholder and a government that recognized a claim of property in a veteran of the Civil War.[49]

The United States government compensated slaveholders whose slaves became soldiers, but it failed to provide system-wide educational benefits for black soldiers. With limited success, John Sweney and Henry McNeal Turner implored the government to furnish books and teachers for soldiers eager to learn. When the war ended, the government neither gave black soldiers forty acres and a mule nor institutionalized education to prepare them for the new roles they would play when they returned to their communities. Still, the government's reluctance was not enough to inhibit some soldiers' pursuit of education. As they prepared to muster out of service, several black soldiers from the Fifty-sixth

Regiment (which had built a school for freed children in Helena, Arkansas) prodded their teacher to help them find a school where they could continue their education. The men had accomplished a great deal in arithmetic, history, geography, and physiology and wished "to continue their education at some well conducted school."[50] Similarly, the superintendent of public instruction in Sparta, Tennessee, wrote to Fisk, a newly established school for freedpeople in Nashville, seeking admission for four "boys" who ranged in age from eighteen to thirty. They were just learning to read, he said, and there had never been a colored school in the county. Two of them had learned to read in the federal army.[51]

At schools such as Fisk, in small freedpeople's schools held in black churches, and at Lincoln Institute, founded by black soldiers of the Sixty-second and Sixty-fifth Regiments, black former soldiers attended classes alongside other freedpeople.[52] Many of the students became teachers. When Elijah Marrs and his brother, Henry Marrs, for example, returned to Shelby, Kentucky, they established schools for freedpeople. In 1867 the Freedmen's Bureau superintendent of education for Virginia noted that "many returned colored soldiers, whose first and only tuition was in their regimental schools, [were] teaching, either as a business or incidentally."[53] As Sergeant John Sweney predicted, education could not be contained.

African American soldiers, even more so than black civilians, expressed a special fervor for literacy. By joining the army they not only freed themselves but also emancipated relatives and the larger black community.[54] They helped to destroy slavery in America and emerged from military service into an irrevocably transformed American South.

Many soldiers viewed literacy as imperative for community leadership. Like Elijah Marrs, who worked among the contrabands, assisting them with material needs and arbitrating their disputes, other literate soldiers believed that their communities would look to them as arbiters and advocates. Indeed, black soldiers' wartime education and experience equipped them to take leadership positions in local and state affairs, thereby fulfilling their concepts of manhood. Former soldiers joined the African American men who convened and attended statewide black political conventions in southern states following the war. Empowered by black men's service in the military, some delegates argued that it was only fair that men who had risked their lives for the Union should be extended full civil rights. Access to education appeared prominently among the rights that many of these black conventions enunciated.[55]

As veterans, Elijah Marrs and his brother enlarged the roles they had played before the war. Whereas they had previously used literacy to enable communication among separated slaves and to inform the black community of local and national news, they now advocated on behalf of fellow African Americans. They intended their literacy to carry the people's thoughts and desires beyond the black community, specifically to the president's cabinet, white men whom they believed had the power to relieve their continuing oppression. In letters to Edwin Stanton, the secretary of war, the brothers pressed the government for protection from the violence that the Ku Klux Klan visited upon assertive black people, and they called upon the government to protect African Americans' rights to testify in court against whites, operate businesses, and have equal access to public accommodations such as hotels. By writing to the secretary of war, the head of the chain of command to which they had belonged as soldiers, they rejected the new system of oppression that southern whites sought to impose. As the freedpeople's representatives, the Marrs brothers articulated demands for agency and self-determination. If southern whites would not allow them into their coffeehouses, they wanted the right to operate their own. If whites would not allow black travelers to stay in their inns and hotels, black communities and individuals wanted the right to provide their own accommodations. Further, they did not want to be forced to work for former masters when they could be industrious and establish their own businesses. The freedpeople of Shelbyville and LaGrange, Kentucky, realized that petitions to the very local whites who sought to exclude them would be meaningless and could be expected to trigger reprisals. In this moment of Reconstruction, with some northern whites still considered allies, literate black men could write these aspirations down and secretly send them north, hoping that powerful northerners would intervene to help them realize their claims for fair treatment and independence.[56] To implement their goals, freed people called upon literate men whose confidence was boosted by service in the army, and the men responded by stepping forward to lead their communities in advocating for full citizenship rights.

NOTES

1. My thinking about freedpeople's emergence into the public sphere is influenced by Jurgen Habermas, *The Structural Transformation of the Public Sphere: An Inquiry into a Category of Bourgeois Society* (Cambridge: MIT Press, 2000). Also helpful were Craig Calhoun, ed., *Habermas and the Public Sphere* (Cambridge: MIT Press, 1992); and Elsa Barkley Brown, "Negotiating and Transforming the Public Sphere: African American Political Life in the Transition from Slavery to Freedom," *Public Culture* 7 (1994): 107–46.
2. For African Americans' use of military service to gain freedom in the Revolutionary War and in the War of 1812, and the federal government's resistance to arming black men during the Civil War, see Ira Berlin, Joseph P. Reidy, and Leslie S. Rowland, eds., *Freedom's Soldiers: The Black Military Experience in the Civil War* (New York:

Cambridge University Press, 1998), 1–19; Dudley Taylor Cornish, *The Sable Arm: Negro Troops in the Union Army, 1861–1865* (New York: Norton, 1965), 1–28; Jack D. Foner, *Blacks and the Military in American History: A New Perspective* (New York: Praeger, 1974), 3–51; Noah Andre Trudeau, *Like Men of War: Black Troops in the Civil War, 1862–1865* (Boston: Little, Brown, 1998), 1–20; Joseph T. Wilson, *The Black Phalanx: A History of the Negro Soldiers of the United States in the Wars of 1775–1812, 1861–1865* (Hartford, Conn.: American Publishing, 1891), 30–40.

3. For a fuller discussion of education in black Union regiments, see Heather A. Williams, "Self-Taught: The Role of African Americans in Educating the Freedpeople, 1861–1871" (Ph.D. diss., Yale University, 2002), 86–143. The limited historiography of the education of African American soldiers during the Civil War casts the Union army as a schoolhouse in which white chaplains, along with white officers and their wives, taught black men. Historian Dudley T. Cornish, for example, argued that the Union army had no coherent educational program for black soldiers and concluded that "what schooling the colored soldier received while in federal service was in general the result of the intelligent interest of his officers, who, aware of the Negro's need and desire for education, tried to provide for that need and fulfill that desire." Cornish correctly asserted that the federal government did not have a plan for teaching soldiers to read and write. It is also true that white chaplains and military wives responded to black soldiers' desire for education. But this is only part of the story. African American soldiers had a far more complex relationship to literacy than Cornish and other historians have suggested. Dudley Taylor Cornish, "The Union Army as a School for Negroes," *Journal of Negro History* 37(1952): 368. John W. Blassingame made a similar argument in "The Union Army as an Educational Institution for Negroes, 1862–1865," *Journal of Negro Education* 34 (1965): 152–59. More recently, Edward G. Longacre repeated this limited depiction in his reference to education in black Union regiments; see "Black Troops in the Army of the James, 1863–1865," in *A Question of Manhood: A Reader in U.S. Black Men's History and Masculinity,* ed. Darlene Clark Hine and Earnestine Jenkins, vol. 1, *"Manhood Rights": The Construction of Black Male History and Manhood, 1750–1870* (Bloomington: Indiana University Press, 1999), 532–49.

4. For discussions of the shifting nature of the concept of manhood or masculinity over time, see Gail Bederman, *Manliness and Civilization: A Cultural History of Gender and Race in the United States, 1880–1917* (Chicago: University of Chicago Press, 1995), 5–23; Christopher B. Booker, *"I Will Wear No Chain!": A Social History of African American Males* (Westport, Conn.: Praeger, 2000), viii–xii; Hine and Jenkins, *A Question of Manhood,* 1–58; Michael Kimmel, *Manhood in America: A Cultural History* (New York: Free Press, 1996), 1–10.

5. Elijah P. Marrs, *Life and History of Rev. Elijah P. Marrs* (Louisville: Bradley and Gilbert, 1885), 18. Marrs was born to a free father and enslaved mother in Shelby County, Kentucky, in 1840. His older brother, Henry Marrs, enlisted in the Union army a few months before him.

6. Compiled Military Service Record of Elijah Mars, RG 94, M1818, microfilm roll 233, National Archives; and review of the Regimental Records of Company L, 12th United States Colored Troops, RG 94, National Archives.

7. Marrs, *Life and History*, 17.

8. Ibid., 18.

9. Ibid., 20. Marrs mustered in on 26 September 1864 and was assigned to Company L, 12th U.S. Colored Artillery; Compiled Military Service Record of Elijah Marrs. In his autobiography Marrs spelled his name Marrs, but it is spelled Mars in his military records. I have adopted his spelling.

10. Peter Bruner, *A Slave's Adventure toward Freedom: Not Fiction but the True Story of a Struggle* (Oxford, Ohio: n.p., 1919), 43. Robert Anderson, a former slave from Green County, Kentucky, ran away after being punished unjustly and enlisted in the army. He was inspired in this action by several friends who had escaped and enlisted; see Disy Anderson Leonard and Robert Anderson, *From Slavery to Affluence* (1927; reprint, Steamboat Springs: Steamboat Pilot, 1967), 4–43.

11. Berlin, Reidy, and Rowland, *Freedom's Soldiers*, 13–15.

12. Marrs, *Life and History*, 22. Hereafter cited in text.

13. According to Adjutant General Lorenzo Thomas, who held responsibility for the administration of the Bureau of Colored Troops, noncommissioned officers were usually appointed from within white regiments, "but as intelligent blacks are found they are made seargeants and corporals"; Report of L. Thomas to H. M. Stanton, Secretary of War, 7 November 1864, *The War of the Rebellion: A Compilation of the Official Records of the Union and Confederate Armies*, ser. 3, vol. 4 (Washington, D.C.: Government Printing Office, 1900), 921–22.

14. Berlin, Reidy, and Rowland, *Freedom's Soldiers*, 13–15.

15. Marrs, *Life and History*, 24–25.

16. Recruitment broadside over the name of Frederick Douglass and fifty-four other men, Philadelphia, 1863, GLC 2752, Gilder Lehrman Collection, Pierpont Morgan Library.

17. Frederick Douglass, "Why Should a Colored Man Enlist?" *Douglass' Monthly*, April 1863, reprinted in *Frederick Douglass: Selected Speeches and Writings*, ed. Philip S. Foner, abridged and adapted by Yuval Taylor (Chicago: Lawrence Hill Books, 1999), 528–31. As Jim Cullen and Gail Bederman have pointed out, for the sixty years before the Civil War, manhood was indistinguishable from white supremacy. Most states withheld from black men manhood rights, the rights of citizenship that Douglass referred to, such as voting or jury service; Jim Cullen, "'I's a Man Now': Gender and African American Men," in *Divided Houses: Gender and the Civil War*, ed. Catherine Clinton and Nina Silber (New York: Oxford University Press, 1992), 76–91; Bederman, *Manliness and Civilization*, 20–22.

18. A. H. Newton, *Out of the Briars: An Autobiography and Sketch of the Twenty-ninth Regiment Connecticut Volunteers* (1910; reprint, Miami: Mnemosyne, 1969), 39.

19. Ibid.

20. For discussions of manhood in the Civil War period see Cullen, "'I's a Man Now,'" and LeeAnn Whites, "The Civil War as a Crisis in Gender," in Clinton and Silber, *Divided Houses*, 3–21.

21. Marrs, *Life and History*, 28.

22. Marrs eventually moved approximately 750 of the contrabands to Camp Nelson. Adjutant General Lorenzo Thomas wrote the following about contrabands at Camp Nelson: "I found it necessary to order shelter for the helpless women and children at Camp Nelson, where there is quite a number, and that number constantly increasing. On Christmas day a large number arrived, stating they were driven from their homes, and in some instances they stated their master had their cabins pulled down over their heads. I have no reason to suppose that the thorough Union men treat their helpless slaves with any inhumanity, but it is the southern sympathizers, who are opposed to the policy of arming the blacks such of them as have lost their able-bodied men are anxious to get rid of those who are an expense to them, and in many cases drive them off to seek shelter where they best can"; L. Thomas to Edwin M. Stanton, Secretary of War, 27 December 1864, *War of the Rebellion: A Compilation of the Official Records of the Union and Confederate Armies*, ser. 3, vol. 4, 1018. Thomas's own office had taken steps to halt pervasive "cruelties practiced" by Kentucky slave owners on black men who had tried to enlist and were rejected on medical grounds. To prevent the violent retaliation, the adjutant general's office asked the secretary of war to instruct those in charge of recruiting in Kentucky to enlist any slave who presented himself, even if he had to be placed into an "invalid colored regiment"; C. W. Foster, Assistant Adjutant General of Volunteers to Edwin M. Stanton, Secretary of War, 7 June 1864, *War of the Rebellion*, ser. 3, vol. 4, 422.

23. Marrs, *Life and History*, 65.

24. Ibid., 61–62.

25. The idea of "positioning" is borrowed from Bederman, *Manliness and Civilization*, 7.

26. Berlin, Reidy, and Rowland, *Freedom's Soldiers*, 29–30.

27. Laura Edwards, *Gendered Strife and Confusion: The Political Culture of Reconstruction* (Urbana: University of Illinois Press, 1997). LeeAnn Whites made the argument that southern white elite men derived some of their sense of manhood from their position as heads of dependent households; "Crisis in Gender," 3–21.

28. Sweney enlisted in September 1863 and was promoted to the rank of first sergeant in Company F of the Thirteenth Regiment on 20 November 1863; Regimental Records, 13 United States Colored Infantry, RG 94, National Archives. Sweney's military service record was missing from the National Archives in spring 2000.

29. John Sweney's letter appears in *Freedom: A Documentary History of Emancipation, 1861–1867*, ser. 2, *The Black Military Experience*, ed. Ira Berlin, Joseph P. Reidy, and Leslie S. Rowland (New York: Cambridge University Press, 1982), 615.

30. Berlin, Reidy, and Rowland, *Freedom*, 615.

31. Henry McNeal Turner, "Emancipation Day," in *Respect Black: The Writings and Speeches of Henry McNeal Turner*, ed. Edwin S. Redkey (New York: Arno, 1971), 2.

32. Edwin S. Redkey, "Black Chaplains in the Union Army," *Civil War History* 33 (1987): 331–50; Redkey, *Respect Black,* viii; Henry McNeal Turner Military Service Record, RG 94, M1819, National Archives. As the war progressed, 13 other black men took on the role of chaplain among the 133 chaplains of black regiments. Most of the African American chaplains came from northern states, but some were southerners, including three who were born into slavery. The men represented Baptist, African Methodist Episcopal, Congregational, and Presbyterian denominations. Even as they ministered to the spiritual and educational needs of enlisted men, black chaplains fought for recognition of their own status as officers. For example, they successfully petitioned the United States War Department for uniforms to clearly identify them as officers, thus gaining access to military hospitals from which they were previously turned away, mistaken for privates or civilians. Black chaplain Benjamin Randolph made a written request for a clear identifier for chaplains, saying that "with ordinary clergyman's dress," chaplains "frequently suffer indignities because they are not recognized as chaplains"; B. F. Randolph to Abraham Lincoln, 24 August 1864, Randolph Military Service Record, RG 94, National Archives; Redkey, "Black Chaplains" 331–50.

33. James C. Scott, *Domination and the Arts of Resistance: Hidden Transcripts* (New Haven: Yale University Press, 1990), 9.

34. According to a report prepared by R. D. Mussey, colonel, One Hundredth United States Colored Infantry, and commissioner for organization, U.S. Colored Troops, chaplains were required to make the instruction of the regiment a principal part of their duties. Mussey to Maj. C. W. Foster, Assistant Adjutant General, chief of the Colored Bureau, Washington, D.C., 10 October 1864, *War of the Rebellion,* ser. 3, vol. 4, 772.

35. Henry McNeal Turner to Adjutant General, United States Army, 24 June 1865, Adjutant General Letters Received, RG 94, M619, 736, T1865, National Archives.

36. Ibid.

37. Henry McNeal Turner to Adjutant General, United States Army, 14 August 1865, Adjutant General Letters Received, RG 94, M619, 591, T1865, National Archives.

38. Henry McNeal Turner to Adjutant General, United States Army, 31 August 1865, Adjutant General Letters Received, RG 94, M619, 695, T1865, National Archives. Several other black chaplains also implored the government to support regimental schools for African American soldiers. William Waring to Adjutant General, 21 June 1864, RG 94, M619, 876, W1864, National Archives; William Waring to Brigadier General L. Thomas, Adjutant General, United States Colored Troops, 10 November 1864, RG 94, M619, 2042, W1864, National Archives; Benjamin Randolph to E. D. Townsend, 1 November 1864, Benjamin Randolph Military Service Record, RG 94, M619, 972, 1864, National Archives; Military Service Record of Francis A. Boyd, RG 94, National Archives; Francis A. Boyd to Adjutant General Lorenzo Thomas, 31 December 1864; Francis A. Boyd to Major General B. Butler, 5 January 1865, Military Service Record of Francis A. Boyd, RG 94, M619, 1861, 1864; Affidavit of L. W. Gratigny, 6 January 1865; Francis A. Boyd to Colonel O. A. Bartholomew, 3 January 1865, all in Boyd Military Service Record, National Archives.

39. Thomas Wentworth Higgenson, *Army Life in a Black Regiment* (New York: Penguin, 1997), 19.

40. Ibid., 42. Higgenson was not alone in scrutinizing black men's bodies. Abolitionist missionary John Fee wrote admiringly of the soldiers whom he saw at Camp Nelson in Kentucky. He quoted a doctor who examined the men as saying, "sometimes we actually stood still in admiration of the wonderfully developed chests and muscles of some of these men"; John Fee to Simeon Jocelyn, [n.d.], American Missionary Association Archives, Amistad Research Center, New Orleans (hereafter AMA). For a discussion of northern whites' attitudes toward African Americans in the mid-nineteenth century, see George M. Fredrickson, *The Black Image in the White Mind: The Debate on Afro-American Character and Destiny, 1817–1914* (Middletown, Conn.: Wesleyan University Press, 1971), 97–129.

41. Higgenson, *Army Life*, 7, 25–26.

42. Ibid., 22.

43. Ibid., 24.

44. South Carolina outlawed teaching slaves to read or write as early as 1740. Other states enacted statutes in the eighteenth and nineteenth centuries that prohibited teaching slaves and, in some instances any African American, to read or write. Some statutes punished both the teacher and student.

45. Report submitted by Rev. Warren on 10 April 1865, in John Eaton, *Grant, Lincoln and the Freedmen: Reminiscences of the Civil War* (New York: Longmans, Green, 1907), 208–9.

46. John Fee to Simeon Jocelyn, 18 July 1864 and 8 August 1864, AMA; *Freedmen's Record* 1, no. 1 (12 December 1865), 12; handwritten statement of Jason Spratley, Warwick County, Virginia, n.d., Hampton University Archives, Hampton, Va.

47. John McCline, *Slavery in the Clover Bottoms*, ed. Jan Furman (Knoxville: University of Tennessee Press, 1998), 81–83.

48. Abraham Lincoln to O. H. Browning, 22 September 1861, in *Complete Works of Abraham Lincoln*, ed. John G. Nicolay and John Hay, 12 vols. (n.p.: Lincoln Memorial University, 1894), 6: 360.

49. Military Service Record of Elijah Marrs, RG 94, M1818, microfilm roll 233. Robinson also filed a claim for Henry Marrs, RG 94, M1817, microfilm roll 69.

50. M. M. Anthony to Mr. Ogden, 8 April 1866, AMA. For additional information on Southland College and the black regiment's role in building it, see Williams, "Self-Taught," 37–52; Thomas C. Kennedy, "Southland College: The Society of Friends and Black Education in Arkansas," *Southern Friend* 7 (1985): 39–69; Thomas C. Kennedy, "The Last Days at Southland," *Southern Friend* 8 (1986): 3–19; idem, "The Rise and Decline of a Black Monthly Meeting: Southland, Arkansas, 1864–1925," *Southern Friend* 19 (1997): 3–29; Linda B. Selleck, *Gentle Invaders: Quaker Women Educators and Racial Issues during the Civil War and Reconstruction* (Richmond, Ind.: Friends United Press, 1995), 191–217.

51. W. F. Carter to John Ogden, 17 February 1868, AMA.

52. Regarding the regiments' involvement in the founding of Lincoln University, see

Richard Baxter Foster, *Historical Sketch of Lincoln Institute, Jefferson City, Missouri: Full History of its Conception, Struggles, and Triumph* (Jefferson City, Mo.: n.p., 1871); Williams, "Self-Taught," 35–37.

53. John W. Alvord, *Fourth Semi-Annual Report on Schools for Freedmen, July 1, 1867* (Washington, D.C.: Government Printing Office, 1867), 18–19.

54. Berlin, Reidy, and Rowland, *Freedom's Soldiers*, 15.

55. Williams, "Self-Taught," 163, 172–76.

56. Application of the Colored People of Shelbyville to Secretary Stanton, 14 May 1866, Freedmen and Southern Society Project, University of Maryland; Elijah Marrs to Secretary of War Stanton, 1 February 1868, Freedmen and Southern Society Project, University of Maryland.

# CONTRIBUTORS

EDWARD E. BAPTIST is an assistant professor of history at Cornell University. He is the author of *Creating an Old South: Middle Florida's Plantation Frontier before the Civil War.*

L. DIANE BARNES is an assistant professor of history at Youngstown State University and an associate editor with the Frederick Douglass Papers. She is a co-editor of *My Bondage and My Freedom.*

CRAIG THOMPSON FRIEND is an associate professor of history and editor of the *Florida Historical Quarterly* at the University of Central Florida. He is the editor of *The Buzzel about Kentuck: Settling the Promised Land* and the author of a forthcoming book on the Maysville Road in the early American Republic.

LORRI GLOVER is an associate professor of history at the University of Tennessee. She is the author of *All Our Relations: Blood Ties and Emotional Bonds among the Early South Carolina Gentry.*

JENNIFER R. GREEN is an assistant professor of history at Central Michigan University. She is the author of "From West Point to the Virginia Military Institute: The Educational Life of Stonewall Jackson" *(Virginia Cavalcade).*

HARRY S. LAVER is an assistant professor of history at Southeastern Louisiana University. He is the author of "Rethinking the Social Role of the Militia: Community Building in Antebellum Kentucky" *(Journal of Southern History).*

JOHN MAYFIELD is a professor of history at Samford University. He is the author of *The New Nation: 1800–1845* and *Rehearsal for Republicanism: Free Soil and the Politics of Antislavery.*

GREG O'BRIEN is an associate professor of history at the University of Southern Mississippi. He is the author of *Choctaws in a Revolutionary Age, 1750–1830.*

HEATHER ANDREA WILLIAMS is a Woodrow Wilson Postdoctoral Fellow at Smith College. She is the author of "'Clothing Themselves in Intelligence': The Freedpeople, Schooling and Northern Teachers, 1861–1871" (*Journal of African American History*).

# SELECTED BIBLIOGRAPHY

Allardice, Bruce. "West Points of the Confederacy: Southern Military Schools and the Confederate Army." *Civil War History* 43 (1997): 310–31.

Andrew, Rod, Jr. *Long Gray Lines: The Southern Military School Tradition, 1839–1915.* Chapel Hill: University of North Carolina Press, 2001.

Appleby, Joyce. *Inheriting the Revolution: The First Generation of Americans.* Cambridge: Harvard University Press, 2000.

Aron, Stephen. *How the West Was Lost: The Transformation of Kentucky from Daniel Boone to Henry Clay.* Baltimore: Johns Hopkins University Press, 1996.

Ayers, Edward L. *Vengeance and Justice: Crime and Punishment in the Nineteenth-Century South.* New York: Oxford University Press, 1984.

Baptist, Edward E. *Creating an Old South: Middle Florida's Plantation Frontier before the Civil War.* Chapel Hill: University of North Carolina Press, 2002.

———. "'Cuffy,' 'Fancy Maids,' and 'One-Eyed Men': Rape, Commodification, and the Domestic Slave Trade in the United States." *American Historical Review* 106 (2001): 1619–50.

Barnes, L. Diane. "Hammer and Hand in the Old South: Artisan Workers in Petersburg, Virginia, 1820–1860." Ph.D. diss., West Virginia University, 2000.

———. "Southern Artisans, Organization, and the Rise of a Market Economy in Antebellum Petersburg." *Virginia Magazine of History and Biography* 107 (1999): 159–88.

Basso, Matthew, Laura McCall, and Dee Garceau, eds. *Across the Great Divide: Cultures of Manhood in the American West.* New York: Routledge, 2001.

Bederman, Gail. *Manliness and Civilization: A Cultural History of Gender and Race in the United States, 1880–1917.* Chicago: University of Chicago Press, 1995.

———. "Manly Civilizations / Primitive Masculinity: Race, Gender, and Evolutions of Middle-Class American Manhood." Ph.D. diss., Brown University, 1992.

Bell, Amelia. "Separate People: Speaking of Creek Men and Women." *American Anthropologist* 92 (1990): 332–45.

Berlin, Ira. *Many Thousands Gone: The First Two Centuries of Slavery in North America.* Cambridge: Harvard University Press, 1998.

223

————. *Slaves without Masters: The Free Negro in the Antebellum South.* New York: Vintage, 1974.

Berlin, Ira, and Herbert G. Gutman. "Native and Immigrants, Free Men and Slaves: Urban Workingmen in the Antebellum American South." *American Historical Review* 88 (1983): 1175–1200.

Berlin, Ira, Joseph P. Reidy, and Leslie S. Rowland, eds. *Freedom's Soldiers: The Black Military Experience in the Civil War.* New York: Cambridge University Press, 1998

Berry, Stephen W., II. *All That Makes a Man: Love and Ambition in the Civil War South.* New York: Oxford University Press, 2003.

Bingham, Emily. *Mordecai: An Early American Family.* New York: Hill and Wang, 2003.

Blassingame, John W. *The Slave Community: Plantation Life in the Antebellum South.* New York: Oxford University Press, 1972.

Bleser, Carol, ed. *Secret and Sacred: The Diaries of James Henry Hammond, a Southern Slaveholder.* New York: Oxford University Press, 1988.

Bloch, Ruth H. "American Feminine Ideals in Transition: The Rise of the Moral Mother, 1785–1815." *Feminist Studies* 4 (1978): 100–126.

Block, Sharon. "Lines of Color, Sex, and Service: Comparative Sexual Coercion in Early America." In *Sex, Love, Race: Crossing Boundaries in North American History,* edited by Martha Hodes, 141–63. New York: New York University Press, 1999.

Blumin, Stuart M. *The Emergence of the Middle Class: Social Experience in the American City, 1760–1900.* New York: Cambridge University Press, 1989.

Bontemps, Alex. *The Punished Self: Surviving Slavery in the Colonial South.* Ithaca: Cornell University Press, 2001.

Booker, Christopher B. *"I Will Wear No Chain!": A Social History of African American Males.* Westport, Conn.: Praeger, 2000.

Brown, Elsa Barkley. "Negotiating and Transforming the Public Sphere: African American Political Life in the Transition from Slavery to Freedom." *Public Culture* 7 (1994): 107–46.

Brown, Kathleen M. *Good Wives, Nasty Wenches, and Anxious Patriarchs: Gender, Race, and Power in Colonial Virginia.* Chapel Hill: University of North Carolina Press, 1996.

Bruce, Dickson D., Jr. *Violence and Culture in the Antebellum South.* Austin: University of Texas Press, 1979.

Burgett, Bruce. *Sentimental Bodies: Sex, Gender, and Citizenship in the Early Republic.* Princeton: Princeton University Press, 1998.

Burton, Orville Vernon. *In My Father's House Are Many Mansions: Family and Community in Edgefield, South Carolina.* Chapel Hill: University of North Carolina Press, 1985.

Bushman, Richard L. *The Refinement of America: Persons, Houses, Cities.* New York: Knopf, 1992.

Bynum, Victoria. *Unruly Women: The Politics of Social and Sexual Control in the Old South.* Chapel Hill: University of North Carolina Press, 1992.

Calloway, Colin G. *The American Revolution in Indian Country: Crisis and Diversity in Native American Communities.* New York: Cambridge University Press, 1995.

Carnes, Mark C. *Secret Ritual and Manhood in Victorian America*. New Haven: Yale University Press, 1989.

Carnes, Mark C., and Clyde Griffin, eds. *Meanings for Manhood: Constructions of Masculinity in Victorian America*. Chicago: University of Chicago Press, 1990.

Carson, James Taylor. *Searching for the Bright Path: The Mississippi Choctaws from Prehistory to Removal*. Lincoln: University of Nebraska Press, 1999.

Cash. W. J. *The Mind of the South*. New York: Knopf, 1941.

Cashin, Joan E. *A Family Venture: Men and Women on the Southern Frontier*. New York: Oxford University Press, 1991.

Censer, Jane Turner. *North Carolina Planters and Their Children, 1800–1860*. Baton Rouge: Louisiana State University Press, 1984.

Clawson, Mary Ann. *Constructing Brotherhood: Class, Gender, and Fraternalism*. Princeton: Princeton University Press, 1989.

Click, Patricia C. *The Spirit of the Times: Amusements in Nineteenth-Century Baltimore, Norfolk, and Richmond*. Charlottesville: University Press of Virginia, 1989.

Clinton, Catherine. *The Plantation Mistress: Woman's World in the Old South*. New York: Pantheon, 1982.

Clinton, Catherine, and Nina Silber, eds. *Divided Houses: Gender and the Civil War*. New York: Oxford University Press, 1992.

Cohen, Patricia Cline. "Unregulated Youth: Masculinity and Murder in the 1830s City." *Radical History Review* 52 (1992): 33–52.

Connell, R. W. *Masculinities*. Berkeley: University of California Press, 1995.

Cott, Nancy. *The Bonds of Womanhood: "Women's Sphere" in New England, 1780–1835*. New Haven: Yale University Press, 1977.

Courtwright, David T. *Violent Land: Single Men and Social Disorder from the Frontier to the Inner City*. Cambridge: Harvard University Press, 1996.

Cremin, Lawrence A. *American Education: The National Experience, 1783–1876*. New York: Harper and Row, 1980.

Cress, Lawrence Delbert. *Citizens in Arms: The Army and Militia in American Society to the War of 1812*. Chapel Hill: University of North Carolina Press, 1982.

Crowther, Edward R. "Holy Honor: Sacred and Secular in the Old South." *Journal of Southern History* 58 (1992): 617–36.

Cullen, Jim. "'I's a Man Now': Gender and African American Men." In Clinton and Silber, *Divided Houses*, 76–96.

Cunliffe, Marcus. *Soldiers and Civilians: The Martial Spirit in America, 1775–1865*. Boston: Little, Brown, 1968.

Davis, Richard Beale. *Intellectual Life in Jefferson's Virginia*. Chapel Hill: University of North Carolina Press, 1964.

Ditz, Toby L. "Shipwrecked; or, Masculinity Imperiled: Mercantile Representations of Failure and the Gendered Self in Eighteenth-Century Philadelphia." *Journal of American History* 81 (1994): 51–80.

Eaton, Clement. *The Growth of Southern Civilization, 1790–1860*. New York: Harper, 1961.

Edwards, Laura. *Gendered Strife and Confusion: The Political Culture of Reconstruction.* Urbana: University of Illinois Press, 1997.

Eubank, Damon. "A Time for Heroes, A Time for Honor: Kentucky Soldiers in the Mexican War." *Filson Club Historical Quarterly* 72 (1998): 174–92.

Faust, Drew Gilpin. *James Henry Hammond and the Old South: A Design for Mastery.* Baton Rouge: Louisiana State University Press, 1982.

Filine, Peter G. *Him/Her/Self: Gender Identities in Modern America.* 3d ed. Baltimore: Johns Hopkins University Press, 1974.

Fogel, Robert W., and Stanley L. Engerman. *Time on the Cross: The Economics of American Negro Slavery.* Boston: Little, Brown, 1974.

Foner, Jack D. *Blacks and the Military in American History: A New Perspective.* New York: Praeger, 1974.

Ford, Lacy, Jr. "Making the 'White Man's Country' White: Race, Slavery, and State-Building in the Jacksonian South." *Journal of the Early Republic* 19 (1999): 713–37.

———. *Origins of Southern Radicalism: The South Carolina Upcountry, 1800–1860.* New York: Oxford University Press, 1988.

Forgie, George B. *Patricide in the House Divided: A Psychological Interpretation of Lincoln and His Age.* New York: Norton, 1979.

Fox-Genovese, Elizabeth. *Within the Plantation Household: Black and White Women of the Old South.* Chapel Hill: University of North Carolina Press, 1988.

Frank, Stephen M. *Life with Father: Parenthood and Masculinity in the Nineteenth-Century American North.* Baltimore: Johns Hopkins University Press, 1998.

Franklin, John Hope. *The Militant South, 1800–1861.* Cambridge: Belknap Press, 1956.

Fredrickson, George M. *The Black Image in the White Mind: The Debate on Afro-American Character and Destiny, 1817–1914.* New York: Harper and Row, 1971.

Freeman, Joanne B. *Affairs of Honor: National Politics in the New Republic.* New Haven: Yale University Press, 2001.

Gebhard, Caroline. "Reconstructing Southern Manhood: Race, Sentimentality, and Camp in the Plantation Myth." In Jones and Donaldson, *Haunted Bodies.*

Genovese, Eugene D. *The Political Economy of Slavery.* New York: Pantheon, 1961.

———. *Roll, Jordan, Roll: The World the Slaves Made.* New York: Pantheon, 1974.

———. *The Slaveholder's Dilemma: Freedom and Progress in Southern Conservative Thought, 1820–1860.* Columbia: University of South Carolina Press, 1992.

———. *The World the Slaveholders Made: Two Essays in Interpretation.* 1969. Reprint, Middletown: Wesleyan University Press, 1988.

Gillespie, Michele. *Free Labor in an Unfree World: White Artisans in Slaveholding Georgia, 1789–1860.* Athens: University of Georgia Press, 2000.

———. "Planters in the Making: Artisanal Opportunity in Georgia, 1790–1830." In Rock, Gilje, and Asher, *American Artisans,* 33–34.

Gilmore, David. *Manhood in the Making: Cultural Concepts of Masculinity.* New Haven: Yale University Press, 1990.

Glover, Lorri. *All Our Relations: Blood Ties and Emotional Bonds Among the Early South Carolina Gentry.* Baltimore: Johns Hopkins University Press, 2000.

————. "An Education in Southern Masculinity: The Ball Family of South Carolina in the New Republic." *Journal of Southern History* 69 (2003): 39–70.

Goldfield, David R. *Cotton Fields and Skyscrapers: Southern City and Region, 1607–1980.* Baton Rouge: Louisiana State University Press, 1982.

Gorn, Elliott J. "'Gouge and Bite, Pull Hair and Scratch': The Social Significance of Fighting in the Southern Backcountry" *American Historical Review* 90 (1985): 18–43.

Greenberg, Kenneth S. *Honor and Slavery: Lies, Duels, Noses, Masks, Dressing as a Woman, Gifts, Strangers, Humanitarianism, Death, Slave Rebellions, the Proslavery Argument, Baseball, Hunting, and Gambling in the Old South.* Princeton: Princeton University Press, 1996.

————. *Masters and Statesmen: The Political Culture of American Slavery.* Baltimore: Johns Hopkins University Press, 1985.

Griswold, Robert. *Fatherhood in America: A History.* New York: Basic Books, 1993.

Gundersen, Joan R. "Independence, Citizenship, and the American Revolution." *Signs: Journal of Women in Culture and Society* 13 (1987): 59–77.

Gutman, Herbert. *The Black Family in Slavery and Freedom, 1750–1925.* New York: Pantheon, 1976.

Habermas, Jurgen. *The Structural Transformation of the Public Sphere: An Inquiry into a Category of Bourgeois Society.* Cambridge: MIT Press, 2000.

Halttunen, Karen. *Confidence Men and Painted Women: A Study of Middle-Class Culture in America, 1830–1870.* New Haven: Yale University Press, 1982.

Hansen, Karen. "'Our Eyes Beheld Each Other': Masculinity and Intimate Friendship in Antebellum New England." In Nardi, *Men's Friendships,* 35–58.

Harris, J. William. *Plain Folk and Gentry in a Slave Society: White Liberty and Black Slavery in Augusta's Hinterlands.* Middletown: Wesleyan University Press, 1985.

Harrison, Lowell H., and James C. Klotter. *A New History of Kentucky.* Lexington: University Press of Kentucky, 1997.

Hartsock, Nancy C. M. "Masculinity, Heroism, and the Making of War." In *Rocking the Ship of State: Toward a Feminist Peace Politics,* edited by Adrienne Harris and Ynestra King, 135–45. Boulder: Westview Press, 1989.

Hatley, Tom. *The Dividing Paths: Cherokees and South Carolinians through the Revolutionary Era.* New York: Oxford University Press, 1995.

Hatt, Michael. "'Making a Man of Him': Masculinity and the Black Body in Mid-Nineteenth-Century American Sculpture." *Oxford Art Journal* 15 (1992): 21–35.

Heglar, Charles J. *Rethinking the Slave Narrative: Slave Marriage and the Narratives of Henry Bibb and William and Ellen Craft.* Westport, Conn.: Greenwood Press, 2001.

Hemphill, C. Dallett. *Bowing to Necessities: A History of Manners in America, 1620–1860.* New York: Oxford University Press, 1999.

————. "Class, Gender, and the Regulation of Emotional Expression in Revolutionary Era Conduct Literature." In *An Emotional History of the United States,* edited by Jan Lewis and Peter Stearns, 33–51. New York: New York University Press, 1998.

Heyrman, Christine Leigh. *Southern Cross: The Beginnings of the Bible Belt.* New York: Knopf, 1997.

Hine, Darlene Clark, and Earnestine Jenkins, eds. *A Question of Manhood: A Reader in U.S. Black Men's History and Masculinity.* Vol. 1: *"Manhood Rights": The Construction of Black Male History and Manhood, 1750–1870.* Bloomington: Indiana University Press, 1999.

Horton, James O., and Lois Horton. "Violence, Protest, and Identity: Black Manhood in Antebellum America." In Hine and Jenkins, *A Question of Manhood,* 382–98.

Hudson, Larry. *To Have and To Hold: Slave Work and Family Life in Antebellum South Carolina.* Athens: University of Georgia Press, 1997.

Inge, M. Thomas, and Edward J. Piacentino, eds. *The Humor of the Old South.* Lexington: University Press of Kentucky, 2001.

Inscoe, John. *Mountain Masters: Slavery and the Sectional Crisis in Western North Carolina.* Knoxville: University of Tennessee Press, 1989.

Jabour, Anya. "Male Friendship and Masculinity in the Early National South: William Wirt and His Friends." *Journal of the Early Republic* 20 (2000): 83–111.

————. *Marriage in the Early Republic: Elizabeth and William Wirt and the Companionate Ideal.* Baltimore: Johns Hopkins University Press, 1998.

————. "Masculinity and Adolescence in Antebellum America: Robert Wirt at West Point, 1820–1821." *Journal of Family History* 23 (1998): 393–416.

Johansen, Shawn. *Family Men: Middle-Class Fatherhood in Early Industrializing America.* New York: Routledge, 2001.

Johnson, Guion Griffis. "Courtship and Marriage Customs in Antebellum North Carolina." *North Carolina Historical Review* 8 (1931): 384.

Johnson, Walter. *Soul by Soul: Life in the Antebellum Slave Market.* Cambridge: Harvard University Press, 1999.

Jones, Anne Goodwyn, and Susan V. Donaldson, eds. *Haunted Bodies: Gender and Southern Texts.* Charlottesville: University Press of Virginia, 1997.

Jones, Jacqueline. *Labor of Love, Labor of Sorrow: Black Women, Work, and the Family from Slavery to the Present.* New York: Basic Books, 1985.

Kann, Mark E. *On the Man Question: Gender and Civic Virtue in America.* Philadelphia: Temple University Press, 1991.

————. *A Republic of Men: The American Founders, Gendered Language, and Patriarchal Politics.* New York: New York University Press, 1998.

Kerber, Linda. *Women of the Republic: Intellect and Ideology in Revolutionary America.* Chapel Hill: University of North Carolina Press, 1980.

Kett, Joseph F. *Rites of Passage: Adolescence in America, 1790 to the Present.* New York: Basic Books, 1977.

Kierner, Cynthia A. *Beyond the Household: Women's Place in the Early South, 1700–1835.* Ithaca: Cornell University Press, 1998.

————. "Genteel Balls and Republican Parades: Gender and Early Southern Civic Rituals, 1677–1826." *Virginia Magazine of History and Biography* 104 (1996): 185–210.

Kilbride, Daniel. "Southern Medical Students in Philadelphia, 1800–1861: Science and Sociability in the 'Republic of Medicine.'" *Journal of Southern History* 65 (1999): 697–732.

Kimmel, Michael. *Manhood in America: A Cultural History*. New York: Free Press, 1996.

Klein, Rachel. *Unification of a Slave State: The Rise of the Planter Class in the South Carolina Backcountry, 1760–1808*. Chapel Hill: University of North Carolina Press, 1990.

Kolchin, Peter. "Whiteness Studies: The New History of Race in America." *Journal of American History* 89 (2002): 154–73.

Kreyling, Michael. "The Hero in Antebellum Southern Narrative." *Southern Literary Journal* 16 (1984): 3–20.

Laurie, Bruce. *Artisans into Workers: Labor in Nineteenth-Century America*. New York: Noonday Press, 1989.

Laver, Harry S. "Rethinking the Social Role of the Militia: Community Building in Antebellum Kentucky." *Journal of Southern History* 58 (2002): 777–816.

Lebsock, Suzanne. *The Free Women of Petersburg: Status and Culture in a Southern Town, 1784–1860*. New York: Norton, 1984.

Leverenz, David. *Manhood and the American Renaissance*. Ithaca: Cornell University Press, 1989.

Levine, Lawrence. *Black Culture and Black Consciousness: Afro-American Folk Thought from Slavery to Freedom*. New York: Oxford University Press, 1977.

Lewis, Charlene M. Boyer. *Ladies and Gentlemen on Display: Planter Society at the Virginia Springs, 1790–1860*. Charlottesville: University Press of Virginia, 2002.

Lewis, Jan. *The Pursuit of Happiness: Family and Values in Jefferson's Virginia*. Cambridge: Cambridge University Press, 1983.

Lewis, Johanna Miller. *Artisans in the North Carolina Backcountry*. Lexington: University Press of Kentucky, 1995.

Lindman, Janet Moore. "Acting the Manly Christian: White Evangelical Masculinity in Revolutionary Virginia." *William and Mary Quarterly* 57 (2000): 393–416.

Lockridge, Kenneth A. "Colonial Self-Fashioning: Paradoxes and Pathologies in the Construction of Genteel Identity in Eighteenth-Century America." In *Through a Glass Darkly: Reflections on Personal Identity in Early America*, edited by Ronald Hoffman, Mechal Sobel, and Fredrika J. Teute, 274–339. Chapel Hill: University of North Carolina Press, 1997.

———. *The Diary, and Life, of William Byrd II of Virginia, 1674–1744*. Chapel Hill: University of North Carolina Press, 1987.

———. *On the Sources of Patriarchal Rage: The Commonplace Books of William Byrd and Thomas Jefferson and the Gendering of Power in the Eighteenth Century*. New York: New York University Press, 1992.

Lyerly, Cynthia Lynn. *Methodism and the Southern Mind, 1770–1810*. New York: Oxford University Press, 1998.

Lynn, Kenneth S. *Mark Twain and Southwestern Humor*. Boston: Little, Brown, 1959.

Malone, Ann Patton. *Sweet Chariot: Slave Family and Household Structure in Nineteenth-Century Louisiana*. Chapel Hill: University of North Carolina Press, 1992.

Mangan, J. A., and James Walvin, eds. *Manliness and Morality: Middle-Class Masculinity in Britain and America, 1800–1940*. New York: St. Martin's, 1987.

Marten, James. "Fatherhood in the Confederacy: Southern Soldiers and Their Children." *Journal of Southern History* 63 (1997): 269–92.

Mayfield, John. "George Washington Harris: The Fool from the Hills." In *The Human Tradition in Antebellum America*, edited by Michael A. Morrison, 229–43. Wilmington: Scholarly Resources, 2000.

———. "'The Soul of a Man!': William Gilmore Simms and the Myths of Southern Manhood." *Journal of the Early Republic* 15 (1995): 477–500

———. "The Theater of Public Esteem: Ethics and Values in Longstreet's *Georgia Scenes*." *Georgia Historical Quarterly* 75 (1991): 566–86.

McCall, Laura, and Donald Yacovone, eds. *A Shared Experience: Men, Women, and the History of Gender*. New York: New York University Press, 1998.

McCardell, John. *The Idea of a Southern Nation: Southern Nationalists and Southern Nationalism, 1830–1860*. New York: Norton, 1979.

McCormick, Richard P. *The Second American Party System: Party Formation in the Jacksonian Era*. Chapel Hill: University of North Carolina Press, 1966.

McCurry, Stephanie. *Masters of Small Worlds: Yeoman Households, Gender Relations, and the Political Culture of the Antebellum South Carolina Low Country*. New York: Oxford University Press, 1995.

McWhiney, Grady. *Cracker Culture: Celtic Ways in the Old South*. Tuscaloosa: University of Alabama Press, 1988.

Mitchell, Reid. "Soldiering, Manhood, and Coming of Age: A Northern Volunteer." In Clinton and Silber, *Divided Houses*.

———. *The Vacant Chair: The Northern Soldier Leaves Home*. New York: Oxford University Press, 1993.

Morgan, Edmund S. *American Slavery-American Freedom: The Ordeal of Colonial Virginia*. New York: Norton, 1975.

Morgan, Philip D. *Slave Counterpoint: Black Culture in the Eighteenth-Century Chesapeake and Lowcountry*. Chapel Hill: University of North Carolina Press, 1998.

Morris, Christopher. "What's So Funny? Southern Humorists and the Market Revolution." In Morris and Reinhardt, *Southern Writers*, 9–26.

Morris, Christopher, and Stephen G. Reinhardt, eds. *Southern Writers and Their Worlds*. College Station: Texas A&M University Press, 1996.

Mosse, George L. *The Image of Man: The Creation of Modern Masculinity*. New York: Oxford University Press, 1996.

Mrozak, Donald. "The Habit of Victory: The American Military and the Cult of Manliness." In Mangan and Walvin, *Manliness and Morality*, 220–39.

Nardi, Peter M., ed. *Men's Friendships*. London: Sage, 1992.

Nelson, Dana D. *National Manhood: Capitalist Citizenship and the Imagined Fraternity of White Men*. Durham: Duke University Press, 1998.

Newman, Simon P. *Parades and the Politics of the Street: Festive Culture in the Early American Republic*. Philadelphia: University of Pennsylvania Press, 1997.

Newton, Sarah E. *Learning to Behave: A Guide to American Conduct Books before 1900*. Westport, Conn.: Greenwood Press, 1994.

Norton, Mary Beth. *Liberty's Daughters: The Revolutionary Experience of American Women, 1750–1800*. Boston: Little, Brown, 1980.

Novak, Steven. *The Rights of Youth: American Colleges and Student Revolt, 1798–1815*. Cambridge: Harvard University Press, 1977.

Oakes, James. *The Ruling Race: A History of American Slaveholders*. New York: Knopf, 1982.

O'Brien, Greg. *Choctaws in a Revolutionary Age, 1750–1830*. Lincoln: University of Nebraska Press, 2002.

O'Brien, Michael. *Rethinking the South: Essays in Intellectual History*. Baltimore: Johns Hopkins University Press, 1988.

Olsen, Christopher J. *Political Culture and Secession in Mississippi: Masculinity, Honor, and the Antiparty Tradition, 1830–1860*. New York: Oxford University Press, 2000.

Ownby, Ted. *Subduing Satan: Religion, Recreation, and Manhood in the Rural South, 1865–1920*. Chapel Hill: University of North Carolina Press, 1990.

Owsley, Frank L. *Plain Folk of the Old South*. Baton Rouge: Louisiana State University Press, 1949.

Owsley, Frank L., and Harriet C. Owsley. "The Economic Basis of Society in the Late Ante-Bellum South." *Journal of Southern History* 6 (1940): 24–45

Pace, Robert F., and Christopher A. Bjornsen. "Adolescent Honor and College Student Behavior in the Old South." *Southern Cultures* 6 (2000): 9–28.

Perdue, Theda. *Cherokee Women: Gender and Culture Change, 1700–1835*. Lincoln: University of Nebraska Press, 1998.

———, ed. *Sifters: Native American Women's Lives*. New York: Oxford University Press, 2001.

Perkins, Elizabeth. *Border Life: Experience and Memory in the Revolutionary Ohio Valley*. Chapel Hill: University of North Carolina Press, 1998.

———. "The Consumer Frontier: Household Consumption in Early Kentucky." *Journal of American History* 78 (1991): 486–510

Phillips, Ulrich B. *American Negro Slavery: A Survey of the Supply, Employment, and Control of Negro Labor as Determined by the Plantation Regime*. 1918. Reprint, Baton Rouge: Louisiana State University, 1966.

Proctor, Nicholas. *Bathed in Blood: Hunting and Mastery in the Old South*. Charlottesville: University Press of Virginia, 2002.

Pugh, David G. *Sons of Liberty: The Masculine Mind in Nineteenth-Century America*. Westport, Conn.: Greenwood Press, 1983.

Rock, Howard B. "'All Her Sons Join as One Social Band': New York City's Artisanal Societies in the Early Republic." In Rock, Gilje, and Asher, *American Artisans*, 155–75.

Rock, Howard B., Paul A. Gilje, and Robert Asher, eds. *American Artisans: Crafting Social Identity, 1750–1850*. Baltimore: Johns Hopkins University Press, 1995.

Rodgers, Daniel T. "Republicanism: The Career of a Concept." *Journal of American History* 79 (1992): 11–38.

Roediger, David R. "The Pursuit of Whiteness: Property, Terror, and Expansion, 1790–1860." *Journal of the Early Republic* 19 (1999): 579–600.

————. *The Wages of Whiteness: Race and the Making of the American Working Class.* London: Verso, 1991.

Rohrbough, Malcolm J. *The Trans-Appalachian Frontier: People, Societies, and Institutions, 1775–1850.* New York: Oxford University Press, 1978.

Root, R. K., ed. *Lord Chesterfield's Letters to His Son.* London: J. M. Dent, 1929.

Rothman, Ellen K. *Hands and Hearts: A History of Courtship in America.* New York: Basic Books, 1984.

Rotundo, E. Anthony. *American Manhood: Transformations in Masculinity from the Revolution to the Modern Era.* New York: Basic Books, 1993.

Royster, Charles. *A Revolutionary People at War: The Continental Army and American Character, 1775–1783.* Chapel Hill: University of North Carolina Press, 1979.

Rozbicki, Michal J. *The Complete Colonial Gentleman: Cultural Legitimacy in Plantation America.* Charlottesville: University Press of Virginia, 1998.

Rutman, Darrett B., and Anita Rutman. "The Village South." In *Small Worlds, Large Questions: Explorations in Early American Social History, 1600–1850,* edited by Darrett B. Rutman, 231–72. Charlottesville, University Press of Virginia, 1994.

Schwartz, Marie Jenkins. *Born in Bondage: Growing Up Enslaved in the Antebellum South.* Cambridge: Harvard University Press, 2000.

Sellers, Charles. *The Market Revolution: Jacksonian America, 1815–1846.* New York: Oxford University Press, 1991.

Shade, William G. *Democratizing the Old Dominion: Virginia and the Second Party System, 1824–1861.* Charlottesville: University Press of Virginia, 1996.

Sheidley, Nathaniel. "Unruly Men: Indians, Settlers, and the Ethos of Frontier Patriarchy in the Upper Tennessee Watershed, 1763–1815." Ph.D. diss., Princeton University, 1999.

Shields, Johanna Nichol. "A Sadder Simon Suggs: Freedom and Slavery in the Humor of Johnson Hopper." *Journal of Southern History* 56 (1990): 641–64.

Shoemaker, Nancy. "An Alliance between Men: Gender Metaphors in Eighteenth-Century American Indian Diplomacy East of the Mississippi River." *Ethnohistory* 46 (1999): 239–64.

Shore, Laurence. *Southern Capitalists: The Ideological Leadership of an Elite, 1832–1885.* Chapel Hill: University of North Carolina Press, 1986.

Sinha, Manisha. *The Counterrevolution in Slavery: Politics and Ideology in Antebellum South Carolina.* Chapel Hill: University of North Carolina Press, 2000.

Smith, Daniel Blake. *Inside the Great House: Planter Family Life in Eighteenth-Century Chesapeake Society.* Ithaca: Cornell University Press, 1980.

Smith-Rosenberg, Carroll. "The Female World of Love and Ritual: Relations between Women in Nineteenth-Century America." *Signs: Journal of Women in Culture and Society* 1 (1975): 1–29.

Snyder, R. Claire. *Citizen-Soldiers and Manly Warriors: Military Service and Gender in the Civic Republican Tradition.* Lanham, Md.: Rowman and Littlefield, 1999.

Stampp, Kenneth. *The Peculiar Institution.* New York: Knopf, 1956.

Stanley, Amy Dru. "Home Life and the Morality of the Market." In Stokes and Conway, *Market Revolution*, 74–96.

Stearns, Peter N. *Be a Man! Males in Modern Society*. New York: Holmes and Meier, 1979.

Stevenson, Brenda. *Life in Black and White: Family and Community in the Slave South*. New York: Oxford University Press, 1996.

Stokes, Melvin, and Stephen Conway, eds. *The Market Revolution in America*. Charlottesville: University Press of Virginia, 1996.

Stowe, Steven M. *Intimacy and Power in the Old South: Ritual in the Lives of the Planters*. Baltimore: Johns Hopkins University Press, 1987.

———. "The Rhetoric of Authority: The Making of Social Values in Planter Family Correspondence." *Journal of American History* 73 (1987): 913–33.

———. "'The *Thing* Not Its Vision': A Woman's Courtship and Her Sphere in the Southern Planter Class." *Feminist Studies* 9 (1983): 113–30.

Sydnor, Charles S. *The Development of Southern Sectionalism, 1819–1848*. 1948. Reprint, Baton Rouge: Louisiana State University Press, 1968.

Tadman, Michael. *Speculators and Slaves: Masters, Traders, and Slaves in the Old South*. Madison: University of Wisconsin Press, 1989.

Tolbert, Lisa. *Constructing Townscapes: Space and Society in Antebellum Tennessee*. Chapel Hill: University of North Carolina Press, 1999.

Traister, Bruce. "Academic Viagra: The Rise of American Masculinity Studies." *American Quarterly* 52 (2000): 274–304.

Travers, Len. *Celebrating the Fourth: Independence Day and the Rites of Nationalism in the Early Republic*. Amherst: University of Massachusetts Press, 1997.

Tripp, Steven Elliott. *Yankee Town, Southern City: Race and Class Relations in Civil War Lynchburg*. New York: New York University Press, 1997.

Trudeau, Noah Andre. *Like Men of War: Black Troops in the Civil War, 1862–1865*. Boston, Little, Brown, 1998.

Wakelyn, Jon. "Antebellum College Life and the Relations between Fathers and Sons." In *The Web of Southern Social Relations: Women, Family, and Education*, edited by Walter J. Fraser, R. Frank Saunders Jr., and Jon L. Wakelyn, 107–26. Athens: University of Georgia Press, 1985.

Waldstreicher, David. *In the Midst of Perpetual Fetes: The Making of American Nationalism, 1776–1820*. Chapel Hill: University of North Carolina Press, 1997.

Watson, Harry L. *Liberty and Power: The Politics of Jacksonian America*. New York: Hill and Wang, 1990.

Watson, Samuel J. "Flexible Gender Roles during the Market Revolution: Family, Friendship, Marriage, and Masculinity among U.S. Army Officers, 1815–1846." *Journal of Social History* 29 (1995): 81–106.

Watts, Steven. *The Republic Reborn: War and the Making of Liberal America, 1790–1820*. Baltimore: Johns Hopkins University Press, 1987.

Welter, Barbara. "The Cult of True Womanhood: 1820–1860." *American Quarterly* 18 (1966): 151–74.

White, Deborah Gray. *Ar'n't I a Woman? Female Slaves in the Plantation South.* New York: Norton, 1985.

White, Richard. *The Roots of Dependency: Subsistence, Environment, and Social Change among the Choctaws, Pawnees, and Navajos.* Lincoln: University of Nebraska Press, 1983.

Whites, LeeAnn. "The Civil War as a Crisis in Gender." In Clinton and Silber, *Divided Houses*, 3–21.

Wilentz, Sean. *Chants Democratic: New York City and the Rise of the American Working Class, 1788–1850.* New York: Oxford University Press, 1984.

Williams, Heather. "Self-Taught: The Role of African Americans in Educating the Freedpeople, 1861–1871." Ph.D. diss., Yale University, 2002.

Wilson, Lisa. *Ye Heart of a Man: The Domestic Lives of Men in Colonial New England.* New Haven: Yale University Press, 1999.

Wood, Gordon. *The Radicalism of the American Revolution.* New York: Knopf, 1992.

Wyatt-Brown, Bertram. "The Ideal Typology and Antebellum Southern History." *Societas* 5 (1975): 5–28.

———. *The Shaping of Southern Culture: Honor, Grace, and War, 1760s–1880s.* Chapel Hill: University of North Carolina Press, 2001.

———. *Southern Honor: Ethics and Behavior in the Old South.* New York: Oxford University Press, 1982.

Yacovone, Donald. "'Surpassing the Love of Women': Victorian Manhood and the Language of Fraternal Love." In McCall and Yacovone, *A Shared Experience*, 195–221.

Yarborough, Richard. "Race, Violence, and Manhood: The Masculine Ideal in Frederick Douglass's 'The Heroic Slave.'" In *Frederick Douglass: New Literary and Historical Essays*, edited by Eric Sundquist, 166–88. New York: Cambridge University Press, 1990.

Young, Jeffrey Robert. *Domesticating Slavery: The Master Class in Georgia and South Carolina, 1670–1837.* Chapel Hill: University of North Carolina Press, 1999.

Young, R. J. *Antebellum Black Activists: Race, Gender, and Self.* New York: Garland, 1996.

Zuckerman, Michael. "Penmanship Exercises for Saucy Sons: Some Thoughts on the Colonial Southern Family." *South Carolina Historical Magazine* 84 (1983): 152–66.

CPSIA information can be obtained
at www.ICGtesting.com
Printed in the USA
LVOW12s2056081216
516419LV00001B/127/P